Do the Math workbook

ELEMENTARY & INTERMEDIATE ALGEBRA

SECOND EDITION

Michael Sullivan, III
Joliet Junior College

Katherine R. Struve
Columbus State Community College

Janet Mazzarella
Southwestern College

Prentice Hall
is an imprint of

PEARSON

2 3 4 5 6 BB 11 10 09

ISBN-13:   978-0-321-59359-7   Standalone
ISBN-10:   0-321-59359-6   Standalone

ISBN-13:   978-0-321-59360-3   Component
ISBN-10:   0-321-59360-X   Component

Prentice Hall
is an imprint of

www.pearsonhighered.com

Do the Math
workbook

Elementary & Intermediate Algebra, Second Edition

Table of Contents

Five-Minute Warm-Up 1.2
Fractions, Decimals, and Percents

Definitions and vocabulary. In your own words, write a brief definition for each of the following.

1. Natural numbers _____

2. Natural numbers that are *prime* _____

3. Natural numbers that are *composite* _____

4. Least common multiple _____

5. In the statement $4 \bullet 9 = 36$,

    (a) list the factor(s).   **(b)** list the product(s).   5a. _____

                                                                 5b. _____

6. List three common multiples of 8 and 12.   6. _____

7. List three common factors of 8 and 12.   7. _____

8. List all possible factors of 18.   8. _____

9. Write the prime factorization of 18.   9. _____

Guided Practice 1.2
Fractions, Decimals, and Percents

Objective 1: Factor a Number as a Product of Prime Factors

1. We use a *factor tree* to find the prime factorization of a number. The process begins with finding two factors of the given number. Continue to factor until all factors are prime.

Find the prime factorization of each natural number. *(See textbook Example 1)*

  (a) 30   **(b)** 120   1a. _____

                                                           1b. _____

Objective 2: Find the Least Common Multiple of Two or More Numbers

2. Find the least common multiple of the numbers 8 and 12: *(See textbook Examples 2 and 3)*

Step 1: Write each number as the product of prime factors, aligning common factors vertically.	Factor 8 as the product of primes: **(a)** _____ Factor 12 as the product of primes: **(b)** _____
Step 2: Write down the factor(s) that the numbers share, if any. Then write down the remaining factors the greatest number of times that the factors appear in any number.	List the common factors: **(c)** _____ List the remaining factors: **(d)** _____
Step 3: Multiply the factors listed in Step 2. The product is the least common multiple (LCM).	Multiply. LCM = **(e)** _____

Objective 3: Write Equivalent Fractions

3. *Equivalent fractions* are fractions that represent the same part of a whole. Sometimes we simplify fractions, using smaller numbers to represent an equivalent part of a whole. Other times we multiply by one, written as a quantity over itself, to find larger numbers to represent the equivalent fraction.

Write the fraction $\dfrac{5}{8}$ as an equivalent fraction with a denominator of 24. *(See textbook Example 4)*

  (a) Determine the missing numerator and denominator to multiply by 1: $\dfrac{5}{8} \cdot \dfrac{\boxed{?}}{\boxed{?}} = \dfrac{}{24}$ 3a. _____

  (b) Find the equivalent fraction by determining the product: $\dfrac{5}{8} \cdot 1 = \dfrac{5}{8} \cdot \dfrac{\Box}{\Box} = \dfrac{?}{24}$ 3b. _____

4. Write $\dfrac{7}{36}$ and $\dfrac{11}{24}$ as equivalent fractions with the least common denominator. *(See textbook Example 5)*

Step 1: Find the least common denominator of the fractions.

Factor 36 as the product of primes: **(a)** _____

Factor 24 as the product of primes: **(b)** _____

Write the factors in the LCD: **(c)** _____

Multiply to determine the LCD: **(d)** _____

Step 2: Rewrite each fraction with the least common denominator.

To write $\dfrac{7}{36}$ on the LCD, multiply by?

(e) _____

To write $\dfrac{11}{24}$ on the LCD, multiply by?

(f) _____

Multiply to find the equivalent fractions.

(g) $\dfrac{7}{36} \cdot \dfrac{\square}{\square} = $ ___ ; $\dfrac{11}{24} \cdot \dfrac{\square}{\square} = $ ___

Objective 5: Round Decimals

5. It is important to identify the place value of digits in a number and to be able to round to a specific place.

Use the number 94,204.6375 to round to the required place. *(See textbook Examples 7 and 8)*

    (a) thousands   **(b)** tens

5a. _____

5b. _____

    (c) whole number (or ones)   **(d)** tenth

5c. _____

5d. _____

    (e) hundreds   **(f)** hundredth

5e. _____

5f. _____

Objective 7: Convert a Percent to a Decimal and a Decimal to a Percent

6. Write 75% as a decimal. *(See textbook Example 12)*

6. _____

7. Write 0.005 in percent form. *(See textbook Example 13)*

7. _____

Do the Math Exercises 1.2
Fractions, Decimals, and Percents

In Problems 1–2, find the prime factorization of each number.

1. 54   **2.** 63

1._____

2._____

In Problems 3–4, find the LCM of each set of numbers.

3. 8 and 70   **4.** 9, 15, and 20

3._____

4._____

In Problems 5–6, write each fraction with the given denominator.

5. Write $\dfrac{4}{5}$ with denominator 15.   **6.** Write $\dfrac{5}{14}$ with denominator 28.

5._____

6._____

In Problems 7–8, write the equivalent fractions with the least common denominator.

7. $\dfrac{1}{12}$ and $\dfrac{5}{18}$ **8.** $\dfrac{5}{12}$ and $\dfrac{7}{15}$

7._____

8._____

In Problems 9–10, write each fraction in lowest terms.

9. $\dfrac{9}{15}$ **10.** $\dfrac{24}{27}$

9._____

10._____

In Problems 11–12, tell the place value of the digit in the given number.

11. 9124.786; the 7   **12.** 539.016; the 9   11. _____

                                                                                     12. _____

In Problems 13–14, round each number to the given place.

13. 7298.0845 to the nearest hundred   **14.** 37.439 to the nearest tenth   13. _____

                                                                                     14. _____

In Problems 15–16, write each fraction as a terminating or repeating decimal.

15. $\dfrac{2}{9}$ **16.** $\dfrac{11}{32}$ 15. _____

                                                                                     16. _____

In Problems 17–18, write each decimal as a fraction in lowest terms.

17. 0.4   **18.** 0.358   17. _____

                                                                                     18. _____

19. Write 59% as a decimal.   **20.** Write 0.349 as a percent.   19. _____

                                                                                     20. _____

Five-Minute Warm-Up 1.3
The Number Systems and the Real Number Line

In Problems 1 – 4, simplify each of the following expressions.

1. $\dfrac{0}{7}$ **2.** $\dfrac{12}{0}$ **3.** $\dfrac{9}{9}$ **4.** $\dfrac{3}{1}$

1._____

2._____

3._____

4._____

5. In the fraction $\dfrac{3}{7}$, identify **(a)** the numerator and **(b)** the denominator.

5a._____

5b._____

In Problems 6 – 9, use the set of numbers $\left\{\dfrac{15}{0}, -100, \dfrac{3}{6}, 0.001, \dfrac{0}{1}, -1, \dfrac{4}{2}\right\}$. *List all the elements that are...*

6. Nonnegative   **7.** Positive

6._____

7._____

8. Positive and less than one   **9.** Neither positive nor negative

8._____

9._____

In Problems 10 and 11, write the fraction as either a repeating decimal or a terminating decimal.

10. $\dfrac{5}{6}$ **11.** $\dfrac{4}{5}$

10._____

11._____

Guided Practice 1.3
The Number Systems and the Real Number Line

1. A *set* is a collection of objects. We use braces { } to indicate the set and enclose the objects, or *elements*, in the set. When the set has no elements in it, we say that the set is an *empty set* and use the notation ∅ or { } to indicate an empty set. It is incorrect to use {∅} to denote an empty set.

If set A is the set of digits $\{0, 1, 2, 3, 4, 5, 6, 7, 8, 9\}$, *(See textbook Example 1)*

   (a) write a set B which contains elements from set A which are even.   1a. _____

   (b) write a set C which contains elements from set A which are odd.   1b. _____

Objective 1: Classify Numbers

2. Review the definitions of the sets of numbers listed in textbook Section 1.3. These sets are:

   $\mathbb{N}$ = Natural numbers W = Whole numbers $\mathbb{Z}$ = Integers
   $\mathbb{Q}$ = Rational numbers Ir = Irrational numbers $\mathbb{R}$ = Real numbers

List the numbers in the set $\left\{\dfrac{-8}{2}, 2.\overline{6}, \dfrac{0}{3}, 14, -10, \dfrac{7}{0}, -1.050050005...\right\}$ that are... *(See textbook Example 2)*

   (a) Natural _____   (b) Whole _____

   (c) Integer _____   (d) Rational _____

   (e) Irrational _____   (f) Real _____

3. List the sets of numbers to which the given number belongs. *(See textbook Example 2)*

   (a) π _____   (b) $\dfrac{12}{-6}$ _____

   (c) $1.25252525...$ _____   (d) $\dfrac{-100}{-20}$ _____

Objective 2: Plot Points on the Real Number Line

4. On the real number line, label the points with coordinates: $-\dfrac{5}{2}$, 3, 1.75, -0.5 *(See textbook Example 3)*

Objective 3: Use Inequalities to Order Real Numbers

5. An important property of the real number line follows from the fact that given two numbers (points) a and b, either a is to the left of b ($a < b$), a is equal to b ($a = b$), or a is to the right of b ($a > b$). It is also possible that a is less than or equal to b ($a \leq b$) or a is greater than or equal to b ($a \geq b$).

Replace the question mark by <, >, or =, whichever is correct. *(See textbook Example 4)*

(a) $-10 \,?\, -10.5$ (b) $\dfrac{3}{4} \,?\, 0.75$ (c) $\dfrac{8}{6} \,?\, \dfrac{18}{15}$

5a. _____

5b. _____

5c. _____

6. Determine whether the statement is True or False.

(a) $0 > -2$ (b) $5 \geq \dfrac{-10}{-2}$ (c) $-5 \leq -5.\overline{1}$

6a. _____

6b. _____

6c. _____

7. If x represents any real number, how would you use inequality symbols to write

(a) x is positive?   (b) x is negative?

7a. _____

7b. _____

Objective 4: Compute the Absolute Value of a Real Number

8. The *absolute value* of a number a, written $|a|$, is the distance from 0 to a on the real number line. Because distance is always positive, the absolute value of a any non-zero number is always

8. _____

9. Evaluate each of the following: *(See textbook Example 5)*

(a) $\left| \dfrac{0}{-5} \right|$ (b) $\left| -4.2 \right|$ $\left| 120 \right|$

9a. _____

9b. _____

9c. _____

Do the Math Exercises 1.3
The Number Systems and the Real Number Line

In Problems 1–3, write each set.

1. *B* is the set of *natural* numbers less than 25.

1. _____

2. *C* is the set of *integers* between –6 and 4, not including –6 or 4.

2. _____

3. *F* is the set of odd *natural* numbers less than 1.

3. _____

In Problems 4–6, list the elements in the set $\left\{-4, 3, -\dfrac{13}{2}, 0, 2.303003000...\right\}$ *that are described.*

4. whole numbers

5. rational numbers

4. _____

5. _____

6. real numbers

6. _____

7. Plot the points in the set $\left\{\dfrac{3}{4}, \dfrac{0}{2}, -\dfrac{5}{4}, -0.5, 1.5\right\}$ on a real number line.

In Problems 8–9, determine whether the statement is True or False.

8. $0 < -5$

9. $-3 \geq -5$

8. _____

9. _____

In Problems 10–12, replace the ? with the correct symbol: $>, <, =$.

10. $-8 \; ? \; -8.5$

11. $\dfrac{5}{12} \; ? \; \dfrac{2}{3}$

10. _____

11. _____

12. $\dfrac{5}{11} \; ? \; 0.\overline{45}$

12. _____

In Problems 13–15, evaluate each expression.

13. $|-8|$

14. $|7|$

13. _____

14. _____

15. $\left| -\dfrac{13}{9} \right|$

15. _____

Five-Minute Warm-Up 1.4
Adding, Subtracting, Multiplying, and Dividing Integers

In Problems 1 – 4, what operation is indicated by each of the following words?

1. Quotient   **2.** Difference   1. _____

                                                                                2. _____

3. Sum   **4.** Product   3. _____

                                                                                4. _____

5. Write an expression for 9 divided by 18 using each of the following symbols:

   (a) $\dfrac{a}{b}$ **(b)** a/b **(c)** $a \div b$ **(b)** $a\overline{)b}$ 5a. _____

                                                                                5b. _____

                                                                                5c. _____

                                                                                5d. _____

6. Evaluate each of the following:

   (a) $\left|-13\right|$ **(b)** $\left|\dfrac{15}{4}\right|$ **(c)** $\left|0\right|$ 6a. _____

                                                                                6b. _____

                                                                                6c. _____

7. Write $\dfrac{90}{36}$ as a fraction in lowest terms.   7. _____

Guided Practice 1.4
Adding, Subtracting, Multiplying, and Dividing Integers

Objective 1: Add Integers

1. To add two integers that are the same sign, add their absolute values.

  (a) If both numbers are positive, the sign of the sum is _____.   1a. _____

  (b) If both numbers are negative, the sign of the sum is _____.   1b. _____

2. To add two integers that are different signs, subtract the absolute value of the smaller number from the absolute value of the larger number. The sign of the sum is _____.

3. Find the sum: $-45 + (-22)$ *(See textbook Example 5)*

Step 1: Add the absolute values of the two integers.	Find the absolute value of $\left|-45\right|$: **(a)** _____
	Find the absolute value of $\left|-22\right|$: **(b)** _____
	Add (a) and (b): **(c)** _____
Step 2: Attach the common sign, either positive or negative.	The sign of both numbers is negative so the sign of the sum is: **(d)** _____
	Write the sum: **(e)** _____

4. Find the sum: $73 + (-81)$ *(See textbook Example 6)*

Step 1: Subtract the smaller absolute value from the larger absolute value.	Find the absolute value of $\left|73\right|$: **(a)** _____
	Find the absolute value of $\left|-81\right|$: **(b)** _____
	Subtract (a) from (b): **(c)** _____
Step 2: Attach the sign of the integer with the larger absolute value.	Which number has the larger absolute value: **(d)** _____
	What is the sign of (d): **(e)** _____
	Therefore, the sign of the sum is: **(f)** _____
	Write the sum: **(g)** _____

Objective 2: Determine the Additive Inverse of a Number

5. For any real number a other than 0, there is a real number $-a$, called the *additive inverse*, or *opposite*, of a, having the property: $a + (-a) = -a + a = 0$.

Determine the additive inverse of the given real number. *(See textbook Example 7)*

(a) $\dfrac{9}{2}$

(b) -10.3

5a. _____

5b. _____

Objective 3: Subtract Integers

6. Find the difference: $-32 - (-61)$ *(See textbook Example 8)*

Step 1: Change the subtraction problem to an equivalent addition problem.	Write the equivalent addition problem: **(a)** _____
Step 2: Find the sum.	Use the rules from Objective 1 to find the sum from (a): **(b)** _____

Objective 4: Multiply Integers

7. To multiply two integers, multiply the numbers without regard to the sign.

(a) If both numbers have the same sign, the sign of the product is _____.

7a. _____

(b) If both numbers have different signs, the sign of the product is _____.

7b. _____

(c) _____ is neither positive nor negative.

7c. _____

8. Find the product. *(See textbook Example 11)*

(a) $6(-12)$

(b) $(-4)(-15)$

(c) $-13 \bullet 9$

8a. _____

8b. _____

8c. _____

Objective 5: Divide Integers

In Problems 9 – 10, identify the (a) dividend, (b) divisor, and (c) the quotient.

9a. _____   9b. _____   9c. _____

9. $\dfrac{36}{12}$

10. $(-72) \div 72$

10a. _____   10b. _____   10c. _____

11. Find the multiplicative inverse (reciprocal) of -3. *(See textbook Example 14)*

11. _____

Do the Math Exercises 1.4
Adding, Subtracting, Multiplying, and Dividing Integers

In Problems 1–4, find the sum.

1. $-4 + 12$

2. $-13 + (-5)$

1._____

2._____

3. $-145 + (-68)$

4. $(-13) + 37 + (-22)$

3._____

4._____

In Problems 5–6, determine the additive inverse of each real number.

5. -34

6. 7

5._____

6._____

In Problems 7–9, find the difference.

7. $12 - 19$

8. $-15 - 9$

7._____

8._____

9. $46 - (-25)$

9._____

In Problems 10–13, find the product.

10. $7 \cdot 9$

11. $(-22)(-5)$

10._____

11._____

12. (−128)7

13. −6 • 4 • 8

12. _____

13. _____

In Problems 14–15, find the multiplicative inverse (or reciprocal) of each number.

14. 10

15. −3

14. _____

15. _____

In Problems 16–18, find the quotient.

16. 36 ÷ 9

17. $\dfrac{-144}{6}$

16. _____

17. _____

18. $\dfrac{-80}{-12}$

18. _____

In Problems 19–20, write each expression using mathematical symbols. Then evaluate the expression.

19. the sum of 32 and −64

20. −40 divided by 100

19. _____

20. _____

Sullivan/Struve/Mazzarella, *Elementary & Intermediate Algebra*, 2e

Five-Minute Warm-Up 1.5
Adding, Subtracting, Multiplying, and Dividing Rational Numbers

In Problems 1 – 4, perform the indicated operations.

1. $(-15)(-6)$

2. $\dfrac{125}{-5}$

1. _____

2. _____

3. $-36 - 42$

4. $27 + (-163)$

3. _____

4. _____

5. Write $\dfrac{24}{96}$ as a fraction in lowest terms.

5. _____

6. Find the least common denominator of $\dfrac{4}{15}$ and $\dfrac{5}{24}$.

6. _____

7. Rewrite $\dfrac{5}{12}$ as an equivalent fraction with a denominator of 60.

7. _____

Guided Practice 1.5
Adding, Subtracting, Multiplying, and Dividing Rational Numbers

1. Write each rational number in lowest terms.

(a) $\dfrac{-12}{15}$ 　　　　　(b) $-\dfrac{24}{3}$ 　　　　　(c) $\dfrac{-5}{-25}$

1a. _____

1b. _____

1c. _____

Objective 1: Multiply Rational Numbers Expressed as Fractions

2. Find the product: $-\dfrac{7}{72} \cdot \dfrac{81}{35}$ *(See textbook Example 1)*

2. _____

Objective 2: Divide Rational Numbers Expressed as Fractions

3. Find the quotient: $\dfrac{8}{15} \div \dfrac{4}{45}$ *(See textbook Example 2)*

Step 1: Write the equivalent multiplication problem.

$$\dfrac{8}{15} \div \dfrac{4}{45} =$$

(a) _____

Step 2: Write the product in factored form and divide out common factors.

Write the prime factorization of the numerator and denominator:

(b) _____

Divide out common factors:

(c) _____

Step 3: Multiply the remaining factors.

$$\dfrac{8}{15} \div \dfrac{4}{45} =$$ (d) _____

Objective 3: Add and Subtract Rational Numbers Expressed as Fractions

4. Adding or subtracting fractions with the same denominator use the following properties:

$$\dfrac{a}{c} + \dfrac{b}{c} = \dfrac{a+b}{c}, c \neq 0 \qquad \dfrac{a}{c} - \dfrac{b}{c} = \dfrac{a-b}{c}, c \neq 0$$

Find the difference and write in lowest terms, if necessary: $\dfrac{7}{12} - \dfrac{11}{12}$ *(See textbook Example 4)*

(a) Use the property $\dfrac{a}{c} - \dfrac{b}{c} = \dfrac{a-b}{c}$ to write the difference over a single denominator:

4a. _____

(b) Rewrite as an addition problem:

4b. _____

(c) Add the numerators:

4c. _____

(d) Factor and divide out common factors. State the difference: $\dfrac{7}{12} - \dfrac{11}{12} =$

4d. _____

5. Find the sum: $\dfrac{5}{12} + \dfrac{4}{9}$ *(See textbook Example 5)*

Step 1: Find the least common denominator of the denominators.

Write 12 as the product of primes: **(a)** _____

Write 9 as the product of primes: **(b)** _____

Write the factors in the LCD: **(c)** _____

Multiply to determine the LCD: **(d)** _____

Step 2: Write each rational number with the denominator found in Step 1.

To write $\dfrac{5}{12}$ on the LCD, multiply by? **(e)** _____

To write $\dfrac{4}{9}$ on the LCD, multiply by? **(f)** _____

Multiply to find the equivalent fractions.

(g) $\dfrac{5}{12} \cdot \dfrac{\square}{\square} =$; $\dfrac{4}{9} \cdot \dfrac{\square}{\square} =$

Step 3: Add the numerators and write the result over the common denominator.

Add the fractions: **(h)** _____

Step 4: Write in lowest terms.

The result is already in lowest terms. State the sum $\dfrac{5}{12} + \dfrac{4}{9}$: **(i)** _____

6. Evaluate and write in lowest terms, if necessary: $-3 + \dfrac{5}{8}$ *(See textbook Example 7)*

(a) Write the integer -3 as a fraction: 6a. _____

(b) Write each fraction as an equivalent fraction over the common denominator: 6b. _____

(c) Add the numerators and write the result over the common denominator: 6c. _____

(d) Write the fractions in lowest terms, if necessary. State the sum of $-3 + \dfrac{5}{8}$:   6d. _____

Objective 4: Add, Subtract, Multiply, and Divide Rational Numbers Expressed as Decimals

7. To add or subtract decimals, we arrange the numbers in a column with the decimals aligned. Place the decimal point in the answer directly below the decimal point in the problem. When adding or subtracting decimals, any number that has no decimal point has an implied decimal located _____.

8. The number of digits to the right of the decimal point in the product is the same as the _____ of the number of digits to the right of the decimal point in the factors.

Do the Math Exercises 1.5
Adding, Subtracting, Multiplying, and Dividing Rational Numbers

In Problems 1–4, find the product, and write in lowest terms.

1. $\dfrac{7}{8} \cdot \dfrac{10}{21}$

2. $-\dfrac{3}{7} \cdot 63$

1. _____

2. _____

3. $-\dfrac{5}{2} \cdot \dfrac{16}{25}$

4. $-\dfrac{60}{75} \cdot \left(-\dfrac{25}{36}\right)$

3. _____

4. _____

In Problems 5–6, find the reciprocal of each number.

5. $\dfrac{9}{4}$

6. -8

5. _____

6. _____

In Problems 7–10, find the quotient, and write in lowest terms.

7. $\dfrac{1}{2} \div \dfrac{3}{6}$

8. $-\dfrac{1}{4} \div 4$

7. _____

8. _____

9. $\dfrac{4}{3} \div \left(-\dfrac{9}{10}\right)$

10. $\dfrac{44}{63} \div \dfrac{11}{21}$

9. _____

10. _____

In Problems 11–14, find the sum or difference and write in lowest terms.

11. $\dfrac{6}{11} + \dfrac{16}{11}$

12. $-\dfrac{7}{8} + 4$

11. _____

12. _____

13. $-\dfrac{2}{5} + \left(-\dfrac{2}{3}\right)$

14. $-\dfrac{29}{6} - \left(-\dfrac{29}{20}\right)$

13. _____

14. _____

In Problems 15–20, perform the indicated operation.

15. $-(-32.9) + 10.3$

16. $32 - 5.68$

15. _____

16. _____

17. $3.1 \bullet 10.9$

18. $0.065 \bullet 340$

17. _____

18. _____

19. $\dfrac{332.59}{7.9}$

20. $\dfrac{48}{0.03}$

19. _____

20. _____

Five-Minute Warm-Up 1.6
Properties of Real Numbers

In Problems 1 – 4, perform the indicated operations.

1. $-5 + 5 + (-2)$

1. _____

2. $\dfrac{5}{9} \bullet \dfrac{9}{5} \bullet (-12)$

2. _____

3. $\dfrac{8}{1} \bullet \dfrac{1}{12}$

3. _____

4. $-33 \bullet \left(-\dfrac{15}{11}\right)$

4. _____

5. $\dfrac{-75}{-15}$

5. _____

Guided Practice 1.6
Properties of Real Numbers

Objective 1: Understand and Use the Identity Properties of Addition and Multiplication

1. Based on the stated property, write the right side of the equation.

(a) $\frac{4}{7} + 0 =$ ——— ; Identity Property of Addition   1a. _____

(b) $\frac{9}{9} \cdot \left(-\frac{1}{4}\right) =$ ——— ; Multiplicative Identity   1b. _____

2. Perform the following conversions. *(See textbook Example 1)*

(a) 198 inches = ? feet [1 foot = 12 inches]   2b. _____

(b) 15 minutes = ? seconds [1 minute = 60 seconds]   2b. _____

Objective 2: Understand and Use the Commutative Properties of Addition and Multiplication

3. The commutative properties of addition and multiplication say that the _____ in which a   3. _____
problem is written will not change the result.

4. The following operations are *not* commutative: _____ and _____

5. Based on the stated property, write the right side of the equation. *(See textbook Example 2)*

(a) $(-12) + 6 =$ _____ ; Commutative Property of Addition   5a. _____

(b) $(4 + 20) \cdot \frac{1}{2} =$ _____ ; Commutative Property of Multiplication   5b. _____

6. Evaluate the following expressions. *(See textbook Examples 3 and 4)*

(a) $(-17) + 4 + 17$ 6a. _____

(b) $42 \cdot 5 \cdot \left(\frac{3}{7}\right)$ 6a. _____

Objective 3: Understand and Use the Associative Properties of Addition and Multiplication

7. The associative properties of addition and multiplication say that if a problem contains only addition or contains only multiplication, we can keep the order the same but change the _____ of the numbers in the problem and the result will not change.

7. _____

8. Based on the stated property, write the right side of the equation. *(See textbook Example 5)*

(a) $(-9 + 12) + 2 =$ _____ ; Associative Property of Addition

8a. _____

(b) $3 \bullet \left(\dfrac{2}{3} \bullet 15 \right) =$ _____ ; Associative Property of Multiplication

8b. _____

9. Use an Associative Property to evaluate the following expressions. *(See textbook Examples 6 and 7)*

(a) $(-7) + 17 + 10$

9a. _____

(b) $12 \bullet \left(\dfrac{5}{6} \bullet 5 \right)$

9a. _____

Objective 4: Understand the Multiplication and Division Properties of 0

10. Complete the following. *(See textbook Example 8)*

(a) $a \bullet 0 = 0 \bullet a =$ _____

(b) $\dfrac{0}{a} =$ _____ ; $a \neq 0$

(c) $\dfrac{a}{0} =$ _____ ; $a \neq 0$

Do the Math Exercises 1.6
Properties of Real Numbers

In Problems 1–4, convert each measurement to the indicated unit of measurement. Use the following conversions:

1 gallon = 4 quarts   *3 feet = 1 yard*
16 ounces = 1 pound   *100 centimeters = 1 meter*

1. 130 feet to yards   **2.** 5900 centimeters to meters   1. _____

2. _____

3. 58 quarts to gallons   **4.** 120 ounces to pounds   3. _____

4. _____

In Problems 5–8, state the property of real numbers that is being illustrated.

5. $4 \bullet 63 \bullet \frac{1}{4} = 4 \bullet \frac{1}{4} \bullet 63$ **6.** $(4 \bullet 5) \bullet 7 = 4 \bullet (5 \bullet 7)$ 5. _____

6. _____

7. $\frac{-8}{0}$ **8.** $\frac{5}{12} \bullet \frac{12}{5} = 1$ 7. _____

8. _____

In Problems 9–17, evaluate each expression by using the properties of real numbers.

9. $46 + 59 + (-46)$ **10.** $\frac{4}{9} \bullet \frac{9}{4} \bullet 28$ 9. _____

10. _____

11. $36 \cdot (-12) \cdot \dfrac{1}{6}$

12. $\dfrac{13}{2} \cdot \dfrac{8}{39} \cdot \dfrac{39}{4}$

11. _____

12. _____

13. $\dfrac{0}{100}$

14. $4000(0.5)(0.001)$

13. _____

14. _____

15. $104 \cdot \dfrac{1}{104}$

16. $30 \cdot \dfrac{4}{4}$

15. _____

16. _____

17. $\dfrac{7}{48} \cdot \left(-\dfrac{21}{4} \right) \cdot \dfrac{12}{7}$

17. _____

Sullivan/Struve/Mazzarella, *Elementary & Intermediate Algebra*, 2e

Five-Minute Warm-Up 1.7
Exponents and the Order of Operations

1. Find the sum: $-56 + (-25)$

1. _____

2. Find the difference: $-17 - 31$

2. _____

3. Find the product: $-36 \bullet \left(\dfrac{8}{9}\right)$

3. _____

4. Find the quotient: $\dfrac{135}{-3}$

4. _____

5. Evaluate the expression: $35 - 43 + (-18) + 96$

5. _____

6. Find the product: $(-3) \bullet (-3) \bullet (-3) \bullet (-3)$

6. _____

Guided Practice 1.7
Exponents and the Order of Operations

Objective 1: Evaluate Exponential Expressions

1. Integer exponents provide a shorthand device for representing repeated multiplications of a real number. In the expression 2^5,

(a) 2 is called the _____   1a. _____

(b) 5 is called the _____   1b. _____

(c) To evaluate the expression, multiply _____ = _____.   1c. _____

(See textbook Example 2)

2. Identify the base for each expression. *(See textbook Example 1)*

(a) -9^2 (b) $(-9)^4$ 2a. _____

                                                                     2b. _____

3. Consider the number -6.

(a) Another word for raising the number -6 to the second power is to say -6 ___.   3a. _____

(b) This is written _____.   3b. _____

(c) To evaluate the expression, multiply _____ = _____.   3c. _____

(See textbook Example 4)

4. Consider the number -5.

(a) Another word for raising the number -5 to the third power is to say -5 ____.   4a. _____

(b) This is written _____.   4b. _____

(c) To evaluate the expression, multiply _____ = _____.   4c. _____

(See textbook Example 3)

Objective 2: Apply the Rules for Order of Operations

5. Complete the following table.

			Order of Operations
(a)	**P**	_____	This includes all possible grouping symbols.
(b)	**E**	_____	Work from left to right.
(c)	**M/D**	_____	Work from left to right.
(d)	**A/S**	_____	Work from left to right.

6. We use a variety of grouping symbols. When multiple pairs of grouping symbols exist and are nested inside one another, we evaluate the information in the innermost grouping symbol first and work our way outward.

Besides nested parentheses, what grouping symbols might appear in an expression with multiple operations?

6. _____

7. Evaluate the expression: $5 - 24 \div 6 \bullet 9$ *(See textbook Example 5)*

7. _____

8. Evaluate the expression: $\dfrac{4 \bullet 2^3 + (-16)}{3(4-6)^2}$ *(See textbook Examples 9 and 10)*

Step 1: Evaluate the expression in parentheses first.

$\dfrac{4 \bullet 2^3 + (-16)}{3(4-6)^2}$ = **(a)** _____

Step 2: Evaluate the exponents.

= **(b)** _____

Step 3: Find products.

= **(c)** _____

Step 4: Add terms in numerator.

= **(d)** _____

Step 5: Write in lowest terms.

= **(e)** _____

Do the Math Exercises 1.7
Exponents and the Order of Operations

In Problems 1–2, write in exponential form.

1. $4 \bullet 4 \bullet 4 \bullet 4 \bullet 4$ **2.** $(-8)(-8)(-8)$

1. _____

2. _____

In Problems 3–8, evaluate each exponential expression.

3. 2^5 **4.** $\left(\dfrac{5}{2}\right)^4$

3. _____

4. _____

5. $(0.04)^2$ **6.** -5^4

5. _____

6. _____

7. 1^6 **8.** $\left(-\dfrac{3}{2}\right)^5$

7. _____

8. _____

In Problems 9–19, evaluate each expression.

9. $12 + 8 \bullet 3$ **10.** $50 \div 5 \bullet 4$

9. _____

10. _____

11. $(7-5) \bullet \dfrac{5}{2}$

12. $\dfrac{5+3}{3+15}$

11. _____

12. _____

13. $12 - [7 + (-6)3]$

14. $(-11.8 - 15.2) \div (-2)$

13. _____

14. _____

15. $-10 - 4^2$

16. $-5^2 + 3^2 \div \left(3^2 + 9\right)$

15. _____

16. _____

17. $\left(\dfrac{7 - 5^2}{8 + 4 \bullet 2}\right)^2$

18. $3 \bullet \left[6 \bullet (5-2) - 2 \bullet 5\right]$

17. _____

18. _____

19. $\left(\dfrac{3}{4} + \dfrac{1}{2}\right)\left(\dfrac{2}{3} - \dfrac{1}{2}\right)$

19. _____

Sullivan/Struve/Mazzarella, *Elementary & Intermediate Algebra*, 2e

Five-Minute Warm-Up 1.8
Simplifying Algebraic Expressions

1. Find the sum: $-14 + 37$ 1. _____

2. Find the difference: $-26 - (-16)$ 2. _____

3. Find the product: $72 \cdot \left(-\dfrac{5}{8}\right)$ 3. _____

4. Find the quotient: $\dfrac{-105}{-15}$ 4. _____

5. Evaluate each of the following:
   (a) $(-4)^2$ (b) -4^2 5a. _____

                                                                                          5b. _____

6. Simplify: $\left(-13 + (-2)\right)^2$ 6. _____

Guided Practice 1.8
Simplifying Algebraic Expressions

Objective 1: Evaluate Algebraic Expressions

1. A letter that represents any number from a set of numbers is called a(n) _____.   1._____

2. A fixed number, such as 3, or a letter or symbol that represents a fixed number is
a(n) _____.   2._____

3. Any combination of variables, constants, grouping symbols, and mathematical operations
is called a(n) _____ _____.   3._____

4. When we substitute a numerical value for each variable in an expression and then
simplify the result, we are _____ an algebraic expression.   4._____

5. Evaluate the algebraic expression $2x^2 - 5x + 3$ for $x = -2$. *(See textbook Example 1)*   5._____

Objective 2: Identify Like Terms and Unlike Terms

6. A constant or the product of a constant and one or more variables raised to a power is
called a _____.   6._____

7. The numerical factor of a term is called a(n) _____.   7._____

8. When terms have the same variable(s) and the same exponent(s) on the variables, we say
that the expressions are _____ _____.   8._____

9. Identify the terms in the algebraic expression $x^2 - 2xy - y^2$. *(See textbook Example 3)*   9._____

10. Determine the coefficient of each term. *(See textbook Examples 4 and 5)*

   (a) $\dfrac{x}{2}$ **(b)** $-y$ **(c)** 14   **(d)** $-\dfrac{2z}{5}$ 10a._____

                                                                                            10b._____

                                                                                            10c._____

                                                                                            10d._____

11. Determine if the following pairs of terms are *like* or *unlike*. *(See textbook Example 6)*

(a) $4xy^2$ and $2x^2y$ (b) $\dfrac{3}{4}n^3$ and $5n^3$

11a. _____

11b. _____

Objective 3: Use the Distributive Property

12. Use the Distributive Property to remove the parentheses. *(See textbook Example 7)*

(a) $2(3x-1)$ (b) $-\dfrac{1}{5}(10y+5)$

12a. _____

12b. _____

Objective 4: Simplify Algebraic Expressions by Combining Like Terms

13. Combine like terms. *(See textbook Examples 8 and 9)*

(a) $x+3x$ (b) $4x^2 - x + 2 - 4x^2 + 7x + 1$

13a. _____

13b. _____

14. Simplify the algebraic expression: $5 + 2(6x+1) - (3x-5)$ *(See textbook Example 10)* 14. _____

Do the Math Exercises 1.8
Simplifying Algebraic Expressions

In Problems 1–2, evaluate each expression using the given values of the variables.

1. $n^2 - 4n + 3$ for $n = 2$

2. $-2p^2 + 5p + 1$ for $p = -3$

1. _____

2. _____

In Problems 3–4, for each expression, identify the terms and then name the coefficient of each term.

3. $3m^4 - m^3 n^2 + 4n - 1$

4. $t^3 - \dfrac{t}{4}$

3. _____

4. _____

In Problems 5–6, determine if the terms are like or unlike.

5. -13 and 38

6. $x^2 y^3$ and $y^2 x^3$

5. _____

6. _____

In Problems 7–8, use the Distributive Property to remove the parentheses.

7. $3(4s + 2)$

8. $-5(k - n)$

7. _____

8. _____

In Problems 9–14, simplify each expression by using the Distributive Property to remove parentheses and combining like terms.

9. $x + 2y + 5x + 7y$

10. $-7p^5 + 2p^5$

9. _____

10. _____

11. $-(-6m + 9n - 8p)$

12. $18m - (6 + 9m)$

11. _____

12. _____

13. $\dfrac{3}{5}y + \dfrac{7}{10}y$

14. $\dfrac{1}{5}(60 - 15x) + \dfrac{3}{4}(12 - 24x)$

13. _____

14. _____

15. Ticket Sales A community college theatre group sold tickets to a recent production. Student tickets cost \$5 and nonstudent tickets cost \$8. The algebraic expression $5s + 8n$ represents the total revenue from selling s student tickets and n nonstudent tickets. Evaluate $5s + 8n$ for $s = 76$ and $n = 63$.

15. _____

Five-Minute Warm-Up 2.1
Linear Equations: The Addition and Multiplication Properties of Equality

1. Determine the additive inverse of $-\dfrac{2}{3}$.   1. _____

2. Determine the multiplicative inverse of 14.   2. _____

3. Evaluate: $-\dfrac{5}{2}\left(-\dfrac{2}{5}\right)$ 3. _____

4. Use the Distributive Property to simplify: $-3(6x+5)$ 4. _____

5. Simplify: $9-\dfrac{1}{2}(12x-4)$ 5. _____

6. Evaluate $\dfrac{7}{4}x+2$ for $x=-16$.   6. _____

Guided Practice 2.1
Linear Equations: The Addition and Multiplication Properties of Equality

Objective 1: Determine If a Number Is a Solution of an Equation

1. How do you determine if a value of a variable is a solution to an equation?

2. Determine if the given value of the variable is a solution of the equation $-3x + 5 = -10$.
(See textbook Example 1)

  (a) $x = 5$ **(b)** $x = -5$ 2a. _____

                                                2b. _____

Objective 2: Use the Addition Property of Equality to Solve linear Equations

3. In your own words, state the Addition Property of Equality.

4. Will the Addition Property of Equality allow you to subtract the same number from both sides of an equation to form an equivalent equation? Explain your reasoning.

5. The goal in solving a linear equation is to get the variable by itself with a coefficient of 1. We call this

process _____ _____ _____.

6. Solve the linear equation: $x + 13 = -11$ *(See textbook Example 2)*

Step 1: Isolate the variable x on the left side of the equation.		$x + 13 = -11$
	Subtract 13 from both sides:	**(a)** $x + 13 - \underline{\quad} = -11 - \underline{\quad}$
Step 2: Simplify the left and right sides of the equation.	Apply the Additive Inverse Property, $a + (-a) = 0$:	**(b)** _____
	Apply the Additive Identity Property, $a + 0 = a$	**(c)** _____
Step 3: Check Verify your value for x in the original equation.	Replace x in the original equation to see if a true statement results.	$x + 13 = -11$
	State the solution set:	**(d)** _____

Objective 3: Use the Multiplication Property of Equality

7. In your own words, state the Multiplication Property of Equality. Do you believe this property will hold true for division as well? Why or why not?

8. Solve the linear equation: $-9x = 324$ *(See textbook Example 5)*

Step 1: Get the coefficient of the variable *x* to be 1.		$-9x = 324$
	Multiply both sides by the reciprocal of the coefficient, $-\dfrac{1}{9}$:	**(a)** _____ $\bullet (-9x) =$ _____ $\bullet (324)$
Step 2: Simplify the left and right sides of the equation.	Regroup factors using the Associative Property of Multiplication:	**(b)** _____
	Apply the Multiplicative Inverse Property, $a \bullet \dfrac{1}{a} = 1$:	**(c)** _____
	Apply the Multiplicative Identity, $1 \bullet a = a$:	**(d)** _____
Step 3: Check Verify your value for *x* in the original equation.	Replace *x* in the original equation to see if a true statement results.	$-9x = 324$
	State the solution set:	**(e)** _____

9. State the first step necessary to isolate the variable. *(See textbook Examples 6 – 9)*

(a) $3p = -45$

9a. _____

(b) $\dfrac{x}{15} = -15$

9b. _____

(c) $-18 = -\dfrac{2}{3}y$

9c. _____

(d) $\dfrac{8}{3} = \dfrac{4}{9}n$

9d. _____

Do the Math Exercises 2.1
Linear Equations: The Addition and Multiplication Properties of Equality

In Problems 1–4, determine if the given value is a solution to the equation. Answer Yes or No.

1. $4t + 2 = 16$; $t = 3$ **2.** $3(x + 1) - x = 5x - 9$; $x = -3$ 1. _____

2. _____

3. $-15 = 3x - 16$; $x = \dfrac{1}{3}$ **4.** $3s - 6 = 6s - 3.4$; $s = -1.2$ 3. _____

4. _____

In Problems 5–8, solve the equation using the Addition Property of Equality. Be sure to check your solution.

5. $13 = u - 6$ **6.** $-2 = y + 13$ 5. _____

6. _____

7. $x - \dfrac{1}{8} = \dfrac{3}{8}$ **8.** $\dfrac{3}{8} = y - \dfrac{1}{6}$ 7. _____

8. _____

Do the Math Exercises 2.1

In Problems 9–14, solve the equation using the Multiplication Property of Equality. Be sure to check your solution.

9. $4z = 30$ **10.** $-8p = 20$

9. _____

10. _____

11. $\dfrac{4}{3}b = 16$ **12.** $-\dfrac{6}{5}n = -36$

11. _____

12. _____

13. $\dfrac{1}{4}w = \dfrac{7}{2}$ **14.** $\dfrac{3}{10}q = -\dfrac{1}{6}$

13. _____

14. _____

15. New Kayak The total cost for a new kayak is \$862.92, including sales tax of \$63.92. To find the cost of the kayak without tax, solve the equation $k + 63.92 = 862.92$, where k represents the cost of the kayak.

15. _____

Five-Minute Warm-Up 2.2
Linear Equations: Using the Properties Together

1. Simplify by combining like terms: $3x - 2(5x + 4) - 4x$

1. _____

2. Evaluate the expression $-7(4x - 3) - 12$ for $x = -3$.

2. _____

3. Simplify: $\dfrac{4}{3} \bullet \left(\dfrac{3}{4}x\right)$

3. _____

4. Simplify by combining like terms: $8x + 3 - 12 - 6x$

4. _____

5. Simplify: $\dfrac{-12}{-28}$

5. _____

6. Divide: $\dfrac{106}{0.8}$

6. _____

Guided Practice 2.2
Linear Equations: Using the Properties Together

Objective 1: Apply the Addition and the Multiplication Properties of Equality to Solve Linear Equations

1. Solve the equation: $6x - 9 = -27$ *(See textbook Example 1)*

Step 1: Isolate the term containing the variable.		$6x - 9 = -27$
	Apply the Addition Property of Equality and add ___ to both sides of the equation:	**(a)** _____
		(b) $6x - 9 + $ ___ $ = -27 + $ ___
	Simplify:	**(c)** _____
Step 2: Get the coefficient of the variable to be 1.	Apply the Multiplication Property of Equality and divide both sides of the equation by ___ (this is the same as multiplying both sides by ___):	**(d)** _____ ; _____
		(e) $\dfrac{6x}{\_\_} = \dfrac{-18}{\_\_}$
	Simplify:	**(f)** _____
Step 3: Check Verify your value for x in the original equation.	Replace x in the original equation to see if a true statement results.	$6x - 9 = -27$
	State the solution set:	**(g)** _____

2. Solve the equation: $\dfrac{5}{4}n + 3 = -12$ *(See textbook Example 2)* $\dfrac{5}{4}n + 3 = -12$

 (a) Subtract 3 from both sides of the equation: **(a)** _____

 (b) Simplify: **(b)** _____

 (c) Multiply both sides of the equation by $\dfrac{4}{5}$:   **(c)** _____

 (d) Simplify: **(d)** _____

 (e) State the solution set: **(e)** _____

Objective 2: Combine Like Terms and Apply the Distributive Property to Solve Linear Equations

3. Before using the Addition or Multiplication Property of Equality to solve an equation, we must begin by simplifying each side of the equation. If a side of the equation has two or more like terms, we begin by

4. When an equation contains parentheses, we use the _____ Property to remove the parentheses before we use the Addition or Multiplication Property of Equality to solve the equation.

5. In the following equations, combine like terms and/or use the Distributive Property to remove the parentheses. What equation is left to solve? *DO NOT SOLVE THE EQUATION.* *(See textbook Examples 3 and 4)*

   (a) $5x + 3 - 7x + 2 = -4$ **(b)** $4 + 8(3n + 4) = -2(n - 1) - 3$ 5a. _____

                                                                         5b. _____

Objective 3: *Solve a Linear Equation with the Variable on Both Sides of the Equation*

6. Our goal is to get the terms that contain the variable on one side of the equation and the constant terms on the other side. In the equation $6 - 5x = 4 + 3x$, what steps would accomplish this goal? **Hint:** There is more than one option. *(See textbook Example 5)*

7. Solve the equation: $3(z + 5) - 16z = 2 - (z + 3)$ *(See textbook Example 6)*

Step 1: Remove any parentheses using the Distributive Property.		$3(z + 5) - 16z = 2 - (z + 3)$
	Use the Distributive Property:	**(a)** _____
Step 2: Combine like terms on each side of the equation.	Combine like terms:	**(b)** _____
Step 3: Use the Addition Property of Equality to get the terms with the variable on one side of the equation and the constants on the other side.	Add z to both sides of the equation:	**(c)** _____
	Simplify:	**(d)** _____
	Subtract 15 from both sides:	**(e)** _____
	Simplify:	**(f)** _____
Step 4: Use the Multiplication Property of Equality to get the coefficient of the variable to be 1.	Divide both sides by -12:	**(g)** _____
	Simplify:	**(h)** _____
Step 5: Check the solution to verify that is satisfies the original equation.	We leave the check to you.	
	State the solution set:	**(i)** _____

Do the Math Exercises 2.2
Linear Equations: Using the Properties Together

In Problems 1–4, solve the equation. Check your solution.

1. $-4x + 3 = 15$

2. $6z - 7 = 3$

1. _____

2. _____

3. $\dfrac{5}{4}a + 3 = 13$

4. $\dfrac{1}{5}p - 3 = 2$

3. _____

4. _____

In Problems 5–8, solve the equation. Check your solution.

5. $5r + 2 - 3r = -14$

6. $2b + 5 - 8b = 23$

5. _____

6. _____

7. $3(t - 4) = -18$

8. $-5(6 + z) = -20$

7. _____

8. _____

In Problems 9–12, solve the equation. Check your solution.

9. $3 + 8x = 21 - x$

10. $6 - 12m = -3m + 3$

9. _____

10. _____

11. $-4(10 - 7x) = 3x + 10$

12. $-8 + 4(p + 6) = 10p$

11. _____

12. _____

13. Wendy's A Wendy's Mandarin Chicken salad contains 10 grams of fat less than a Taco   13. _____
Bell Zesty Chicken Border Bowl. If there are 60 grams of fat in the two salads, find the
number of grams of fat in the Taco Bell Zesty Chicken Border Bowl by solving the
equation $x + (x - 10) = 60$, where x represents the number of grams of fat in a Taco Bell
Border Bowl and $x - 10$ represents the number of grams of fat in the Wendy's Mandarin
Chicken salad.

14. Overtime Pay Juan worked a total of 50 hours last week and earned $498.75. He   14. _____
earned 1.5 times his regular hourly rate for 6 hours, and double his hourly rate for 4
holiday hours. Solve the equation $40x + 6(1.5x) + 4(2x) = \$498.75$, where x is Juan's
regular hourly rate.

15. Perimeter of a Triangle The perimeter of a triangle is 210 inches. If the sides are made   15. _____
up of 3 consecutive even integers, find the lengths of each of the 3 sides by solving the
equation $x + (x + 2) + (x + 4) = 210$, where x represents the length of the shortest side.

Five-Minute Warm-Up 2.3
Solving Linear Equations Involving Fractions and Decimals; Classifying Equations

1. Find the LCD of $\dfrac{6}{7}$ and $\dfrac{2}{5}$.   1. _____

2. Find the LCD of $-\dfrac{4}{25}$ and $\dfrac{7}{45}$.   2. _____

3. Use the Distributive Property to simplify: $-4\left(\dfrac{3}{4}x - 1\right)$ 3. _____

4. Multiply: $100(0.43x - 2.7)$ 4. _____

5. Simplify by combining like terms: $3 - 0.5(10x - 50) + 6x$

   5. _____

6. Simplify by combining like terms: $\dfrac{4}{3}\left[9 + 3(x - 5)\right]$ 6. _____

7. Simplify by combining like terms: $6\left(\dfrac{5x + 1}{3} - 2\right)$ 7. _____

Guided Practice 2.3
Solving Linear Equations Involving Fractions and Decimals; Classifying Equations

Objective 1: Use the Least Common Denominator to Solve a Linear Equation Containing Fractions

1. Solve the linear equation: $\frac{3}{2}x - \frac{4}{3}x = -\frac{9}{4}$ *(See textbook Example 1)*

Step 1: Apply the Distributive Property to remove parentheses.

Determine the LCD: **(a)** _____

Use the Multiplication Property of Equality: **(b)** ___ $\bullet \left(\frac{3}{2}x - \frac{4}{3}x \right) =$ ___ $\bullet \left(-\frac{9}{4} \right)$

Use the Distributive Property: **(c)** ___ $\bullet \left(\frac{3}{2}x \right) -$ ___ $\bullet \left(\frac{4}{3}x \right) =$ ___ $\bullet \left(-\frac{9}{4} \right)$

Simplify (c):   **(d)** _____

Step 2: Combine like terms.

Combine like terms: **(e)** _____

Step 3: Use the Addition Property of Equality to get the terms with the variable on one side of the equation and the constants on the other side.

This step is not necessary as the variable term is on the left side and the constant term on right.

Step 4: Get the coefficient of the variable to be 1.

Divide both sides by 2:   **(f)** _____

Simplify: **(g)** _____

Step 5: Check Verify your value for *x* in the original equation.

Replace *x* in the original equation to see if a true statement results.

State the solution set: **(h)** _____

2. Solve the equation $\frac{4x+3}{9} + 1 = \frac{2x+1}{2}$. *(See textbook Example 2)*

We will multiply both sides of the equation by the LCD to remove the fractions from the equation. *DO NOT FINISH SOLVING THE EQUATION.*

(a) Identify the LCD of the denominators in the equation: **(a)** _____

(b) Apply the Multiplication Property of Equality.   **(b)** _____

(c) Distribute the LCD to each terms and divide out common factors: **(c)** _____

(d) Use the Distributive Property to remove parentheses: **(d)** _____

(e) Combine like terms on each side of the equation: **(e)** _____

Objective 2: Solve a Linear Equation Containing Decimals

3. When encountering an equation that contains decimals, an option is to multiply both sides of the equation by some power of 10 that will clear the decimals. Try solving an equation that contains decimals using this technique and alternately leaving the decimals in the equation. Which method do you prefer?

Solve: $0.06x + 0.075(7500 - x) = 517.5$ *(See textbook Example 5)*   3. _____

Objective 3: Classify a Linear Equation as an Identity, Conditional, or a Contradiction

4. Solve the linear equation $-2(3x - 1) = 4 - 6(x + 3)$. State whether the equation is an identity, contradiction or conditional equation. *(See textbook Example 6)*

(a) Is the last statement of the solution true or false? _____

(b) Therefore the solution set is _____

(c) Is this equation an identity, contradiction or a conditional equation? _____

Objective 4: Use Linear Equations to Solve Problems

5. Martina saves dimes and quarters in a piggy bank. She opened the bank and discovered that she had $24.85 from a total of 127 coins. Martina wants to know how many dimes and how many quarters are in the bank….apparently, she doesn't want to just count them. To find the number of quarters, q, she solves the equation: $0.10(127 - q) + 0.25q = 24.85$. *(See textbook Example 9)*

(a) Solve the equation. What value did you find for the value of q? _____

(b) Check. Number of dimes plus number of quarters = 127? _____ Total value of $24.85? _____

(c) Answer the question: How many dimes were there?_____ How many quarters were there?_____

Do the Math Exercises 2.3
Solving Linear Equations Involving Fractions and Decimals; Classifying Equations

In Problems 1–4, solve the equation. Check your solution.

1. $\dfrac{3}{2}n - \dfrac{4}{11} = \dfrac{91}{22}$

2. $\dfrac{3m}{8} - 1 = \dfrac{5}{6}$

1. _____

2. _____

3. $\dfrac{3}{2}b - \dfrac{4}{5}b = \dfrac{28}{5}$

4. $\dfrac{2}{3}(6 - x) = \dfrac{5x}{6}$

3. _____

4. _____

In Problems 5–8, solve the equation. Check your solution.

5. $0.3z = 6$

6. $p + 0.04p = 260$

5. _____

6. _____

7. $0.7y - 4.6 = 0.4y - 2.2$

8. $5 - 0.2(m - 2) = 3.6m + 1.6$

7. _____

8. _____

In Problems 9–12, solve the equation. State whether the equation is a contradiction, an identity, or a conditional equation.

9. $4(y - 2) = 5y - (y + 1)$

10. $-3x + 2 + 5x = 2(x + 1)$

9. _____

10. _____

11. $7b + 2(b - 4) = 8b - (3b + 2)$

12. $\dfrac{2m+1}{4} - \dfrac{m}{6} = \dfrac{m}{3} - 1$

11.

12. _____

13. Team Sweatshirt Your favorite college has logo sweatshirts on sale for $33.60. The sweatshirt has been marked down by 30%. To find the original price of the sweatshirt, x, solve the equation $x - 0.30x = 33.60$.

13.

14. Clean Car Pablo cleaned out his car and found nickels and quarters in the car seats. He found $4.25 in change and noticed that the number of quarters was 5 less than twice the number of nickels. Solve the equation $0.05n + 0.25(2n - 5) = 4.25$ to find n, the number of nickels Pablo found.

14. _____

15. Paying Your Taxes You are married and just determined that you paid $12,200 in federal income taxes in 2008. The solution to the equation $12,200 = 0.15(x - 14,600) + 1460$ represents the adjusted gross income of you and your spouse in 2008. Determine the adjusted gross income of you and your spouse in 2008.

15.

Five-Minute Warm-Up 2.4
Evaluating Formulas and Solving Formulas for a Variable

1. Evaluate the expression $2L + 2W$ for $L = 10.5$ and $W = 3.5$

1. _____

2. Round the expression 12.3762 to the hundredths place.

2. _____

3. Write the percent as a decimal: 7.25%

3. _____

4. Multiply and round your answer to the nearest tenth: $25 \bullet \pi$

4. _____

5. Solve: $-4x + 5 = -11$

5. _____

Guided Practice 2.4
Evaluating Formulas and Solving Formulas for a Variable

Objective 1: Evaluate a Formula

1. A formula is an equation that describes how two or more variables are related. If you travel in Europe and the temperature is $20°$ Celsius, use the formula $F = \frac{9}{5}C + 32$ to find the equivalent temperature in degrees Fahrenheit. *(See textbook Example 1)*

1. _____

2. Many times we solve problems that involve simple interest. Simple interest is money that is paid for the use of money, without any effect of compounding (receiving interest on the interest). For each of the variables in the simple interest formula, identify what the variable represents.

$I = Prt$			
I		r	
P		t	

3. List the formulas for each of the following geometric figures. *(Refer to textbook Section 2.4, as necessary.)*

(a) **Square**	(b) **Rectangle**
Area:_____ Perimeter: _____	Area:_____ Perimeter: _____
(c) **Triangle**	(d) **Trapezoid**
Area:_____ Perimeter: _____	Area:_____ Perimeter: _____
(e) **Parallelogram**	(f) **Circle**
Area:_____ Perimeter: _____	Area:_____ Circumference: _____
(g) **Cube**	(h) **Rectangular Solid**
Volume:_____ Surface Area: _____	Volume:_____ Surface Area: _____
(i) **Sphere**	(j) **Right Circular Cylinder**
Volume:_____ Surface Area:_____	Volume:_____ Surface Area: _____
(k) **Cone**	
Volume:_____	

4. Find the number of meters of fencing that must be purchased to enclose a dog run that is 8.5 meters long and 6.75 meters wide. If fencing cost $15 per meter, how much will it cost to install the fence?

(a) What formula will you need to solve this problem? *(See textbook Examples 4 and 5)* 4a. _____

(b) Substitute the values in the problem into the formula to find how much fencing is required.

4b. _____

(c) Multiply to find the cost.

4c. _____

Objective 2: Solve a formula for a Variable

5. Solve $6x - 12y = -24$ for y. *(See textbook Examples 7 and 8)*

Step 1: Isolate the term containing the variable, y.

$$6x - 12y = -24$$

Subtract $6x$ from both sides of the equation to isolate the term $-12y$: **(a)** _____

Simplify: **(b)** _____

Step 2: Get the coefficient of the variable to be 1.

Divide both sides of the equation by -12: **(c)** _____

Simplify using $\dfrac{a-b}{c} = \dfrac{a}{c} - \dfrac{b}{c}$: **(d)** $y = $ _____

6. The amount of profit P, earned by a manufacturer is given by the formula $P = R - C$, where R represents the manufacturer's revenue and C represents the manufacturer's costs. *(See textbook Example 9)*

   (a) Solve the equation for C, the manufacturer's costs.   6a. _____

   (b) Find the amount of costs incurred if the manufacturer has a $5200 profit and $7300   6b. _____
   in revenue.

Do the Math Exercises 2.4
Evaluating Formulas and Solving Formulas for a Variable

In Problems 1–5, substitute the given values into the formula and then evaluate to find the unknown quantity. Label units in the answer. If the answer is not exact, round your answer to the nearest hundredth.

1. **Length of a Bridge** The formula $m = 0.3048f$ converts length in feet f to length in meters m. The George Washington Bridge in New York City is 3500 feet long. How long is the George Washington Bridge in meters?

    1.

2. **Salesperson's Earnings** The formula $E = 750 + 0.07S$ is a formula for the earnings, E, of a salesperson who receives $750 per week plus 7% commission on all sales, S. Find the earnings of a salesperson who had weekly sales of $1200.

    2.

3. **Investing an Inheritance** Christopher invested his $5000 inheritance from his grandmother in a 9-month Certificate of Deposit that earns 4% simple interest per annum. Use the formula $I = Prt$ to find the amount of interest Christopher's investment will earn.

    3. _____

4. Consider the rectangle below.

    20
    32

    a) Find the perimeter of the rectangle.

    4a. _____

    (b) Find the area of the rectangle.

    4b. _____

5. For the problems below, use $\pi \approx 3.14$.

    $r = 2.8$

    (a) Find the circumference of the circle.

    5a. _____

    (b) Find the area of the circle.

    5b. _____

In Problems 6–9, solve each formula for the stated variable.

6. $F = mv^2$; solve for m

7. $V = \dfrac{1}{3}Bh$; solve for B

6. _____

7. _____

8. $S = a + b + c$; solve for b

9. $P = 2l + 2w$; solve for l

8. _____

9. _____

In Problems 10–13, solve each formula for y.

10. $-2x + y = 18$

11. $12x - 6y = 18$

10. _____

11. _____

12. $5x + 6y = 18$

13. $\dfrac{2}{3}x - \dfrac{5}{2}y = 5$

12. _____

13. _____

In Problems 14–15, (a) solve for the indicated variable, and then (b) find the value of the unknown quantity. When given, label units in the answer.

14. **Profit = Revenue – Cost:** $P = R - C$

   (a) Solve for R.

   14a. _____

   (b) Find R when $P = \$4525$ and $C = \$1475$.

   14b. _____

15. **Simple Interest:** $I = Prt$

   (a) Solve for t.

   15a. _____

   (b) Find t when $I = \$42$, $P = \$525$, and $r = 4\%$.

   15b. _____

Five-Minute Warm-Up 2.5
Introduction to Problem Solving: Direct Translation Problems

1. Solve the equation: $x - 17.38 = -72.1$ 1. _____

2. Solve the equation: $x + 0.05x = 33.6$ 2. _____

3. Each of the following words or phrases can be replaced with one of the symbols: $+ \, / - / \times / \div$.
Select the correct symbol for each word or phrase.

(a) twice	**(b)** less than	**(c)** of	**(d)** sum	3a. _____
				3b. _____
				3c. _____
				3d. _____
(e) per	**(f)** increased by	**(g)** difference	**(h)** quotient	3e. _____
				3f. _____
				3g. _____
				3h. _____
(i) fewer	**(j)** greater than	**(k)** ratio	**(l)** decreased by	3i. _____
				3j. _____
				3k. _____
				3l. _____
(m) product	**(n)** exceeds by	**(o)** more than	**(p)** double	3m. _____
				3n. _____
				3o. _____
				3p. _____
(q) less	**(r)** times	**(s)** half	**(t)** altogether	3q. _____
				3r. _____
				3s. _____
				3t. _____

Guided Practice 2.5
Introduction to Problem Solving: Direct Translation Problems

Objective 1: Translate English Phrases to Algebraic Expressions

1. Express each English phrase as an algebraic expression. *(See textbook Example 1)*

(a) The sum of -5 and $3x$ (b) 5 times the sum of r and 25   1a. _____

1b. _____

(c) The sum of 3 times a number x and 12   (d) The ratio of twice a number p and 7   1c. _____

1d. _____

(e) 18 less than half of a number z (f) The difference of w and 900   1e. _____

1f. _____

2. Order matters when subtracting and dividing. Translate the English phrase as an algebraic expression.

(a) a less than b (b) a less b (c) a subtracted from b 2a. _____

2b. _____

2c. _____

(d) a divided by b (e) a divided into b 2d. _____

2e. _____

Objective 2: Translate English Sentences to Equations

3. Translate each sentence into an equation. Do not solve the equation. *(See textbook Example 4)*

(a) The sum of 5 and x is 19.   (b) 14 less than twice y is 30.   3a. _____

3b. _____

(c) The difference of z and 9 is the same as 6 more than two-fifths of z.   3c. _____

4. List six steps for solving problems with mathematical models.

_____   _____

_____   _____

_____   _____

Objective 3: Build Models for Solving Direct Translation Problems

5. If n represents the first of three unknown consecutive integers, how would you represent the next two

integers? (a) _____   (b) _____

6. If x represents the first of four unknown consecutive even integers, how would you represent the next

three even integers? (a) _____   (b) _____   (c) _____

7. If p represents the first of four unknown consecutive odd integers, how would you represent the next three

odd integers? **(a)** _____ **(b)** _____ **(c)** _____

8. The sum of three consecutive odd integers is 453. Find the integers. *(See textbook Example 6)*

Step 1: **Identify** We are looking for three consecutive odd integers whose sum is 453.

(a) Step 2: **Name** Let n represent the first integer. What expression represents the next

odd integer? _____ the third odd integer? _____

(b) Step 3: **Translate** Write an equation for the sum of the three odd integers. _____

(c) Step 4: **Solve** your equation from Step 3. What value did you find for n? _____

Step 5: **Check** Find the other integers. Do they meet the criteria in the problem?

(d) Step 6: **Answer the Question** _____

9. Lucky you! A long-lost uncle left you $20,000 in his will. You have decided to invest the money in two different accounts, a conservative bond fund and a more aggressive stock account. If you will invest $5000 less in the bond fund than the stock account, how much of the $20,000 will you invest in each account? *(See textbook Example 8)*

Step 1: **Identify** We want to know how much to invest in each account.

(a) Step 2: **Name** Let x represent the amount in the stock account. What algebraic expression

represents $5000 less going in the bond fund? _____

(b) Step 3: **Translate** Write an equation for the sum of the two accounts: _____

(c) Step 4: **Solve** your equation from Step 3. What value did you find for x? _____

Step 5: **Check** Use your value for the stock account and Step 2 to find how much is in the bond account. Do these answers seem reasonable? Do they meet all of the criteria?

(d) Step 6: **Answer the Question** _____

Do the Math Exercises 2.5
Introduction to Problem Solving: Direct Translation Problems

In Problems 1–4, translate each phrase to an algebraic expression. Let x represent the unknown number.

1. double a number

2. 8 less than a number

    1. _____

    2. _____

3. the quotient of −14 and a number

4. 21 more than 4 times a number

    3. _____

    4. _____

In Problems 5–7, choose a variable to represent one quantity. State what that quantity represents and then express the second quantity in terms of the first.

5. The Toronto Blue Jays scored 3 fewer runs than the Cleveland Indians.

    5. _____

6. Beryl has $0.25 more than 3 times the amount Ralph has.

    6. _____

7. There were 12,765 fans at a recent NBA game. Some held paid admission tickets and some held special promotion tickets.

    7. _____

In Problems 8–11, translate each statement into an equation. Let x represent the unknown number. DO NOT SOLVE.

8. The sum of 43 and a number is −72.

9. 49 is 3 less than twice a number.

    8. _____

    9. _____

10. The quotient of a number and –6, decreased by 15, is 30.

11. Twice the sum of a number and 5 is the same as 7 more than the number.

10. _____

11. _____

In problems 12–15, translate the given information into an equation and solve.

12. Consecutive Integers The sum of three consecutive odd integers is 81. Find the numbers.

12. _____

13. Towers The tallest buildings in the world (those having the most stories) are the Sears Tower in Chicago, Illinois, and the Ryugyong Hotel in Pyongyang, North Korea. The Ryugyong Hotel has 5 fewer stories than the Sears Tower. The two buildings together have 215 stories. Find the number of stories in each building.

13. _____

14. Investments Jack and Diane have $40,000 to invest. Their financial advisor has recommended that they diversify by placing some of the money in stocks and some in bonds. Based upon current market conditions, he has recommended that the amount in bonds should equal two-thirds of the amount invested in stocks. How much should be invested in stocks? How much should be invested in bonds?

14. _____

15. Cellular Telephones You need a new cell phone for emergencies only. Company A charges $12 per month plus $0.10 per minute, while Company B charges $0.15 per minute with no monthly service charge. For how many minutes will the monthly cost be the same?

15. _____

Five-Minute Warm-Up 2.6
Problem Solving: Direct Translation Problems Involving Percent

1. Write as a decimal.   1a. _____

   (a) 62%   **(b)** 1.75%   1b. _____

2. Write as a percent.   2a. _____

   a) 0.055   **(b)** 1.5   2b. _____

3. Combine like terms: $p + 0.75p$ 3. _____

4. Solve: $x - 0.20x = 10.60$ 4. _____

Guided Practice 2.6
Problem Solving: Direct Translation Problems Involving Percent

Objective 1: Solve Direct Translation Problems Involving Percent

1. Percent means "divided by 100". For instance, 20% means $\dfrac{20}{100}$ or $\dfrac{1}{5}$. Write each of these percents as fractions. Simplify, if possible.

    (a) 75%   **(b)** 100%   **(c)** $5\dfrac{1}{4}\%$ 1a. _____

1b. _____

1c. _____

2. To divide by 100, shift the decimal point 2 decimal places to the left. Write each of these percents as decimals.

    (a) 68%   **(b)** 2.5%   **(c)** 150%   2a. _____

2b. _____

2c. _____

3. If a question says, "what percent" and the solution to our equation is either a fraction or a decimal, we convert the result to percent by reversing the processes above. Write each of the following as a percent.

    (a) 0.08   **(b)** $\dfrac{7}{10}$ **(c)** 0.3   3a. _____

3b. _____

3c. _____

4. A number is 72% of 30. Find the number. *(See textbook Example 1)*
    (a) Translate the statement into an equation.   4a. _____

    (b) Solve the equation and answer the question.   4b. _____

5. The number 150 is what percent of 120? *(See textbook Example 2)*
    (a) Translate the statement into an equation.   5a. _____

    (b) Solve the equation and answer the question.   5b. _____

Objective 2: Model and Solve Direct Translation Problems from Business That Involve Percent

6. You just purchased a new computer. The price of the computer, including 7.5% sales tax, was $1343.75. How much did the computer cost before sales tax? *(See textbook Example 5)*

  Step 1: Identify We want to know the price of the computer before sales tax.

  Step 2: Name Let p represent the price of the computer before sales tax.

(a) **Step 3: Translate** If p is the price of the computer, what algebraic expression calculates the amount of sales tax on the computer?

_____

(b) Write the equation: the original price plus the sales tax equals the total price: _____

(c) **Step 4: Solve** Solve your equation from Step 3. _____

  Step 5: Check Does your answer seem reasonable? Have you satisfied the criteria in the question?

(d) **Step 6: Answer** Always be careful to answer the question that is being asked. _____

7. Suppose you just learned that the local sporting goods store is having an end-of-the-season sale on ski equipment. Everything has been marked down by 60%. The sale price on a pair of Black Diamond skis is $224. What was the original price? *(See textbook Example 6)*

  Step 1: Identify We are looking for the original price of the skis, which have been marked down by 60%, and we know that the sale price is $224.

  Step 2: Name Let p represent the original price of the skis.

(a) **Step 3: Translate** If p is the original price of the skis, what algebraic expression calculates the amount of discount?

_____

(b) Write the equation: the original price less the discount equals the sale price:

_____

(c) **Step 4: Solve** Solve your equation from Step 3. _____

  Step 5: Check Does your answer seem reasonable? Have you satisfied the criteria in the question?

(d) **Step 6: Answer** Always be careful to answer the question that is being asked. _____

Do the Math Exercises 2.6
Problem Solving: Direct Translation Problems Involving Percent

In Problems 1–8, find the unknown in each percent question.

1. What is 85% of 50?

2. 75% of 20 is what number?

1. _____

2. _____

3. What number is 150% of 9?

4. 40% of what number is 122?

3. _____

4. _____

5. 45% of what number is 900?

6. 11 is 5.5% of what number?

5. _____

6. _____

7. 4 is what percent of 25?

8. What percent of 16 is 12?

7. _____

8. _____

9. **Sales Tax** The sales tax in Franklin County, Ohio, is 5.75%. The total cost of purchasing a used Honda Civic, including sales tax, is $8460. Find the cost of the car before sales tax.

9. _____

10. **Pay Raise** MaryBeth works from home as a graphic designer. Recently she raised her hourly rate by 5% to cover increased costs. Her new hourly rate is $23.70. Find MaryBeth's previous hourly rate.

10. _____

11. Good Investment Perry just learned that his house increased in value by 4% over the past year. The value of the house is now $208,000. What was the value of the home one year ago?

11. _____

12. Hailstorm Toyota Town had a 15%-off sale on cars that had been damaged in a hailstorm. A new Toyota truck is on sale for $13,217.50. What was the price of the truck before the hailstorm discount?

12. _____

13. Business: Marking up the Price of Books A college bookstore marks up the price that it pays the publisher for a book by 35%. If the selling price of a book is $56.00, how much did the bookstore pay for the book?

13. _____

14. Vacation Package The Liberty Travel Agency advertised a 5-night vacation package in Jamaica for 30% off the regular price. The sale price of the package is $1139. To the nearest dollar, how much was the vacation package before the 30% off sale?

14. _____

15. Census Data Based on data obtained from the U.S. Census Bureau, 22% of the 113 million females aged 18 years or older have never married. How many females aged 18 years or older have never married?

15. _____

Five-Minute Warm-Up 2.7
Problem Solving: Geometry and Uniform Motion

1. Solve: $a + 2(a - 30) = 90$ 1. _____

2. Solve: $2(x + 5) + 2(3x - 8) = 22$ 2. _____

3. If x represents the unknown quantity, translate each of the following English phrases to an algebraic expression.

    (a) 12 more than twice an unknown number   3a. _____

    (b) 25 less than half of the width   3b. _____

    (c) double the difference of 45 and the measure of an angle   3c. _____

    (d) the sum of 15 and twice the cost   3d. _____

    (e) twice the sum of the speed and 30   3e. _____

4. If an 8-foot board is cut into two pieces and one piece has length p, express the length of the other piece in terms of p.   4. _____

Guided Practice 2.7
Problem Solving: Geometry and Uniform Motion

Objective 1: Set Up and Solve Complementary and Supplementary Angle Problems

1. Two angles are *complementary* if the sum of their measures is _____. Each angle is called the *complement* of the other.

2. Two angles are *supplementary* if the sum of their measures is _____. Each angle is called the *supplement* of the other.

3. Find the measures of two supplementary angles such that the measure of the smaller angle is $20°$ less than the measure of the larger angle. *(See textbook Example 1)*

> **Step 1: Identify** Since the angles are supplementary, we know the sum of their measures is $180°$.

> **Step 2: Name** Let x represent the measure of the larger angle.

(a) Step 3: Translate If x is the measure of the larger angle, what algebraic expression calculates the measure of the smaller angle?

_____

(b) Write the equation: the sum of the measures is equal to 180:   _____

(c) Step 4: Solve your equation from Step 3.   _____

> **Step 5: Check** Does your answer seem reasonable? Have you satisfied the criteria in the question?

(d) Step 6: Answer Always be careful to answer the question that is being asked. _____

Objective 2: Set Up and Solve Angles of a Triangle Problem

4. The sum of the measures of the three angles of a triangle is always _____.

5. The measure of the third angle of a triangle is $30°$ more than measure of the second angle of a triangle and the measure of the second angle is twice the measure the first angle. Find the measure of each angle of the triangle. *(See textbook Example 2)*

> **Step 1: Identify** Since these are angles of a triangle, we know the sum of their measures is $180°$.

> **Step 2: Name** Let x represent the measure of the first angle.

(a) Step 3: Translate If x is the measure of the first angle, what algebraic expression calculates the measure of the second angle?

_____

5. (b) What algebraic expression calculates the measure of the third angle? _____

    (c) Write the equation: the sum of the measures is equal to 180: _____

    (d) Step 4: Solve your equation from Step 3. _____

        Step 5: Check Does your answer seem reasonable? Have you satisfied the criteria in the question?

    (e) Step 6: Answer Always be careful to answer the question that is being asked. _____

Objective 3: Use Geometry Formulas to Solve Problems

6. Tablecloth Mary is making a rectangular tablecloth that is 20 inches longer than it is wide. If she has 200 inches of trim that will just fit around the edge of the tablecloth, find the dimensions of the tablecloth. *(See textbook Example 3)*

    (a) If x is width of the tablecloth, what algebraic expression represents the length? _____

    (b) What formula from geometry is needed to solve this problem? _____

    (c) Write an equation that models the information in the problem: _____

    (d) Solve your equation from (c) and answer the question: _____

Objective 4: Set Up and Solve Uniform Motion Problems

7. Boats Two boats are traveling toward the same port from opposite directions. They are 50 miles apart and one boat is traveling 4 mph faster than the other. If the boats both reach the port in 2 hours and 30 minutes, find the speed for each boat. *(See textbook Example 6)*

    (a) What do you know about the distances traveled by the two boats? _____

    (b) Complete the following table.

	Rate, mph	Time, hours	Distance, miles
Slower boat			
Faster boat			
Total			

    (c) Write and solve an equation that models the distance traveled by the boats.

    (d) Answer the question._____

Do the Math Exercises 2.7
Problem Solving: Geometry and Uniform Motion

Find the value of x and then identify the measure of each of the angles.

1. Find two complementary angles such that the measure of the first angle is 25° less than   1. _____
the measure of the second.

Find the measures of the angles of the triangle.

2. In a triangle, the second angle measures four times the first. The measure of the third   2. _____
angle is 18° more than the second. Find the measures of the three angles.

Use a formula from geometry to solve for the unknown quantity.

3. The width of a rectangle is 10 m less than half of the length. If the perimeter is 52   3. _____
meters, find the length of each side of the rectangle.

Solve the uniform motion problem. Set up the uniform motion problem following steps 4a–4d.

4. Two trains leave Albuquerque, traveling the same direction on parallel tracks. One train
is traveling at 72 mph and the other is traveling at 66 mph. How long before they are 45
miles apart?

(a) Write an algebraic expression for the distance traveled by the faster train.   4a. _____

(b) Write an algebraic expression for the distance traveled by the slower train.   4b. _____

(c) Write an algebraic expression for the difference in distance between the two.   4c. _____

(d) Write an equation to answer the question.   4d. _____

Fill in the table from the information given. Then write the equation that will solve the problem. DO NOT SOLVE.

5. A 580-mile trip in a small plane took a total of 5 hours. The first two hours were flown at one rate and then the plane encountered a headwind and was slowed by 10 mph.

5. _____

	Rate	•	Time	=	Distance
Beginning of trip					
Rest of the trip					
Total					

Write an equation that will solve each problem. Then solve.

6. **Garden** The length of a rectangular garden is 9 feet. If 26 feet of fencing are required to fence the garden, find the width of the garden.

6. _____

7. **Buying Fertilizer** Melinda has to buy fertilizer for a flower garden in the shape of a right triangle. If the area of the garden is 54 square feet and the base of the garden measures 9 feet, find the height of the triangular garden.

7. _____

8. **Table** The Jacksons are having a custom rectangular table made for a small dining area. The length of the table is 18 inches more than the width, and the perimeter is 180 inches. Find the length and width of the table.

8. _____

9. **Cyclists** Two cyclists leave a city at the same time, one going east and the other going west. The west-bound cyclist bikes at 4 mph faster than the east-bound cyclist. After 5 hours they are 200 miles apart. How fast is the east-bound cyclist riding?

9. _____

10. **River Trip** Max lives on a river, 30 miles from town. Max travels downstream (with the current) at 20 mph. Returning upstream (against the current) his rate is 12 mph. If the total trip to town and back took 4 hours, how long did he spend returning from town?

10. _____

Five-Minute Warm-Up 2.8
Solving Linear Inequalities in One Variable

In Problems 1 – 6, replace the question mark by <, >, or = to make the statement true.

1. −0.2 ? 0

2. −5 ? −4.5

3. $\dfrac{7}{12}$? $\dfrac{9}{16}$

4. 0.625 ? $\dfrac{5}{8}$

5. $\dfrac{-13}{8}$? $\dfrac{-11}{4}$

6. 0.003 ? 0.0031

1._____

2._____

3._____

4._____

5._____

6._____

7. Plot the set of points $\left\{-3.5, \dfrac{3}{2}, -\dfrac{2}{3}, 3\right\}$ on the number line.

Name: Date:
Instructor: Section:

Guided Practice 2.8
Solving Linear Inequalities in One Variable

Objective 1: Graph Inequalities on a Real Number Line

1. When representing an inequality on a number line, we graph the inequality using a(n) _____

if the endpoint in included and a(n) _____ if the endpoint is not included.

2. Graph $x > -2$ on a real number line. *(See textbook Example 1)*

Objective 2: Use Interval Notation

3. Write the inequality in interval notation. *(See textbook Example 2)*

   (a) $x < -5$ **(b)** $x \geq 10$ 3a. _____

                                                                    3b. _____

Objective 3: Solve Linear Inequalities Using Properties of Inequalities

4. *True or False:* The Addition Property of Inequality states that the direction of the inequality does not change regardless of the quantity that is added to each side of the inequality.   4. _____

5. *True or False:* When multiplying both sides of an inequality by a negative number, we reverse the direction of the inequality.   5. _____

6. *True or False:* When multiplying both sides of an inequality by a positive number, we reverse the direction of the inequality.   6. _____

7. Solve the inequality $3x + 10 > 1$. Graph the solution set. *(See textbook Examples 3 and 4)*

Step 1: Get the expression containing the variable on the left side of the inequality.	This is already done.	$3x + 10 > 1$
Step 2: Isolate the variable *x* on the left side.	Subtract 10 from both sides:	**(a)** $3x + 10$ _____ > 1 _____
	Simplify:	**(b)** _____
	Divide both sides by 3 and simplify:	**(c)** _____
	Write the answer in set-builder notation:	**(d)** _____
	Write the answer using interval notation:	**(e)** _____
	Graph the solution set:	**(f)**

8. When multiplying or dividing both sides of an inequality by a negative real number, remember to reverse the direction of the inequality symbol. Solve the inequality and state the solution using interval notation. *(See textbook Example 6)*

(a) $-6x < -72$

(b) $-\dfrac{2}{5}x \geq 10$

8a. _____

8b. _____

9. Solve the inequality $\dfrac{1}{6}(4x - 5) \leq \dfrac{1}{2}(2x + 3)$. *(See textbook Examples 7 and 8)*

Step 1: To rewrite the inequality as an equivalent inequality without fractions, we multiply both sides of the inequality by the LCD. Then remove parentheses.	$\dfrac{1}{6}(4x - 5) \leq \dfrac{1}{2}(2x + 3)$ Multiply both sides by the LCD: (a) ___ $\cdot \dfrac{1}{6}(4x - 5) \leq$ ___ $\cdot \dfrac{1}{2}(2x + 3)$ Divide out common factors: **(b)** _____ Use the Distributive Property: **(c)** _____
Step 2: Combine like terms on each side of the inequality.	This is already done.
Step 3: Get the variable expressions on the left side of the inequality and the constants on the right side.	Subtract $6x$ from both sides: **(d)** _____ Add 5 to both sides: **(e)** _____
Step 4: Get the coefficient of the variable to be one.	Divide both sides by -2: Remember to reverse the inequality symbol! **(f)** _____ Write the answer in set-builder notation: **(g)** _____ Write the answer using interval notation: **(h)** _____

Objective 4: Model Inequality Problems

10. Write the appropriate inequality symbol for each phrase.

Phrase	Inequality Symbol	Phrase	Inequality Symbol
(a) At least	(a) _____	(b) No less than	(b) _____
(c) More than	(c) _____	(d) Greater than	(d) _____
(e) No more than	(e) _____	(f) At most	(f) _____
(g) Fewer than	(g) _____	(h) Less than	(h) _____

Do the Math Exercises 2.8
Solving Linear Inequalities in One Variable

In Problems 1–4, graph each inequality on a number line, and write each inequality in interval notation.

1. $n > 5$ **2.** $x \le 6$ 1._____

                                                                                                          2._____

3. $x \ge -2$ **4.** $y < -3$ 3._____

                                                                                                          4._____

In Problems 5–6, use interval notation to express the inequality shown in each graph.

5.   **6.**   5._____

                                                                                                          6._____

In Problems 7–8, fill in the blank with the correct symbol. State which property of inequality is being utilized.

7. If $3x - 2 > 7$, then $3x$____9 **8.** If $\dfrac{5}{3}x \ge -10$, then x____-6 7._____

                                                                                                          8._____

In Problems 9–17, solve the inequality and express the solution set in set-builder notation and interval notation Graph the solution set on a real number line.

9. $x - 2 < 1$ **10.** $4x > 12$ 9._____

                                                                                                          10._____

11. $-7x \geq 28$

12. $2x + 5 > 1$

11. _____

12. _____

13. $2x - 2 \geq 3 + x$

14. $2 - 3x \leq 5$

13. _____

14. _____

15. $-3(1 - x) > x + 8$

16. $2y - 5 + y < 3(y - 2)$

15. _____

16. _____

17. $3(p + 1) - p \geq 2(p + 1)$

17. _____

In Problems 18–19, write the given statement using inequality symbols. Let x represent the unknown quantity.

18. The cost of a new lawnmower is at least $250.

18. _____

19. There are fewer than 25 students in your math class on any given day.

19. _____

20. Truck Rental A truck can be rented from Acme Truck Rental for $80 per week plus $0.28 per mile. How many miles can be driven if you have at most $100 to spend on truck rental?

20. _____

Sullivan/Struve/Mazzarella, *Elementary & Intermediate Algebra,* 2e

Name: Date:
Instructor: Section:

1. Plot the following points on the real number line: $-1, \dfrac{3}{2}, 3, -2.5$

2. Evaluate: $-2x - 3$ 2a. _____
    (a) for $x = -5$ **(b)** for $x = 0$
                                          2b. _____

3. Evaluate: $7x + 3y$ 3a. _____
    (a) for $x = -1, y = -6$ **(b)** for $x = 3, y = -4$
                                          3b. _____

4. Solve: $-2x + 9 = -1$ 4. _____

5. Solve: $4(2x - 1) - 6x = 2 - 5(x - 3)$ 5. _____

Guided Practice 3.1
The Rectangular Coordinate System and Linear Equations in Two Variables

Objective 1: Plot Points in the Rectangular Coordinate System

1. Label each quadrant and axis in the rectangular or Cartesian coordinate system.

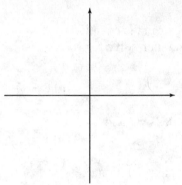

2. What name do we give the ordered pair $(0, 0)$? _____

In Problem 3, circle one answer for each underlined choice.

3. To plot the ordered pair $(-3, 2)$, you would move 3 units <u>up, down, left or right</u> from the origin?

4. Identify the coordinates of each point labeled below. (*See textbook Example 2*)

4.

A _____

B _____

C _____

Objective 2: Determine If an Ordered Pair Satisfies an Equation

5. Determine which, if any, of the following ordered pairs satisfy the equation $2x - y = -5$.
(See textbook Example 3)

   (a) $(1, -3)$ **(b)** $(-5, -5)$

5a. _____

5b. _____

6. Find an ordered pair that satisfies the equation $4x + 2y = 7$. *(See textbook Example 4)*

Step 1: Choose any value for one of the variables in the equation.	You may choose any value of x or y that you wish. In this example, we will let $x = 3$.	
Step 2: Substitute the value of the variable chosen in Step 1 into the equation and then use the techniques learned in Chapter 2 to solve for the remaining variable.	Substitute 3 for x in the equation $4x + 2y = 7$ and then solve for y:	$4x + 2y = 7$ $4(3) + 2y = 7$ **(a)** $2y = 7 - 4(3) =$ _____
	Divide both sides by 2 and simplify:	**(b)** $y =$ _____
	Write the complete solution as an ordered pair:	**(c)** $(x, y) =$ _____

Objective 3: Create a Table of Values That Satisfy an Equation

7. To create a table of values that satisfy an equation, choose any value for one of the variables in the equation. Substitute the value of the variable into the equation and then use the techniques learned in Chapter 2 to solve for the remaining variable. Complete the table of values for $y = 3x - 1$. *(See textbook Example 5)*

	x	y	(x, y)
(a)	-2	$3(\underline{}) - 1 = \underline{}$	$(-2, \underline{})$
(b)	-1	$3(\underline{}) - 1 = \underline{}$	$(-1, \underline{})$
(c)	0	$3(\underline{}) - 1 = \underline{}$	$(0, \underline{})$
(d)	1	$3(\underline{}) - 1 = \underline{}$	$(1, \underline{})$
(e)	2	$3(\underline{}) - 1 = \underline{}$	$(2, \underline{})$

Do the Math Exercises 3.1
The Rectangular Coordinate System and Linear Equations in Two Variables

In Problems 1–2, plot the following ordered pairs in the rectangular coordinate system. Tell which quadrant each point lies in or state that the point lies on the x-axis or y-axis.

1. $P(-3, -2)$; $Q(2, -4)$; $R(4, 3)$; $S(-1, 4)$; $T(-2, -4)$; $U(3, -3)$

2. $P\left(\frac{3}{2}, -2\right)$; $Q\left(0, \frac{5}{2}\right)$; $R\left(-\frac{9}{2}, 0\right)$; $S(0, 0)$; $T\left(-\frac{3}{2}, -\frac{9}{2}\right)$; $U\left(3, \frac{1}{2}\right)$ $V\left(\frac{5}{2}, -\frac{7}{2}\right)$

1. _____

2. _____

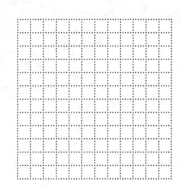

Identify the coordinates of each point labeled in the figure. Name the quadrant in which each point lies or state that the point lies on the x- or y-axis.

3.

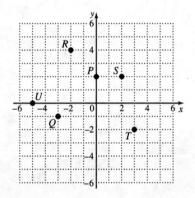

3. _____

In Problems 4–5, determine whether or not the ordered pair satisfies the equation.

4. $y = 2x - 3$ $A(-1, -5)$ $B(4, -5)$ $C(-2, -7)$

5. $5x - y = 12$ $A(2, 0)$ $B(0, 12)$ $C(-2, -22)$

4. _____

5. _____

6. Find an ordered pair that satisfies the equation $x + y = 7$ by letting $x = 2$.

7. Find an ordered pair that satisfies the equation $5x - 3y = 11$ by letting $y = 3$.

6. _____

7. _____

In Problems 8–9, use the equation to complete the table. Use the table to list some of the ordered pairs that satisfy the equation.

8. $y = 4x - 5$

x	y	(x, y)
–3		
1		
2		

9. $3x + 4y = 2$

x	y	(x, y)
–2		
2		
4		

In Problems 10–11, for each equation find the missing value in the ordered pair.

10. $y = 5x - 4$ $A(-1, \underline{\quad})$ $B(\underline{\quad}, 31)$ $C\left(-\dfrac{2}{5}, \underline{\quad}\right)$

11. $\dfrac{1}{3}x + 2y = -1$ $A(-4, \underline{\quad})$ $B\left(\underline{\quad}, -\dfrac{3}{4}\right)$ $C(0, \underline{\quad})$

10. _____

11. _____

12. Taxi Ride The cost to take a taxi is $1.70 plus $2.00 per mile for each mile driven. The total cost, C, is given by the equation $C = 1.7 + 2m$ where m represents the total miles driven.

(a) How much will it cost to take a taxi 5 miles?

12a. _____

(b) How much will it cost to take a taxi 20 miles?

12b. _____

(c) If you spent $32.70 on cab fare, how far was your trip?

12c. _____

(d) If (m, C) represents any ordered pair that satisfies $C = 1.7 + 2m$, interpret the meaning of $(14, 29.7)$ in the context of this problem.

12d. _____

Five-Minute Warm-Up 3.2
Graphing Linear Equations in Two Variables

1. Solve: $-5x = 45$

1. _____

2. Solve: $12y = -40$

2. _____

3. Solve: $5y + 12 = 2$

3. _____

4. Evaluate: $-2x + 8y$
   (a) for $x = -3$, $y = 2$ **(b)** for $x = 10$, $y = 4$

4a. _____

4b. _____

5. Solve using the given information: $y = \dfrac{3}{2}x + 5$
   (a) If $x = -4$, find y.   **(b)** If $y = -1$, find x.

5a. _____

5b. _____

6. Plot the ordered pairs: $(0, -3)$; $(2, 0)$; $(-3, 2)$; $(1, -4)$; $(-2, -1)$

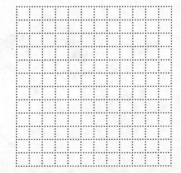

Guided Practice 3.2
Graphing Linear Equations in Two Variables

Objective 1: Graph a Line by Plotting Points

1. Point-plotting is one method we use to graph a line. Find several ordered pairs that satisfy the equation. Plot the points in a rectangular coordinate system and then connect the points in a smooth curve or line.

Graph the equation $y = -2x - 3$ using the point-plotting method. *(See textbook Example 1)*

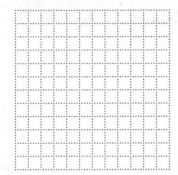

2. When a linear equation in two variables is written in the form $Ax + By = C$ where A, B, and C are real

numbers and both A and B cannot be 0, we say the linear equation is written in _____ form.

Objective 2: Graph a Line Using Intercepts

3. To find the x-intercept(s), if any, of the graph of an equation, let _____ in the equation and solve for x.

4. To find the y-intercept(s), if any, of the graph of an equation, let _____ in the equation and solve for y.

5. Graph the linear equation $3x - 2y = -6$ by finding its intercepts. *(See textbook Example 6)*

   (a) Identify the x-intercept: _____   **(b)** Identify the y-intercept: _____

   (c) Draw the axes. Plot the intercepts and connect the points in a straight line to obtain the graph.

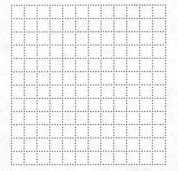

Objective 3: Graph Vertical and Horizontal Lines

6. A vertical line is given by an equation of the form $x = a$ where a is the x-intercept.

Graph the equation $x = -2$. *(See textbook Example 9)*

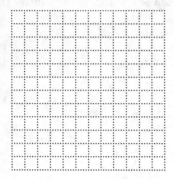

7. A horizontal line is given by an equation of the form $y = b$ where b is the y-intercept.

Graph the equation $y = 3$. *(See textbook Example 10)*

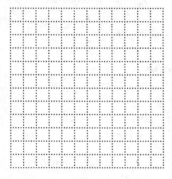

Sullivan/Struve/Mazzarella, *Elementary & Intermediate Algebra*, 2e

Do the Math Exercises 3.2
Graphing Linear Equations in Two Variables

In Problems 1–2, determine whether or not the equation is a linear equation in two variables.

1. $y^2 = 2x + 3$

2. $y - 2x = 9$

1. _____

2. _____

In Problems 3–4, graph each linear equation using the point-plotting method.

3. $y = -3x - 1$

4. $y = x - 6$

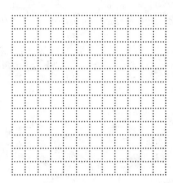

In Problems 5–8, find the intercepts of each graph.

5.

6.

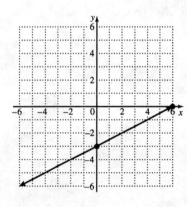

5. _____

6. _____

7.

8.

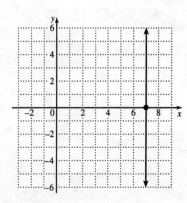

7. _____

8. _____

In Problems 9–10, find the intercepts of each equation.

9. $3x - 5y = 30$

10. $\dfrac{x}{2} - \dfrac{y}{8} = 1$

9. _____

10. _____

In Problems 11–12, graph each linear equation by finding its intercepts.

11. $3x - 5y = 15$

12. $\dfrac{1}{3}x - y = 0$

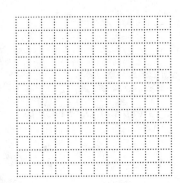

In Problems 13–14, graph each horizontal or vertical line.

13. $x = -7$

14. $y = 2$

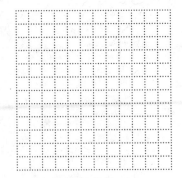

Five-Minute Warm-Up 3.3
Slope

In Problems 1 – 7, simplify each expression.

1. $\dfrac{9-3}{15-3}$

2. $\dfrac{6-15}{2-5}$

1. _____

2. _____

3. $\dfrac{-2-8}{4-(-2)}$

4. $\dfrac{-5-(-9)}{3-5}$

3. _____

4. _____

5. $\dfrac{5-12}{-6-(-6)}$

6. $\dfrac{-18-(-18)}{4-(-4)}$

5. _____

6. _____

7. $\dfrac{\dfrac{1}{2}-\left(-\dfrac{3}{4}\right)}{-\dfrac{2}{3}-\dfrac{5}{6}}$

7. _____

Guided Practice 3.3
Slope

Objective 1: Find the Slope of a Line Given Two Points

1. The ratio of the rise (vertical change) to the run (horizontal change) is called the _____ of the line.

2. The slope of a line which passes through the ordered pairs (x_1, y_1) and (x_2, y_2) is given by the formula:

$$m = \frac{\rule{3cm}{0.4pt}}{\rule{3cm}{0.4pt}}$$

3. Find the slope of the line containing the points $(-1, 7)$ and $(3, -13)$. *(See textbook Example 1)*

3. _____

Objective 2: Find the Slope of vertical and Horizontal Lines

4. Calculate the slope of the line through the points $(-8, 3)$ and $(-8, -1)$. *(See textbook Example 3)*

4. _____

5. Is the graph of the line in #4 vertical or horizontal?

5. _____

6. Calculate the slope of the line through the points $(-1, 5)$ and $(4, 5)$. *(See textbook Example 4)*

6. _____

7. Is the graph of the line in #6 vertical or horizontal?

7. _____

8. *Properties of Slope* Describe the graph of the line with the following slope:

    (a) Positive _____   **(b)** Negative _____

    (c) Zero _____   **(d)** Undefined _____

Objective 3: Graph a Line Using Its Slope and a Point on the Line

9. Draw a graph of the line that contains the point $(-1, 3)$ and has slope $-\dfrac{3}{4}$. *(See textbook Example 5)*

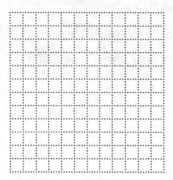

Do the Math Exercises 3.3
Slope

In Problems 1–2, find the slope of the line whose graph is given.

1.

2.

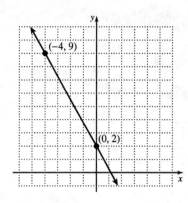

1. _____

2. _____

In Problems 3–4, (a) plot the points in a rectangular coordinate system, (b) draw a line through the points, (c) and find and interpret the slope of the line.

3. (2, 6) and (–2, –4)

4. (4, –5) and (–2, –4)

3c. _____

4c. _____

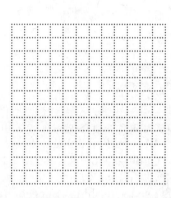

In Problems 5–6, find the slope of the line whose graph is given.

5.

6.

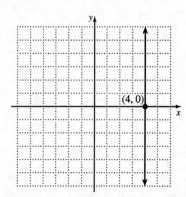

5. _____

6. _____

In Problems 7–8, draw a graph of the line that contains the given point and has the given slope.

7. $(3, -1)$; $m = -1$

8. $(-2, -3)$; $m = \dfrac{5}{2}$

9. Roof Pitch A canopy is set up on the football field. On the 45-yard line, the height of the canopy is 68 inches. The peak of the canopy is at the 50-yard marker where the height is 84 inches. What is the pitch of the roof of the canopy?

9. _____

10. Earning Potential On average, a person who graduates from high school can expect to have lifetime earnings of 1.2 million dollars. It takes four years to earn a bachelor's degree, but the lifetime earnings will increase to 2.1 million dollars. Use the ordered pairs (0, 1.2 million) and (4, 2.1 million) to find and interpret the slope of the line representing the increase in earnings due to finishing college.

10. _____

Five-Minute Warm-Up 3.4
Slope-Intercept Form of a Line

1. Solve $7x + 5y = -35$ for y.   1. _____

2. Solve $3x - 8y = 12$ for y.   2. _____

3. Solve: $15 = 3 - 9x$ for x.   3. _____

4. Identify the following information using: $y = -\dfrac{5}{3}x - \dfrac{1}{2}$ 4a. _____

   (a) the coefficient of x **(b)** the constant

                                                         4b. _____

Guided Practice 3.4
Slope-Intercept Form of a Line

Objective 1: Use the Slope-Intercept Form to Identify the Slope and y-Intercept of a Line

1. The *Slope-Intercept Form* of a line is an equation written in the form
$y = mx + b$, where the slope of the line is ____, the coefficient of x, and the
y-intercept is ____, the constant.

1. _____

_____

2. Find the slope and y-intercept of the line whose equation is $y = -\dfrac{1}{2}x + 6$.

(See textbook Example 1)

2. slope = _____

y-intercept = _____

3. Find the slope and y-intercept of the line whose equation is $6x + 3y = 15$.
(See textbook Example 2)

3. slope = _____

y-intercept = _____

Objective 2: Graph a Line Whose Equation Is in Slope-Intercept Form

4. Graph the line $y = \dfrac{2}{5}x - 1$ using the slope and y-intercept. *(See textbook Example 4)*

(a) What is the slope? _____

(b) What is the y-intercept? _____

(c) Graph the line.

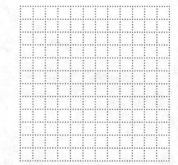

Objective 3: Graph a Line Whose Equation Is in the Form Ax + By = C

5. Graph the line $2x + 3y = 6$ using the slope and y-intercept. *(See textbook Example 5)*

(a) Write the equation in slope-intercept form.

_____

(b) What is the slope? _____

(c) What is the y-intercept? _____

(d) Graph the line.

Objective 4: *Find the Equation of a Line Given Its Slope and y-Intercept*

6. Find the equation of a line whose slope is $-\dfrac{1}{4}$ and whose y-intercept is 3. *(See textbook Example 6)*

6. _____

7. The cost of renting a particular car for a day is $22 plus $0.07 per mile. Find the following. *(See textbook Example 8)*

(a) Write a linear equation that relates the daily cost of renting the car, y, to the number of miles driven in a day.

7a. _____

(b) What is the cost of driving this car 100 miles?

7b. _____

Do the Math Exercises 3.4
Slope-Intercept Form of a Line

In Problems 1–4, find the slope and y-intercept of the line whose equation is given.

1. $y = -6x + 2$

2. $y = -x - 12$

1. _____

2. _____

3. $6x - 8y = -24$

4. $10x + 6y = 24$

3. _____

4. _____

In Problems 5–6, use the slope and y-intercept to graph each line whose equation is given.

5. $y = -4x - 1$

6. $y = \dfrac{4}{3}x - 3$

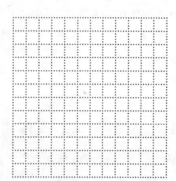

In Problems 7–8, graph each line using the slope and y-intercept.

7. $x - 2y = -4$

8. $4x + 3y = -6$

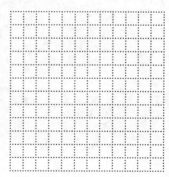

In Problems 9–14, find the equation of the line with the given slope and intercept.

9. slope is 1; y-intercept is 10

10. slope is $\dfrac{4}{7}$; y-intercept is –9

9. _____

10. _____

11. slope is $\dfrac{1}{4}$; y-intercept is $\dfrac{3}{8}$

12. slope is 0; y-intercept is –2

11. _____

12. _____

13. slope is undefined; x-intercept is 4

14. slope is –3; y-intercept is 0

13. _____

14. _____

15. Counting Calories According to a 1989 National Academy of Sciences Report, the recommended daily intake of calories for males between the ages of 7 and 15 can be calculated by the equation $y = 125x + 1125$, where x represents the boy's age and y represents the recommended calorie intake.

(a) What is the recommended caloric intake for a 12-year-old boy?

15a. _____

(b) What is the age of a boy whose recommended caloric intake is 2250 calories?

15b. _____

(c) Interpret the slope of $y = 125x + 1125$.

15c. _____

(d) Why would this equation not be accurate for a 3-year-old male?

15d. _____

(e) Graph the equation in a rectangular coordinate system. Label the axes appropriately.

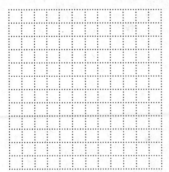

Five-Minute Warm-Up 3.5
Point-Slope Form of a Line

1. Solve $y - (-2) = -4(x - 3)$ for y.   1. _____

2. Solve $9x - 3y = -12$ for y.   2. _____

3. Evaluate: $\dfrac{8 - 5}{2 - 11}$ 3. _____

4. Evaluate: $\dfrac{0.4 - (-0.2)}{9.9 - 10.2}$ 4. _____

5. Use the Distributive Property to simplify: $-\dfrac{7}{4}(4x - 12)$ 5. _____

6. Find the slope of the line that contains $(-7, 10)$ and $(-3, 6)$.   6. _____

Guided Practice 3.5
Point-Slope Form of a Line

Objective 1: Find the Equation of a Line Given a Point and a Slope

1. What equation do we use to write the *Point-Slope Form* of a line with slope m and containing (x_1, y_1)?

_____

2. Find the equation of a line whose slope is 9 and that contains the point $(-2, -1)$. *(See textbook Example 1)*

    (a) Identify values: $m =$ _____; $x_1 =$ _____; $y_1 =$ _____

    (b) Point-slope form of a line: _____

    (c) Substitute the values from (a) into the equation from (b): _____

    (d) Simplify: _____

    (e) Use the Distributive Property: _____

    (f) Simplify and write the equation in slope-intercept form: _____

3. Find the equation of a line whose slope is $-\dfrac{5}{6}$ and that contains the point $(0, 12)$. *(See textbook Example 2)*

    (a) Identify values: $m =$ _____; $x_1 =$ _____; $y_1 =$ _____

    (b) Point-slope form of a line: _____

    (c) Substitute the values from (a) into the equation from (b): _____

    (d) Simplify and use the Distributive Property: _____

4. Find the equation a horizontal line that contains the point $(5, -11)$. *(See textbook Example 3)*

    (a) Identify values: $m =$ _____; $x_1 =$ _____; $y_1 =$ _____

    (b) Point-slope form of a line: _____

    (c) Substitute the values from (a) into the equation from (b): _____

    (d) Simplify: _____

                                   _____

Objective 2: Find the Equation of a Line Given Two Points

5. To find the equation of a line given two points, the first step is to find _____.

6. Find the equation of the line through the points $(1, 5)$ and $(-1, -1)$. If possible, write the equation in slope-intercept form. *(See textbook Example 4)*

Step 1: Find the slope of the line containing the points.	Formula for the slope of a line through two points:	**(a)** _____
	Identify values:	**(b)** $x_1 =$ _____; $y_1 =$ _____
		$x_2 =$ _____; $y_2 =$ _____
	Substitute values into (a) and simplify:	**(c)** _____
Step 2: Substitute the slope found in Step 1 and either point into the point-slope form of a line to find the equation.	Point-slope form of a line:	**(d)** _____
	Identify values:	**(e)** $m =$ _____; $x_1 =$ _____; $y_1 =$ _____
	Substitute values into (e):	**(f)** _____
Step 3: Solve the equation for *y*.	Distribute the 3:	**(g)** _____
	Add _____ to both sides:	**(h)** _____
	Is the equation in slope-intercept form?	**(i)** _____
	Try using (x_2, y_2) in (d). Does this change the equation of the line found in (i)?	**(j)** _____
	Identify the slope:	**(k)** _____
	Identify the *y*-intercept:	**(l)** _____

7. Find the equation of a line through the points $(-5, -1)$ and $(-5, 3)$. *(See textbook Example 5)*

(a) Find the slope of the line: _____

(b) What do we know about the graph of this line? _____

(c) No matter what value of *y* we choose, the *x*-coordinate of the point on the line will be _____

(d) Write the equation of the line: _____

Do the Math Exercises 3.5
Point-Slope Form of a Line

In Problems 1–4, find the equation of the line that contains the given point and with the given slope. Write the equation in slope-intercept form and graph the line.

1. (4, 1); slope = 6

2. (6, –3); slope = –5

1. _____

2. _____

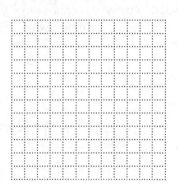

3. (–8, 2); slope = $-\dfrac{1}{2}$

4. (–7, –1); slope = 0

3. _____

4. _____

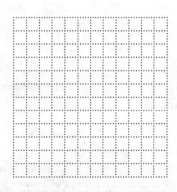

In Problems 5–6, find the equation of the line that contains the given point and satisfies the given information. Write the equation in slope-intercept form, if possible.

5. Horizontal line that contains (–6, –1)

6. Vertical line that contains (4, –3)

5. _____

6. _____

In Problems 7–10, find the equation of the line that contains the given points. Write the equation in slope-intercept form, if possible.

7. (–2, 4) and (2, –2)

8. (4, 18) and (–1, 3)

7. _____

8. _____

9. (–6, 5) and (7, 5) **10.** (–3, 8) and (–3, 1) 9. ____

10. ____

11. Retirement Plans Based on the retirement plan available by his employer, Kei knows that if he retires after 20 years, his monthly retirement income will be $3150. If he retires after 30 years, his monthly income increases to $3600. Let *x* represent the number of years of service and *y* represent the monthly retirement income.

(a) Interpret the meaning of the point (30, 3600) in the context of this problem. 11a. ____

(b) Plot the ordered pairs (20, 3150) and (30, 3600) in a rectangular coordinate system and graph the line through the points.

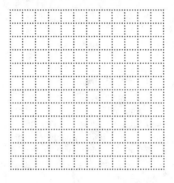

(c) Find the linear equation, in slope-intercept form, that relates the monthly retirement income, *y*, to the number of years of service, *x*. 11c. ____

(d) Use the equation found in part **(c)** to find the monthly income for 15 years of service. 11d. ____

(e) Interpret the slope. 11e. ____

Five-Minute Warm-Up 3.6
Parallel and Perpendicular Lines

1. Determine the reciprocal of -5.

1. _____

2. Determine the reciprocal of $\frac{1}{3}$.

2. _____

3. Determine the reciprocal of $-\frac{9}{4}$.

3. _____

4. Solve $-4x - y = 12$ for y.

4. _____

5. Identify the following information using: $-x + 4y = -2$

   (a) the slope of the line   (b) the y-intercept of the line

5a. _____

5b. _____

6. Find the equation of the line that has slope $-\frac{3}{2}$ and contains the point $(5, -2)$.

6. _____

Guided Practice 3.6
Parallel and Perpendicular Lines

Objective 1: *Determine Whether Two Lines Are Parallel*

1. In your own words, write a definition of parallel lines.

2. Two lines are parallel if and only if they have the same _____ and different _____.

3. If $L_1 : y = m_1 x + b_1$ and $L_2 : y = m_2 x + b_2$ and L_1 is parallel to L_2, then m_1 _____ m_2 and b_1 _____ b_2.

4. Determine whether the line $4x - y = 1$ is parallel to $8x - 2y = -10$. *(See textbook Example 2)*

To find the slope and y-intercept, we solve each equation for y so that each is in slope-intercept form.

(a) Equation 1, $4x - y = 1$, written in slope-intercept form: _____

(b) Determine the slope and y-intercept of the line in equation 1:   slope: _____; y-intercept: _____

(c) Equation 2, $8x - 2y = -10$, written in slope-intercept form: _____

(d) Determine the slope and y-intercept of the line in equation 2:   slope: _____; y-intercept: _____

(e) Conclusion: _____

Objective 2: *Find the Equation of a Line Parallel to a Given Line*

5. Find an equation for the line that is parallel to $5x - 2y = -1$ and contains the point $(-3, -4)$.
(See textbook Example 3)

Step 1: Find the slope of the given line by putting the equation in slope-intercept form.

(a)_____

Step 2: Use the point-slope form of a line with the given point and the slope found in Step 1 to find the equation of the parallel line.

Slope of the line found in Step 1:   **(b)**_____

Slope of the parallel line: **(c)**_____

Identify values: **(d)** $m =$ _____; $x_1 =$ _____; $y_1 =$ _____

Point-slope form of a line: **(e)**_____

Substitute values into (e):   **(f)**_____

Step 3: Put the equation in slope-intercept form by solving for y.

Solve for y: **(g)**_____

Objective 3: Determine Whether Two Lines are Perpendicular

6. In your own words, write a definition of perpendicular lines.

7. Two lines are perpendicular if and only if the product of their slopes is _____.

8. If $L_1 : y = m_1 x + b_1$ and $L_2 : y = m_2 x + b_2$ and L_1 is perpendicular to L_2, then $m_1 \cdot m_2 =$ ___ or $m_1 =$ ___.

9. Determine whether the line $y = \dfrac{3}{4}x + 6$ is perpendicular to $y = \dfrac{4}{3}x - 2$. *(See textbook Example 6)*

   (a) Determine the slope and y-intercept of the line in equation 1:   slope: _____; y-intercept: _____

   (b) Determine the slope and y-intercept of the line in equation 2:   slope: _____; y-intercept: _____

   (c) What is the product of the slopes of the two lines?   _____

   (d) Conclusion: _____

10. Find an equation of the line that is perpendicular to the line $-2x + y = 7$ and contains the point $(3, -12)$. Write the equation in slope-intercept form. *(See textbook Example 8)*

Step 1: Find the slope of the given line by putting the equation in slope-intercept form.		**(a)**_____
Step 2: Find the slope of the perpendicular line.	Slope of the line found in Step 1:	**(b)**_____
	Slope of the perpendicular line:	**(c)**_____
	Identify values:	**(d)** $m =$ ____; $x_1 =$ ____; $y_1 =$ ____
Step 3: Use the point-slope form of a line with the given point and the slope found in Step 2 to find the equation of the perpendicular line.	Point-slope form of a line:	**(e)**_____
	Substitute values into (e):	**(f)**_____
Step 4: Put the equation in slope-intercept form by solving for y.	Solve for y:	**(g)**_____

Do the Math Exercises 3.6
Parallel and Perpendicular Lines

In Problems 1–3, fill in the chart with the missing slopes.

	Slope of the Given Line	Slope of a Line Parallel to the Given Line	Slope of a Line Perpendicular to the Given Line
1.	$m = 4$		
2.	$m = -\dfrac{1}{8}$		
3.	$m = \dfrac{5}{2}$		

In Problems 4–7, determine if the lines are parallel, perpendicular, or neither.

4. $L_1 : y = -4x + 3$
$L_2 : y = 4x - 1$

5. $L_1 : y = 3x - 1$
$L_2 : y = 6 - \dfrac{x}{3}$

4. _____

5. _____

6. $L_1 : x - 4y = 24$
$L_2 : 2x - 8y = -8$

7. $L_1 : x - 2y = -8$
$L_2 : x + 2y = 2$

6. _____

7. _____

In Problems 8–11, find the equation of the line that contains the given point and is parallel to the given line. Write the equation in slope-intercept form, if possible.

8. $(7, -5); y = 2x + 6$

9. $(-4, 5); x = -3$

8. _____

9. _____

10. $(4, -8); y = -1$ **11.** $(6, 7); 2x + 3y = 9$ 10. _____

11. _____

In Problems 12–15, find the equation of the line that contains the given point and is perpendicular to the given line. Write the equation in slope-intercept form, if possible.

12. $(4, 7); y = \dfrac{1}{3}x - 3$ **13.** $(-2, -5); y = -2x + 5$ 12. _____

13. _____

14. $(3, -6);$ *y*-axis   **15.** $(11, -6);$ *x*-axis   14. _____

15. _____

Five-Minute Warm-Up 3.7
Linear Inequalities in Two Variables

1. Solve: $x + 5 < -3$ 1. _____

2. Solve: $5x - 2 \geq -17$ 2. _____

3. Solve: $-3 + 7(x - 2) \geq -2(1 - 5x)$ 3. _____

4. Graph: $y = 2x - 1$

Guided Practice 3.7
Linear Inequalities in Two Variables

Objective 1: Determine Whether an Ordered Pair Is a Solution to a Linear Inequality

1. *True or False:* To determine if an ordered pair is a solution to the linear inequality, substitute the values for the variables into the inequality. If a true statement results, then the ordered pair is a solution to the inequality.

1. _____

2. Determine if $(1, 3)$ is a solution to $y \leq 2x + 1$. *(See textbook Example 1)*

2. _____

Objective 2: Graph Linear Inequalities

3. To graph any linear inequality in two variables, you must first graph the corresponding equation. If the inequality is strict (< or >), you should use a _____ line. If the inequality is nonstrict $(\leq$ or $\geq)$, you should use a _____ line.

4. The graph of a line separates the xy-plane into two _____.

5. If a test point satisfies the inequality, then every ordered pair that lies in that half plane also satisfies the inequality. To represent this solution set, we _____ the half plane containing the test point.

6. Graph the linear inequality $y \geq x + 2$. *(See textbook Example 2)*

Step 1: We replace the inequality symbol with an equal sign and graph the corresponding line.	Write the equation:	**(a)** _____
	Identify the slope:	**(b)** _____
	Identify the y-intercept:	**(c)** _____
	Graph the line on the grid provided in (h). Is the line connecting these points solid or dashed?	**(d)** _____
Step 2: We select any test point that is not on the line and determine whether the test point satisfies the inequality. When the line does not contain the origin, it is usually easiest to choose the origin, (0, 0), as the test point.	Select a test point:	**(e)** _____ $y \geq x + 2$
	Substitute the values for the variables into the inequality. Is the statement true or false?	**(f)** _____
	Which half plane should be shaded; the half plane containing the test point or the opposite half plane?	**(g)** _____
	Graph the solution set by using the slope and y-intercept, graphing the line, and shading the appropriate half plane.	$y \geq x + 2$ **(h)**

7. Graph the linear inequality $4x - y > 0$. *(See textbook Example 4)*

Replace the inequality symbol with an equal sign to obtain the graph of $4x - y > 0$. Is the line solid or dashed?

(a) _____

Select a test point. Can you use $(0, 0)$?

(b) _____

Determine if the inequality is satisfied by your test point? If the statement is true, shade the half plane containing the test point. If the statement is false, shade the opposite half plane.

(c)

Objective 3: Solve Problems Involving Linear Inequalities

8. Wood Flooring Mary Jo owns a discount flooring store and sells two different grades of wood flooring. There is a domestic cherry wood that sells for $4.32 per square foot and a reclaimed Douglas fir that sells for $2.50 per square foot. How many square feet of wood flooring does she need to sell to have an income of at least $5000? *(See textbook Example 6)*

(a) Write a linear inequality that describes Mary Jo's options for selling wood flooring.

> **Step 1: Identify** We want to determine how many square feet of each she should sell to earn at least $5000. This requires an inequality in two variables.

> **Step 2: Name the Unknowns** Let x represent the number of square feet of cherry flooring sold and let y represent the number of square feet of Douglas fir sold.

> **Step 3: Translate** If cherry wood sells for $4.32 per square foot and Douglas fir sells for $2.50 per square foot, write an inequality the represents her total income greater than or equal to $5000.

(a) _____

(b) Will Mary Jo make her sales goal if she sells 600 square feet of cherry wood and 850 square feet of Douglas fir?

(b)_____

Do the Math Exercises 3.7
Linear Inequalities in Two Variables

In Problems 1–4, determine which of the following ordered pairs, if any, are solutions to the given linear inequality in two variables.

1. $y \leq x - 5$ $A(-4, -6)$ $B(0, -8)$ $C(3, 10)$ **2.** $y > -2x + 1$ $A(0, 0)$ $B(-2, 3)$ $C(2, -1)$ 1. _____

2. _____

3. $3x + 5y \geq 4$ $A(2, 0)$ $B(-3, 4)$ $C(6, -2)$ **4.** $x > 10$ $A(3, 12)$ $B(11, -6)$ $C(10, 16)$ 3. _____

4. _____

In Problems 5–12, graph each linear inequality.

5. $y \leq 4x + 2$

6. $y > x - 3$

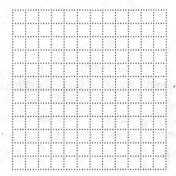

7. $y < 4$

8. $y \geq \dfrac{3}{2}x - 2$

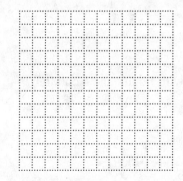

9. $2x + 6y < -6$

10. $6x - 8y \geq 24$

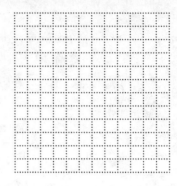

11. $x - y > 0$

12. $x \geq 2$

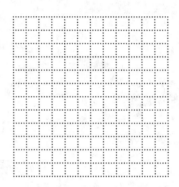

13. Fishing Trip Patrick's rowboat can hold a maximum of 500 pounds. In Patrick's circle of friends, the average adult weighs 160 pounds and the average child weighs 75 pounds.

(a) Write a linear inequality that describes the various combinations of the number of adults a and children c that can go on a fishing trip in the rowboat.

13a. _____

(b) Will the boat sink with 2 adults and 4 children?

13b. _____

(c) Will the boat sink with 1 adult and 5 children?

13c. _____

Five-Minute Warm-Up 4.1
Solving Systems of Linear Equations by Graphing

1. Graph each of the following linear equations.

   (a) $6x - 3y = -12$ **(b)** $y = -\dfrac{3}{2}x - 1$

 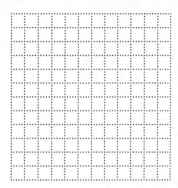

2. Determine whether $2x + 3y = -3$ is parallel to $-4x - 6y = 18$.

2.

3. Determine whether $3x + 2y = 6$ is parallel to $y = -\dfrac{3}{2}x + 3$.

3.

Guided Practice 4.1
Solving Systems of Linear Equations by Graphing

Objective 1: Determine If an Ordered Pair Is a Solution of a System of Linear Equations

1. Determine whether the given ordered pairs are solutions of the system of equations. *(See textbook Example 2)*

$$\begin{cases} x + y = 0 \\ 2x - 3y = 5 \end{cases}$$

(a) $(-2, 2)$ **(b)** $(1, -1)$

1a. _____

1b. _____

Objective 2: Solve a System of Linear Equations by Graphing

2. Solve the following system by graphing: $\begin{cases} x - y = -5 \\ 2x + y = -1 \end{cases}$ *(See textbook Example 3)*

Step 1: Graph the first equation in the system.	The equation $x - y = -5$ can be graphed using the intercepts or by writing the equation in slope-intercept form. We will use the intercepts. Name the x and y-intercept and then graph the line in the coordinate plane below.	**(a)** x-intercept _____ **(b)** y-intercept _____
Step 2: **Graph** the second equation in the system.	The equation $2x + y = -1$ can also be graphed by either method. This time we will use slope-intercept form. Write the equation in slope-intercept form. Name the slope and y-intercept and then graph the line in the coordinate plane below.	**(c)** equation _____ **(d)** slope _____ **(e)** y-intercept _____
Step 3: Determine the point of intersection of the two lines, if any.	Name the point where the lines appear to intersect.	**(f)** _____
Step 4: Verify that the point of intersection determined in Step 3 is a solution of the system.	Check that the point satisfies both of the equations in the system.	**(g)**

State the solution to the system: **(h)** _____

3. Solve the system by graphing: $\begin{cases} 2x + y = 1 \\ -4x - 2y = 6 \end{cases}$ *(See textbook Example 5)*　　3. _____

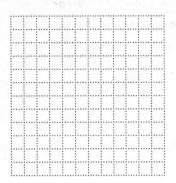

Objective 3: Classify Systems of Linear Equations as Consistent or Inconsistent

4. Complete the following chart which describes the solutions to a system of linear equations in two variables.

Number of Solutions	Classification of the System	Appearance of the Graph of the Two Lines
(a) no solution		
(b) infinitely many solutions		
(c) exactly one solution		

5. **(a)** Without graphing, determine the number of solutions of the system:

$\begin{cases} 4x - 3y = -6 \\ 8x - 6y = -12 \end{cases}$ *(See textbook Example 7)*　　5a. _____

(b) State whether the system is consistent or inconsistent.　　5b. _____

(c) If the system is consistent, state whether the equations are dependent or independent. 5c. _____

Do the Math Exercises 4.1
Solving Systems of Linear Equations by Graphing

In Problems 1–2, determine whether the ordered pair is a solution of the system of equations.

1. $\begin{cases} 2x+5y=0 \\ x-3y=11 \end{cases}$

    (a) $(5, -2)$
    (b) $(-5, 2)$
    (c) $(2, -3)$

2. $\begin{cases} x-4y=2 \\ 5x-8y=-6 \end{cases}$

    (a) $(-8, -2)$
    (b) $(2, 2)$
    (c) $\left(\dfrac{-10}{3}, -\dfrac{4}{3} \right)$

1a. _____

1b. _____

1c. _____

2a. _____

2b. _____

2c. _____

In Problems 3–6, solve each system of equations by graphing.

3. $\begin{cases} y=-4x+6 \\ y=-2x \end{cases}$

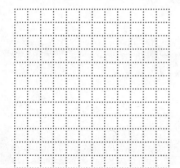

4. $\begin{cases} -2x+5y=-20 \\ 4x-10y=10 \end{cases}$

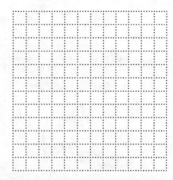

5. $\begin{cases} 2x+5y=2 \\ -x+2y=-1 \end{cases}$

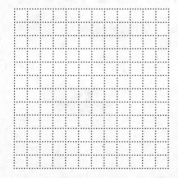

6. $\begin{cases} 3y=-4x-4 \\ 8x+2=-6y-6 \end{cases}$

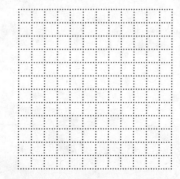

In Problems 7–10, without graphing, determine the number of solutions of each system of equations. State whether the system is consistent or inconsistent. For those systems that are consistent, state whether the equations are dependent or independent.

7. $\begin{cases} 2x + y = -3 \\ -2x - y = 6 \end{cases}$

8. $\begin{cases} -x + y = 5 \\ x - y = -5 \end{cases}$

7. _____

8. _____

9. $\begin{cases} y - 3 = 0 \\ x - 3 = 0 \end{cases}$

10. $\begin{cases} 5x + y = -1 \\ 10x + 2y = -2 \end{cases}$

9. _____

10. _____

Set up a system of linear equations in two variables that models the problem. Then solve the system of linear equations by graphing.

11. **Car Rental** The Speedy Car Rental agency charges $60 per day plus $0.14 per mile while the Slow-but-Cheap Car Rental agency charges $30 per day plus $0.20 per mile. Determine the number of miles for which the cost of the car rental will be the same for both companies. If you plan to drive the car for 400 miles, which company should you use?

11. _____

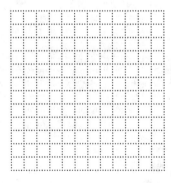

Five-Minute Warm-Up 4.2
Solving Systems of Linear Equations Using Substitution

1. Solve $5x - 3y = -18$ for y.

1. _____

2. Solve $3x + 8y = -12$ for x.

2. _____

3. Solve: $\dfrac{3}{2}x - \dfrac{5}{2}(x + 6) = -8$

3. _____

4. Solve: $-\left(\dfrac{7}{3}y + 6\right) - \dfrac{2}{3}y = -15$

4. _____

Guided Practice 4.2
Solving Systems of Linear Equations Using Substitution

Objective 1: Solve a System of Linear Equations Using the Substitution Method

1. Solve the following system by substitution: $\begin{cases} 4x + 3y = -23 & (1) \\ y = -x - 7 & (2) \end{cases}$ *(See textbook Example 1)*

Step 1: Solve one of the equations for one of the unknowns.

Equation (2) is already solve for *y*: $y = -x - 7$

Step 2: Substitute the expression for *y* into equation (1).

Equation (1):   **(a)** _____

Substitute into equation (1):   **(b)** _____

Step 3: Solve the equation for *x*.

Distribute the 3:   **(c)** _____

Combine like terms: **(d)** _____

Add 21 to both sides: **(e)** $x =$ _____

Step 4: Substitute your value for *x* into equation 2 and solve for *y*.

Equation (2):   **(f)** _____

Substitute for *x*:   **(g)** _____

Solve for *y*:   **(h)** _____

Step 5: Verify your solution.

Check that your ordered pair satisfies both of the equations.

State the solution: **(i)** _____

2. Solve the following system by substitution: $\begin{cases} 3x - 2y = -8 \\ x + 3y = 34 \end{cases}$ *(See textbook Example 3)*   2. _____

3. Solve the following system by substitution: $\begin{cases} 5x + 8y = 4 \\ y = -\dfrac{5}{8}x + \dfrac{1}{2} \end{cases}$ *(See textbook*

4. _____

Example 5)

Objective 2: Solve Applied Problems Involving Systems of Linear Equations

4. Unknown Integers The sum of two numbers is -11 and their difference is -101. Find the numbers. *(See textbook Example 6)*

> **Step 1: Identify** This is a direct translation problem involving unknown integers.
>
> **Step 2: Name** Let the two unknown numbers be identified as x and y.
>
> **Step 3: Translate**
> **(a)** Write an equation showing the sum of the two numbers is -11: 4a. _____
>
> **(b)** Write an equation showing the difference of the two numbers is -101: 4b. _____
>
> **Step 4: Solve**
> **(c)** Write the system to be solved: 4c. _____
>
> **(d)** Solve one of the equations for one of the variables. Substitute this expression into the opposite equation and solve for the unknown. What is the solution to the system? 4d. _____
>
> **Step 5: Check** Verify that the values you found satisfy the system and make sense in the original problem.
>
> **Step 6: Answer** the question: 4e. _____

Do the Math Exercises 4.2
Solving Systems of Linear Equations Using Substitution

In Problems 1–4, solve each system of equations using substitution.

1. $\begin{cases} 5x + 2y = -5 \\ 3x - y = -14 \end{cases}$

2. $\begin{cases} y = \dfrac{2}{3}x + 1 \\ y = -\dfrac{3}{2}x + 40 \end{cases}$

1. _____

2. _____

3. $\begin{cases} y = 5x - 3 \\ y = 2x - \dfrac{21}{5} \end{cases}$

4. $\begin{cases} y = 4x \\ 2x - 3y = 5 \end{cases}$

3. _____

4. _____

In Problems 5–8, solve each system of equations using substitution. State whether the system is inconsistent, or consistent and dependent.

5. $\begin{cases} 2x - y = 3 \\ y - 2x = 3 \end{cases}$

6. $\begin{cases} y = -x + 1 \\ x + y = 1 \end{cases}$

5. _____

6. _____

7. $\begin{cases} 4 + y = 3x \\ 6x - 2y = -2 \end{cases}$

8. $\begin{cases} x + y = 2 \\ 2x + 2y = 2 \end{cases}$

7. _____

8. _____

In Problems 9–14, solve each system of equations using substitution.

9. $\begin{cases} y = \dfrac{3}{4}x \\ x = 4(y-1) \end{cases}$

10. $\begin{cases} x = 3y + 6 \\ y - \dfrac{1}{3}x = -2 \end{cases}$

9. _____

10. _____

11. $\begin{cases} 3x + 2y = 1 \\ x + 3y = -\dfrac{5}{3} \end{cases}$

12. $\begin{cases} -4x + y = 3 \\ 8x - 2y = 1 \end{cases}$

11. _____

12. _____

13. $\begin{cases} 18x - 6y = -7 \\ x + 2y = 0 \end{cases}$

14. $\begin{cases} \dfrac{2}{3}x + \dfrac{1}{3}y = 1 \\ \dfrac{1}{2}x + \dfrac{1}{4}y = \dfrac{3}{4} \end{cases}$

13. _____

14. _____

15. Investment Elaine wants to invest part of her $24,000 Virginia Lottery winnings in an international stock fund that yields 4% annual interest and the remainder in a domestic growth fund that yields 6.5% annually. Use the system of equations to determine the amount Elaine should invest in each account to earn $1360 interest at the end of one year, where x represents the amount invested in the international stock fund and y represents the amount invested in the domestic growth fund.

15. _____

$$\begin{cases} x + y = 24{,}000 \\ 0.04x + 0.065y = 1360 \end{cases}$$

Sullivan/Struve/Mazzarella, *Elementary & Intermediate Algebra*, 2e

Five-Minute Warm-Up 4.3
Solving Systems of Linear Equations Using Elimination

1. What is the additive inverse of $\dfrac{5}{4}$?   1. _____

2. What is the additive inverse of -6?   2. _____

3. Distribute: $-\dfrac{7}{4}(-12x + 8y)$ 3. _____

4. Solve: $-6x + 7 = 3(-2x + 1)$ 4. _____

5. Simplify: $8x - 7y + 3 + -8x - 2y - 12$ 5. _____

6. **(a)** Find the LCM of 8 and 12.   6a. _____

    (b) By what factor must 8 be multiplied so that the product of the factor and 8   6b. _____
    equal the LCM?

    (c) By what factor must 12 be multiplied so that the product of the factor and 12   6c. _____
    equal the LCM?

Guided Practice 4.3
Solving Systems of Linear Equations Using Elimination

Objective 1: Solve a System of Linear Equations Using the Elimination Method

1. This method is called "elimination" because one of the variables is eliminated through the process of addition. The elimination method is also sometimes referred to as the *addition method*.

Solve the following system by elimination: $\begin{cases} -x + y = 12 \\ x - 3y = -26 \end{cases}$ *(See textbook Example 1)*   1. _____

2. Solve the following system by elimination: $\begin{cases} 2x + y = -4 & (1) \\ 3x + 5y = 29 & (2) \end{cases}$ *(See textbook Example 2)*

Step 1: Write each equation in standard form, $Ax + By = C$.

Both equations are already in standard form.

Step 2: Our first goal is to get the coefficients on one of the variables to be additive inverses. In looking at this system, we can make the coefficients of y be additive inverses by multiplying equation (1) by -5.

Multiply both sides of (1) by -5, use the Distributive Property, and then write the equivalent system of equations.

$\begin{cases} 2x + y = -4 \\ 3x + 5y = 29 \end{cases}$

(a) $\begin{cases} \underline{\hspace{3cm}} & (1) \\ \underline{\hspace{3cm}} & (2) \end{cases}$

Step 3: We now add equations (1) and (2) to eliminate the variable y and then solve for x.

Add (1) and (2):

(b) _____

Divide both sides by -7:

(c) $x =$ _____

Step 4: Substitute your value for x into either equation (1) or equation (2). We will use equation (1) as it looks like less work.

Equation (1):

Substitute your value for x and solve for y.

$2x + y = -4$

(d) $y =$ _____

Step 5: Check your answer in both of the original equations. If both equations yield a true statement, you have the correct answer.

Write the ordered pair that is the solution to the system.

(e) _____

3. Solve the following system by elimination:
$$\begin{cases} \dfrac{1}{2}x - \dfrac{1}{5}y = \dfrac{2}{5} & (1) \\[2mm] -\dfrac{3}{8}x + \dfrac{5}{4}y = -\dfrac{5}{2} & (2) \end{cases}$$

(See textbook Example 3)

    (a) Multiply both sides of equation (1) by the LCD of 2 and 5:   3a. _____

    (b) Multiply both sides of equation (2) by the LCD of 2, 4, and 8:   3b. _____

    (c) Solve this equivalent system by elimination and state the solution: 3c. _____

4. When solving a system of linear equations by elimination, if both variables were eliminated and the statement $0 = 6$ was left, what is the solution to this system?   4. _____
(See textbook Example 4)

5. When solving a system of linear equations by elimination, if both variables were eliminated and the statement $0 = 0$ was left, what is the solution to this system?   5. _____
(See textbook Example 5)

Objective 2: Solve Applied Problems Involving Systems of Linear Equations

6. Ticket Prices Admission to the movie theatre costs $4.50 per child and $7.50 per adult. If the theatre took in $3337.50 and had 525 patrons, how many of each ticket were sold? *(See textbook Example 6)*

    (a) If *a* represents the number of adult tickets sold and *c* represents the number of children's tickets sold, write an equation that shows that the total number of tickets sold   6a. _____
is 525.

    (b) Use the rate for a child's ticket and number of children's tickets sold plus the rate for an adult ticket and the number of adult tickets sold to write an equation showing the total 6b. _____
revenue for this performance is $3337.50.

    (c) Solve the system.   6c. _____

    (d) Answer the question in the problem.   6d. _____

Do the Math Exercises 4.3
Solving Systems of Linear Equations Using Elimination

In Problems 1–2, solve each system of equations using elimination.

1. $\begin{cases} 2x + 6y = 6 \\ -2x + y = 8 \end{cases}$

2. $\begin{cases} 3x + 2y = 7 \\ -3x + 4y = 2 \end{cases}$

1. _____

2. _____

In Problems 3–4, solve each system of equations using elimination. State whether the system is inconsistent or consistent and dependent.

3. $\begin{cases} x - y = -4 \\ -2x + 2y = -8 \end{cases}$

4. $\begin{cases} 2x + 5y = 15 \\ -6x - 15y = -45 \end{cases}$

3. _____

4. _____

In Problems 5–10, solve each system of equations using elimination.

5. $\begin{cases} 5x - y = 3 \\ -10x + 2y = 2 \end{cases}$

6. $\begin{cases} 2x + 3y = 2 \\ 5x + 7y = 0 \end{cases}$

5. _____

6. _____

7. $\begin{cases} x + 3y = 6 \\ 9y = -3x + 18 \end{cases}$

8. $\begin{cases} 5x + 7y = 6 \\ 2x - 3y = 11 \end{cases}$

7. _____

8. _____

9. $\begin{cases} 12x + 15y = 55 \\ \dfrac{1}{2}x + 3y = \dfrac{3}{2} \end{cases}$

10. $\begin{cases} -2.4x - 0.4y = 0.32 \\ 4.2x + 0.6y = -0.54 \end{cases}$

9. _____

10. _____

In Problems 11–14, solve by any method: graphing, substitution, or elimination.

11. $\begin{cases} 2x - 3y = -10 \\ -3x + y = 1 \end{cases}$

12. $\begin{cases} 0.25x + 0.10y = 3.70 \\ x + y = 25 \end{cases}$

11. _____

12. _____

13. **Carbs** Yvette and José go to McDonald's for breakfast. Yvette orders two sausage biscuits and one 16-ounce orange juice. The entire meal had 98 grams of carbohydrates. José orders three sausage biscuits and two 16-ounce orange juices and his meal had 168 grams of carbohydrates. How many grams of carbohydrates are in a sausage biscuit? How many grams of carbohydrates are in a 16-ounce orange juice? Solve the system

13. _____

$$\begin{cases} 2b + u = 98 \\ 3b + 2u = 168 \end{cases}$$

where b represents the number of grams of carbohydrates in a sausage biscuit and u represents the number of grams of carbohydrates in an orange juice to find the answers.

Five-Minute Warm-Up 4.4

Solving Direct Translation, Geometry, and Uniform Motion Problems Using Systems of Linear Equations

1. If you are traveling at an average speed of 65 miles per hour (mph),

   (a) how far will you travel in 5 hours?   **(b)** If you went 195 miles, how long were you traveling?

   1a. _____

   1b. _____

2. Suppose that you have \$7000 in a Certificate of Deposit (CD) that pays 4.5% annual simple interest. What is the amount of interest paid

   (a) after 3 years?   **(b)** after two months?

   2a. _____

   2b. _____

3. Translate each of the following sentences into an equation. *DO NOT SOLVE.*

   (a) Seven less than twice a number is 45.   3a. _____

   (b) 5 times the sum of 3 and some number is the same as half the number.   3b. _____

   (c) The quotient of a number and 3 is equal to the number subtracted from 20.   3c. _____

Guided Practice 4.4
Solving Direct Translation, Geometry, and Uniform Motion Problems Using Systems of Linear Equations

Objective 1: Model and Solve Direct Translation Problems

1. Fun with Numbers The sum of four times a first number and a second number is 68. If the first number is decreased by twice the second number the result is −1. Find the numbers. *(See textbook Example 1)*

Step 1: Identify We are looking for the two unknown numbers.

Step 2: Name Let x represent the first number and y represent the second number.

Step 3: Translate

(a) Write the equation for the sum of four times a first number and a second number is 68:   1a. _____

(b) Write the equation for the first number decreased by twice the second number results in −1:   1b. _____

(c) **Step 4: Solve** Use either substitution or elimination to find the solution to your system of equations. What is the solution to the system?   1c. _____

Step 5: Check Verify that the values you found satisfy the system and make sense in the original problem.

(d) **Step 6: Answer** the question in the problem: 1d. _____

Objective 2: Model and Solve Geometry Problems

2. Two angles are supplementary if the sum of the measures of the angles is: 2. _____

3. If one angle is 30° more than its supplement, find the measures of the two angles. *(See textbook Example 3)*

(a) If one angle has x degrees and the supplement has y degrees, write an equation showing the sum of the measures of the two angles: 3a. _____

(b) Write an equation showing one angle is 30° more than its supplement: 3b. _____

(c) Solve your system of two linear equations.   3c. _____

(d) Answer the question in the problem.   3d. _____

Objective 3: Model and Solve Uniform Motion Problems

4. Airplane Speed A plane can fly 2400 miles east, with the wind, in 6 hours. The return trip west to the same point, against the wind, takes 8 hours. Find the airspeed of the plane and the effect wind resistance has on the plane. *(See textbook Example 4)*

Step 1: Identify This is a uniform motion problem. We want to determine the airspeed of the plane and the effect of wind resistance.

Step 2: Name We will let *a* represent the airspeed of the plane and *w* represent the effect of wind resistance.

Step 3: Translate
(a) Flying east, with the wind, the ground speed of the plane is: 4a. _____

(b) Flying west, against the wind, the ground speed of the plane is: 4b. _____

Complete the table from the information given, using *a* for speed of the plane and *w* for speed of the wind.

	Distance (miles)	Rate (mph)	Time (hours)
(c) With the wind			
(d) Against the wind			

(e) Write a system of equations using the information in your table: 4e. _____

(f) **Step 4: Solve** Use either substitution or elimination to find the solution to your system of equations.   4f. _____

Step 5: Check Does your solution satisfy each of the equations in the system? Does your answer seem reasonable?

(g) **Step 6: Answer** the question in the problem: 4g. _____

Do the Math Exercises 4.4
Solving Direct Translation, Geometry, and Uniform Motion Problems Using Systems of Linear Equations

Complete the system of equations. Do not solve the system.

1. The sum of two numbers is 90. If 20 is added to 3 times the smaller number, the result exceeds twice the larger number by 50. Let a represent the smaller number and let b represent the larger number.

$$\begin{cases} a+b=90 \\ \\ \underline{\hspace{2cm}} = \underline{\hspace{2cm}} \end{cases}$$

Complete the system of equations. Do not solve the system.

2. The perimeter of a rectangle is 212 centimeters. The length is 8 centimeters less than three times the width. Let l represent the length of the rectangle and let w represent the width of the rectangle.

$$\begin{cases} 2w+2l=212 \\ \\ \underline{\hspace{2cm}} = \underline{\hspace{2cm}} \end{cases}$$

Complete the system of equations. Do not solve the system.

3. A plane flew with the wind for 3 hours, covering 1200 miles. It then returned over the same route to the airport against the wind in 4 hours. Let a represent the airspeed of the plane and w represent the effect of wind resistance.

$$\begin{cases} 3(a+w)=1200 \\ \\ \underline{\hspace{2cm}} = \underline{\hspace{2cm}} \end{cases}$$

4. **Fun with Numbers** Find two numbers whose sum is 55 and whose difference is 17.   4. _____

5. **Fun with Numbers** The sum of two numbers is 32. Twice the larger subtracted from the smaller is –22. Find the numbers.   5. _____

6. **Perimeter of a Parking Lot** A rectangular parking lot has a perimeter of 125 feet. The length of the parking lot is 10 feet more than the width. What is the length of the parking lot? What is the width?

6. _____

7. **Working with Complements** The measure of one angle is 10° less than the measure of three times its complement. Find the measures of the two angles.

7. _____

8. **Finding Supplements** The measure of one angle is 20° more than two-thirds the measure of its supplement. Find the measures of the two angles.

8. _____

9. **Southwest Airlines Plane** A Southwest Airlines plane can fly 455 mph against the wind and 515 mph when it flies with the wind. Find the effect of the wind and the groundspeed of the airplane.

9. _____

10. **Rowing** On Monday afternoon, Andrew rowed his boat with the current for 4.5 hours and covered 27 miles, stopping in the evening at a campground. On Tuesday morning he returned to his starting point against the current in 6.75 hours. Find the speed of the current and the rate at which Andrew rowed in still water.

10. _____

11. **Horseback Riding** Monica and Gabriella enjoy riding horses at a dude ranch in Colorado. They decide to go down different trails, agreeing to meet back at the ranch later in the day. Monica's horse is going 4 mph faster than the Gabriella's, and after 2.5 hours, they are 20 miles apart. Find the speed of each horse.

11. _____

Five-Minute Warm-Up 4.5
Solving Mixture Problems Using Systems of Linear Equations

1. Suppose that Sherry has a credit card balance of $2000. Each month, the credit card charges 18% annual simple interest on any outstanding balances.

   (a) What is the interest that Sherry will be charged on this loan after one month?

   1a. _____

   (b) What is the balance on Sherry's credit card after one month?

   1b. _____

2. Write the percent as a decimal.

   2a. _____

   (a) 40%   (b) 0.15%

   2b. _____

3. Solve by any appropriate method: $\begin{cases} 2x + 5y = -11 \\ 3x + 2y = 11 \end{cases}$

   3. _____

Guided Practice 4.5
Solving Mixture Problems Using Systems of Linear Equations

Objective 1: Draw Up a Plan for Modeling Mixture Problems

1. The cost of an adult ticket to the art museum is $7.50 and student tickets cost $4.00. When a group of 40 adults and students entered the museum, the total receipts were $202. How many adults and how many students were in the group that entered the museum? *(See textbook Example 1)*

Fill in the chart that summarizes the information in the problem.

	Number	Cost per Person in Dollars	Amount
(a) Adults			
(b) Students			
(c) Total			

(d) Write a system of equations to solve this problem. Do not solve the system.   1d. _____

Objective 2: Set Up and Solve Money Problems Using the Mixture Model

2. Johnny has $6.75 in dimes and quarters. If he has 42 coins, how many quarters does Johnny have? *(See textbook Example 2)*

Fill in the chart that summarizes the information in the problem.

	Number of Coins	Value per Coin in Dollars	Total Value
(a) Quarters			
(b) Dimes			
(c) Total			

(d) Write a system of equations to solve this problem.   2d. _____

(e) Solve the system and answer the question in the problem.   2e. _____

Objective 3: Set Up and Solve Dry Mixture and Percent Mixture Problems

3. A candy store sells chocolate-covered almonds for $6.50 per pound and chocolate-covered peanuts for $4.00 per pound. The manager decides to make a bridge mix that combines the almonds with the peanuts. She wants the bridge mix to sell for $6.00 per pound, and there should be no loss in revenue from selling the bridge mix versus the almonds and peanuts alone. How many pounds of chocolate-covered almonds and chocolate-covered peanuts are required to create 50 pounds of bridge mix? *(See textbook Example 4)*

Complete the chart that summarizes the information in the problem.

	Price $/Pound	Number of Pounds	Revenue
(a) Almonds			
(b) Peanuts			
(c) Mix			

(d) Write a system of equations to solve this problem. Do not solve the system.   3d. _____

4. The Chemistry stockroom has a jar labeled 25% hydrochloric acid and another labeled 40% hydrochloric acid. If 90 ml of 30% solution are needed for today's lab experiment, how much of each should the stockroom assistant mix together? *(See textbook Example 5)*

Complete the chart that summarizes the information in the problem.

	Number of ml	Concentration	Amount of Pure HCl
(a) 25% HCl Solution			
(b) 40% HCl Solution			
(c) 30% HCl Solution			

(d) Write a system of equations to solve this problem. Do not solve the system.   4d. _____

Do the Math Exercises 4.5
Solving Mixture Problems Using Systems of Linear Equations

In Problems 1–3, fill in the table from the information given. Then write the system that models the problem. DO NOT SOLVE.

1. John Murphy sells jewelry at art shows. He sells bracelets for $10 and necklaces for $15.   1. _____
   At the end of one day John found that he had sold 69 pieces of jewelry and had receipts
   of $895.

	Number •	Cost per Item =	Total Value
Bracelets			
Necklaces			
Total			

2. Sherry has a savings account that earns 2.75% simple interest per year and a certificate   2. _____
   of deposit (CD) that earns 2% simple interest annually. At the end of one year, Sherry
   received $37.75 in interest on a total investment of $1700 in the two accounts.

	Principal •	Rate =	Interest
Savings Account			
Certificate of Deposit			
Total			

3. A merchant wishes to mix peanuts worth $5 per pound and trail mix worth $2 per pound   3. _____
   to yield 40 pounds of a nutty mixture that will sell for $3 per pound.

	Number of Pounds •	Price per Pound =	Total Value
Peanuts			
Trail Mix			
Total			

In Problems 4–6, complete the system of linear equations to solve the problem. Do not solve.

4. On a school field trip, 22 people attended a dress rehearsal of the Broadway play,
   "Avenue Q." They paid $274 for the tickets, which cost $15 for each adult and $7 for
   each child. How many adults and how many children attended "Avenue Q"? Let a
   represent the number of adult tickets purchased and let c represent the number of
   children's tickets purchased.

$$\begin{cases} a + c = 22 \\ \underline{\hspace{1cm}} + \underline{\hspace{1cm}} = 274 \end{cases}$$

5. You have a total of $2650 to invest. Account A pays 5% annual interest and account B pays 6.5% annual interest. How much should you invest in each account if you would like the investment to earn $155 at the end of one year? Let A represent the amount of money invested in the account that earns 5% annual interest and let B represent the amount of money invested in the account that earns 6.5% annual interest.

$$\begin{cases} A \ + \ B \ = \underline{\hspace{1.5cm}} \\ \\ \underline{\hspace{1cm}} + \underline{\hspace{1cm}} = 155 \end{cases}$$

6. The Latte Shoppe sells Bold Breakfast coffee for $8.60 per pound and Wake-Up coffee for $5.75 per pound. One day, the amount of Bold Breakfast coffee sold was 2 pounds less than twice the amount of Wake-Up coffee and the revenue received from selling both types of coffee was $143.45. How many pounds of each type of coffee were sold that day? Let B represent the number of pounds of Bold Breakfast coffee sold and let W represent the number of pounds of Wake-Up sold. Complete the system of equations:

$$\begin{cases} 8.60B + \ 5.75W \ = \underline{\hspace{1.5cm}} \\ \\ B \ \ = \underline{\hspace{1cm}} - \underline{\hspace{1cm}} \end{cases}$$

In Problems 7–9, write a system of equations.

7. **Ticket Pricing** A ticket on the roller coaster is priced differently for adults and children. 7. _____
One day there were 5 adults and 8 children in a group and the cost of their tickets was
$48.50. Another group of 4 adults and 12 children paid $57.What is the price of each type
of ticket?

8. **Investments** Ann has $5000 to invest. She invests in two different accounts, one   8. _____
expected to return 4.5% and the other expected to return 9%. In order to earn $382.50 for
the year, how much should she invest at each rate?

9. **Alcohol** A laboratory assistant is asked to mix a 30% alcohol solution with 21 liters of   9. _____
an 80% alcohol solution to make a 60% alcohol solution. How many liters of the 30%
alcohol solution should be used?

Five-Minute Warm-Up 4.6
Systems of Linear Inequalities

1. Solve $18x + 30 \leq -6$ and write your answer in interval notation.

2. Solve $\dfrac{5}{2}(4x - 12) < 15x - 25$ and write your answer in interval notation.

2.

3. Graph each of the following linear inequalities.

   (a) $y \geq -x + 2$ **(b)** $8x - 4y < -16$

                    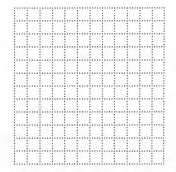

Guided Practice 4.6
Systems of Linear Inequalities

Objective 1: Determine Whether an Ordered Pair Is a Solution of a System of Linear Inequalities

1. Determine which of the following points, if any, satisfy the system of linear inequalities. *(See textbook Example 1)*

$$\begin{cases} 2x - y \geq -3 \\ x + 5y < 4 \end{cases}$$

    (a) $(-1, 1)$ **(b)** $(-4, -3)$ **(c)** $(1, -1)$ 1. _____

Objective 2: Graph a System of Linear Inequalities

2. The only way to show the solution of a system of linear inequalities is by _____.

3. To graph the inequality $x - 8y > 4$, we use a _____ line as the boundry. *Refer to textbook Section 3.7.*

4. To graph the inequality $3x + 2y \geq -6$, we use a _____ line as the boundry.

5. To graph a linear inequality, we first graph the equation to determine the boundary line. This line divides the plane into two half-planes. To decide which half-plane to shade, we use a test point such as (0, 0), provided that this point does not lie on the line. If the test point satisfies the inequality, we shade the half-plane that contains the point. If the test point does not satisfy the inequality, we shade

_____.

6. When graphing a system of linear inequalities, we are looking for the ordered pairs that satisfy both

inequalties simultaneously. Therefore, the solution of the system is the _____ of the graphs of the linear inequalties.

7. Graph the system: $\begin{cases} 2x + 3y > -3 \\ -3x + y \leq 2 \end{cases}$ *(See textbook Examples 2 and 3)*

Objective 3: Solve Applied Problems Involving Systems of Linear Inequalities

8. Party Planning Alexis and Sarah are planning a barbeque for their friends. They plan to serve grilled fish and carne asada and want to spend at most $40 on the meat. The fish sells for $8 per pound and the carne asada is $5 per pound. Since most of their friends do not eat red meat, they plan to buy at least twice as much fish as carne asada. Let x represent the amount of carne asada purchased and y represent the amount of fish purchased. *(See textbook Example 5)*

(a) Write an inequality that describes how much Alexis and Sarah will spend on meat.   8a. _____

(b) Write an inequality that describes that amount of carne asada that will be purchased   8b. _____
relative to the amount of fish that will be purchased.

(c) Since Alexis and Sarah will purchase a positive quantity of meat, write the two   8c. _____
inequalities that describe this constraint.

_____

(d) Graph the system of inequalities.

(e) Can Alexis and Sarah purchase 5 pounds of carne asada and 12 pounds of fish and stay   8e. _____
within their budget?

Do the Math Exercises 4.6
Systems of Linear Inequalities

In Problems 1–2, determine which of the following point(s), if any, is a solution of the system of linear inequalities.

1. $\begin{cases} 2x - 3y < 3 \\ 2x + y < -5 \end{cases}$

    (a) $(-4, 1)$

    (b) $\left(-\dfrac{3}{2}, -2\right)$

    (c) $(-1, -2)$

2. $\begin{cases} x - 2y > 2 \\ -3x - 2y \leq 6 \end{cases}$

    (a) $\left(-1, -\dfrac{3}{2}\right)$

    (b) $(0, -4)$

    (c) $(4, -1)$

1a. _____

1b. _____

1c. _____

2a. _____

2b. _____

2c. _____

In Problems 3–6, graph each system of linear inequalities.

3. $\begin{cases} y > 2 \\ y > \dfrac{2}{3}x - 1 \end{cases}$

4. $\begin{cases} x + y < 2 \\ 3x - 5y \geq 0 \end{cases}$

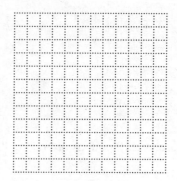

5. $\begin{cases} -y < \dfrac{2}{3}x + 1 \\ -3x + y \le 2 \end{cases}$

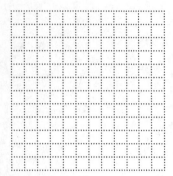

6. $\begin{cases} x - y \le 3 \\ 2x + 3y \le -9 \end{cases}$

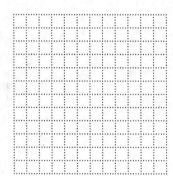

7. Party Food Steven and Christopher are planning a party. They plan to buy bratwurst for $4.00 per pound and hamburger patties that cost $3.00 per pound. They can spend at most $70 and think they should have no more than 20 pounds of bratwurst and hamburger patties. A system of inequalities that models the situation is given by

$$\begin{cases} 4b + 3h \le 70 \\ b + h \le 20 \\ b \ge 0 \\ h \ge 0 \end{cases}$$

where b represents the number of pounds of bratwurst and h represents the number of pounds of hamburger patties.

(a) Graph the system of linear inequalities.

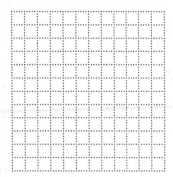

(b) Is it possible to purchase 10 pounds of bratwurst and 10 pounds of hamburger patties? 7b. _____

(c) Is it possible to purchase 15 pounds of bratwurst and 5 pounds of hamburger patties? 7c. _____

Sullivan/Struve/Mazzarella, *Elementary & Intermediate Algebra*, 2e

Five-Minute Warm-Up 5.1
Adding and Subtracting Polynomials

1. What is the coefficient of $-a^3$?

1. _____

2. Combine like terms: $-3x^2 + x - 5 + x^2 - x + 9$

2. _____

3. Simplify the expression: $5 - 2(x + 3y) - 4(2x - 1)$

3. _____

4. Use the Distributive Property to simplify: $\dfrac{5}{3}(-9x + 6)$

4. _____

5. Simplify: $x^2 y + 6xy^2 - \left(3xy^2 + 2x^2 y\right)$

5. _____

6. Evaluate $-\dfrac{3}{4}x^2 - 5x$ for $x = -2$.

6. _____

Guided Practice 5.1
Adding and Subtracting Polynomials

Objective 1: Define Monomial and Determine the Degree of a Monomial

1. For our study of polynomials, we begin with some definitions regarding monomials. *(See textbook Example 1)*

   (a) In your own words, what is a *monomial*? _____

   (b) What is the coefficient of a monomial? _____

   (c) How do you determine the degree of a monomial in one variable? _____

   (d) How do you determine the degree of a monomial in more than one variable? *(See textbook Example 3)*

   _____

Objective 2: Define Polynomial and Determine the Degree of a Polynomial

2. Next, we move on to some definitions used with polynomials. *(See textbook Example 4)*

   (a) In your own words, define *polynomial*. _____

   (b) When is a polynomial in *standard form*? _____

   (c) How do you determine the degree of a polynomial? _____

3. Some polynomials have special names. Always simplify the polynomial first, if possible, before determining if the polynomial has one of the following specific names:

   (a) a polynomial with exactly one term is a _____

   (b) a polynomial with two different monomials is a _____

   (c) a polynomial with exactly three different monomials is a _____

   (d) a polynomial with more than three terms is called a _____

Objective 3: Simplify Polynomials by Combining Like Terms

4. In your own words, define *like terms*. _____

5. To add two polynomials, we need to combine the like terms of the polynomials. Parentheses are included to indicate the first polynomial added to a second polynomial.

Find the sum using horizontal addition: $\left(6x^3 + 3x^2 - 5x + 2\right) + \left(x^3 - 4x^2 + 3\right)$ *(See textbook Example 6)*

5. _____

6. Find the sum using vertical addition: $\left(x^2 y - 5x^2 y^2 - 3xy^2\right) + \left(-2x^2 y - 9x^2 y^2 + 4xy^2\right)$ *(See textbook Example 7)*

6. _____

7. Find the difference: $\left(6z^3 + 2z^2 - 5\right) - \left(-3z^3 + 9z^2 - z + 1\right)$ *(See textbook Example 8)*

7. _____

8. Perform the indicated operations: $\left(6n^3 - 2n^2 + n - 1\right) - \left(4n^2 - 1\right) + \left(-6n^3 + 5n^2 + n\right)$ *(See textbook Example 10)*

8. _____

Objective 4: Evaluate Polynomials

9. Evaluate the polynomial $2x^3 - x^2 - 3x + 5$ for *(See textbook Example 11)*

   (a) $x = -1$ **(b)** $x = 3$

9a. _____

9b. _____

10. Evaluate the polynomial $-a^2 b^2 + 2ab - b^3$ for $a = 2$ and $b = -1$. *(See textbook Example 12)*

10. _____

Do the Math Exercises 5.1
Adding and Subtracting Polynomials

In Problems 1–2, determine whether the given expression is a monomial (Yes or No). For those that are monomials, state the coefficient and degree.

1. $-x^6 y$ **2.** y^{-1}

1. _____

2. _____

In Problems 3–4, determine whether the algebraic expression is a polynomial (Yes or No). If it is a polynomial, write the polynomial in standard form, determine its degree, and state if it is a monomial, binomial, or trinomial. If it is a polynomial with more than three terms, identify the expression as a polynomial.

3. $4y^{-2} + 6y - 1$ **4.** $p^5 - 3p^4 + 7p + 8$

3. _____

4. _____

In Problems 5–8, add the polynomials. Express your answer in standard form.

5. $(x^2 - 2) + (6x^2 - x - 1)$ **6.** $(3 - 12w^2) + (2w^2 - 5 + 6w)$

5. _____

6. _____

7. $\left(\dfrac{3}{8}b^2 - \dfrac{3}{5}b + 1\right) + \left(\dfrac{5}{6}b^2 + \dfrac{2}{15}b - 1\right)$ **8.** $(4a^2 + ab - 9b^2) + (-6a^2 - 4ab + b^2)$

7. _____

8. _____

In Problems 9–12, subtract the polynomials. Express your answer in standard form.

9. $(3x^2 + x - 3) - (x^2 - 2x + 4)$

10. $(m^4 - 3m^2 + 5) - (3m^4 - 5m^2 - 2)$

9. _____

10. _____

11. $\left(\dfrac{7}{4}x^2 - \dfrac{5}{8}x - 1\right) - \left(\dfrac{7}{6}x^2 + \dfrac{5}{12}x + 5\right)$

12. $(4m^2n - 2mn - 4) - (10m^2n - 6mn - 3)$

11. _____

12. _____

In Problems 13–16, evaluate the polynomials for each of the given value(s).

13. $-x^2 + 10$

   (a) $x = 0$
   (b) $x = -1$
   (c) $x = 1$

14. $2 + \dfrac{1}{2}n^2$

   (a) $n = 4$
   (b) $n = 0.5$
   (c) $n = -\dfrac{1}{4}$

13a. _____

13b. _____

13c. _____

14a. _____

14b. _____

14c. _____

15. $-2ab^2 - 2a^2b - b^3$
   for $a = 1$ and $b = -2$

16. $m^2n^2 - mn^2 + 3m^2 - 2$
   for $m = \dfrac{1}{2}$ and $n = -1$

15. _____

16. _____

Five-Minute Warm-Up 5.2
Multiplying Monomials: The Product and Power Rules

1. Write each expression in exponential form.

   (a) $\left(\dfrac{3}{4}\right) \bullet \left(\dfrac{3}{4}\right) \bullet \left(\dfrac{3}{4}\right)$ (b) $(-5)(-5)(-5)(-5)$

   1a. _____

   1b. _____

2. Evaluate each exponential expression.

   (a) -3^2 (b) $\left(\dfrac{3}{2}\right)^3$ (c) $(-4)^2$

   2a. _____

   2b. _____

   2c. _____

   (d) $\left(-\dfrac{4}{3}\right)^3$ (e) $(-2)^5$ (f) $-(-6)^2$

   2d. _____

   2e. _____

   2f. _____

3. Evaluate: $-\dfrac{5}{3} \bullet (-18) \bullet \left(-\dfrac{2}{5}\right)$

   3. _____

4. Use the Distributive Property to simplify: $5(4-2x)$

   4. _____

Guided Practice 5.2
Multiplying Monomials: The Product and Power Rules

Objective 1: Simplify Exponential Expressions Using the Product Rule

1. To multiply exponential expressions which have the same base, the product will have the
common base and an exponent which is the _____ of the exponents of the two factors.   1. _____

2. Simplify each expression. *(See textbook Examples 2 and 3)*

   (a) $r^3 \bullet r^5$ **(b)** $m^2 \bullet n \bullet n^4 \bullet m$ 2a. _____

                                                         2b. _____

Objective 2: Simplify Exponential Expressions Using the Power Rule

3. To raise exponential expressions containing a power to a power, keep the base and   3. _____
  _____ the powers.

4. Simplify each expression. Write the answer in exponential form. *(See textbook Examples 4 and 5)*

   (a) $\left(p^6\right)^3$ **(b)** $\left[(-x)^3\right]^4$ 4a. _____

                                                          4b. _____

5. Raising a negative number to an even exponent results in a _____ number.   5. _____

6. Raising a negative number to an odd exponent results in a _____ number.   6. _____

Objective 3: Simplify Exponential Expressions Containing Products

7. When we raise a product to a power, each factor is _____.

8. Simplify each expression. *(See textbook Example 6)*

   (a) $\left(5xy^2\right)^3$ **(b)** $\left(-m^2n^3\right)^4$ 8a. _____

                                                          8b. _____

Objective 4: Multiply a Monomial by a Monomial

9. Multiply and simplify each expression. *(See textbook Example 7)*

   (a) $\left(-x^4\right)\left(12x^7\right)$ **(b)** $\left(\dfrac{7}{4}q^2\right)\left(\dfrac{12}{21}q^5\right)$

9a. _____

9b. _____

10. Multiply and simplify each expression. *(See textbook Example 8)*

   (a) $\left(-5m^4n^4\right)\left(-2mn^3\right)$ **(b)** $\left(8pq^4\right)\left(-2p^2\right)\left(-3pq^6\right)$

10a. _____

10b. _____

Do the Math Exercises 5.2
Multiplying Monomials: The Product and Power Rules

In Problems 1–4, simplify each expression.

1. $3 \cdot 3^3$

2. $a^3 \cdot a^7$

1. _____

2. _____

3. $b^5 \cdot b \cdot b^7$

4. $(-z)(-z)^5$

3. _____

4. _____

In Problems 5–8, simplify each expression.

5. $(3^2)^2$

6. $[(-n)^7]^3$

5. _____

6. _____

7. $(k^8)^3$

8. $[(-a)^6]^3$

7. _____

8. _____

In Problems 9–12, simplify each expression.

9. $(4y^3)^2$

10. $\left(\dfrac{3}{4}n^2\right)^3$

9. _____

10. _____

11. $(-4ab^2)^3$

12. $(-3a^6bc^4)^4$

11. _____

12. _____

In Problems 13–16, multiply the monomials.

13. $(7b^5)(-2b^4)$

14. $\left(\dfrac{3}{8}y^5\right)\left(\dfrac{4}{9}y^6\right)$

13. _____

14. _____

15. $(6a^2b^3)(2a^5b)$

16. $\left(\dfrac{1}{2}b\right)(-20a^2b)\left(-\dfrac{2}{3}a\right)$

15. _____

16. _____

Five-Minute Warm-Up 5.3
Multiplying Polynomials

In Problems 1 – 6, simplify each expression.

1. $x^6 \cdot x$ **2.** $\left(5y^2\right)\left(4y^6\right)$ 1._____

2._____

3. $\left(2z\right)^6$ **4.** $\left(-3a^4\right)^2$ 3._____

4._____

5. $\left(\dfrac{5}{2}x\right)^2$ **6.** $\left(-4xy^2\right)^2\left(-x^3y^4\right)^3$ 5._____

6._____

7. Use the Distributive Property to simplify: $11(4a - 3b)$ 7._____

8. Simplify: $\dfrac{2}{3}\left(\dfrac{6x}{5} + \dfrac{9}{8}\right)$ 8._____

Guided Practice 5.3
Multiplying Polynomials

Objective 1: Multiply a Polynomial by a Monomial

1. To multiply a monomial and a polynomial we use _____.

2. Multiply and simplify. *(See textbook Examples 2 and 3)*

   (a) $-3ab^2\left(5a^2 - 2ab + 3b^2\right)$

   (b) $\left(\dfrac{7}{3}x^2 - \dfrac{1}{6}x - \dfrac{4}{9}\right)18x^5$

2a. _____

2b. _____

Objective 2: Multiply Two Binomials Using the Distributive Property

3. Find the product using the Distributive Property. *(See textbook Examples 4 and 5)*

   (a) $(x - 4)(x - 2)$

   (b) $(3x - 5)(2x + 1)$

3a. _____

3b. _____

Objective 3: Multiply Two Binomials Using the FOIL Method

4. (a) What process does FOIL tell how to do? _____

   (b) What does each of the letters stand for?

       F _____ O _____ I _____ L _____

   (c) Can the FOIL method be extended to multiply other types of polynomials? _____

5. Use the FOIL Method to find the product. *(See textbook Examples 6 – 9)*

   (a) $(u - 5)(u + 3)$

   (b) $(7x - 2y)(x - 3y)$

5a. _____

5b. _____

Objective 4: Multiply the Sum and Difference of Two Terms

6. Find the product: $(A - B)(A + B) =$

6. _____

7. Find each product. *(See textbook Example 11)*

 (a) $(x-9)(x+9)$

 (b) $(2a+5b)(2a-5b)$

7a. _____

7b. _____

Objective 5: Square a Binomial

8. Find the product:

 (a) $(A+B)^2 = $ _____

 (b) $(A-B)^2 = $ _____

9. Find the product: $(x-3)^2$ *(See textbook Example 12)*

Step 1: Use the $(A-B)^2$ pattern.

Write out the pattern for
$(A-B)^2$:

(a) _____

Identify the components. What is the expression for A?

(b) $A = $ _____

What is the expression for B?

(c) $B = $ _____

Step 2: Find each product.

Find each of the components in the pattern.

(d) $A^2 = $ _____

(e) $2AB = $ _____

(f) $B^2 = $ _____

Use the pattern to write the product: $(x-3)^2 = $

(g) _____

10. Find the product using the special products patterns. *(See textbook Examples 13 and 14)*

 (a) $(12-x)^2$

 (b) $(4x+5y)^2$

10a. _____

10b. _____

Objective 6: Multiply a Polynomial by a Polynomial

11. When we find the product of two polynomials, we make repeated use of the Extended Form of the Distributive Property. These multiplication problems can be formatted either horizontally, like textbook Example 15, or vertically, like textbook Example 16. Try each method and see which you prefer.

Find the product. *(See textbook Examples 15 and 16)*

 (a) $(3x-1)(x^2+2x-4)$

 (b) $(4x+3)(2x^2-5x-3)$

11a. _____

11b. _____

Do the Math Exercises 5.3
Multiplying Polynomials

In Problems 1–4, use the Distributive Property to find each product.

1. $3m(2m-7)$

2. $\dfrac{3}{5}b(15b-5)$

1. _____

2. _____

3. $4w(2w^2+3w-5)$

4. $(7r+3s)(2r^2s)$

3. _____

4. _____

In Problems 5–6, use the Distributive Property to find each product.

5. $(n-7)(n+4)$

6. $(5n-2y)(2n-3y)$

5. _____

6. _____

In Problems 7–10, find the product using the FOIL method.

7. $(x+3)(x+7)$

8. $(3z-2)(4z+1)$

7. _____

8. _____

9. $(x^2-5)(x^2-2)$

10. $(3r+5s)(6r+7s)$

9. _____

10. _____

In Problems 11–12, find the product of the sum and difference of two terms.

11. $(6r-1)(6r+1)$

12. $(8a-5b)(8a+5b)$

11. _____

12. _____

In Problems 13–16, find the product.

13. $(x+4)^2$

14. $(6b-5)^2$

13. _____

14. _____

15. $(3x+2y)^2$

16. $\left(y-\dfrac{1}{3}\right)^2$

15. _____

16. _____

In Problems 17–20, find the product.

17. $(3a-1)(2a^2-5a-3)$

18. $-\dfrac{4}{3}k(k+7)(3k-9)$

17. _____

18. _____

19. $(2m^2-m+4)(-m^3-2m-1)$

20. $(2a-1)(a+4)(a+1)$

19. _____

20. _____

Five-Minute Warm-Up 5.4
Dividing Monomials: The Quotient Rule and Integer Exponents

1. Find the product: $\left(7x^3 y\right)^2$ 1. _____

2. Evaluate: $\left(\dfrac{6}{5}\right)^2$ 2. _____

3. Find the reciprocal:

  (a) -3 **(b)** $\dfrac{7}{8}$ 3a. _____

                                                                    3b. _____

4. Simplify: $\dfrac{72}{40}$ 4. _____

5. Simplify: $\dfrac{3}{8} - \dfrac{5}{6}$ 5. _____

Guided Practice 5.4
Dividing Monomials: The Quotient Rule and Integer Exponents

Objective 1: Simplify Exponential Expressions Using the Quotient Rule

1. To divide exponential expressions which have the same base, the quotient will have the common base and to determine the exponent, _____ the exponent in the denominator from the exponent in the numerator.

1. _____

2. Simplify each expression. *(See textbook Examples 1 and 2)*

(a) $\dfrac{x^{11}}{x^4}$

(b) $\dfrac{-27a^5b^2}{12a^3b}$

2a. _____

2b. _____

Objective 2: Simplify Exponential Expressions Using the Quotient to a Power Rule

3. In your own words, describe the rule for raising a quotient to a power. State (a) if you should simplify the quotient first, if possible, and then raise this quotient to a power; (b) apply the power first, and then simplify, if possible; or (c) it does not matter which occurs first. Be sure to state any restrictions on your rule.

4. Simplify each expression. *(See textbook Examples 3 and 4)*

(a) $\left(-\dfrac{v}{2}\right)^3$

(b) $\left(\dfrac{28a^6}{16ab^4}\right)^2$

4a. _____

4b. _____

Objective 3: Simplify Exponential Expressions Using Zero as an Exponent

5. If a is a nonzero real number, $a^0 =$ _____.

5. _____

6. Simplify each expression. *(See textbook Example 5)*

(a) n^0

(b) $\left(9p^2\right)^0$

(c) $12x^0$

6a. _____

6b. _____

6c. _____

(d) -8^0

(e) $(-6x)^0$

(f) $-4x^0$ if $x = 2$

6d. _____

6e. _____

6f. _____

Objective 4: Simplify Exponential Expressions Involving Negative Exponents

7. If n is a positive integer and if a is a nonzero real number, then

(a) $a^{-n} =$ _____   (b) $\dfrac{1}{a^{-n}} =$ _____   (c) $\left(\dfrac{a}{b}\right)^{-n} =$ _____

7a. _____

7b. _____

7c. _____

From this point forward, assume all variables are nonzero. Always leave your final answer with only positive exponents.

8. Simplify each expression. *(See textbook Examples 6 – 8)*

(a) $(-2)^{-5}$ (b) $6^{-2} - 3^{-2}$ (c) $5a^{-2}$

8a. _____

8b. _____

8c. _____

Objective 5: Simplify Exponential Expressions Using the Laws of Exponents

9. Simplify: $\left(\dfrac{4}{3}x^{-2}y^4\right)\left(-18x^5y^{-7}\right)$ *(See textbook Example 13)*

Step 1: Rearrange factors.

Use the commutative and associative properties of multiplication to group together the coefficients, the variables with base x and the variables with base y:

$\left(\dfrac{4}{3}x^{-2}y^4\right)\left(-18x^5y^{-7}\right) =$

(a) _____

Step 2: Find each product.

Evaluate the product of the coefficients:

(b) _____

Use $a^n \bullet a^m = a^{n+m}$ for x:

(c) _____

Use $a^n \bullet a^m = a^{n+m}$ for y:

(d) _____

Step 3: Simplify. Write the product so that the exponents are positive.

Use $a^{-n} = \dfrac{1}{a^n}$ for y:

(e) _____

Do the Math Exercises 5.4
Dividing Monomials: The Quotient Rule and Integer Exponents

In Problems 1–4, use the Quotient Rule to simplify. All variables are nonzero.

1. $\dfrac{10^5}{10^2}$

2. $\dfrac{x^{20}}{x^{14}}$

1. _____

2. _____

3. $\dfrac{-36x^2y^5}{24xy^4}$

4. $\dfrac{-15r^9s^2}{-5r^8s}$

3. _____

4. _____

In Problems 5–8, use the Quotient to a Power Rule to simplify. All variables are nonzero.

5. $\left(\dfrac{4}{9}\right)^2$

6. $\left(\dfrac{7}{x^2}\right)^2$

5. _____

6. _____

7. $\left(-\dfrac{a^3}{b^{10}}\right)^5$

8. $\left(\dfrac{2mn^2}{q^3}\right)^4$

7. _____

8. _____

In Problems 9–12, use the Zero Exponent Rule to simplify. All variables are nonzero.

9. -100^0

10. $\left(\dfrac{2}{5}\right)^0$

9. _____

10. _____

11. $(-11xy)^0$ **12.** $-11xy^0$

11. _____

12. _____

In Problems 13–16, use the Negative Exponent Rules to simplify. Write answers with only positive exponents. All variables are nonzero.

13. $-7z^{-5}$ **14.** $\left(\dfrac{4}{p^2}\right)^{-2}$

13. _____

14. _____

15. $\dfrac{4}{b^{-3}}$ **16.** $\dfrac{9}{(4t)^{-1}}$

15. _____

16. _____

In Problems 17–20, use the Laws of Exponents to simplify. Write answers with positive exponents. All variables are nonzero.

17. $\left(\dfrac{3}{5}ab^{-3}\right)\left(\dfrac{5}{3}a^{-1}b^3\right)$ **18.** $\dfrac{30ab^{-4}}{15a^{-1}b^{-2}}$

17. _____

18. _____

19. $(5x^{-4}y^3)^{-2}$ **20.** $(5a^3b^{-4})\left(\dfrac{2ab^{-1}}{b^{-3}}\right)^2$

19. _____

20. _____

Five-Minute Warm-Up 5.5
Dividing Polynomials

1. Find the quotient: $\dfrac{-135x^5}{5x}$

1. _____

2. Find the quotient: $\dfrac{12n}{108n^4}$

2. _____

3. Find the product: $-9z\left(3z^2 + 2z - 1\right)$

3. _____

4. Given the polynomial $5x + x^4 - 3x^2 - 7x^3 - x^4 + 13$,

    (a) state the degree.

4a. _____

    (b) Write the polynomial in standard form.

4b. _____

5. Simplify: $\dfrac{3}{4} + \dfrac{2}{4} - \dfrac{9}{4} = \dfrac{3 + 2 - 9}{4} =$

5. _____

6. Subtract: $x^2 + 5x - 2 - \left(x^2 + 6x\right)$

6. _____

Guided Practice 5.5
Dividing Polynomials

Objective 1: Divide a Polynomial by a Monomial

To divide a polynomial by a monomial, divide each of the terms of the polynomial numerator (dividend) by the monomial denominator (divisor). We will be using the Quotient Rule for Exponents and the fact that $\frac{a+b}{c} = \frac{a}{c} + \frac{b}{c}$. **You should continue to reduce fractions to lowest terms, use only positive exponents, and assume all variables are nonzero.**

1. Divide and simplify each expression. *(See textbook Examples 1 – 3)*

(a) $\dfrac{8x^4 + 36x^3}{4x^2}$

(b) $\dfrac{5x^2y + 20xy^3 - 5xy}{5xy}$

1a. _____

1b. _____

Objective 2: Divide a Polynomial by a Binomial

2. How do you check that long division has been done correctly?

To divide the polynomials, we use a process called long division. This is exactly the same process that you use to divide integers. Due to the tremendous popularity of hand-held calculators, this particular skill has diminished over the years. It is important to practice this process so that the steps are easy to recall while performing long division on polynomials.

3. Divide 8047 by 71. *(See textbook Example 4)*

(a) Name the divisor.

3a. _____

(b) Name the dividend.

3b. _____

(c) Perform the division. What is the quotient?

3c. _____

(d) What is the remainder?

3d. _____

(e) Express the quotient as a mixed number.

3e. _____

4. Find the quotient and remainder when $\left(x^3 - 2x^2 + x + 6\right)$ is divided by $\left(x + 1\right)$. *(See textbook Example 5)*

Step 1: Divide the leading term of the dividend, x^3, by the leading term of the divisor, x. Enter the result over the term x^3.

(a) $\dfrac{x^3}{x} = $ _____

Step 2: Multiply ☐ by $x + 1$. Be sure to vertically align like terms.

(b) $x + 1 \overline{\smash{)}\, x^3 - 2x^2 + x + 6}$

_____

Step 3: Subtract your product from the dividend.

(c) $x + 1 \overline{\smash{)}\, x^3 - 2x^2 + x + 6}$ with x^2 above

_____

Subtract and continue with Steps 4 and 5:

Step 4: Repeat Steps 1 – 3 treating $-3x^2 + x + 6$ as the dividend and dividing x into $-3x^2$ to obtain the next term in the quotient.

Step 5: Repeat Steps 1 – 3 treating $4x + 6$ as the dividend and dividing x into $4x$ to obtain the next term in the quotient.

When the degree of the remainder is less than the degree of the divisor, you are finished dividing.

Express the answer as the

$\text{Quotient} + \dfrac{\text{Remainder}}{\text{Divisor}}$.

(d) _____

Step 6: Check Verify that (Quotient)(Divisor) + Remainder = Dividend.

We leave it to you to verify the solution.

5. Before beginning long division, be sure that both the divisor and dividend are written in _____ form.

5. _____

6. *True or False:* The following alternate approach correctly finds the quotient when a polynomial is divided by a binomial.

$\dfrac{2x^4 - 8x}{2x + 4} = \dfrac{\cancel{2}x^4 - \cancel{8}x}{\cancel{2}x + \cancel{4}} = x^3 - 2x$

6. _____

Sullivan/Struve/Mazzarella, *Elementary & Intermediate Algebra*, 2e

Do the Math Exercises 5.5
Dividing Polynomials

In Problems 1–8, divide and simplify.

1. $\dfrac{3x^3 - 6x^2}{3x^2}$

2. $\dfrac{16m^3 + 8m^2 - 4}{8m^2}$

1. _____

2. _____

3. $\dfrac{16a^5 - 12a^4 + 8a^3}{20a^4}$

4. $\dfrac{7p^4 + 21p^3 - 3p^2}{-6p^4}$

3. _____

4. _____

5. $\dfrac{-5y^2 + 15y^4 - 16y^5}{5y^2}$

6. $\dfrac{35x + 20y}{-5}$

5. _____

6. _____

7. $\dfrac{21y^2 + 35x^2}{-7x^2}$

8. $\dfrac{16m^2n^3 - 24m^4n^3}{-8m^3n^4}$

7. _____

8. _____

In Problems 9–14, find the quotient using long division.

9. $\dfrac{x^2 + 4x - 32}{x - 4}$

10. $\dfrac{x^3 - x^2 - 40x + 12}{x + 6}$

9. _____

10. _____

11. $\dfrac{x^4 - 2x^3 + x^2 + x - 1}{x - 1}$

12. $\dfrac{x^3 - 7x^2 + 15x - 11}{x - 3}$

11. _____

12. _____

13. $\dfrac{9x^2 - 14}{2 + 3x}$

14. $\dfrac{64x^6 - 27}{4x^2 - 3}$

13. _____

14. _____

Five-Minute Warm-Up 5.6
Applying the Exponent Rules: Scientific Notation

1. Find the product: $(2x^3)(9.5x^2)$

1. _____

2. Find the product: $(1.6n^{-2})(1.6n^{-4})$

2. _____

3. Find the quotient: $\dfrac{0.04p^{-3}}{0.2p^{-7}}$

3. _____

4. Multiply each of the following:

    (a) 4.2×1000 **(b)** 3.05×0.001 **(c)** $7 \times 3 \times 0.1$

4a. _____

4b. _____

4c. _____

5. Simplify each of the following:

    (a) $\dfrac{10^6}{10^{-2}}$ **(b)** $\dfrac{10^{-5}}{10^4}$ **(c)** $\dfrac{10^{-1}}{10^{-6}}$

5a. _____

5b. _____

5c. _____

    (d) $10^{-5} \times 10^{-3}$ **(e)** $10^{-4} \times 10^9$

5d. _____

5e. _____

Guided Practice 5.6
Applying the Exponent Rules: Scientific Notation

Objective 1: Convert Decimal Notation to Scientific Notation

1. A number is written in scientific notation when it is of the form $x \times 10^N$.

    (a) x must be _____   1a. _____

    (b) N is _____   1b. _____

    (c) When 3,700 is written in scientific notation, the power of 10 is _____ (positive or   1c. _____
    negative).

                                                                   1d. _____

    (d) When 0.002 is written in scientific notation, the power of 10 is _____ (positive or
    negative).

2. Write 45,000,000 in scientific notation. *(See textbook Example 1)*

Step 1: The "understood" decimal point in 45,000,000 follows the last 0.
Therefore, we will move the decimal point to the left until it is between
the 4 and the 5. Do you see why? This requires that we move the   **(a)** _____
decimal $N =$ _____ places.

Step 2: The original number is greater than 1, so the power of 10 is
_____ (positive or negative).   **(b)** _____

Now write 45,000,000 in scientific notation.   **(c)** _____

3. Write 0.00003 in scientific notation. *(See textbook Example 2)*

Step 1: Because 0.00003 is less than 1, we shall move the decimal
point until it is to the right of the 3. This requires that we move the
decimal $N =$ _____ places.   **(a)** _____

Step 2: The original number is between 0 and 1, so the power of 10 is
_____ (positive or negative).   **(b)** _____

Now write 0.00003 in scientific notation.   **(c)** _____

Objective 2: Convert Scientific Notation to Decimal Notation

4. To convert a number from scientific notation to decimal notation, determine the
exponent, N, on the number 10.

    (a) If the exponent is positive, move the decimal N decimal places to the _____.   4a. _____

    (b) If the exponent is negative, then move the decimal $|N|$ decimal places to the _____.   4b. _____

5. Write 6.02×10^4 in decimal notation. *(See textbook Example 3)*

Step 1: Determine the exponent on the number 10.   **(a)** _____

Step 2: Since the exponent is positive, we move the decimal point N places to the ____.   **(b)** _____

Now write 6.02×10^4 in decimal notation.   **(c)** _____

6. Write 9.1×10^{-3} in decimal notation. *(See textbook Example 4)*

Step 1: Determine the exponent on the number 10.   **(a)** _____

Step 2: Since the exponent is negative, we move the decimal point $|N|$ places to the ____.   **(b)** _____

Now write 9.1×10^{-3} in decimal notation.   **(c)** _____

Objective 3: Use Scientific Notation to Multiply and Divide

7. Perform the indicated operation. Express the answer in scientific notation. *(See textbook Examples 5 and 6)*

   (a) $\left(2 \times 10^5\right) \bullet \left(4 \times 10^8\right)$ **(b)** $\left(9 \times 10^{-15}\right) \bullet \left(6 \times 10^{10}\right)$ 7a. _____

    7b. _____

8. Perform the indicated operation. Express the answer in scientific notation. *(See textbook Example 7)*

   (a) $\dfrac{\left(8 \times 10^{12}\right)}{\left(2 \times 10^7\right)}$ **(b)** $\dfrac{\left(7.2 \times 10^{24}\right)}{\left(8 \times 10^{-13}\right)}$ 8a. _____

    8b. _____

Do the Math Exercises 5.6
Applying the Exponent Rules: Scientific Notation

In Problems 1–6, write each number in scientific notation.

1. 8,000,000,000

2. 0.0000001

1. _____

2. _____

3. 0.0000283

4. 401,000,000

3. _____

4. _____

5. 8

6. 120

5. _____

6. _____

In Problems 7–12, write each number in decimal notation.

7. 3.75×10^2

8. 6×10^6

7. _____

8. _____

9. 5×10^{-4}

10. 4.9×10^{-1}

9. _____

10. _____

11. 5.4×10^5

12. 5.123×10^{-3}

11. _____

12. _____

In Problems 13–18, perform the indicated operations. Express your answer in scientific notation.

13. $(3 \times 10^{-4})(8 \times 10^{-5})$

14. $(4 \times 10^7)(2.5 \times 10^{-4})$

13. _____

14. _____

15. $\dfrac{6 \times 10^3}{1.2 \times 10^5}$

16. $\dfrac{4.8 \times 10^7}{1.2 \times 10^2}$

15. _____

16. _____

17. $\dfrac{0.000275}{2500}$

18. $\dfrac{24,000,000,000}{0.00006 \times 2000}$

17. _____

18. _____

Five-Minute Warm-Up 6.1
Greatest Common Factor and Factoring by Grouping

1. Write as the product of prime numbers.
   (a) 36   (b) 225

   1a. _____

   1b. _____

2. Use the Distributive Property to simplify: $-3(4x - 9)$

   2. _____

3. Find the product: $(x + 4)(2x - 3)$

   3. _____

4. Find the product: $4x^2(x - 3)(x + 3)$

   4. _____

5. Given $\dfrac{1}{2} \bullet 10 = 5$,

   (a) list the factors.

   5a. _____

   (b) identify the product.

   5b. _____

6. Identify the missing factor: $10x^4 \bullet ? = 40x^6 y$

   6. _____

Guided Practice 6.1
Greatest Common Factor and Factoring by Grouping

Objective 1: Find the Greatest Common Factor of Two or More Expressions

1. The *greatest common factor (GCF)* of a list of polynomials is the largest expression that divides evenly into all of the polynomials.

Find the GCF of 27, 36 and 45. *(See textbook Examples 1 and 2)*

Step 1: Write each number as a product of prime factors.

(a) $27 =$ _____

(b) $36 =$ _____

(c) $45 =$ _____

Step 2: Determine the common prime factors.

(d) common factors are: _____

Step 3: Find the product of the common factors found in Step 2. This number is the GCF.

(e) GCF = _____

2. Find the greatest common factor (GCF) of each of the following. *(See textbook Examples 3 and 4)*

(a) $12x^2, 30x^6$

(b) $6a^2b^3, 15ab^4c, 27a^3bc^2$

2a. _____

2b. _____

Objective 2: Factor Out the Greatest Common Factor in Polynomials

3. Factor out the great common factor: $6m^4n^2 + 18m^3n^4 - 22m^2n^5$ *(See textbook Example 6)*

Step 1: Find the GCF.

(a) GCF = _____

Step 2: Rewrite each term as the product of the GCF and remaining factor.

(b) $6m^4n^2 + 18m^3n^4 - 22m^2n^5 =$ _____

Step 3: Factor out the GCF.

(c) $6m^4n^2 + 18m^3n^4 - 22m^2n^5 =$ _____

Step 4: Check   Distribute to verify that the factorization is correct.

4. Factor out the greatest common factor. *(See textbook Examples 9 and 10)*

(a) $-24x^5 - 9x^3$

(b) $4x(x + 3) + 7(x + 3)$

4a. _____

4b. _____

Objective 3: Factor Polynomials by Grouping

5. Factor by grouping is commonly used when a polynomial has _____ terms.

5. _____

6. *True or False:* You may need to rearrange the terms in order to be able to identity a common binomial factor.

6. _____

7. Factor by grouping: $2x^2 - 4x + 3xy - 6y$ *(See textbook Example 11)*

Step 1: Group terms with common factors. In this problem the first two terms have a common factor and the last two terms have a common factor.

(a) common factor of $2x^2 - 4x$: _____

(b) common factor of $3xy - 6y$: _____

Step 2: In each grouping, factor out the common factor.

(c) $2x^2 - 4x + 3xy - 6y =$ _____

Step 3: Factor out the common factor that remains.

(d) $2x^2 - 4x + 3xy - 6y =$ _____

Step 4: Check Multiply to verify that the factorization is correct.

8. Factor by grouping: $9x - 18y - 4ax + 8ay$ *(See textbook Example 12)*

8. _____

9. Factor by grouping: $4x^3 + 6x^2 - 12x - 18$ *(See textbook Example 13)*

9. _____

Do the Math Exercises 6.1
Greatest Common Factor and Factoring by Grouping

In Problems 1–5, find the greatest common factor, GCF, of each group of expressions.

1. 35, 42, 63

2. $26xy^2, 39x^2y$

1. _____

2. _____

3. $2x^2yz, xyz^2, 5x^3yz^2$

4. $8(x+y)$ and $9(x+y)$

3. _____

4. _____

5. $6(a-b)$ and $15(a-b)^3$

5. _____

In Problems 6–11, factor the GCF from the polynomial.

6. $-9b^2 - 6ab$

7. $8a^3b^2 + 12a^5b^2$

6. _____

7. _____

8. $5x^4 + 10x^3 - 25x^2$ **9.** $-2y^2 + 10y - 14$ 8. _____

9. _____

10. $-22n^4 + 18n^2 + 14n$ **11.** $a(a - 5) + 6(a - 5)$ 10. _____

11. _____

In Problems 12–15, factor by grouping.

12. $x^2 + ax + 2a + 2x$ **13.** $mn - 3n + 2m - 6$ 12. _____

13. _____

14. $z^3 + 4z^2 + 3z + 12$ **15.** $x^3 - x^2 - 5x + 5$ 14. _____

15. _____

Five-Minute Warm-Up 6.2
Factoring Trinomials of the Form $x^2 + bx + c$

1. List all possible combinations of factors for the given product.

    (a) -12 **(b)** 36 1a. _____

                                                                   1b. _____

*In Problems 2 and 3, find **(a)** the sum of the numbers and **(b)** the product of the numbers.*

  2. -3 and -12 **3.** 8 and -2 2a. _____

                                                                   2b. _____

                                                                     3a. _____

                                                                     3b. _____

4. Find two integers with the following properties.

    (a) sum of -5 and product of -36 4a. _____

    (b) sum of -5 and product of 6 4b. _____

    (c) sum of -4 and product of -5 4c. _____

    (d) sum of 9 and product of 18 4d. _____

5. Determine the coefficients of $-x^2 + 7x - 2$.   5. _____

6. Find the product: $(x - 6)(x - 4)$ 6 _____

Guided Practice 6.2
Factoring Trinomials of the Form $x^2 + bx + c$

Objective 1: Factor Trinomials of the Form $x^2 + bx + c$

Step 1: Find the pair of integers whose product is c and whose sum is b. That is, determine m and n such that $mn = c$ and $m + n = b$.

Step 2: Write $x^2 + bx + c = (x + m)(x + n)$.

Step 3: Check your work by multiplying out the factored form.

1. Factor: $y^2 + 11y + 18$ *(See textbook Example 1)*

Step 1: We are looking for factors of $c = 18$ whose sum is $b = 11$. We begin by listing all factors of 18 and computing the sum of these factors.

(a)

Factors whose product is 18	1, 18	2, 9	3, 6	–1, –18	–2, -9	–3, –6
Sum of factors						

Which two factors sum to 11 and multiply to 18?   **(b)** _____

Step 2: We write the trinomial in the form $(y + m)(y + n)$.

(c) $y^2 + 11y + 18 =$ _____

Step 3: Check We multiply to verify our solution.

We leave it to you to verify the factorization.

2. Factor: $z^2 - 15z + 36$ *(See textbook Example 2)*

(a) Make a list of factors.

Factors whose product is 36	1, 36	2, 18	3, 12	4, 9	–1,– 36	–2,–18	–3,–12	–4, – 9
Sum of factors								

(b) Use the two factors whose sum is -15 to write the factorization of $z^2 - 15z + 36$.

2b. _____

Guided Practice 6.2

3. Factor: $x^2 + x - 56$ *(See textbook Example 3)*

(a) Make a list of factors.

Factors whose product is −56							
Sum of factors							

(b) Use the two factors whose sum is 1 to write the factorization of $x^2 + x - 56$.

3b. _____

4. Factor: $n^2 - 2n - 24$ *(See textbook Example 4)*

(a) Make a list of factors.

Factors whose product is −24							
Sum of factors							

(b) Use the two factors whose sum is −2 to write the factorization of $n^2 - 2n - 24$.

4b. _____

5. Show that $x^2 + 3x - 6$ is prime. *(See textbook Example 5)*

Objective 2: Factor Out the GCF, Then Factor $x^2 + bx + c$

6. Factor: $3p^3 - 9p^2 - 54p$ *(See textbook Example 8)*

6. _____

Do the Math Exercises 6.2
Factoring Trinomials of the Form $x^2 + bx + c$

In Problems 1–5, factor each trinomial completely. If the trinomial cannot be factored, say it is prime.

1. $n^2 + 12n + 20$

2. $y^2 - 8y - 9$

1. _____

2. _____

3. $y^2 + 6y - 40$

4. $t^2 + 2t - 38$

3. _____

4. _____

5. $x^2 - 14xy + 24y^2$

5. _____

In Problems 6–9, factor each trinomial completely by factoring out the GCF first and then factoring the resulting trinomial.

6. $4p^4 - 4p^3 - 8p^2$

7. $30x - 2x^2 - 100$

6. _____

7. _____

8. $-3x^2 - 18x - 15$

9. $-75x + x^3 + 10x^2$

8. _____

9. _____

In Problems 10–15, factor each polynomial completely. If the polynomial cannot be factored, say that it is prime.

10. $-2z^3 - 2z^2 + 24z$

11. $-r^2 - 12r - 36$

10. _____

11. _____

12. $x^2 - x + 6$

13. $-16x + x^3 - 6x^2$

12. _____

13. _____

14. $x^2 + 7xy + 12y^2$

15. $25 + 10x + x^2$

14. _____

15. _____

Five-Minute Warm-Up 6.3
Factoring Trinomials of the Form $ax^2 + bx + c$, $a \neq 1$

1. Determine the coefficients of $4n^2 + n - 1$?

1. _____

2. Write as the product of prime numbers.
   (a) 18
   (b) 150

2a. _____

2b. _____

3. Find the product: $(2x + 1)(3x - 2)$

3. _____

4. Factor by grouping: $4x - 4y + ax - ay$

4. _____

5. Factor out the GCF: $12r^3s^2 + 3rs - 6rs^4$

5. _____

6. Factor out the greatest common binomial factor: $7z(2z + 1) - 4(2z + 1)$

6. _____

Guided Practice 6.3
Factoring Trinomials of the Form $ax^2 + bx + c$, $a \neq 1$

Objective 1: Factor $ax^2 + bx + c$, $a \neq 1$ ***Using Trial and Error***

1. Factor using trial and error: $3x^2 + 7x + 2$ *(See textbook Example 1)*

Step 1: List the possibilities for the first terms of each binomial whose product is ax^2.

(a) We list the possible ways of representing the first term, $3x^2$. Since 3 is a prime number, we have only one possiblity:

$$(\underline{\quad\quad} + \text{?})(\underline{\quad\quad} + \text{?})$$

Step 2: List the possibilities for the last terms of each binomial whose product is c.

(b) The last term, 2, is also prime. List the choices of pairs of factors that multiply to 2.

$$\underline{\quad\quad\quad\quad} \qquad \underline{\quad\quad\quad\quad}$$

(c) However, did you notice that the coefficient of x, 7, is positive? To produce a positive sum, $7x$, we must have two positive factors. What is the only option for factors of 2?

$$\underline{\quad\quad\quad\quad}$$

Step 3: Write out all the combinations of factors found in Steps 1 and 2. Multiply the binomials until a product is found that equals the trinomial.

(d) The order of the terms will change the product when the leading coefficient is not one. Once testing the possibilities produces the required product, write the factorization:

$$3x^2 + 7x + 2 = \underline{\quad\quad\quad\quad\quad\quad\quad}$$

You may continue to practice the trial and error method following textbook Examples 2–4. Do the Quick Check exercises after each textbook example and see if you can find the factorization easily. If it becomes too frustrating, move on to the second method for factoring trinomials whose leading coefficient is not one.

2. Factor using trial and error: $18a^2 - 35ab + 12b^2$ *(See textbook Example 5)*   2. _____

3. Factor: $-6x^2 + 17x + 14$ *(See textbook Example 6)*   3. _____

Objective 2: Factor $ax^2 + bx + c, a \neq 1$ Using Grouping

4. Factor by grouping: $3x^2 - 13x + 12$ *(See textbook Example 7)*

Step 1: Find the value of *ac.* **(a)** Identify the coefficients: $a =$ _____, $c =$ _____

(b) The value of $a \bullet c =$ _____

Step 2: Find the pair of integers, *m* and *n,* whose product is *ac* and whose sum is *b.*

(c)

Factors whose product is 36	−1, −36	−2, −18	−3, −12	−4, −9	−6, −6
Sum of factors					

(d) Which two factors multiply to 36 and sum to -13? _____

Step 3: Write
$$ax^2 + bx + c = ax^2 + mx + nx + c$$

(e) $3x^2 - 13x + 12 =$ _____

Step 4: Factor by expression in Step 3 by grouping.

(f) _____

Step 5: Check

Multiply to verify that the factorization is correct.

5. Factor by grouping: $13x^2 + 9x - 4$ *(See textbook Example 8)*

5. _____

Sullivan/Struve/Mazzarella, *Elementary & Intermediate Algebra,* 2e

Do the Math Exercises 6.3
Factoring Trinomials of the Form $ax^2 + bx + c$, $a \neq 1$

In Problems 1–6, factor each polynomial completely using the trial and error method. Hint: None of the polynomials is prime.

1. $3x^2 + 16x - 12$

2. $5x^2 + 16x + 3$

1. _____

2. _____

3. $11p^2 - 46p + 8$

4. $3x^2 + 7xy + 2y^2$

3. _____

4. _____

5. $6x^2 - 14xy - 12y^2$

6. $-6x^2 - 3x + 45$

5. _____

6. _____

In Problems 7–12, factor each polynomial completely using the grouping method. Hint: None of the polynomials is prime.

7. $7n^2 - 27n - 4$

8. $25t^2 + 5t - 2$

7. _____

8. _____

9. $20t^2 + 21t + 4$

10. $12p^2 - 23p + 5$

9. _____

10. _____

11. $18x^2 + 6xy - 4y^2$

12. $-10y^2 + 47y + 15$

11. _____

12. _____

In Problems 13–15, factor completely. If a polynomial cannot be factored, say it is prime.

13. $18x^2 + 88x - 10$

14. $9x^3y + 6x^2y + 3xy$

13. _____

14. _____

15. $8x^2 + 14x - 7$

15. _____

Five-Minute Warm-Up 6.4
Factoring Special Products

1. Evaluate: $(-10)^2$ 1. _____

2. Evaluate: $(-3)^3$ 2. _____

3. Find the product: $(4x^2)^3$ 3. _____

4. Find the product: $(2p + 5)^2$ 4. _____

5. Find the product: $(4a + 9b)(4a - 9b)$ 5. _____

6. List the perfect squares that are less than 100. That is, find $1^2, 2^2, 3^2$ etc.

_____

7. List the perfect cubes that are less than 100. That is, find $1^3, 2^3, 3^3$ etc.

_____

Guided Practice 6.4
Factoring Special Products

Objective 1: Factor Perfect Square Trinomials

1. Find the product:

(a) $(A + B)^2 =$ _____

(b) $(A - B)^2 =$ _____

2. Factor completely: $z^2 - 8z + 16$ *(See textbook Example 1)*

Step 1: Determine whether the first term and the third term are perfect squares.	**(a)** What is the first term? _____ To be a perfect square, the first term must be of the form $(A)^2$. In this case case, $A =$ _____.
	(b) What is the third term? _____ To be a perfect square, the third term must be of the form $(B)^2$. In this case case, $B =$ _____.
Step 2: Determine whether the middle term is 2 times or –2 times the product of the expression being squared in the first and last term.	**(c)** What is the middle term? _____ Is this equal to the product of 2 or – 2 times A times B? _____
Step 3: Use $A^2 - 2AB + B^2 = (A - B)^2$	**(d)** $z^2 - 8z + 16 =$ _____

3. Factor each perfect square trinomial. *(See textbook Examples 2 and 4)*

(a) $p^2 + 22p + 121$ **(b)** $12m^2n - 36mn^2 + 27n^3$ 3a. _____

3b. _____

Objective 2: Factor the Difference of Two Squares

4. Find the product: $(A - B)(A + B) =$ _____

5. Factor each difference of two squares completely. *(See textbook Examples 5 – 7)*

(a) $x^2 - 49$ **(b)** $25m^6 - 36n^4$ 5a. _____

5b. _____

(c) $a^8 - 256$ **(d)** $12x^2y - 75y^3$ 5c. _____

5d. _____

Objective 3: Factor the Sum or Difference of Two Cubes

6. Find the product:

(a) $(A + B)(A^2 - AB + B^2) = $ _____

(b) $(A - B)(A^2 + AB + B^2) = $ _____

(c) $(A + B)^3 = $ _____

7. Factor the sum or difference of two cubes. *(See textbook Examples 8 and 9)*

(a) $p^3 - 64$ **(b)** $8x^6 + 27y^3$ 7a. _____

                      7b. _____

8. Factor completely. *(See textbook Example 10)*

(a) $24x^4 + 375x$ **(b)** $250x^4y - 16xy^4$ 8a. _____

                       8b. _____

Do the Math Exercises 6.4
Factoring Special Products

In Problems 1–4, factor each perfect square trinomial completely.

1. $m^2 + 12m + 36$ **2.** $9a^2 - 12a + 4$

1. _____

2. _____

3. $16y^2 - 72y + 81$ **4.** $4a^2 + 20ab + 25b^2$

3. _____

4. _____

In Problems 5–6, factor each difference of two squares completely.

5. $36m^2 - 25n^2$ **6.** $a^4 - 16$

5. _____

6. _____

In Problems 7–10, factor each sum or difference of two cubes completely.

7. $64r^3 - 125s^3$ **8.** $m^9 - 27n^6$

7. _____

8. _____

9. $125y^3 + 27z^6$ **10.** $40x^3 + 135y^6$ 9. _____

10. _____

In Problems 11–15, factor completely. If the polynomial is prime, state so.

11. $12n^3 - 36n^2 + 27n$ **12.** $32a^3 + 4b^6$ 11. _____

12. _____

13. $x^4 - 225x^2$ **14.** $12m^2 - 14m + 21$ 13. _____

14. _____

15. $3x^2 + 18x + 27$ 15. _____

Five-Minute Warm-Up 6.5
Summary of Factoring Techniques

In Problems 1 – 2, find each product.

1. $(4x + 3y)(5x - 2y)$ 1. _____

2. $(a + 4b)^2$ 2. _____

In Problems 3 – 5, factor completely.

3. $-27a^3 + 9a^2 - 18a$ 3. _____

4. $6m(2n - 1) - 9(2n - 1)$ 4. _____

5. $4p^2 - 8pq + 3p - 6q$ 5. _____

Guided Practice 6.5
Summary of Factoring Techniques

Objective 1: Factor Polynomials Completely

1. Review the **Steps for Factoring** listed at the beginning of textbook Section 6.5. Step 1 should always be

_____, if possible.

2. Factor: $4x^2 + 16x - 84$ *(See textbook Example 1)*

Step 1: Factor out the greatest common factor (GCF), if any exists.	Determine the GCF:	**(a)** GCF = _____
	Factor out the GCF:	**(b)** $4x^2 + 16x - 84 =$
		_____
Step 2: Identify the number of terms in the polynomial in parentheses.	How many terms are in the polynomial in parentheses?	**(c)** _____
Step 3: We concentrate on the trinomial in parentheses. It is not a perfect square trinomial. The trinomial has a leading coefficient of 1 so we try $(x + m)(x + n)$, where $mn = c$ and $m + n = b$.	Factor the trinomial:	**(d)** _____
Step 4: Check		We leave it to you to multiply the binomials and then distribute to verify that the factorization is correct.

3. Factor: $64a^2 - 81b^2$ *(See textbook Example 2)*

Step 1: Factor out the greatest common factor (GCF), if any exists.	There is no GCF.	
Step 2: Identify the number of terms in the polynomial.	How many terms are in the polynomial?	**(a)** _____
Step 3: Because the first term $64a^2 = (8a)^2$, and the second term, $81b^2 = (9b)^2$, are both perfect squares, we have the difference of two squares.	Factor the binomial:	**(b)** _____
Step 4: Check		We leave it to you to verify that the factorization is correct.

4. Factor: $8a^2 + 24ab + 18b^2$ *(See textbook Example 3)*

Step 1: Factor out the greatest common factor (GCF), if any exists.	What is the GCF of 8, 24, and 18? **(a)** _____
	Factor out the GCF: **(b)** _____
Step 2: Identify the number of terms in the polynomial in parentheses.	How many terms are in the polynomial? **(c)** _____
Step 3: We concentrate on the polynomial in parentheses. Is it a perfect square trinomial?	**(d)** What is the first term? _____ To be a perfect square, the first term must be of the form $(A)^2$. In this case case, $A =$ _____.
	(e) What is the third term? _____ To be a perfect square, the thrid term must be of the form $(B)^2$. In this case case, $B =$ _____.
	(f) What is the middle term? _____ Is this equal to the product of 2 or -2 times A times B? _____
Use $A^2 - 2AB + B^2 = (A - B)^2$	Write the factorization: **(g)** _____
Step 4: Check	We leave it to you to verify that the factorization is correct.

5. Factor completely: $27p^6 + 1$ *(See textbook Example 4)*   5. _____

6. Factor completely: $2n^3 - 10n^2 - 6n + 30$ *(See textbook Example 6)*   6. _____

7. Factor completely: $-3xy^2 - 12xy - 9x$ *(See textbook Example 7)*   7. _____

Do the Math Exercises 6.5
Summary of Factoring Techniques

In Problems 1–15, factor completely. If a polynomial cannot be factored, say it is prime.

1. $x^2 - 256$ **2.** $1 - y^9$

1. _____

2. _____

3. $x^2 + 5x - 6$ **4.** $2x^3 - x^2 - 18x + 9$

3. _____

4. _____

5. $100x^2 - 25y^2$ **6.** $6s^2t^2 + st - 1$

5. _____

6. _____

7. $8x^6 + 125y^3$ **8.** $48m - 3m^9$

7. _____

8. _____

9. $4t^4 + 16t^2$

10. $8n^3 - 18n$

9. _____

10. _____

11. $n^2 + 2n + 8$

12. $24p^3q + 81q^4$

11. _____

12. _____

13. $x^2(x+y) - 16(x+y)$

14. $-9x - 3x^3 - 12x^2$

13. _____

14. _____

15. $6a^3 - 5a^2b + ab^2$

15. _____

Five-Minute Warm-Up 6.6
Solving Polynomial Equations by Factoring

1. Solve: $2x - 1 = 0$

1. _____

2. Solve: $-3(x - 2) + 15 = 0$

2. _____

3. Evaluate $3n^2 + 4n - 5$ for
    (a) $n = 2$ **(b)** $n = -3$

3a. _____

3b. _____

In Problems 4 – 7, factor completely.

4. $x^2 + 2x - 63$

4. _____

5. $4p^2 + 4p - 3$

5. _____

6. $x^2 - 81$

6. _____

7. $n^2 - 16n + 64$

7. _____

Guided Practice 6.6
Solving Polynomial Equations by Factoring

Objective 1: Solve Quadratic Equations Using the Zero-Product Property

1. State the **Zero-Product Property**. _____

_____

_____

2. Solve $(x+1)(2x-3) = 0$ *(See textbook Example 1)*   2. _____

3. A second-degree equation is also called a _____

4. What does it mean to write a quadratic equation in *standard form*? _____

_____

5. Solve: $x^2 + 5x - 24 = 0$ *(See textbook Example 2)*

Step 1: Is the quadratic equation in standard form? Yes, it is written in the form $ax^2 + bx + c = 0.$	$x^2 + 5x - 24 = 0$
Step 2: Factor the expression on the left side of the equation.	**(a)** _____
Step 3: Set each factor to 0. **(b)** _____	**(c)** _____
Step 4: Solve each first-degree equation. **(d)** _____	**(e)** _____
Step 5: Check Substitute your values into the original equation.	We leave it to you to verify the solutions.
Write the solution set:	**(f)** _____

6. Solve: $3t^2 + 11t = 4$ *(See textbook Example 3)*

(a) Write the quadratic equation in standard form: _____

(b) Factor the polynomial on the left side of the equation: _____

(c) Solve and state the solution set. _____

7. Solve: $(x-2)(x-3) = 56$ *(See textbook Example 5)*

   (a) To solve this equation, the first step is _____

   (b) Next, write the quadratic equation in _____

   (c) Factor the polynomial on the left side of the equation: _____

   (d) Solve and state the solution set. _____

8. Solve: $4x^2 + 36 = 24x$ *(See textbook Examples 6 and 7)*

   (a) Write the quadratic equation in standard form: _____

   (b) Factor the polynomial on the left side of the equation: _____

   (c) Solve and state the solution set. _____

Objective 2: Solve Polynomial Equations of Degree Three or Higher Using the Zero-Product Property

9. Solve: $p^3 + 2p^2 - 9p - 18 = 0$ *(See textbook Example 9)*

Step 1: Write the equation in standard form.	The polynomial is already in standard form.	$p^3 + 2p^2 - 9p - 18 = 0$
Step 2: Factor the expression on the left side of the equation. Begin with the GCF, if any.	Does the equation contain a GCF?	**(a)** _____
	How many terms are in the polynomial?	**(b)** _____
	What technique should you use?	**(c)** _____
	Factor the polynomial:	**(d)** _____
Step 3: Set each factor to 0.	**(e)** _____ **(f)** _____	**(g)** _____
Step 4: Solve each first-degree equation.	**(h)** _____ **(i)** _____	**(j)** _____
Step 5: Check Substitute your values into the original equation.		We leave it to you to verify the solutions.
	Write the solution set:	**(k)** _____

Sullivan/Struve/Mazzarella, *Elementary & Intermediate Algebra*, 2e

Do the Math Exercises 6.6
Solving Polynomial Equations by Factoring

In Problems 1–2, solve each equation using the Zero-Product Property.

1. $3x(x + 9) = 0$

2. $(4z - 3)(z + 4) = 0$

1. _____

2. _____

In Problems 3–4, identify each equation as a linear equation or a quadratic equation.

3. $2x + 1 - (x + 7) = 3x + 1$

4. $(x + 2)(x - 2) = 14$

3. _____

4. _____

In Problems 5–12, solve each quadratic equation by factoring.

5. $p^2 - 5p - 24 = 0$

6. $14x - 49x^2 = 0$

5. _____

6. _____

7. $3x^2 + x - 14 = 0$

8. $k^2 + 12k + 36 = 0$

7. _____

8. _____

9. $a^2 - 6a = 16$

10. $m^2 - 30 = 7m$

9. _____

10. _____

11. $4p - 3 = -4p^2$

12. $(x + 5)(x - 3) = 9$

11. _____

12. _____

In Problems 13–14, solve each polynomial equation by factoring.

13. $3x^3 + x^2 - 14x = 0$

14. $m^3 + 2m^2 - 9m - 18 = 0$

13. _____

14. _____

15. Tossing a Ball A ball is thrown vertically upward from the ground with an initial velocity of 64 feet per second. Solve the equation $-16t^2 + 64t = 48$ to find the time t (in seconds) at which the ball is 48 feet from the ground.

15. _____

Five-Minute Warm-Up 6.7
Modeling and Solving Problems with Quadratic Equations

1. Solve: $x(x+4) = 45$

1. _____

2. Solve: $p^2 + 12p + 36 = 0$

2. _____

3. Solve: $6x^2 + 17x + 5 = 0$

3. _____

4. The lengths of the two legs of a right triangle are 9 and 12 inches. Find the length of the hypotenuse.

4. _____

5. Find the product: $(x-5)^2$

5. _____

6. Factor out the GCF: $-18h^3 + 27h^2 - 9h$

6. _____

Guided Practice 6.7
Modeling and Solving Problems with Quadratic Equations

Objective 1: Model and Solve Problems Involving Quadratic Equations

1. A ball is thrown off a cliff from a height of 64 feet above sea level. The height h of the ball above the water (in feet) at any time t (in seconds) can be modeled by the equation

$$h = -16t^2 + 48t + 64$$

(See textbook Example 1)

(a) When will the height of the ball be 64 feet above sea level?   1a. _____

(b) When will the ball strike the water?   1b. _____

2. The length and width of two sides of a rectangle are consecutive odd integers. The area of the rectangle is 255 square centimeters. Find the dimensions of the rectangle. *(See textbook Example 2)*

Step 1: Identify This is a geometry problem involving the area of a rectangle. It also involves consecutive odd integers.

(a) If n represents one of the odd integers, express the next consecutive odd integer: 2a. _____

(b) In general, what formula do we use to calculate the area of a rectangle?   2b. _____

(c) **Step 2: Name** Use the variables from (a) to identify an expression that   2c.
represents the length and width of the rectangle.   width = _____

length = _____

(d) **Step 3: Translate** Write an equation that will model the area of this rectangle.   2d. _____

(e) **Step 4: Solve** the equation from step 3.   2e. _____

Step 5: Check Is your answer reasonable? Does it meet the necessary conditions?

(f) **Step 6: Answer** the question. _____

Objective 2: Model and Solve Problems Using the Pythagorean Theorem

3. In your own words, state the Pythagorean Theorem.

4. If x and y are the lengths of the legs and z is the length of the hypotenuse, write an equation which uses these variables to state the Pythagorean Theorem.

4. _____

5. Use the Pythagorean Theorem to find the missing length in the right triangle. *(See textbook Example 4)*

    (a) one leg = 18 cm; second leg = 24 cm, find the hypotenuse.   **(b)** one leg is 24 ft; hypotenuse is 25 ft, find the second leg.

5a. _____

5b. _____

6. In a right triangle, the hypotenuse measures $(2x - 3)$ meters. If one leg measures x meters and the other leg measures $(x + 3)$ meters,

    (a) solve for x.

6a. _____

    (b) What are the lengths of the sides of the right triangle?

6b. _____

Do the Math Exercises 6.7
Modeling and Solving Problems with Quadratic Equations

In Problems 1–2, use the given area to find the missing sides of the rectangle.

1.
$A = 250$
$3x - 5$
x

2.
$A = 364$
x
$x + 12$

1. _____

2. _____

In Problems 3–4, use the given area to find the height and base of the triangle.

3.
$A = 42$
$3x - 4$
x

4.
$A = 84$
$x + 4$
$2x - 8$

3. _____

4. _____

In Problems 5–6, use the given area to find the dimensions of the quadrilateral.

5.
$A = 77$
$2x + 1$
$3x + 2$

6.
$2x + 1$
x
$A = 70$
$3x + 2$

5. _____

6. _____

In Problems 7–8, use the Pythagorean Theorem to find the lengths of the sides of the triangle.

7.

8.

7. _____

8. _____

9. Projectile Motion If $h = -16t^2 + 96t$ represents the height of a rocket, in feet, t seconds after it was fired, when will the rocket be 144 feet high?

9. _____

10. Rectangular Room The width of a rectangular room is 4 feet less than the length. If the area of the room is 21 square feet, find the dimensions of the room.

10. _____

11. Triangle The base of a triangle is 2 meters more than the height. If the area of the triangle is 24 square meters, find the base and height of the triangle.

11. _____

12. Playing Field Dimensions The length of a rectangular playing field is 3 yards less than twice the width. If the area of the field is 104 square yards, what are its dimensions?

12. _____

13. Jasper's Big-Screen TV Jasper purchased a new big-screen TV. The TV screen is 10 inches taller than it is wide and is surrounded by a casing that is 2 inches wide.

(a) Jasper lost his tape measure but sees on the box that the TV measures 50 inches on the diagonal, including the casing. What are the dimensions of the TV screen?

13a. _____

(b) Jasper knows that the size of the opening where he wants the TV installed is 29 by 42 inches. Will this TV fit into his space?

13b. _____

Five-Minute Warm-Up 7.1
Simplifying Rational Expressions

1. Evaluate $\dfrac{-4a + 2b}{3}$ for $a = -2$ and $b = -7$.   1. _____

2. Factor: $4x^2 + x - 3$ 2. _____

3. Solve: $2x^2 - x - 15 = 0$ 3. _____

4. Write $\dfrac{30}{63}$ in lowest terms.   4. _____

5. Divide: $\dfrac{24x^2 y}{36xy^3}$ 5. _____

Guided Practice 7.1
Simplifying Rational Expressions

Objective 1: Evaluate a Rational Expression

1. Evaluate the following rational expressions. *(See textbook Example 1)*

  (a) $\dfrac{3}{2x+4}$ for $x = 3$ **(b)** $\dfrac{5x-3}{x+1}$ for $x = 7$ 1a. _____

                                                                                     1b. _____

2. Evaluate the following rational expressions. *(See textbook Examples 2 and 3)*

  (a) $\dfrac{x+9}{x^2+8x-12}$ for $x = -3$ **(b)** $\dfrac{-3a+2b}{-a-b}$ for $a = 6$ and $b = 2$ 2a. _____

                                                                                               2b. _____

Objective 2: Determine Values for which a Rational Expression is Undefined

3. To determine the undefined values of a rational expression, find the values where _____.

4. Find the value(s) of x for which the expression is undefined. *(See textbook Examples 4 and 5)*

  (a) $\dfrac{x-3}{x+8}$ **(b)** $\dfrac{x^2-2x-3}{x^2-9x+18}$ 4a. _____

                                                                                          4b. _____

Objective 3: Simplify Rational Expressions

5. To simplify a rational expression always use the following steps:

  (a) Completely _____ the numerator and denominator of the rational expression.

  (b) _____ _____ the common factors.

6. Simplify: $\dfrac{6x - 18}{x^2 - 5x + 6}$, $x \neq 2$, $x \neq 3$ *(See textbook Example 6)*

Step 1: Completely factor the numerator and the denominator.	This problem has included the restrictions on the variable. These excluded values cause the denominator to equal zero and will not affect our work.	
	Factor each expression:	**(a)** $\dfrac{6x - 18}{x^2 - 5x + 6} = $ _____
Step 2: Divide out common factors. The rational expression is completely simplified if the numerator and the denominator share no common factor other than 1.	Divide out common factors:	**(b)** _____
	Write the simplified expression:	**(c)** _____

7. Simplify: $\dfrac{2x^2 + 12x + 10}{4x^2 + 28x + 40}$ *(See textbook Example 8)*   7. _____

8. Simplify: $\dfrac{50 - 2x^2}{4x^2 + 28x + 40}$ *(See textbook Example 9)*   8. _____

Do the Math Exercises 7.1
Simplifying Rational Expressions

In Problems 1–4, evaluate each expression for the given values.

1. $\dfrac{x}{x+4}$

    (a) $x = 8$

    (b) $x = -4$

    (c) $x = 0$

2. $\dfrac{2m-1}{m}$

    (a) $m = 4$

    (b) $m = 1$

    (c) $m = -1$

1a. _____

1b. _____

1c. _____

2a. _____

2b. _____

2c. _____

3. $\dfrac{a^2 - 2a}{a - 4}$

    (a) $a = 5$

    (b) $a = -1$

    (c) $a = -4$

4. $\dfrac{b^2 - a^2}{(a - b)^2}$

    (a) $a = 3$, $b = 2$

    (b) $a = 5$, $b = 4$

    (c) $a = -2$, $b = 2$

3a. _____

3b. _____

3c. _____

4a. _____

4b. _____

4c. _____

In Problems 5–8, find the value(s) of the variable for which the rational expression is undefined.

5. $\dfrac{5m^3}{m+8}$

6. $\dfrac{12}{4a-3}$

5. _____

6. _____

7. $\dfrac{2x^2}{x^2 + x - 2}$

8. $\dfrac{3h+2}{h^3 + 5h^2 + 4h}$

7. _____

8. _____

In Problems 9–16, simplify each rational expression. Assume that no variable has a value which results in a denominator with a value of zero.

9. $\dfrac{6p^2 + 3p}{3p}$

10. $\dfrac{4 - z}{z - 4}$

9. _____

10. _____

11. $\dfrac{x^2 - 9}{x^2 + 5x + 6}$

12. $\dfrac{x^3 + 3x^2 + 2x}{x^3 - 2x^2 - 3x}$

11. _____

12. _____

13. $\dfrac{a - b}{b^2 - a^2}$

14. $\dfrac{z^3 + 3z^2 + 2z + 6}{z^2 + 5z + 6}$

13. _____

14. _____

15. $\dfrac{2x^2 + 5x - 3}{4x^2 - 8x + 3}$

16. $\dfrac{5 + 4x - x^2}{x^2 - 25}$

15. _____

16. _____

Five-Minute Warm-Up 7.2
Multiplying and Dividing Rational Expressions

1. Find the product: $\dfrac{21}{4} \cdot \dfrac{18}{49}$

1. _____

2. Find the reciprocal of $-\dfrac{5}{2}$.

2. _____

3. Find the quotient: $\dfrac{15}{36} \div \dfrac{70}{24}$

3. _____

4. Factor: $-5x^2 + 25x$

4. _____

5. Simplify the rational expression: $\dfrac{x^2 - 9}{x^2 - 3x - 18}$

5. _____

Guided Practice 7.2
Multiplying and Dividing Rational Expressions

Objective 1: Multiply Rational Expressions

1. Multiply $\dfrac{x+3}{8} \cdot \dfrac{4x-12}{x^2-9}$. Simplify the result, if possible. *(See textbook Example 1)*

Step 1: Completely factor the polynomials in each numerator and denominator.

$$\dfrac{x+3}{8} \cdot \dfrac{4x-12}{x^2-9} =$$

Factor the numerator and denominator: **(a)** _____

Step 2: Multiply using
$$\dfrac{a}{b} \cdot \dfrac{c}{d} = \dfrac{ac}{bd}$$

Write the product: **(b)** _____

Step 3: Divide out common factors in the numerator and denominator.

Divide out common factors and express the answer as a simplified rational expression in factored form. **(c)** _____

Write the simplified result: **(d)** _____

2. Multiply $\dfrac{x^2-4x}{x^2-4} \cdot \dfrac{x^2-x-6}{x-4}$. Simplify the result, is possible. *(See textbook Example 2)*

(a) Completely factor the polynomials in each numerator and denominator.

(a) _____

(b) Multiply.

(b) _____

(c) Divide out common factors in the numerator and denominator.

(c) _____

(d) Express the answer as a simplified rational expression in factored form.

(d) _____

3. Find the product and simplify: $\dfrac{x^2-y^2}{13x^2-13xy} \cdot \dfrac{26y-26x}{x^2+2xy+y^2}$ *(See textbook Example 4)* 3. _____

Objective 2: Divide Rational Expressions

4. Divide $\dfrac{3x+15}{36} \div \dfrac{5x+25}{24}$. Simplify the result, is possible. *(See textbook Example 5)*

Step 1: Multiply the dividend by the reciprocal of the divisor.

$$\dfrac{3x+15}{36} \div \dfrac{5x+25}{24} =$$

Rewrite the quotient as a product: **(a)** _____

Step 2: Completely factor the polynomials in each numerator and denominator.

Factor each expression: **(b)** _____

Step 3: Multiply.

Write the product: **(c)** _____

Step 4: Divide out common factors in the numerator and denominator.

Divide out the common factors: **(d)** _____

Express the answer as a simplified rational expression in factored form: **(e)** _____

5. Find the quotient and simplify: $\dfrac{x^2-4x+3}{2x^2-5x+3} \div (x-3)$ *(See textbook Example 7)*

5. _____

6. Find the quotient and simplify: $\dfrac{\dfrac{3y^2-3x^2}{x^2+2xy+y^2}}{\dfrac{6x^2-6xy}{3y+3x}}$ *(See textbook Example 8)*

6. _____

Do the Math Exercises 7.2
Multiplying and Dividing Rational Expressions

In Problems 1–4, multiply.

1. $\dfrac{x-4}{4} \cdot \dfrac{12x}{x^2-16}$

2. $\dfrac{8n-8}{n^2-3n+2} \cdot \dfrac{n+2}{12}$

1. _____

2. _____

3. $\dfrac{z^2-4}{3z-2} \cdot \dfrac{3z^2+7z-6}{z^2+z-6}$

4. $(x-3) \cdot \dfrac{x+2}{x^2-5x+6}$

3. _____

4. _____

In Problems 5–8, divide.

5. $\dfrac{p+7}{3p+21} \div \dfrac{p}{6}$

6. $\dfrac{z^2-25}{10z} \div \dfrac{z^2-10z+25}{5z}$

5. _____

6. _____

7. $\dfrac{3y^2+6y}{8} \div \dfrac{y+2}{12y-12}$

8. $\dfrac{4z^2+12z+9}{8z+16} \div \dfrac{(2z+3)^2}{12z+24}$

7. _____

8. _____

Do the Math Exercises 7.2

In Problems 9–16, perform the indicated operation.

9. $\dfrac{x-4}{12x-18} \cdot \dfrac{6}{x^2-16}$

10. $\dfrac{x+5}{3} \div \dfrac{30x}{4x+20}$

9. _____

10. _____

11. $\dfrac{2r^2+rs-3s^2}{r^2-s^2} \cdot \dfrac{r^2-2rs-3s^2}{2r+3s}$

12. $\dfrac{2x^2-5x+3}{x^2-1} \cdot \dfrac{x^2+1}{2x^2-x-3}$

11. _____

12. _____

13. $\dfrac{(x-3)^2}{8xy^2} \div \dfrac{x^2-9}{(4x^2y)^2}$

14. $\dfrac{p^2-49}{p^2-5p-14} \cdot \dfrac{p-7}{14-5p-p^2}$

13. _____

14. _____

15. $\dfrac{1}{b^2+b-12} \div \dfrac{1}{b^2-5b-36}$

16. $\dfrac{\dfrac{t^2}{t^2-16}}{\dfrac{t^2-3t}{t^2-t-12}}$

15. _____

16. _____

Five-Minute Warm-Up 7.3
Adding and Subtracting Rational Expressions with a Common Denominator

1. Write $\dfrac{27}{45}$ in lowest terms.

1. _____

2. Find each sum and simplify:

   (a) $\dfrac{8}{3} + \dfrac{5}{3}$

   (b) $\dfrac{11}{8} + \dfrac{9}{8}$

   2a. _____

   2b. _____

3. Find each difference and simplify:

   (a) $\dfrac{9}{2} - \dfrac{7}{2}$

   (b) $\dfrac{13}{24} - \left(-\dfrac{2}{24}\right)$

   3a. _____

   3b. _____

4. Determine the additive inverse of $\dfrac{1}{2}$.

4. _____

5. Simplify: $-(2x - 3)$

5. _____

Guided Practice 7.3
Adding and Subtracting Rational Expressions with a Common Denominator

Objective 1: Add Rational Expressions with a Common Denominator

1. Find the sum and simplify, if possible: $\dfrac{2x}{x^2 - 3x} + \dfrac{5x}{x^2 - 3x}$ *(See textbook Example 1)*

Step 1: Add the numerators and write the result over the common denominator.	Use $\dfrac{a}{c} + \dfrac{b}{c} = \dfrac{a+b}{c}$:	**(a)** _____
Step 2: Simplify the rational expression.	Factor the numerator and denominator:	**(b)** _____
	Divide out the common factors:	**(c)** _____
	Express the answer in simplified form:	**(d)** _____

2. Find the sum and simplify, if possible: $\dfrac{3x - 10}{x^2 - 25} + \dfrac{2x - 15}{x^2 - 25}$ *(See textbook Example 3)*   2. _____

Objective 2: Subtract Rational Expressions with a Common Denominator

3. Find the difference and simplify, if possible: $\dfrac{x^2}{x^2 - 5x - 6} - \dfrac{1}{x^2 - 5x - 6}$ *(See textbook Example 4)*

Step 1: Subtract the numerators and write the result over the common denominator.	Use $\dfrac{a}{c} - \dfrac{b}{c} = \dfrac{a-b}{c}$:	**(a)** _____
Step 2: Simplify the rational expression.	Factor the numerator and denominator:	**(b)** _____
	Divide out the common factors:	**(c)** _____
	Express the answer in simplified form:	**(d)** _____

4. Find the difference and simplify if possible: $\dfrac{2x^2 + 3x}{x - 2} - \dfrac{x^2 + 3x + 4}{x - 2}$ *(See textbook*

4. _____

Example 5)

Objective 3: Add or Subtract Rational Expressions with Opposite Denominators

5. Find the sum and simplify, if possible: $\dfrac{6n - 5}{n - 5} + \dfrac{2n - n^2}{5 - n}$ *(See textbook Example 6)*

5. _____

6. Find the difference and simplify, if possible: $\dfrac{x^2 + 1}{x^2 - 9} - \dfrac{4x + 2}{9 - x^2}$ *(See textbook*

6. _____

Example 7)

Do the Math Exercises 7.3
Adding and Subtracting Rational Expressions with a Common Denominator

In Problems 1–4, add the rational expressions.

1. $\dfrac{4n+1}{8}+\dfrac{12n-1}{8}$

2. $\dfrac{4p-1}{p-1}+\dfrac{p+1}{p-1}$

1. _____

2. _____

3. $\dfrac{3x^2+4}{3x-6}+\dfrac{3x^2-28}{3x-6}$

4. $\dfrac{2x}{2x^2-x-15}+\dfrac{5}{2x^2-x-15}$

3. _____

4. _____

In Problems 5–8, subtract the rational expressions.

5. $\dfrac{4a^2}{3a-1}-\dfrac{a^2+a}{3a-1}$

6. $\dfrac{7x+13}{3x}-\dfrac{x+1}{3x}$

5. _____

6. _____

7. $\dfrac{2z^2+7z}{z^2-1}-\dfrac{z^2-6}{z^2-1}$

8. $\dfrac{2n^2+n}{n^2-n-2}-\dfrac{n^2+6}{n^2-n-2}$

7. _____

8. _____

In Problems 9–12, add or subtract the rational expressions.

9. $\dfrac{4}{x-1} + \dfrac{8x}{1-x}$

10. $\dfrac{x^2+3}{x-1} - \dfrac{x+3}{1-x}$

9. _____

10. _____

11. $\dfrac{x^2+6x}{x^2-1} + \dfrac{4x+3}{1-x^2}$

12. $\dfrac{m^2+2mn}{n^2-m^2} - \dfrac{n^2}{m^2-n^2}$

11. _____

12. _____

In Problems 13–16, perform the indicated operation.

13. $\dfrac{3n^2}{2n-1} - \dfrac{6n}{2n-1}$

14. $\dfrac{x^2}{x^2-9} + \dfrac{6x+9}{x^2-9}$

13. _____

14. _____

15. $\dfrac{2s-3t}{s-t} + \dfrac{6s-4t}{t-s}$

16. $\dfrac{n+3}{2n^2-n-3} - \dfrac{-n^2-3n}{2n^2-n-3}$

15. _____

16. _____

Sullivan/Struve/Mazzarella, *Elementary & Intermediate Algebra*, 2e

Five-Minute Warm-Up 7.4
Finding the Least Common Denominator and Forming Equivalent Rational Expressions

1. Write $\dfrac{7}{15}$ as a fraction with 45 as its denominator.

1. _____

2. Find the least common denominator (LCD) of $\dfrac{9}{20}$ and $\dfrac{2}{45}$.

2. _____

3. Write each of the rational expressions in Problem 2 as equivalent expressions using the LCD.

3. _____

4. Identify the missing factor: $12x^2 y \cdot ? = 36x^2 y^3$

4. _____

5. Factor: $x^2 - 4x + 4$

5. _____

6. Factor: $-3x^2 - 9x$

6. _____

Guided Practice 7.4
Finding the Least Common Denominator and Forming Equivalent Rational Expressions

Objective 1: Find the Least Common Denominator of Two or More Rational Expressions

1. Find the least common denominator (LCD) of $\dfrac{7}{24}$ and $\dfrac{3}{20}$. *(See textbook Example 1)*

Step 1: Write each denominator as the product of prime factors.	Write 24 as the product of prime factors: **(a)** _____
	(b) _____
	Write 20 as the product of prime factors:
Step 2: Write down the factor(s) that the denominators share, if any. Then write down the remaining factors the greatest number of times that the factor occurs in a denominator.	List the shared factors: **(c)** _____
	List the remaining factors the greatest number of times that the factors occurs in a factorization: **(d)** _____
Step 3: Multiply the factors listed in Step 2. The product is the least common denominator (LCD).	Multiply the factors in (c) and (d): **(e)** LCD = _____

2. Find the least common denominator (LCD) of the rational expressions $\dfrac{7}{6x^2}$ and $\dfrac{5}{9x}$. *(See textbook Example 2)*

Step 1: Express each denominator as the product of factors. Write the factored form using exponents, if possible.	Write $6x^2$ as the product of prime factors: **(a)** _____
	Write $9x$ as the product of prime factors: **(b)** _____
Step 2: List the common factors raised to the highest power. Then list the factors that are not common.	List the shared factors, using the highest power: **(c)** _____
	List the remaining factors: **(d)** _____
Step 3: Multiply the factors listed in Step 2. The product is the least common denominator (LCD).	Multiply the factors in (c) and (d): **(e)** LCD = _____

3. Find the LCD of the rational expressions: $\dfrac{7c}{8a^3b}$ and $\dfrac{11d}{10a^2b^2}$ *(See textbook Example 3)*   3. _____

4. Find the LCD of the rational expressions: $\dfrac{8}{7a^2 - 14a}$ and $\dfrac{5}{2a^2}$ *(See textbook Example 4)* 4. _____

5. Find the LCD of the rational expressions: $\dfrac{4x}{x^2 - 9}$ and $\dfrac{x^2}{x^2 - 6x + 9}$ *(See textbook Example 5)* 5. _____

Example 5)

Objective 2: Write a Rational Expression That Is Equivalent to a Given Rational Expression

6. Write the rational expression $\dfrac{x - 2}{3x^2 - x}$ as an equivalent rational expression with denominator $9x^3 - 3x^2$.
(See textbook Example 8)

Step 1: Write each denominator in factored form.	Write $3x^2 - x$ as the product of prime factors:	**(a)** _____
	Write $9x^3 - 3x^2$ as the product of prime factors:	**(b)** _____
Step 2: Determine the "missing factor(s)".	Compare (a) and (b). What is (are) the missing factor(s)?	**(c)** _____
Step 3: Multiply the original rational expression by 1.	Write 1 as $\dfrac{\text{missing factor}}{\text{missing factor}}$.	**(d)** _____
Step 4: Find the product. Leave the denominator in factored form.	Multiply the expression in (d) and the original rational expression. This product is the equivalent rational expression.	**(e)** _____

Objective 3: Use the LCD to Write Equivalent Rational Expressions

7. Find the LCD of the rational expressions $\dfrac{4}{9xy^2}$ and $\dfrac{5}{12x^2}$. Then rewrite each rational   7. _____

expression with the LCD. *(See textbook Example 9)*

_____

_____

Do the Math Exercises 7.4
Finding the Least Common Denominator and Forming Equivalent Rational Expressions

In Problems 1–6, find the LCD of the given rational expressions.

1. $\dfrac{3}{7y^2};\dfrac{4}{49y}$

2. $\dfrac{2}{6x-18};\dfrac{3}{8x-24}$

1. _____

2. _____

3. $\dfrac{5}{2x^2-12x+18};\dfrac{4}{4x^2-36}$

4. $\dfrac{8}{x^2-1};\dfrac{3}{x^2-2x+1}$

3. _____

4. _____

5. $\dfrac{-1}{c^2-49};\dfrac{5}{21-3c}$

6. $\dfrac{3z}{(z+5)(z-4)};\dfrac{-z}{(4-z)(5+z)}$

5. _____

6. _____

In Problems 7–10, write an equivalent rational expression with the given denominator.

7. $\dfrac{7a+1}{abc}$ with denominator a^2b^2c

7. _____

8. $\dfrac{3}{x+2}$ with denominator x^2+5x+6

8. _____

9. $\dfrac{7a}{3a^2+9a+6}$ with denominator $6a^2+18a+12$

9. _____

10. 7 with denominator t^2+1

10. _____

In Problems 11–18, find the LCD of the rational expressions. Then rewrite each as an equivalent rational expression with the LCD.

11. $\dfrac{4}{5n^2}; \dfrac{3}{7n}$

12. $\dfrac{2p^2-1}{6p}; \dfrac{3p^3+2}{8p^2}$

11. _____

12. _____

13. $\dfrac{x+2}{x}; \dfrac{x}{x+2}$

14. $\dfrac{3b}{7a}; \dfrac{2a}{7a+14b}$

13. _____

14. _____

15. $\dfrac{5}{m-6}; \dfrac{2m}{6-m}$

16. $\dfrac{4a}{a^2-1}; \dfrac{7}{a+1}$

15. _____

16. _____

17. $\dfrac{4n}{n^2-n-6}; \dfrac{2}{n^2+4n+4}$

18. $\dfrac{3}{2n^2-7n+3}; \dfrac{2n}{n-3}$

17. _____

18. _____

Five-Minute Warm-Up 7.5
Adding and Subtracting Rational Expressions with Unlike Denominators

1. Determine the least common denominator (LCD) and then write the rational expressions
as equivalent expressions using the LCD.

    (a) $\dfrac{3}{2}$ and $\dfrac{5}{3}$ **(b)** $\dfrac{7}{12}$ and $\dfrac{5}{28}$ 1a. _____

                                                                                      1b. _____

2. Factor: $6z^2 - 7z + 2$ 2. _____

3. Simplify: $\dfrac{8x^2 - 4x}{4x}$ 3. _____

4. Simplify: $\dfrac{16 - x^2}{2x^2 - 8x}$ 4. _____

5. Find the sum: $\dfrac{3}{8x} + \dfrac{1}{8x}$ 5. _____

Guided Practice 7.5
Adding and Subtracting Rational Expressions with Unlike Denominators

Objective 1: Add and Subtract Rational Expressions with Unlike Denominators

1. Find the sum and simplify, if possible: $\dfrac{7}{15} + \dfrac{10}{25}$ *(See textbook Example 1)*

Step 1: Find the least common denominator of 15 and 25.

Write 15 as the product of prime factors: **(a)** _____

Write 25 as the product of prime factors: **(b)** _____

Determine the LCD: **(c)** _____

Step 2: Write each fraction as an equivalent fraction using the LCD.

Find the equivalent fraction: **(d)** $\dfrac{7}{15} \bullet \dfrac{\rule{1cm}{0.4pt}}{\rule{1cm}{0.4pt}} = \dfrac{\rule{1cm}{0.4pt}}{\rule{1cm}{0.4pt}}$

Find the equivalent fraction: **(e)** $\dfrac{10}{25} \bullet \dfrac{\rule{1cm}{0.4pt}}{\rule{1cm}{0.4pt}} = \dfrac{\rule{1cm}{0.4pt}}{\rule{1cm}{0.4pt}}$

Step 3: Find the sum of the numerators, written over the common denominator.

Use $\dfrac{a}{c} + \dfrac{b}{c} = \dfrac{a+b}{c}$:

(f) _____

Step 4: Simplify, if possible.

What is the sum, reduced to lowest terms? **(g)** _____

2. Find the sum and simplify, if possible: $\dfrac{5}{12x} + \dfrac{7x}{18x^2}$ *(See textbook Example 2)*

Step 1: Find the least common denominator.

Write $12x$ as the product of prime factors: **(a)** _____

Write $18x^2$ as the product of prime factors: **(b)** _____

Determine the LCD: **(c)** _____

Step 2: Write each rational expression as an equivalent expression using the LCD.

Find the equivalent expression: **(d)** $\dfrac{5}{12x} \bullet \dfrac{\rule{1cm}{0.4pt}}{\rule{1cm}{0.4pt}} = \dfrac{\rule{1cm}{0.4pt}}{\rule{1cm}{0.4pt}}$

Find the equivalent expression: **(e)** $\dfrac{7x}{18x^2} \bullet \dfrac{\rule{1cm}{0.4pt}}{\rule{1cm}{0.4pt}} = \dfrac{\rule{1cm}{0.4pt}}{\rule{1cm}{0.4pt}}$

Step 3: Add the rational expressions found in Step 2.

Use $\dfrac{a}{c} + \dfrac{b}{c} = \dfrac{a+b}{c}$:

(f) _____

Step 4: Simplify, if possible.

What is the sum, simplified to lowest terms? **(g)** _____

3. Find the sum and simplify, if possible: $\dfrac{4}{x+2} + \dfrac{2}{x+1}$ *(See textbook Example 3)*

3. _____

4. Find the difference and simplify, if possible: $\dfrac{2}{x} - \dfrac{4}{x-2}$ *(See textbook Example 5)*

Step 1: Find the least common denominator.	Determine the LCD:	**(a)** _____
Step 2: Write each rational expression as an equivalent expression using the LCD.	Find the equivalent expression:	**(b)** $\dfrac{2}{x} \cdot \dfrac{\quad}{\quad} = \dfrac{\quad}{\quad}$
	Find the equivalent expression:	**(c)** $\dfrac{4}{x-2} \cdot \dfrac{\quad}{\quad} = \dfrac{\quad}{\quad}$
Step 3: Subtract the rational expressions found in Step 2.	Use $\dfrac{a}{c} - \dfrac{b}{c} = \dfrac{a-b}{c}$:	**(d)** _____
Step 4: Simplify, if possible.	What is the difference, simplified to lowest terms?	**(e)** _____

5. Find the sum and simplify, if possible: $\dfrac{2y^2 + 4y - 5}{y^2 - 9} + \dfrac{y^2 + 4y + 4}{9 - y^2}$ *(See textbook Example 8)*

5. _____

6. Find the difference and simplify, if possible: $3 - \dfrac{x-2}{x-4}$ *(See textbook Example 9)*

6. _____

Sullivan/Struve/Mazzarella, *Elementary & Intermediate Algebra*, 2e

Do the Math Exercises 7.5
Adding and Subtracting Rational Expressions with Unlike Denominators

In Problems 1–6, find each sum and simplify.

1. $\dfrac{7}{12}+\dfrac{3}{4}$

2. $\dfrac{5}{2x}+\dfrac{6}{5}$

1. _____

2. _____

3. $\dfrac{2}{x-1}+\dfrac{x-1}{x+1}$

4. $\dfrac{7}{n-4}+\dfrac{8}{4-n}$

3. _____

4. _____

5. $\dfrac{2x-6}{x^2-x-6}+\dfrac{x+4}{x+2}$

6. $\dfrac{3}{x-4}+\dfrac{x+4}{x^2-16}$

5. _____

6. _____

In Problems 7–10, find each difference and simplify, if necessary.

7. $\dfrac{8}{21}-\dfrac{6}{35}$

8. $\dfrac{x-2}{x+2}-\dfrac{x+2}{x-2}$

7. _____

8. _____

9. $\dfrac{x}{x+4} - \dfrac{-4}{x^2 + 8x + 16}$

10. $\dfrac{p+1}{p^2 - 2p} - \dfrac{2p+3}{2-p}$

9. _____

10. _____

In Problems 11–16, find the LCD of the rational expressions. Then rewrite each as an equivalent rational expression with the LCD.

11. $\dfrac{5}{4n} - \dfrac{3}{n^2}$

12. $\dfrac{x-2}{x+3} + 2$

11. _____

12. _____

13. $\dfrac{-1}{3n - n^2} + \dfrac{1}{3n^2 - 9n}$

14. $\dfrac{a-5}{2a^2 - 6a} - \dfrac{6}{12a^2 - 4a^3}$

13. _____

14. _____

15. $\dfrac{x+1}{x-3} + \dfrac{x+2}{x-2} - \dfrac{x^2+3}{x^2 - 5x + 6}$

16. $\dfrac{7}{w-3} - \dfrac{5}{w} - \dfrac{2w+6}{w^2 - 9}$

15. _____

16. _____

Five-Minute Warm-Up 7.6
Complex Rational Expressions

1. Factor: $2x^2 - 5x - 12$

1. _____

2. Factor: $3x^2 - 75$

2. _____

3. Find the quotient: $\dfrac{x-2}{6} \div \dfrac{x^2-4}{8}$

3. _____

4. Find the product: $\dfrac{x-1}{x-2} \bullet \left(x^2 - 3x + 2\right)$

4. _____

5. Find the product: $\left(\dfrac{3}{x} + \dfrac{2}{x^2}\right) \bullet x^3$

5. _____

Guided Practice 7.6
Complex Rational Expressions

Objective 1: Simplify a Complex Rational Expression by Simplifying the Numerator and Denominator Separately (Method I)

1. In your own words, define a *complex rational expression*.

2. Simplify $\dfrac{\dfrac{5}{x} - \dfrac{x}{5}}{\dfrac{1}{5} - \dfrac{5}{x^2}}$ using Method I. *(See textbook Examples 2 and 3)*

Step 1: Write the numerator of the complex fraction as a single rational expression.	Determine the LCD of x and 5:	**(a)** _____
	Write the equivalent rational expressions on the LCD and then use $\dfrac{a}{c} - \dfrac{b}{c} = \dfrac{a-b}{c}$:	**(b)** _____
Step 2: Write the denominator of the complex fraction as a single rational expression.	Determine the LCD of x^2 and 5:	**(c)** _____
	Write the equivalent rational expressions on the LCD and then add use $\dfrac{a}{c} - \dfrac{b}{c} = \dfrac{a-b}{c}$:	**(d)** _____
Step 3: Rewrite the complex rational expression using the rational expressions determined in Steps 1 and 2.		**(e)** _____
Step 4: Simplify the rational expression using the techniques for dividing rational expressions from textbook Section 7.2.	Rewrite the division problem as a multiplication problem:	**(f)** _____
	Divide out common factors and express the answer as a simplified rational expression in factored form.	**(g)** _____

Objective 2: *Simplify a Complex Rational Expression Using the Least Common Denominator (Method II)*

3. Method II uses the LCD to simplify complex rational expressions. We use several of the properties of real numbers to simplify the complex rational expression; that is, to find an equivalent rational expression which has a single fraction bar. State the property of real numbers that is illustrated below.

(a) $\dfrac{x-9}{x-9} = 1$

3a. _____

(b) $\dfrac{2}{x} \cdot \dfrac{x-9}{x-9} = \dfrac{2}{x}$

3b. _____

(c) $\dfrac{2}{x} \cdot \dfrac{x-9}{x-9} = \dfrac{2x-18}{x^2-9x}$

3c. _____

4. Simplify $\dfrac{1 + \dfrac{1}{x}}{1 - \dfrac{1}{x^2}}$ using Method II. *(See textbook Examples 5 and 6)*

Step 1: Find the least common denominator among all the denominators in the complex rational expression.	Determine the LCD of x and x^2:	**(a)** _____
Step 2: Multiply both the numerator and denominator of the complex rational expression by the LCD found in Step 1.		**(b)** _____
	Distribute the LCD to each term:	**(c)** _____
Step 3: Simplify the rational expression.	Divide out the common factors:	**(d)** _____
	Simplify the expression:	**(e)** _____

Do the Math Exercises 7.6
Complex Rational Expressions

In Problems 1–4, simplify the complex rational expression using Method I.

1. $\dfrac{\dfrac{4}{t^2}-1}{\dfrac{t+2}{t^3}}$

2. $\dfrac{\dfrac{2}{x}+\dfrac{3}{x^2}}{\dfrac{2x+3}{x}}$

1. _____

2. _____

3. $\dfrac{\dfrac{5}{n-1}+3}{n-\dfrac{2}{n-1}}$

4. $\dfrac{\dfrac{2}{a+b}}{\dfrac{1}{a}+\dfrac{1}{b}}$

3. _____

4. _____

In Problems 5–8, simplify the complex rational expression using Method II.

5. $\dfrac{\dfrac{3c}{4}+\dfrac{3d}{10}}{\dfrac{3c}{2}-\dfrac{6d}{5}}$

6. $\dfrac{\dfrac{a}{2}+4}{2-\dfrac{a}{2}}$

5. _____

6. _____

7. $\dfrac{\dfrac{x}{x+1}}{1+\dfrac{1}{x-1}}$

8. $\dfrac{6x+\dfrac{3}{y}}{\dfrac{9x+3}{y}}$

7. _____

8. _____

In Problems 9–14, simplify the complex rational expression using either Method I or Method II.

9. $\dfrac{1-\dfrac{4}{x^2}}{1-\dfrac{1}{x}-\dfrac{6}{x^2}}$

10. $\dfrac{\dfrac{-6}{y^2+5y+6}}{\dfrac{2}{y+3}-\dfrac{3}{y+2}}$

9. _____

10. _____

11. $\dfrac{2-\dfrac{3}{x}-\dfrac{2}{x^2}}{1-\dfrac{5}{x}+\dfrac{6}{x^2}}$

12. $\dfrac{1-\dfrac{n^2}{25m^2}}{1-\dfrac{n}{5m}}$

11. _____

12. _____

13. $\dfrac{\dfrac{x}{x+y}-1}{\dfrac{y}{x+y}-1}$

14. $\dfrac{\dfrac{5}{2b+3}+\dfrac{1}{2b-3}}{\dfrac{6b}{8b^2-18}}$

13. _____

14. _____

15. **Finding the Mean** The arithmetic mean of a set of numbers is found by adding the numbers and then dividing by the number of entries on the list. Write a complex rational expression to find the arithmetic mean of the expressions $\dfrac{n}{6}, \dfrac{n+3}{2}$, and $\dfrac{2n-1}{8}$ and then simplify the complex rational expression.

15. _____

Five-Minute Warm-Up 7.7
Rational Equations

1. Solve: $-8 + 4(x + 6) = 10x$

1. _____

2. Factor: $x^2 - 3x - 28$

2. _____

3. Solve: $4p^2 - 1 = 0$

3. _____

4. Find the values for which the expression $\dfrac{x - 2}{x^2 + 6x - 16}$ is undefined.

4. _____

5. Solve for P: $A = P + Prt$

5. _____

Guided Practice 7.7
Rational Equations

Objective 1: Solve Equations Containing Rational Expressions

1. When solving rational equations it is important to identify the restrictions on the variable. We exclude all

values of the variable that result in _____ .

2. Solve: $\dfrac{x+5}{x-7} = \dfrac{x-3}{x+7}$ *(See textbook Example 2)*

Step 1: Determine the value(s) of the variable that result in an undefined rational expression.	For what values of x will the denominator be equal to zero? **(a)** _____
Step 2: Determine the least common denominator (LCD) of all the denominators.	LCD: **(b)** _____
Step 3: Multiply both sides of the equation by the LCD and simplify the expression on each side of the equation.	Multiply both sides by the LCD: **(c)** _____
	Divide out common factors: **(d)** _____
	Multiply: **(e)** _____
Step 4: Solve the resulting equation.	
	Solve for x: **(f)** _____
Step 5: Check Verify your solution using the original equation.	Write the solution set: **(g)** _____

3. Solve: $\dfrac{9}{x} + \dfrac{4}{5x} = \dfrac{7}{10}$ *(See textbook Example 3)*

   (a) Determine the excluded values of the variable.   3a. _____

   (b) Determine the LCD of all of the denominators.   3b. _____

   (c) Multiply both sides of the equation by the LCD. What is the resulting equation?   3c. _____

   (d) Solve the resulting equation.   3d. _____

4. Solve: $\dfrac{6}{x^2-1}=\dfrac{5}{x-1}-\dfrac{3}{x+1}$ *(See textbook Example 6)*

    (a) Determine the excluded values of the variable.   4a. _____

    (b) Determine the LCD of all of the denominators.   4b. _____

    (c) Multiply both sides of the equation by the LCD and solve the resulting equation.   4c. _____
    What is the solution to this equation?

    (d) What is the solution set?   4d. _____

Objective 2: Solve for a Variable in a Rational Equation

5. Solve: $\dfrac{6}{z}=\dfrac{2}{x}+\dfrac{1}{y}$ for y *(See textbook Examples 8 and 9)*

Step 1: Determine the value(s) of the variable(s) that result in an undefined rational expression.	For what values of the variables will the denominator **(a)** _____ be equal to zero?
Step 2: Determine the least common denominator (LCD) of all the denominators.	LCD: **(b)** _____
Step 3: Multiply both sides of the equation by the LCD and simplify the expression on each side of the equation.	Multiply both sides by the LCD: **(c)** _____
	Divide out common factors: **(d)** _____
Step 4: Solve the resulting equation for *y*.	Subtract $2yz$ from both sides: **(e)** _____
	Factor out *y*: **(f)** _____
	Divide by the coefficient of *y:* **(g)** _____
	Simplify, if possible. Write the solution: **(h)** _____

     Sullivan/Struve/Mazzarella, *Elementary & Intermediate Algebra*, 2e

Do the Math Exercises 7.7
Rational Equations

In Problems 1–10, solve each equation and state the solution set. Remember to identify the values of the variable for which the expressions in each rational equation are undefined.

1. $\dfrac{4}{p} - \dfrac{5}{4} = \dfrac{5}{2p} + \dfrac{3}{8}$

2. $\dfrac{4}{x-4} = \dfrac{5}{x+4}$

1. _____

2. _____

3. $\dfrac{x-2}{4x} - \dfrac{x+2}{3x} = \dfrac{1}{6x} + \dfrac{2}{3}$

4. $\dfrac{6}{t} - \dfrac{2}{t-1} = \dfrac{2-4t}{t^2-t}$

3. _____

4. _____

5. $\dfrac{4}{x-3} - \dfrac{3}{x-2} = \dfrac{4x+9}{x^2-5x+6}$

6. $\dfrac{2x+3}{x-1} - 2 = \dfrac{3x-1}{4x-4}$

5. _____

6. _____

7. $x = \dfrac{6-5x}{6x}$

8. $\dfrac{2x}{x+4} = \dfrac{x+1}{x+2} - \dfrac{7x+12}{x^2+6x+8}$

7. _____

8. _____

9. $\dfrac{2}{b+2} - \dfrac{5b+6}{b^2 - b - 6} = \dfrac{-b}{b-3}$

10. $\dfrac{5}{x-2} - \dfrac{2}{2-x} = \dfrac{4}{x+1}$

9. _____

10. _____

In Problems 10–14, solve the equation for the indicated variable.

11. $\dfrac{a}{b+2} = c$ for b

12. $\dfrac{3}{i} - \dfrac{4}{j} = \dfrac{8}{k}$ for j

11. _____

12. _____

13. $B = \dfrac{k}{x} - \dfrac{m}{cx}$ for x

14. $X = \dfrac{ab}{a-b}$ for a

13. _____

14. _____

15. Drug Concentration The concentration C of a drug in a patient's bloodstream in milligrams per liter t hours after ingestion is modeled by $C = \dfrac{40t}{t^2 + 3}$. When will the concentration of the drug be 10 milligrams per liter?

15. _____

16. Average Cost Suppose that the average daily cost $\overline{C}$ in dollars of manufacturing x bicycles is given by the equation $\overline{C} = \dfrac{x^2 + 75x + 5000}{x}$. Determine the level of production for which the average daily cost will be $240.

16. _____

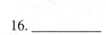

Five-Minute Warm-Up 7.8
Models Involving Rational Equations

1. Solve: $\dfrac{20}{r} = \dfrac{15}{r-3}$

1. _____

2. Solve: $\dfrac{1}{x} + \dfrac{1}{x-2} = \dfrac{3}{4}$

2. _____

3. Solve: $\dfrac{2}{r} + \dfrac{8}{r+3} = 2$

3. _____

Guided Practice 7.8
Models Involving Rational Equations

Objective 1: Model and Solve Ratio and Proportion Problems

1. Write an example of a ratio.

1. _____

2. Write an example of a proportion.

2. _____

3. Solve: $\dfrac{5}{k+4} = \dfrac{2}{k-1}$ *(See textbook Example 1)*

3. _____

4. Flight Accidents According to the Statistical Abstract of the United States, in 2001, there were 1.22 fatal airplane accidents per 100,000 flight hours. Also, in 2001, there were a total of 321 fatal accidents. How many flight hours were flown in 2001? *(See textbook Example 2)*

4. _____

Objective 2: Model and Solve Problems with Similar Figures

5. In your own words, what does it mean if two geometric figures are *similar*?

6. Suppose that a 6-foot-tall man casts a shadow of 3.2 feet. At the same time of day, a tree casts a shadow of 8 feet. How tall is the tree? *(See textbook Example 5)*

   (a) Write a proportion that can be used to solve this problem.

6a. _____

   (b) Solve the proportion. How tall is the tree?

6b. _____

Objective 3: Model and Solve Work Problems

7. Problems of this type involve completing a job or a task when working at a constant rate. We convert the time t that it takes to complete the job into a unit rate. That is, if it takes t hours to complete a job, then $\dfrac{1}{t}$ of the job is completed per hour.

   (a) If it takes 15 minutes to complete a job, what part of the job is completed per minute? 7a. _____

   (b) If it takes t hours to complete a job, what part of the job is completed per hour?   7b. _____

   (c) If it takes $t + 3$ hours to complete a job, what part of the job is competed per hour?   7c. _____

8. Josh can clean the math building on his campus in 3 hours. Ken takes 5 hours to clean the same building. If they work together, how long will it take for Josh and Ken to clean the math building? *(See textbook Example 6)*

    Step 1: Identify We want to know how long it will take Josh and Ken working together to clean the building.

    Step 2: Name We let t represent the time (in hours) that it takes to clean the building when working together.

    Step 3: Translate What fraction of the job is completed in one hour when working individually and when working together? Write the following ratios:

    (a) Part of the job completed by Josh in one hour: 8a. _____

    (b) Part of the job completed by Ken in one hour: 8b. _____

    (c) Part of the job completed when working together in one hour: 8c. _____

    (d) Write the model for this problem:

                                                  8d. _____

    Step 4: Solve the equation from Step 3.

    Step 5: Check Is your answer reasonable?

    (e) Step 6: Answer the question.   8e. _____

Objective 4: Model and Solve Uniform Motion Problems

9. A small plane can travel 1000 miles with the wind in the same time it can go 600 miles against the wind. If the speed of the plane in still air is 180 mph, what is the speed of the wind? *(See textbook Example 8)*

    (a) If w is the speed of the wind, what is the rate (in mph) when travelling with the wind: 9a. _____

    (b) If w is the speed of the wind, what is the rate when travelling against the wind: 9b. _____

    (c) Use $t = \dfrac{d}{r}$ to write a rational expression for the time travelled with the wind:

                                                  9c. _____

    (d) Use $t = \dfrac{d}{r}$ to write a rational expression for the time travelled against the wind:

                                                  9d. _____

    (e) Write an equation that can be used to solve this problem: 9e. _____

    (f) Solve your equation and answer the question.   9f. _____

Do the Math Exercises 7.8
Models Involving Rational Equations

In Problems 1–6, solve the proportion.

1. $\dfrac{6}{5} = \dfrac{8}{3x}$

2. $\dfrac{k}{k+3} = \dfrac{6}{15}$

1. _____

2. _____

3. $\dfrac{n+6}{3} = \dfrac{n+4}{5}$

4. $\dfrac{n-2}{4n+7} = \dfrac{-2}{n+1}$

3. _____

4. _____

5. $\dfrac{4}{x^2} = \dfrac{1}{x+3}$

6. $\dfrac{1}{2z-1} = \dfrac{z+4}{z^2+10z+14}$

5. _____

6. _____

In Problems 7 and 8, write an algebraic expression that represents each phrase.

7. If Brian worked for n days and Kellen worked for half as many days, write an algebraic expression that represents the number of days Kellen worked.

7. _____

8. If the rate of the current in a stream is 3 mph and Betsy can paddle her canoe at a rate of r mph in still water, write an algebraic expression that represents Betsy's rate when she paddles downstream.

8. _____

In Problems 9–14, write an equation that could be used to model each of the following.
SOLVE THE EQUATION.

9. Buying Candy If it costs $3.50 for 2 lb of candy, how much candy can be purchased   9. _____
for $8.75?

_____

10. Comparing Pesos and Pounds If 50 Mexican pesos are worth approximately 2.5   10. _____
British pounds and if Sean takes 80 pounds as spending money in Mexico City, how
many pesos will he have?

_____

11. Telephone Pole Shadow A bush that is 4 m tall casts a shadow that is 1.75 m long.   11. _____
How tall is a telephone pole if its shadow is 8.75 m?

_____

12. Pruning Trees Martin can prune his fruit trees in 4 hours. His neighbor can prune the   12. _____
same trees for him in 7 hours. If they work together on this job, to the nearest tenth of
an hour, how long will it take to prune the trees?

_____

13. Travel by Plane A small plane can travel 1000 miles with the wind in the same time it   13. _____
can go 600 miles against the wind. If the speed of the plane in still air is 180 mph, what
is the speed of the wind?

_____

14. A Bike Trip A bicyclist rides his bicycle 12 miles up a hill and then 16 miles on level   14. _____
terrain. His speed on level ground is 3 miles per hour faster than his speed going uphill.
The cyclist rides for the same amount of time going uphill and on level ground. Find
his speed going uphill.

_____

Five-Minute Warm-Up 8.1
Graphs of Equations

1. Plot the following points on the real number line: $\dfrac{3}{2}, -2, 0, 3$.

2. Determine which of the following are solutions to the equation $4x - 5(x+1) = 6$.

    (a) $x = -1$ **(b)** $x = -11$ **(c)** $x = 1$ **(d)** $x = 11$

2. _____

3. Evaluate the expression $-x^2 - 3x + 4$ for the given values of the variable.

3a. _____

    (a) $x = 3$ **(b)** $x = -2$ **(c)** $x = 0$

3b. _____

3c. _____

4. Solve the equation $4x - 3y = -12$ for y.

4. _____

5. Evaluate each of the following absolute values.

5a. _____

    (a) $|-12|$ **(b)** $|0|$ **(c)** $|125|$

5b. _____

5c. _____

Guided Practice 8.1
Graphs of Equations

Objective 1: Plot Points in the Rectangular Coordinate System

1. Label each quadrant and axis in the rectangular or Cartesian coordinate system.

2. What name do we give the ordered pair $(0, 0)$? _____

In Problems 3 and 4, circle one answer for each underlined choice.

3. To plot the ordered pair $(-3, 2)$, you would move 3 units <u>up, down, left or right</u> from the origin.

4. To plot the ordered pair $(-6, -2)$, you would move <u>6 or 2</u> units down from the origin.

Objective 3: Graph an Equation Using the Point-Plotting Method *(See textbook Example 3)*

5. Graph the equation $y = 3x - 1$ by plotting points.

Step 1: We want to find all the points (x, y) that satisfy the equation. To determine these points we choose values of x and use the equation to determine the corresponding values of y.

	x	$y = 3x - 1$	(x, y)
(a)	-2	$3(\underline{}) - 1 = \underline{}$	$(-2, \underline{})$
(b)	-1	$3(\underline{}) - 1 = \underline{}$	$(-1, \underline{})$
(c)	0	$3(\underline{}) - 1 = \underline{}$	$(0, \underline{})$
(d)	1	$3(\underline{}) - 1 = \underline{}$	$(1, \underline{})$
(e)	2	$3(\underline{}) - 1 = \underline{}$	$(2, \underline{})$

Step 2: Draw the axes in the Cartesian plane and plot the points listed in the third column. Now connect the points to obtain the graph of the equation (a line).

Objective 4: Identify the Intercepts from the Graph of an Equation *(See textbook Example 6)*

6. The point(s), if any, where a graph crosses or touches the x-axis is called the x-intercept. 6._____
Suppose a graph crosses the x-axis at a point a and touches the y-axis at a point b. Write
these points as ordered pairs.   _____

7. The point(s), if any, where a graph crosses or touches the y-axis is called the y-intercept. 7. _____
Suppose a graph crosses the y-axis at a point c. Write this point as an ordered pair.

Objective 5: Interpret Graphs

8. $(1, 5)$ is a point on the graph of $3x - y = -2$. If the x-axis represents the number of picnic tables
manufactured and sold and the y-axis represents the profit (in tens of dollars) from the sale of those tables,
describe the meaning of the ordered pair $(1, 5)$.

_____

9. $(2, 8)$ is a point on the graph of $y = -x^2 + 3x + 6$. If the x-axis represents the time (in seconds) after a
ball leaves the hand of a thrower and the y-axis represents the height (in feet) above the ground, describe the
meaning of the ordered pair $(2, 8)$.

_____

Do the Math Exercises 8.1
Graphs of Equations

1. Determine the coordinates of each of the points plotted. Tell in which quadrant or on what coordinate axis each point lies.

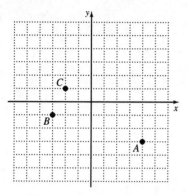

1.

A _____

B _____

C _____

2. Use the graph above to plot each of the following points. Tell in which quadrant or on which coordinate axis each point lies.

$D(0, 5)$ $\qquad$ $E(2, 3)$ $\qquad$ $F(1, 0)$

2.

D _____

E _____

F _____

3. Determine which of the following are points on the graph of the equation $-4x + 3y = 18$.

(a) $(1, 7)$ $\qquad$ **(b)** $(0, 6)$ $\qquad$ **(c)** $(-3, 10)$ $\qquad$ **(d)** $\left(\dfrac{3}{2}, 4\right)$

3. _____

4. Determine which of the following are points on the graph of the equation $x^2 + y^2 = 1$.

(a) $(0, 1)$ $\qquad$ **(b)** $(1, 1)$ $\qquad$ **(c)** $\left(\dfrac{1}{2}, \dfrac{1}{2}\right)$ $\qquad$ **(d)** $\left(\dfrac{\sqrt{3}}{2}, \dfrac{1}{2}\right)$

4. _____

5. The graph of the equation is given. List the intercepts of the graph.

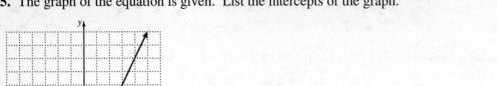

5. *x*-intercept:

_____

y-intercept:

_____

In Problems 6 – 9, graph each equation by plotting points.

6. $y = x - 2$

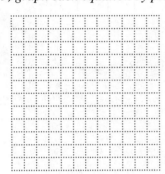

7. $y = x^2 - 2$

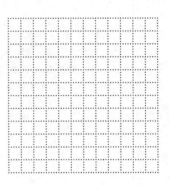

8. $y = |x| + 1$

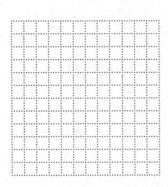

9. $3x + y = -2$

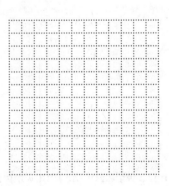

10. If $(a, -2)$ is a point on the graph of $y - 3x = 5$, what is a?

10. _____

11. If $(-2, b)$ is a point on the graph of $y = -2x^2 + 3x + 1$, what is b?

11. _____

Five-Minute Warm-Up 8.2
Relations

1. Write each inequality using interval notation.

    (a) $-1 < x \le 0$ (b) $x > -2$

1a. _____

1b. _____

2. Write each interval in inequality notation involving x.

    (a) $[0, 5]$ (b) $[1, \infty)$

2a. _____

2b. _____

3. Plot the ordered pairs in the rectangular coordinate system.

$$A(0, -3);\ B(-2, -4);\ C(1, -1);\ D(2, 0);\ E(-4, 3)$$

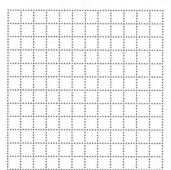

4. Graph the equation $5x + 3y = -15$.   5. Graph the equation $y = -x^2 + 2$ by plotting points.

 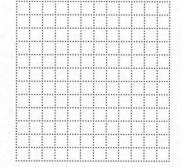

Guided Practice 8.2
Relations

Objective 1: Understand Relations

1. In your own words, write a definition for a *relation*.

Objective 2: Find the Domain and the Range of a Relation

2. The *domain* is the set of all _____ and is the set of _____ -coordinates for the relation which is defined by the set of ordered pairs (x, y).

3. The *range* is the set of all _____ and is the set of _____ -coordinates for the relation which is defined by the set of ordered pairs (x, y).

*In Problems 4 and 5, the figure shows the graph of a relation. Determine (**a**) the domain and (**b**) the range of the relation. (See textbook Example 4)*

4.

5.

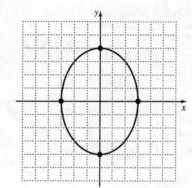

4a. _____

4b. _____

5a. _____

5b. _____

Objective 3: Graph a Relation Defined by an Equation

6. Graph the relation $x = y^2 - 3$. Use the graph to determine **(a)** the domain and **(b)** the range of the relation. *(See textbook Example 5)*

$x = y^2 - 3$	y	(x, y)
	-2	
	-1	
	0	
	1	
	2	

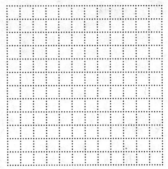

6a. _____

6b. _____

Do the Math Exercises 8.2
Relations

Write the relation as a set of ordered pairs. Then identify the domain and range.

1.

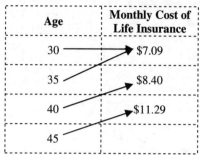

Age	Monthly Cost of Life Insurance
30	$7.09
35	$8.40
40	$11.29
45	

1. _____

domain _____

range _____

In Problems 2 – 4, identify the domain and the range of each relation.

2. $\{(-2, 6), (-1, 3), (0, 0), (1, -3), (2, 6)\}$

domain _____

range _____

3. $\{(-2, -8), (-1, -1), (0, 0), (1, 1), (2, 8)\}$

domain _____

range _____

4. $\{(-3, 0), (0, 3), (3, 0), (0, -3)\}$

domain _____

range _____

In Problems 5 – 8, identify the domain and range of the relation from the graph.

5.

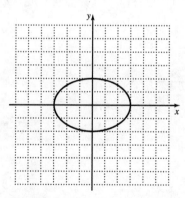

domain _____

range _____

6.

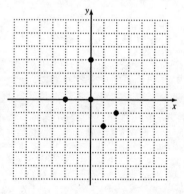

domain _____

range _____

7.

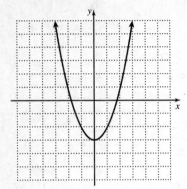

domain _____

range _____

8.

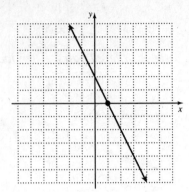

domain _____

range _____

In Problems 9 – 14, identify the domain and range of each relation. You may want to draw a graph by point-plotting or by using your graphing calculator.

9. $y = x - 2$

domain _____

range _____

10. $y = x^2 - 2$

domain _____

range _____

11. $y = -2x^2 + 8$

domain _____

range _____

12. $y = |x| - 2$

domain _____

range _____

13. $x = y^2 + 2$

domain _____

range _____

14. $y = x^3 - 4$

domain _____

range _____

Sullivan/Struve/Mazzarella, *Elementary & Intermediate Algebra,* 2e

Five-Minute Warm-Up 8.3
An Introduction to Functions

In Problems 1 and 2, evaluate the expression for the given value of the variable.

1. $-\dfrac{4}{5}x - 3$ for $x = -25$

2. $-2x^2 + 3x - 1$ for $x = -1$

1. _____

2. _____

3. Express the inequality $x > -16$ using interval notation.

3. _____

4. Express the interval $(-\infty, 100]$ using set-builder notation.

4. _____

5. For the following set of ordered pairs, list **(a)** the domain and **(b)** the range.
$$\{(-2, 1), (-4, 3), (-6, 5), (-8, 7)\}$$

5a. domain _____

5b. range _____

In Problems 6 – 8, evaluate each expression.

6. $\dfrac{2^2 - 5}{-5}$

7. $-4(-1)^2 + 6(-1) + 5$

8. $\left| \dfrac{4 - (-20)}{-2^3} \right|$

6. _____

7. _____

8. _____

9. The volume of a right circular cylinder is given by the formula $V = \pi r^2 (r + 3)$ where r is the radius of the cylinder and whose height is 3 inches more than the radius. Find the volume of a cylinder whose radius is 2.5 inches. Round your answer to the nearest tenth of a cubic inch.

9. _____

Guided Practice 8.3
An Introduction to Functions

Objective 1: Determine Whether a Relation Expressed as a Map or Ordered Pairs Represents a Function

1. In your own words, write a definition for a *function*.

2. Determine whether the relation represents a function. If the relation is a function, then state its domain and range. *(See textbook Example 2)*

   (a) $\{(3, -6), (4, -1), (5, -6)\}$ _____

   (b) $\{(4, 5), (3, -3), (4, -1)\}$ _____

Objective 2: Determine Whether a Relation Expressed as an Equation Represents a Function

3. The symbol $\pm$ is a shorthand device and is read "plus or minus." Write the two equations that are represented by $y = \pm 2x$ and then determine whether the equation shows y is a function of x.

   (a) $y = \pm 2x$ means $y =$ _____ and also $y =$ _____ .   **(b)** Is y a function of x? _____

4. Determine whether each equation shows y as a function of x. *(See textbook Example 4)*
   (a) $y = 9$ **(b)** $x + y^2 = 2$ 4a. _____

                                                                     4b. _____

Objective 3: Determine Whether a Relation Expressed as a Graph Represents a Function

5. We use the Vertical Line Test to determine whether the graph of a relation is a function. In your own words, state the *Vertical Line Test (VLT)*.

6. Which of the graphs are graphs of functions? *(See textbook Example 5)*   6.

   (a)   **(b)**   **(c)**   **(d)**

Objective 4: Find the Value of a Function

7. For the function $y = f(x)$, the variable x is called the _____ variable, because it can be

assigned any of the numbers in the _____.

8. For the function $y = f(x)$, the variable y is called the _____ variable, because it can be

assigned any of the numbers in the _____.

In Problems 9 – 12, find the value of each function. (See textbook Example 6 and Example 7)

9. $f(x) = 2x^2 - 5x$; $f(-4)$ **10.** $g(x) = -3x + 2$; $g(2a)$

9. _____

10. _____

11. $h(t) = 4$; $h(5)$ **12.** $F(z) = -3z + 4$; $F(k+1)$

11. _____

12. _____

Objective 5: Work with Applications of Functions

13. The number N of trucks produced at a certain factory in 1 day after t hours of operation is
given by $N(t) = 80t - 4t^2$, where $0 \le t \le 8$. *(See textbook Example 8)*

(a) Identify the dependent variable.   13a. _____

(b) Identify the independent variable.   13b. _____

(c) Evaluate $N(5)$ and explain the meaning of $N(5)$.   13c. _____

Name: Date:

Instructor: Section:

Do the Math Exercises 8.3
An Introduction to Functions

In Problems 1 – 3, determine whether the relation represents a function (Yes or No).

1.

Grade on exam	Study time (hr)
A	5
B	6
C	4
D	3.5
	1

1. _____

2. $\{(-2, 3), (-2, 1), (-2, -3), (-2, 9)\}$

2. _____

3. $\{(-5, 3), (-2, 1), (5, 1), (7, -3)\}$

3. _____

In Problems 4 – 7, determine whether each equation shows y as a function of x. (Yes or No)

4. $y = -6x + 3$ **5.** $y = \pm 4x$

4. _____

5. _____

6. $y = x^2 + 2$ **7.** $y^2 = x$

6. _____

7. _____

In Problems 8 – 11, determine whether the graph is that of a function (Yes or No).

8.   **9.**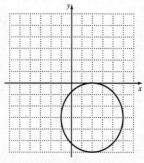

8. _____

9. _____

10.   **11.**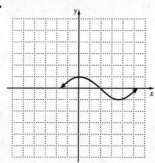

10. _____

11. _____

In Problems 12 and 13, find the following values for each function.

(a) $f(3)$ (b) $f(-2)$ (c) $f(2x)$ (d) $f(x+2)$

12. $f(x) = 3x + 1$ **13.** $f(x) = -2x - 3$

12a. _____

12b. _____

12c. _____

12d. _____

13a. _____

13b. _____

13c. _____

13d. _____

In Problems 14 and 15, find the value of each function.

14. _____

14. $f(x) = -2x^2 + x + 1$; $f(-3)$ **15.** $h(q) = \dfrac{3q^2}{q+2}$; $h(2)$

15. _____

16. If $f(x) = -2x^2 + 5x + C$ and $f(-2) = -15$, what is the value of C?   16. _____

17. If $f(x) = \dfrac{-x + B}{x - 5}$ and $f(3) = -1$, what is the value of B?   17. _____

Five-Minute Warm-Up 8.4
Functions and Their Graphs

In Problems 1 and 2, solve each equation.

1. $-4x + 2 = 0$

2. $-18 + 3y = 0$

1. _____

2. _____

3. Graph the equation $y = -\dfrac{4}{3}x + 2$.

4. Graph the equation $y = x^2 - 4$ by plotting points.

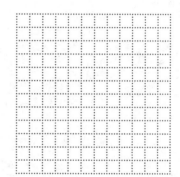

In Problems 5 and 6, determine the (a) domain and (b) the range from the graph.

5.

6.

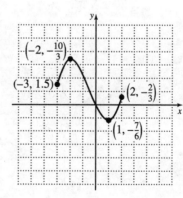

5a. _____

5b. _____

6a. _____

6b. _____

Guided Practice 8.4
Functions and Their Graphs

Objective 1: Find the Domain of a Function

1. The domain of a function is the set of all inputs for which the function gives an output that is a real number or makes sense. When identifying the domain of a function we exclude values of the variable that causes division by _____.

In Problems 2 and 3, find the domain of each of the following functions. (See textbook Example 1)

2. $F(t) = \dfrac{t}{2t + 3}$

3. $g(z) = 6z + 1$

2. _____

3. _____

Objective 2: Graph of a Function

4. Complete the table and graph the function $f(x) = |2x - 4|$. *(See textbook Example 3)*

x	$f(x)$	$(x, f(x))$
-2		
-1		
0		
1		
2		
3		
4		

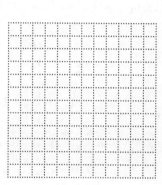

Objective 3: Obtain Information from the Graph of a Function

5. Use the graph of the function to answer parts (a) – (c). *(See textbook Example 4)*

(a) Determine the domain of the function.
(b) Determine the range of the function.
(c) Identify the x and y-intercept(s).

5a. _____
5b. _____
5c. _____

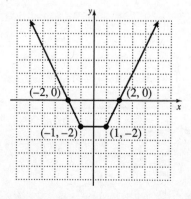

6. Consider the function $f(x) = -\dfrac{5}{2}x + 8$. *(See textbook Example 6)*

    (a) Is the point $(4, -2)$ on the graph of the function?

    6a. _____

    (b) If $x = 6$, what is $f(x)$? What point is on the graph of the function?

    6b. _____
    _____

    (c) If $f(x) = 3$, what is x? What point is on the graph of f?

    6c. _____

7. The zeros of a function are also the ____-intercepts of the graph of the function. To find the zeros of a function we set the function equal to _____ and solve for x.

8. Find the zeros of the function f whose graph is shown below. *(See textbook Example 7)*   8. _____

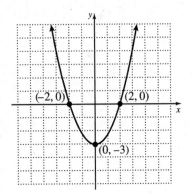

Do the Math Exercises 8.4
Functions and Their Graphs

In Problems 1 –5, find the domain of each function.

1. $G(x) = -8x + 3$

2. $H(x) = \dfrac{x+5}{2x+1}$

3. $s(t) = 2t^2 - 5t + 1$

4. $H(q) = \dfrac{1}{6q+5}$

5. $f(x) = \dfrac{4x-9}{7}$

1. _____

2. _____

3. _____

4. _____

5. _____

In Problems 6 and 7, graph each function.

6. $F(x) = x^2 + 1$

7. $H(x) = |x+1|$

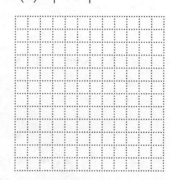

*In Problems 8 and 9, find **(a)** the domain, **(b)** the range, **(c)** the intercepts, if any, and **(d)** the zeros, if any.*

8.

9.

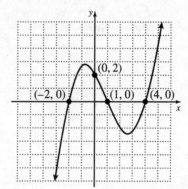

8a. _____

8b. _____

8c. _____

8d. _____

9a. _____

9b. _____

9c. _____

9d. _____

10. *Use the table of values for the function G to answer the following:*

(a) What is $G(3)$?

x	G(x)
−5	−3
−4	0
0	5
3	8
7	5

(b) For what number(s) is $G(x) = 5$?

(c) What is the *x*-intercept of the graph of *G*?

(d) What is the *y*-intercept of the graph of *G*?

(e) Are there any zeros of the function *G*? If so, name the zero(s).

10a. _____

10b. _____

10c. _____

10d. _____

10e. _____

11. *Use the function* $f(x) = 3x + 5$ *to answer the following:*

(a) Is the point (−2, 1) on the graph of the function?

(b) If $x = 4$, what is $f(x)$? What point is on the graph of the function?

(c) If $f(x) = -4$, what is *x*? What point is on the graph of the function?

(d) Is $x = 0$ a zero of the function?

11a. _____

11b. _____

11c. _____

11d. _____

12. Geometry The volume *V* of a sphere as a function of its radius *r* is given by $V(r) = \dfrac{4}{3}\pi r^3$.

(a) What is the domain of this function?

(b) Find the volume of the sphere whose radius is $4\dfrac{1}{2}$ cm. Round your answer to one decimal place.

12a. _____

12b. _____

Five-Minute Warm-Up 8.5
Linear Functions

In Problems 1 and 2, graph each linear equation.

1. $\frac{2}{3}x - \frac{1}{2}y = -2$

2. $x = -1$

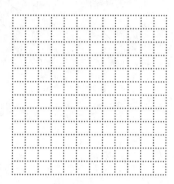

3. Find the equation of the line through $(-1,\ 2)$ and $(2,\ -7)$.

3. _____

In Problems 4 and 5, solve for the given variable.

4. $6.5 - 1.5(x - 4) + 4x = 10.25$

5. $-\frac{7}{8}(2y + 3) \leq \frac{5}{4}(y - 2)$

4. _____

5. _____

Guided Practice 8.5
Linear Functions

Objective 1: Graph Linear Functions

1. A _____ function is a function of the form $f(x) = mx + b$ where m and b are real numbers. The

graph of a linear function is called a _____.

2. To graph a linear function, we compare the function to $y = mx + b$ where m is the _____ and b is

the _____.

3. Graph the linear function $f(x) = \dfrac{3}{2}x - 2$. *(See textbook Example 1)*

   (**a**) Identify the y-intercept.

   (**b**) Identify the slope.

   (**c**) Graph the function.

3a. _____

3b. _____

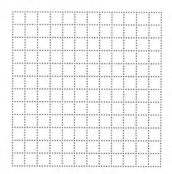

Objective 2: Find the Zero of a Linear Function

4. To find the zero of a linear function $f(x) = mx + b$, we solve the equation _____.

5. Perimeter of a Rectangle In a given rectangle, the length is 3 ft less than twice the
width. If x represents the width of the rectangle, the perimeter can be calculated by the
function $P(x) = 2x + 2(2x - 3)$. *(See textbook Example 3)*

   (**a**) What is the implied domain of the function?   5a. _____

   (**b**) What is the perimeter of a rectangle whose width is 12 ft?   5b. _____

   (**c**) What is the width of a rectangle whose perimeter is 84 ft?   5c. _____

   (**d**) For what width of the rectangle will the perimeter exceed 12 feet?   5d. _____

Objective 3: Build Models from Verbal Descriptions

6. The linear cost function is $C(x) = ax + b$, where b represents the _____ costs of operating a

business and _____ represents the costs associated with manufacturing one additional item. *(See textbook Example 4)*

7. Some companies use *straight-line depreciation* to depreciate their assets so that the value of the asset declines by a constant amount each year. To calculate the amount the asset depreciates each year, divide the total cost by the number of years of useful life. A cab company bought a new car for $22,500 and plans to drive it until there is no scrap value. The life of a car in the cab fleet is 5 years. *(See textbook Example 5)*

(a) By how much does the car depreciate each year?

7a. _____

(b) This rate can be expressed as the slope of a linear function. Is this slope positive or negative?

7b. _____

(c) The *book value* is the value of the asset at a particular time. To find the book value, we take the original value and deduct the amount of depreciation after a given time. Write a linear function that expresses the book value V of the car as a function of its age, x.

7c. _____

(d) What is the implied domain of the linear function?

7d. _____

(e) What is the book value after 4 years?

7e. _____

(f) When will the book value of the car be $10,125?

7f. _____

(g) What is the independent variable?

7g. _____

(h) What is the dependent variable?

7h. _____

Objective 4: Build Linear Models from Data

8. How many points are needed to determine the equation of a line?

8. _____

9. If the data appears to be linearly related, we select two points on the line of best fit. The linear model can be determined by finding the equation of the line through the two points as described in Section 1.6, Example 12.

(a) To find the equation of the line, you must first determine the _____.

(b) Second, use the point-slope form of a line, _____, to find the equation.

Do the Math Exercises 8.5
Linear Functions

In Problems 1 – 4, graph each linear function.

1. $f(x) = 2x - 4$

2. $g(x) = -\dfrac{3}{2}x + 1$

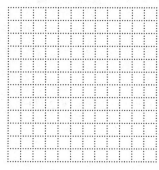

3. $h(x) = \dfrac{1}{4}x + 2$

4. $F(x) = 3$

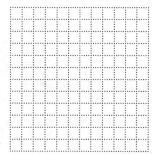

In Problems 5 and 6, find the zeros of the linear function.

5. $f(x) = 3x - 24$

6. $g(x) = -\dfrac{3}{2}x + 6$

5. _____

6. _____

7. Suppose that $f(x) = \dfrac{4}{3}x + 5$ and $g(x) = \dfrac{1}{3}x + 1$.

(a) Solve $f(x) = g(x)$.

7a. _____

(b) What is the value of f at the solution?

7b. _____

(c) What is the value of g at the solution?

7c. _____

(d) Solve $f(x) > g(x)$.

7d. _____

8. Graph $f(x) = \frac{4}{3}x + 5$ and $g(x) = \frac{1}{3}x + 1$ on the same Cartesian plane. Label the intersection point.

9. **(a)** Find a linear function g such that $g(1) = 5$ and $g(5) = 17$. **(b)** What is $g(-3)$?

9a. _____

9b. _____

10. Birth Rate A multiple birth is any birth with 2 or more children born. The birth rate is the number of births per 1,000 women. The birth rate B of multiple births as a function of age a is given by the function $B(a) = 1.73a - 14.56$ for $15 \leq a \leq 44$.

(a) What is the independent variable?

10a. _____

(b) What is the dependent variable?

10b. _____

(c) What is the domain of this linear function?

10c. _____

(d) What is the multiple birth rate of women who are 22 years of age according to the model?

10d. _____

(e) What is the age of women whose multiple birth rate is 49.45?

10e. _____

Five-Minute Warm-Up 8.6
Compound Inequalities

1. Use **(a)** set-builder notation and **(b)** interval notation to list the set of all real numbers x
   such that $-4 \leq x < -1$.

1a. _____

1b. _____

2. Graph the inequality $x < -3$.

3. Use interval notation to express the inequality shown in the graph.

3. _____

4. Solve $2(x+4) = x - (3x+4)$.

4. _____

5. Solve $\dfrac{3}{8}x + 1 \leq -\dfrac{5}{4}$.

5. _____

6. Solve $-2(1-x) + 2x < 7x + 4$.

6. _____

Guided Practice 8.6
Compound Inequalities

Objective 1: Determine the Intersection or Union of Two Sets

1. The *intersection* of two sets A and B, denoted _____, is the set of all elements that belong to both

set A and set B. The word _____ implies intersection.

2. The *union* of two sets A and B, denoted _____, is the set of all elements that are in set A or in set B

or in both A and B. The word _____ implies union.

3. Suppose $A = \{x \mid x > -2\}$, $B = \{x \mid x \leq 1\}$, and $C = \{x \mid x \geq 3\}$. *(See textbook Example 2)*

(a) Determine $A \cap B$. Graph the solution set on a real number line.

    Step 1: Graph $A = \{x \mid x > -2\}$

    Step 2: Graph $B = \{x \mid x \leq 1\}$

    Step 3: Identify where the graph of the inequalities overlap.

(b) Determine $B \cup C$. Graph the solution set on a real number line.

    Step 1: Graph $B = \{x \mid x \leq 1\}$

    Step 2: Graph $C = \{x \mid x \geq 3\}$

    Step 3: Identify the solution as the set that is in either B or C.

Objective 2: Solve Compound Inequalities Involving "and" *(See textbook Example 3)*

4. Solve $5x - 1 < 9$ and $5x \geq -20$. Graph the solution set.

Step 1: Solve each inequality separately.		$5x - 1 < 9$
	Add 1 to both sides:	**(a)** _____
	Divide both sides by 5:	**(b)** _____
		$5x \geq -20$
	Divide both sides by 5:	**(c)** _____
Step 2: Find the intersection of the solution sets, which will represent the solution set to the compound inequality.	Graph (b):	**(d)**
	Graph (c):	**(e)**
	Graph the intersection (overlap)	**(f)**

5. If $a < b$, then we can write $a < x$ and $x < b$ more compactly as _____.

6. Solve $-8 \le 5x - 3 \le 7$ and graph the solution set. *(See textbook Example 6)*

Our goal is to get the variable by itself in the "middle" with a coefficient of 1. Remember that the inequality is always written in order, the smaller number on left and the larger number on the right side of the inequality.

$$-8 \le 5x - 3 \le 7$$

(a) Add 3 to all three parts:

-8 ___ $\le 5x - 3$ ___ ≤ 7 ___

(b) Simplify: _____

(c) Divide all three parts by 5 and simplify: _____

(d) Graph the solution set:

Objective 3: **Solve Compound Inequalities Involving "or"** *(See textbook Example 7)*

7. Solve $-\dfrac{3}{2}x + 6 > 9$ or $7x - 10 > 4$. Write the solution set in interval notation.

Step 1: Solve each inequality separately.		$-\dfrac{3}{2}x + 6 > 9$
	Subtract 6 from both sides:	**(a)** _____
	Multiply both sides by $-\dfrac{2}{3}$: Don't forget to reverse the direction of the inequality.	**(b)** _____
		$7x - 10 > 4$
	Add 10 to both sides:	**(c)** _____
	Divide both sides by 7:	**(d)** _____
Step 2: Find the union of the solution sets, which will represent the solution set to the compound inequality.	Graph (b):	**(e)**
	Graph (d):	**(f)**
	Graph the union:	**(g)**
	Write the solution in interval notation:	**(h)** _____

Do the Math Exercises 8.6
Compound Inequalities

In Problems 1 – 3, use A = {4, 5, 6, 7, 8, 9}, B = {1, 5, 7, 9}, and C = {2, 3, 4, 6} to find each set.

1. $A \cup C$ **2.** $A \cap C$ 1. _____

                                                                                          2. _____

3. $B \cap C$ 3. _____

In Problems 4 and 5, use $E = \{x \mid x \le 2\}$ and $F = \{x \mid x \ge -2\}$ to find each of the following.

4. $E \cap F$ **5.** $E \cup F$ 4. _____

                                                                                          5. _____

In Problems 6 – 17, solve each compound inequality. Express your answer in interval notation.

                                                                                          6. _____

6. $x \le 5$ and $x > 0$ **7.** $x < 0$ or $x \ge 6$

                                                                                          7. _____

                                                                                          8. _____

8. $7x + 2 \ge 9$ and $4x + 3 \le 7$ **9.** $x + 3 \le 5$ or $x - 2 \ge 3$

                                                                                          9. _____

                                                                                          10. _____

10. $-12 < 7x + 2 \le 6$ **11.** $3x \ge 7x + 8$ or $x < 4x - 9$

                                                                                          11. _____

                                                                                          12. _____

12. $-\dfrac{4}{5}x - 5 > 3$ or $7x - 3 > 4$ **13.** $0 < \dfrac{3}{2}x - 3 \le 3$

                                                                                          13. _____

14. $x - \dfrac{3}{2} \le \dfrac{5}{4}$ and $-\dfrac{2}{3}x - \dfrac{2}{9} < \dfrac{8}{9}$

15. $-3 < -4x + 1 < 17$

14. _____

15. _____

16. $-4 \le \dfrac{4x-3}{3} < 3$

17. $-15 < -3(x+2) \le 1$

16. _____

17. _____

In Problem 18, use the Addition Property and/or Multiplication Properties to find a and b.

18. If $-4 < x < 3$, then $a < 2x - 7 < b$.

18. _____

19. Diastolic Blood Pressure Blood pressure is measured using two numbers. One of the numbers measures diastolic blood pressure. The diastolic blood pressure represents the pressure while the heart is resting between beats. In a healthy person, the diastolic blood pressure should be greater than 60 and less than 90. If we let the variable x represent a person's diastolic blood pressure, express the diastolic blood pressure of a healthy person using compound inequality.

19. _____

20. Heating Bills For usage above 300 kilowatt-hours, the non-space heat winter energy charge for Illinois Power residential service was $23.12 plus $0.05947 per kilowatt-hour over 300. During one winter, a customer's charge ranged from a low of $50.28 to a high of $121.43. Over what range of values did electric usage vary (in kilowatt-hours)?

20. _____

Five-Minute Warm-Up 8.7
Absolute Value Equations and Inequalities

1. Evaluate each expression.

(a) $\left|-12\right|$ (b) $\left|0\right|$ (c) $\left|\dfrac{3}{4}\right|$ (d) $\left|-5.2\right|$

1a. _____

1b. _____

1c. _____

1d. _____

2. Express the distance between the origin, 0, and 45 as an absolute value.

2. _____

3. Express the distance between the origin, 0, and -12 as an absolute value.

3. _____

4. Solve each equation.

(a) $-3x + 7 = -5$ (b) $4(x+1) = x + 5x - 10$

4a. _____

4b. _____

5. Solve each inequality.

(a) $6x - 10 < 8x + 2$ (b) $\dfrac{1}{2}(3x-1) \le \dfrac{2}{3}(x+3)$

5a. _____

5b. _____

Guided Practice 8.7
Absolute Value Equations and Inequalities

Objective 1: Solve Absolute Value Equations

1. If a is a positive real number and if u is any algebraic expression, then $|u| = a$ is equivalent to

_____ or _____ .

2. When solving absolute value equations the first step is to _____ .

3. Solve the equation $|3x - 1| - 5 = -3$. *(See textbook Example 2)*

Step 1: Isolate the expression containing the absolute value.

$$|3x - 1| - 5 = -3$$

Add 5 to both sides: **(a)** _____

Step 2: Rewrite the absolute value equation as two equations: $u = a$ and $u = -a$, where u is the algebraic expression in the absolute value symbol. Here $u = 3x - 1$ and $a = 2$.

(b) _____ or _____

Step 3: Solve each equation.

(c) $x =$ _____ or $x =$ _____

Step 4: Check. Verify each solution.

Substitute your values for x into the original equation. If the statement is true, then the value is a solution of the absolute value equation. If the statement is false, delete the value from the solution set.

(d) solution set: _____

4. If u and v are any algebraic expressions, then $|u| = |v|$ is equivalent to

_____ or _____ .

Objective 2: Solve Absolute Value Inequalities Involving $<$ or $\leq$

5. If a is a positive real number and if u is any algebraic expression, then

$|u| < a$ is equivalent to _____ .

$|u| \leq a$ is equivalent to _____ .

6. Solve the inequality $|4x - 3| \leq 9$. Write the solution set in interval notation. *(See textbook Example 6)*

		$|4x - 3| \leq 9$
Step 1: The inequality is in the form $|u| \leq a$ where $u = 4x - 3$ and $a = 9$. We rewrite the inequality as a compound inequality that does not involve absolute value.	Use the fact that $|u| \leq a$ means $-a \leq u \leq a$:	**(a)** _____
Step 2: Solve the resulting compound inequality.	Add 3 to all three parts:	**(b)** _____
	Divide all three parts of the inequality by 4:	**(c)** _____
	Graph the solution:	**(d)**
	Write the solution in interval notation:	**(e)** _____

Objective 3: Solve Absolute Value Inequalities Involving > or ≥

7. If a is a positive real number and if u is any algebraic expression, then

$|u| > a$ is equivalent to _____ or _____.

$|u| \geq a$ is equivalent to _____ or _____.

8. Solve the inequality $3|8x + 3| > 9$. Write the solution set in interval notation. *(See textbook Example 9)*

		$3|8x + 3| > 9$
Step 1: The inequality is in the form $|u| > a$ where $u = 8x + 3$ and $a = 3$. We rewrite the inequality as a compound inequality that does not involve absolute value.	Isolate the absolute value:	**(a)** _____
	Rewrite the inequality:	**(b)** _____
Step 2: Solve each inequality separately.		
		(c) _____ or _____
Step 3: Find the union of the solution sets of each inequality.	Graph the solution:	**(d)** graph
	Write the solution in interval notation:	**(e)** _____

Do the Math Exercises 8.7
Absolute Value Equations and Inequalities

In Problems 1 and 2, solve each absolute value equation.

1. $\left|\dfrac{2x-3}{5}\right| = 2$

2. $3|y-4| + 4 = 16$

1. _____

2. _____

In Problems 3 – 6, solve each absolute value inequality. Express your answer in set-builder notation.

3. $|y+4| < 6$

4. $|-3x+2| - 7 \le -2$

3. _____

4. _____

5. $|x+4| \ge 7$

6. $3|z| + 8 > 2$

5. _____

6. _____

In Problems 7 – 14, solve each absolute value equation or inequality.

7. _____

7. $|2x+1| = x - 3$

8. $|3-5x| < |-7|$

8. _____

9. _____

9. $|3x-4| = -9$

10. $|-9x+2| \ge -1$

10. _____

11. $|4x+3|=1$

12. $|4x-3|>1$

11. _____

12. _____

13. $|7x+5|+4<3$

14. $|4y+3|\geq-3$

13. _____

14. _____

In Problems 15 and 16, write each statement as an absolute value inequality.

15. x differs from -4 by less than 2

16. twice x differs from 7 by more than 3

15. _____

16. _____

17. Tensile Strength The tensile strength of paper used to make grocery bags is about 40 lb/in^2. It can be shown that a paper grocery bag whose tensile strength satisfies the inequality $\left|\dfrac{x-40}{2}\right|>1.96$ has an unusual tensile strength. Determine the tensile strengths that would be considered unusual.

17. _____

Five-Minute Warm-Up 8.8
Variation

1. Solve each equation.

    (a) $-75 = 15x$

    (b) $-\dfrac{2}{3}k = \dfrac{8}{27}$

1a. _____

1b. _____

2. Solve: $-12 = \dfrac{k}{4}$

2. _____

3. Graph the equation $y = \dfrac{1}{2}x$.

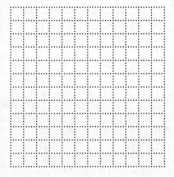

4. Graph the equation $y = 2x$.

Guided Practice 8.8
Variation

Objective 1: Model and Solve Problems Involving Direct Variation

1. We say that y varies directly with x, or y is directly proportional to x, if there is a nonzero number k such

that _____.

2. The number k is called the _____.

3. If y varies directly with x, then y is a _____ function of x and has a y-intercept of _____.

4. Suppose that y is directly proportional to x and when $x = -12$, $y = 5$. Find y when $x = 20$. Write the direct variation equation, calculate the constant k, and then use the given values to solve the unknown.

4. _____

Objective 2: Model and Solve Problems Involving Inverse Variation

5. We say that y varies inversely with x, or y is inversely proportional to x, if there is a nonzero number k

such that _____.

6. Suppose that y varies inversely with x. When $x = 4$, $y = 12$. Find y when $x = 18$. Write   6. _____
the inverse variation equation, calculate the constant, k, and then use the given values to
solve for the unknown. *(See textbook Example 3)*

Objective 3: Model and Solve Problems Involving Combined or Joint Variation

7. Suppose that r varies jointly with s and t. When $r = 12$, $s = 8$ and $t = 3$. Find r when   7. _____
$s = 14$ and $t = 6$. Write the joint variation equation, calculate the constant, k, and then use the
given values to solve for the unknown. *(See textbook Example 4)*

Do the Math Exercises 8.8
Variation

In Problems 1 and 2, (a) find the constant of proportionality, k, (b) write the linear function relating the two variables, and (c) find the quantity indicated.

1. Suppose that y varies directly with x. When $x = 3$, then $y = 15$. Find y when $x = 5$.

2. Suppose that y is directly proportional to x. When $x = 20$, then $y = 4$. Find y when $x = 35$.

1a. _____

1b. _____

1c. _____

2a. _____

2b. _____

2c. _____

In Problems 3 and 4, find the quantity indicated.

3. A is directly proportional to B. If A is 360 when B is 72, find B when A is 400.

4. m varies directly with r. If r is 24 when m is 9, find r when m is 24.

3. _____

4. _____

5. **House of Representatives** The number of representatives that each state has in the U.S. House of Representatives is directly proportional to the state's population. According to the 2000 Census, Ohio's 18 delegates represent a state whose population is 11.375 million. Find the number of representatives from Massachusetts if its population is 6.356 million.

5. _____

6. **Buying Gasoline** The cost to purchase a tank of gasoline varies directly with the number of gallons purchased. You notice that the person in front of you spent $34.50 on 15 gallons of gas. If your SUV needs 35 gallons of gas, how much will you spend?

6. _____

7. Falling Objects The velocity of a falling object (ignoring air resistance) v is directly proportional to the time t of the fall. If, after 2 seconds, the velocity of the object is 64 feet per second, what will its velocity be after 3 seconds?

7. _____

*In Problems 8 – 10, (**a**) find the constant, k; (**b**) write the function relating the two variables; and (**c**) find the quantity indicated.*

8. Suppose that y is inversely proportional to x. When $x = 20$, then $y = 4$. Find y when $x = 35$.

9. Suppose that y varies jointly with x and z. When $y = 20$, $x = 6$ and $z = 10$. Find y when $x = 8$ and $z = 15$.

8a. _____

8b. _____

8c. _____

9a. _____

9b. _____

9c. _____

10a. _____

10b. _____

10c. _____

10. Suppose that Q varies directly with x and inversely with y. When $Q = \dfrac{14}{5}$, $x = 4$ and $y = 3$. Find Q when $x = 8$ and $y = 3$.

11. Resistance The current, I, in a circuit is inversely proportional to its resistance, R, measured in ohms. Suppose that when the current in a circuit is 30 amperes, the resistance is 8 ohms. Find the current in the same circuit when the resistance is 10 ohms.

11. _____

12. Intensity of Light The intensity, I, of light (measured in foot-candles) varies inversely with the square of the distance from the bulb. Suppose the intensity of a 100-watt light bulb at a distance of 2 meters is 0.075 foot-candles. Determine the intensity of the bulb at a distance of 3 meters.

12. _____

Five-Minute Warm-Up 9.1
Square Roots

In Problems 1 – 4, identify which numbers in the set $\left\{\dfrac{-2}{3}, 5, -2.3, \dfrac{21}{7}, 1.\overline{6}, \dfrac{0}{11}, -10, \dfrac{11}{0}, 2.718281828...\right\}$

belong to the sets listed below.

1. Integer _____

2. Rational _____

3. Irrational _____

4. Real _____

In Problems 5 – 10, evaluate the expressions.

5. 5^2

6. 11^2

5. _____

6. _____

7. $(0.8)^2$

8. $(1.2)^2$

7. _____

8. _____

9. $\left(\dfrac{4}{7}\right)^2$

10. $\left(\dfrac{13}{6}\right)^2$

9. _____

10. _____

Guided Practice 9.1
Square Roots

Objective 1: Evaluate Square Roots of Perfect Squares

1. Fill in the blank:

   (a) Every positive real number has two square roots, one _____ and one _____.

   1a. _____

   _____

   (b) We use the symbol $\sqrt{}$, called a _____, to denote the nonnegative square root.

   1b. _____

   (c) The nonnegative square root is called the _____ square root.

   1c. _____

   (d) The number under the radical is called the _____.

   1d. _____

2. Evaluate each square root. *(See textbook Example 1)*

(a) $\sqrt{64}$ (b) $\sqrt{400}$

   2a. _____

   2b. _____

(c) $\sqrt{\dfrac{4}{25}}$ (d) $\left(\sqrt{17}\right)^2$

   2c. _____

   2d. _____

3. Evaluate each expression. *(See textbook Example 2)*

a) $-3\sqrt{49}$ (b) $\sqrt{1+16+64}$

   3a. _____

   3b. _____

(c) $\sqrt{1}+\sqrt{16}+\sqrt{64}$ (d) $\sqrt{49+3\bullet 4\bullet(-2)}$

   3c. _____

   3d. _____

Objective 2: Determine Whether a Square Root is Rational, Irrational, or Not a Real Number

4. Fill in the blank:

   (a) The square root of a perfect square is a _____ number.

   4a. _____

   (b) The square root of a positive rational number that is not a perfect square, such as $\sqrt{20}$, is an _____ number.

   4b. _____

   (c) The square root of a negative real number, such as $\sqrt{-2}$ is not a _____ number.

   4c. _____

5. Determine if each square root is rational, irrational, or not a real number. Then evaluate each real square root. For each square root that is irrational, express the square root as a decimal rounded to two decimal places. *(See textbook Example 4)*

(a) $\sqrt{48}$

((b) $\sqrt{-289}$

5a. _____

5b. _____

(c) $\sqrt{256}$

(d) $-\sqrt{225}$

5c. _____

5d. _____

Objective 3: Find Square Roots of Variable Expressions

For a variable expression, where the variable can be either positive nor negative, the square root of the expression squared is the absolute value of the expression. So, $\sqrt{4x^2} = |2x|$.

6. Evaluate each square root. *(See textbook Example 5)*

(a) $\sqrt{(-23)^2}$

(b) $\sqrt{\left(\dfrac{17}{68}\right)^2}$

6a. _____

6b. _____

6c. _____

(c) $\sqrt{(3y-2)^2}$

(d) $\sqrt{25x^2 - 30x + 9}$

6d. _____

Do the Math Exercises 9.1
Square Roots

In Problems 1 – 4, evaluate each square root.

1. $\sqrt{9}$

2. $\sqrt{\dfrac{4}{81}}$

3. $\sqrt{0.16}$

4. $\left(\sqrt{3.7}\right)^2$

1. _____

2. _____

3. _____

4. _____

In Problems 5 – 8, tell if the square root is rational, irrational, or not a real number. If the square root is rational, find the exact value; if the square root is irrational, write the approximate value rounded to two decimal places.

5. $\sqrt{-50}$

6. $\sqrt{\dfrac{49}{100}}$

7. $\sqrt{24}$

8. $\sqrt{12}$

5. _____

6. _____

7. _____

8. _____

In Problems 9 – 12, simplify each square root.

9. $\sqrt{(-13)^2}$

10. $\sqrt{w^2}$

9. _____

10. _____

11. $\sqrt{(x-8)^2}$

12. $\sqrt{9z^2 - 24z + 16}$

11. _____

12. _____

In Problems 13 – 15, simplify each expression.

13. $2\sqrt{\dfrac{9}{4}} - \sqrt{4}$

14. $\sqrt{9^2 - 4 \cdot 1 \cdot 20}$

13. _____

14. _____

15. $\sqrt{(-3)^2 - 4 \cdot 3 \cdot 2}$

15. _____

Five-Minute Warm-Up 9.2
nth Roots and Rational Exponents

In Problems 1 – 4, simplify each expression.

1. $\sqrt{0.25}$

2. $\left(\sqrt{\dfrac{4}{9}}\right)^2$

1. _____

2. _____

3. $\sqrt{(4x+3)^2}$

4. $\sqrt{x^2 - 2xy + y^2}$

3. _____

4. _____

In Problems 5 – 8, simplify each expression.

5. _____

5. 7^{-2}

6. $\dfrac{1}{x^{-2}}$

6. _____

7. _____

7. $\left(\dfrac{3x}{y^2}\right)^2$

8. $\left(\dfrac{4a^2b^{-1}}{8a^2b^3}\right)^{-3}$

8. _____

Guided Practice 9.2
nth Roots and Rational Exponents

Objective 1: Evaluate nth Roots

1. In the notation $\sqrt[3]{8} = 2$, 3 is called the _____, 8 is called the _____ and 2 is the _____.

2. If the index is even, then the radicand must be _____ in order for the radical to simplify to a real number.

If the index is odd, then the radicand can be _____ and the expression will simplify to any real number.

3. Since $(-4)^2 = 16$ and $4^2 = 16$, it could be interpreted that $\sqrt{16} = -4$ or 4. In fact, $\sqrt{16} = 4$ only, because when the index even, we use the _____ _____, which must be ≥ 0.

4. Evaluate each root without using a calculator. *(See textbook Example 1)*

(a) $\sqrt[3]{-27}$ (b) $\sqrt{-36}$ (c) $\sqrt[4]{\dfrac{16}{81}}$

4a. _____

4b. _____

4c. _____

5. Write $\sqrt[4]{64}$ as a decimal rounded to two decimal places. *(See textbook Example 2)*

5. _____

Objective 2: Simplify Expressions of the form $\sqrt[n]{a^n}$

6. Simplify: $\sqrt[4]{(2x-1)^4}$ *(See textbook Example 3)*

6. _____

Objective 3: Evaluate Expressions of the Form $a^{\frac{1}{n}}$

7. Write each of the following expressions as a radical and simplify, if possible. *(See textbook Example 4)*

(a) $144^{\frac{1}{2}}$ (b) $(-64)^{\frac{1}{2}}$ (d) $2x^{\frac{1}{3}}$

7a. _____

7b. _____

7c. _____

Objective 4: Evaluate Expressions of the Form $a^{\frac{m}{n}}$

8. If a is a real number and $\dfrac{m}{n}$ is a rational number in lowest terms with $n \geq 2$, then

$$a^{\frac{m}{n}} = \underline{\hspace{2cm}} \text{ or } \underline{\hspace{2cm}}, \text{ provided that } \sqrt[n]{a} \text{ exists.}$$

9. Evaluate each of the following expressions, if possible. *(See textbook Example 6)*

(a) $36^{\frac{3}{2}}$ **(b)** $-16^{\frac{5}{2}}$ **(c)** $(-64)^{\frac{2}{3}}$

9a. _____

9b. _____

9c. _____

10. Write $25^{\frac{2}{3}}$ as a decimal rounded to two decimal places. *(See textbook Example 7)*

10. _____

11. Write each radical expression with a rational exponent. *(See textbook Example 8)*

(a) $\sqrt[4]{(2x)^3}$ **(b)** $\left(\sqrt[3]{2x^2 y}\right)^2$

11a. _____

11b. _____

12. Rewrite each of the following with positive exponents, and completely simplify, if possible. *(See textbook Example 9)*

(a) $64^{-\frac{1}{2}}$ **(b)** $\dfrac{2}{16^{-\frac{1}{2}}}$ **(c)** $(4x)^{-\frac{5}{2}}$

12a. _____

12b. _____

12c. _____

Do the Math Exercises 9.2
nth Roots and Rational Exponents

In Problems 1 – 5, simplify each radical.

1. $\sqrt[3]{216}$

2. $-\sqrt[4]{256}$

1. _____

2. _____

3. $\sqrt[3]{\dfrac{8}{125}}$

4. $\sqrt[5]{n^5}$

3. _____

4. _____

5. $\sqrt[6]{(2x-3)^6}$

5. _____

In Problems 6 – 11, evaluate each expression, if possible.

6. $16^{1/2}$

7. $-25^{1/2}$

6. _____

7. _____

8. $(-81)^{1/2}$

9. $-(-32)^{3/5}$

8. _____

9. _____

10. $121^{-1/2}$

11. $\dfrac{1}{49^{-3/2}}$

10. _____

11. _____

In Problems 12 and 13, rewrite each of the following radicals with a rational exponent.

12. $\sqrt[4]{x^3}$

13. $\sqrt[4]{(3pq)^7}$

12. _____

13. _____

In Problems 14 and 15, use a calculator to write each expression as a decimal rounded to two decimal places.

14. $\sqrt[3]{85}$

15. $100^{0.25}$

14. _____

15. _____

Five-Minute Warm-Up 9.3
Simplify Expressions Using the Laws of Exponents

In Problems 1 – 8, simplify each expression.

1. $9z^6 \cdot 6z$

2. $\dfrac{18u^5}{12u^3}$

1. _____

2. _____

3. 25^{-2}

4. $\left(\dfrac{4}{3}\right)^{-3}$

3. _____

4. _____

5. $\dfrac{9}{7}x^5 y^{-2} \cdot \dfrac{28}{12}xy$

6. $\left(-5p^3\right)^{-2}$

5. _____

6. _____

7. $\left(\dfrac{8a^{-1}}{b^{-5}}\right)^2$

8. $\left(\dfrac{2x^{-2}y}{6x^{-3}y^2}\right)^{-1} \cdot \left(\dfrac{xy^{-2}}{9xy^2}\right)^2$

7. _____

8. _____

9. Evaluate: $\sqrt{\dfrac{81}{49}}$

9. _____

Guided Practice 9.3
Simplify Expressions Using the Laws of Exponents

Objective 1: Use the Laws of Exponents to Simplify Expressions Involving Rational Exponents

1. List four characteristics of an expression with rational exponents which is completely simplified.

2. Simplify each of the following expressions involving rational exponents. Express the answer with positive rational exponents, if necessary. *(See textbook Example 1 and Example 2)*

(a) $6^{\frac{12}{5}} \cdot 6^{-\frac{2}{5}}$ **(b)** $\dfrac{\left(-8a^4\right)^{\frac{1}{3}}}{a^{\frac{5}{6}}}$

2a. _____

2b. _____

3. Simplify the following expression involving rational exponents. Express the answer with positive rational exponents, if necessary. *(See textbook Example 3)*

$\left(xy^{-\frac{3}{8}}\right) \cdot \left(x^{\frac{1}{2}}y^{-2}\right)^{\frac{3}{4}}$

3. _____

Objective 2: Use the Laws of Exponents to Simplify Radical Expressions

4. Rewrite the radical as an expression involving a rational exponent and simplify. Express the answer with a simplified radical, if necessary. *(See textbook Example 4)*

(a) $\sqrt[6]{81^3}$

(b) $\sqrt[4]{128x^8 y^4}$

(c) $\dfrac{\sqrt[4]{x^3}}{\sqrt{x}}$

(d) $\sqrt[3]{\sqrt{p}}$

4a. _____

4b. _____

4c. _____

4d. _____

Objective 3: Factor Expressions Containing Rational Exponents

5. Simplify $6x^{\frac{2}{3}} + 2x^{\frac{1}{3}}(5x - 2)$ by factoring out $2x^{\frac{1}{3}}$. Express the answer with positive rational exponents, if necessary. *(See textbook Example 5)*

5. _____

Do the Math Exercises 9.3
Simplify Expressions Using the Laws of Exponents

In Problems 1 – 8, simplify each of the following expressions.

1. $3^{\frac{1}{3}} \cdot 3^{\frac{5}{3}}$

2. $\dfrac{10^{\frac{7}{5}}}{10^{\frac{2}{5}}}$

1. _____

2. _____

3. $\dfrac{y^{\frac{1}{5}}}{y^{\frac{9}{10}}}$

4. $\left(36^{-\frac{1}{4}} \cdot 9^{\frac{3}{4}}\right)^{-2}$

3. _____

4. _____

5. $\left(a^{\frac{5}{4}} \cdot b^{\frac{3}{2}}\right)^{\frac{2}{5}}$

6. $\left(a^{\frac{4}{3}} \cdot b^{-\frac{1}{2}}\right)\left(a^{-2} \cdot b^{\frac{5}{2}}\right)$

5. _____

6. _____

7. $\left(5p^{\frac{2}{3}}q^{\frac{3}{8}}\right)\left(p^{\frac{-7}{15}}q^{\frac{-7}{8}}\right)$

8. $\left(\dfrac{64m^{\frac{1}{2}}n}{m^{-2}n^{\frac{4}{3}}}\right)^{\frac{1}{2}}$

7. _____

8. _____

Do the Math Exercises 9.3

In Problems 9 and 10, distribute and simplify.

9. $x^{\frac{1}{3}}\left(x^{\frac{5}{3}} + 4 \right)$

10. $8p^{\frac{2}{3}}\left(p^{\frac{4}{3}} - 4p^{-\frac{2}{3}} \right)$

9. _____

10. _____

In Problems 11 – 14, use rational exponents to simplify each radical. Assume all variables are positive.

11. $\sqrt[3]{x^6}$

12. $\sqrt[9]{125^6}$

11. _____

12. _____

13. $\sqrt{25x^4 y^6}$

14. $\sqrt[4]{p^3} \cdot \sqrt[3]{p}$

13. _____

14. _____

In Problems 15 and 16, simplify by factoring out the given expression.

15. $3(x-5)^{\frac{1}{2}}(3x+1) + 6(x-5)^{\frac{3}{2}}; (x-5)^{\frac{1}{2}}$

15. _____

16. $x^{-\frac{2}{3}}(3x+2) + 9x^{\frac{1}{3}}; x^{-\frac{2}{3}}$

16. _____

Sullivan/Struve/Mazzarella, _Elementary & Intermediate Algebra_, 2e

Five-Minute Warm-Up 9.4
Simplifying Radical Expressions

1. List the perfect squares that are less than 150. _____

2. List the perfect cubes that are less than 150. _____

3. List the perfect fourths that are less than 150. _____

In Problems 4 – 9, simplify each radical.

4. $\sqrt{-4}$

5. $\sqrt{10^2}$

4. _____

5. _____

6. $\sqrt{x^2}$

7. $\sqrt{(4x+1)^2}$

6. _____

7. _____

8. $\sqrt{4p^2 - 4p + 1}$

9. $\sqrt{144 + 25}$

8. _____

9. _____

Guided Practice 9.4
Simplifying Radical Expressions

Objective 1: Use the Product Property to Multiply Radical Expressions

1. The Product Property of Radicals states that if $\sqrt[n]{a}$ and $\sqrt[n]{b}$ are real numbers and $n \geq 2$ is an integer, then $\sqrt[n]{a} \cdot \sqrt[n]{b} = \sqrt[n]{ab}$. Use this property to multiply each of the following. *(See textbook Example 1)*

(a) $\sqrt{5} \cdot \sqrt{7}$ **(b)** $\sqrt{x-5} \cdot \sqrt{x+5}$ **(c)** $\sqrt[3]{7x} \cdot \sqrt[3]{2x}$

1a. _____

1b. _____

1c. _____

Objective 2: Use the Product Property to Simplify Radical Expressions

2. A radical expression is *simplified* when _____.

3. Simplify: $\sqrt{75}$ *(See textbook Example 2)*

Step 1: Since the index is 2, we write each factor of the radicand as the product of two factors, one of which is a perfect square.   What perfect square is a factor of 75?   **(a)** _____

Step 2: Write the radical as the product of two radicals, one of which contains the perfect square. $\sqrt{75} =$ **(b)** _____

Step 3: Take the square root of each perfect power.   **(c)** _____

4. Simplify: $\dfrac{-6 + \sqrt{48}}{2}$ *(See textbook Example 4)*

$$\dfrac{-6 + \sqrt{48}}{2} =$$

Step 1: Since the index is 2, write each factor of the radicand as the product of the factors, one of which is a perfect square.   **(a)** _____

Step 2: Use $\sqrt{a \cdot b} = \sqrt{a} \cdot \sqrt{b}$.   **(b)** _____

Step 3: Take the square root of each perfect power.   **(c)** _____

Step 4: Factor out the 2 in the numerator.   **(d)** _____

Step 5: Divide out the common factor.   **(e)** _____

5. Explain how to simplify an expression with an index that does not divide evenly into the exponent on the variable in the radicand.

5._____

Objective 3: Use the Quotient Property to Simplify Radical Expressions

6. Simplify $\sqrt{\dfrac{12x^2}{121}}$. Assume $x \geq 0$. *(See textbook Example 8)*

6._____

7. Simplify $\dfrac{\sqrt{72a}}{\sqrt{2a^5}}$. Assume $a > 0$. *(See textbook Example 9)*

7._____

Objective 4: Multiply Radicals with Unlike Indices

8. What is the first step to multiply $\sqrt{6} \cdot \sqrt[4]{48}$? *(See textbook Example 10)*

8._____

Do the Math Exercises 9.4
Simplifying Radical Expression

In Problems 1 – 3, use the Product Rule to multiply. Assume that all variables can be any real number.

1. $\sqrt[4]{6a^2} \cdot \sqrt[4]{7b^2}$ **2.** $\sqrt{p-5} \cdot \sqrt{p+5}$

1. _____

2. _____

3. $\sqrt[3]{\dfrac{-9x^2}{4}} \cdot \sqrt[3]{\dfrac{4}{3x}}$

3. _____

In Problems 4 – 7, simplify each radical using the Product Property. Assume that all variables can be any real number.

4. $\sqrt[4]{162}$ **5.** $\sqrt{20a^2}$

4. _____

5. _____

6. $\sqrt[3]{-64p^3}$ **7.** $\sqrt[5]{x^{12}}$

6. _____

7. _____

In Problems 8 and 9, simplify each expression.

8. $\dfrac{5 - \sqrt{100}}{5}$ **9.** $\dfrac{-6 + \sqrt{48}}{8}$

8. _____

9. _____

In Problems 10 – 13, multiply and simplify. Assume that all variables are greater than or equal to zero.

10. $\sqrt{3} \cdot \sqrt{12}$

11. $\sqrt{6x} \cdot \sqrt{30x}$

10. _____

11. _____

12. $\sqrt[3]{9a} \cdot \sqrt[3]{6a^2}$

13. $\sqrt[3]{16m^2n} \cdot \sqrt[3]{27m^2n}$

12. _____

13. _____

In Problems 14 – 17, simplify. Assume that all variables are greater than zero.

14. $\sqrt{\dfrac{5}{36}}$

15. $\sqrt[4]{\dfrac{5x^4}{16}}$

14. _____

15. _____

16. $\sqrt[3]{\dfrac{-27x^9}{64y^{12}}}$

17. $\dfrac{\sqrt[4]{64}}{\sqrt[4]{4}}$

16. _____

17. _____

In Problems 18 and 19, multiply and simplify.

18. $\sqrt{2} \cdot \sqrt[3]{27}$

19. $\sqrt[4]{3} \cdot \sqrt[8]{5}$

18. _____

19. _____

Five-Minute Warm-Up 9.5
Adding, Subtracting, and Multiplying Radical Expressions

1. Add: $\left(2z^3 - 7z^2 + 1\right) + \left(z^3 + 2z^2 - 4z - 1\right)$

1. _____

2. Subtract: $\left(-2a^2b^2 + ab - 3b^2\right) - \left(a^2b^2 + a^2 - 5ab - 2b^2\right)$

2. _____

3. Multiply: $-4x^2\left(2x^2 + 3xy - 5y^2\right)$

3. _____

4. Multiply: $\dfrac{3}{2}x^2\left(\dfrac{4}{27}x^3 - \dfrac{8}{21}x^2 + \dfrac{2}{3}\right)$

4. _____

5. Multiply: $\left(9c + 2\right)\left(2c - 3\right)$

5. _____

6. Multiply: $\left(ab - 2\right)\left(ab + 2\right)$

6. _____

7. Multiply: $\left(7n - 3\right)^2$

7. _____

Guided Practice 9.5
Adding, Subtracting, and Multiplying Radical Expressions

Objective 1: Add or Subtract Radical Expressions

1. Describe the characteristics of like radicals.

1._____

2. Add or subtract, as indicated. Assume all variables are greater than or equal to zero. *(See textbook Example 1)*

(a) $8\sqrt{x} + \sqrt{x}$

(b) $13\sqrt[3]{3p} - 6\sqrt[3]{3p} + \sqrt[3]{3p}$

2a._____

2b._____

3. Simplify the radicals to make the radicands the same. Assume all variables are greater than or equal to zero. *(See textbook Example 2 and Example 3)*

(a) $3\sqrt{8} - 4\sqrt{32}$

(b) $3n^2\sqrt{54n^4} - 2n\sqrt{150n^6} + 2\sqrt{24n^9}$

3a._____

3b._____

Objective 2: Multiply Radical Expressions

4. Multiply and simplify $\left(9 + 2\sqrt{6}\right)\left(2 - 3\sqrt{2}\right)$. *(See textbook Example 4)*

4. _____

5. Multiply and simplify $\left(7 - \sqrt{3}\right)\left(7 + \sqrt{3}\right)$. *(See textbook Example 5)*

$$\left(7 - \sqrt{3}\right)\left(7 + \sqrt{3}\right)$$

Step 1: What special products formula can be used to multiply $\left(7 - \sqrt{3}\right)\left(7 + \sqrt{3}\right)$?

5a. _____

Step 2: Use the formula from part (a) to multiply and simplify $\left(7 - \sqrt{3}\right)\left(7 + \sqrt{3}\right)$.

5b. _____

Do the Math Exercises 9.5
Adding, Subtracting, and Multiplying Radical Expressions

In Problems 1 – 9, add or subtract as indicated. Assume all variables are positive or zero.

1. $6\sqrt{3} + 8\sqrt{3}$

2. $12\sqrt[4]{z} - 5\sqrt[4]{z}$

1. _____

2. _____

3. $4\sqrt[3]{5} - 3\sqrt{5} + 7\sqrt[3]{5} - 8\sqrt{5}$

4. $6\sqrt{3} + \sqrt{12}$

3. _____

4. _____

5. $7\sqrt[4]{48} - 4\sqrt[4]{243}$

6. $2\sqrt{48z} - \sqrt{75z}$

5. _____

6. _____

7. $3\sqrt{63z^3} + 2z\sqrt{28z}$

8. $\sqrt{48y^3} - 4y\sqrt{12} + \sqrt{108y^3}$

7. _____

8. _____

9. $-2\sqrt[3]{5x^3} + 4x\sqrt[3]{40} - \sqrt[3]{135}$

9. _____

In Problems 10 – 14, multiply and simplify. Assume all variables are positive or zero.

10. $\sqrt{5}\left(5+3\sqrt{3}\right)$

11. $\sqrt[3]{6}\left(\sqrt[3]{2}+\sqrt[3]{12}\right)$

10. _____

11. _____

12. $\left(5+\sqrt{5}\right)\left(3+\sqrt{6}\right)$

13. $\left(9+5\sqrt{10}\right)\left(1-3\sqrt{10}\right)$

12. _____

13. _____

14. $\left(2-\sqrt{3}\right)^2$

14. _____

In Problems 15 – 18, perform the indicated operation and simplify. Assume all variables are positive or zero.

15. $\left(\sqrt{6}-2\sqrt{2}\right)\left(2\sqrt{6}+3\sqrt{2}\right)$

16. $\left(2-\sqrt{3}\right)^2$

15. _____

16. _____

17. $\left(\sqrt[3]{y}-6\right)\left(\sqrt[3]{y}+3\right)$

18. $\dfrac{4}{5}\bullet\left(-\dfrac{\sqrt{5}}{5}\right)+\left(-\dfrac{3}{5}\right)\bullet\left(-\dfrac{2\sqrt{5}}{5}\right)$

17. _____

18. _____

Five-Minute Warm-Up 9.6
Rationalizing Radical Expressions

1. What would be needed to multiply 75 by in order to make it the smallest perfect square that is a multiple of 75?

1.

2. Simplify: $\sqrt{121a^2}$, $a > 0$

2. _____

3. Multiply: $\dfrac{\sqrt{3}}{\sqrt{2}} \cdot \dfrac{\sqrt{6}}{\sqrt{2}}$

3. _____

4. Multiply: $\left(2 + \sqrt{3}\right)\left(2 - \sqrt{3}\right)$

4. _____

5. Multiply: $\left(2\sqrt{5} + \sqrt{3}\right)\left(3\sqrt{5} - 2\sqrt{3}\right)$

5. _____

Guided Practice 9.6
Rationalizing Radical Expressions

Objective 1: Rationalize a Denominator Containing One Term

1. In your own words, what does it mean to rationalize the denominator of a rational expression?

2. To rationalize a denominator containing a single square root, we multiply the numerator and denominator

of the quotient by a square root so that the radicand in the denominator becomes _____.

3. Determine what to multiply each quotient by so that the denominator contains a radicand which is a perfect square. *(See textbook Example 1)*

(a) $\dfrac{3}{\sqrt{3}}$

(b) $\dfrac{4}{\sqrt{20}}$

(c) $\dfrac{1}{\sqrt{8a}}$

3a. _____

3b. _____

3c. _____

4. Determine what to multiply each quotient by so that the denominator contains a radicand which is a perfect power. *(See textbook Example 2)*

(a) $\dfrac{6}{\sqrt[3]{5}}$

(b) $\sqrt[3]{\dfrac{2}{12}}$

(c) $\dfrac{4x}{\sqrt[4]{27x^2 y}}$

4a. _____

4b. _____

4c. _____

Objective 2: Rationalize a Denominator Containing Two Terms

5. To rationalize a denominator containing two terms, we multiply both numerator and denominator by the

_____ of the denominator.

6. Identify the conjugate of each expression. Then multiply the expression by its conjugate. *(See textbook Example 3)*

(a) $3 + \sqrt{5}$ **(b)** $2\sqrt{3} - 5\sqrt{2}$ 6a. _____

6b. _____

7. Determine what to multiply the quotient by to rationalize the denominator $\dfrac{\sqrt{8}}{\sqrt{2} - 3}$.   7. _____

(See textbook Example 3)

Do the Math Exercises 9.6
Rationalizing Radical Expressions

In Problems 1 – 12, rationalize each denominator. Assume all variables are positive.

1. $\dfrac{2}{\sqrt{3}}$

2. $-\dfrac{3}{2\sqrt{3}}$

1. _____

2. _____

3. $\dfrac{\sqrt{3}}{\sqrt{11}}$

4. $\sqrt{\dfrac{5}{z}}$

3. _____

4. _____

5. $\dfrac{\sqrt{32}}{\sqrt{a^5}}$

6. $-\sqrt[3]{\dfrac{4}{p}}$

5. _____

6. _____

7. $-\sqrt[3]{\dfrac{5}{72}}$

8. $\dfrac{8}{\sqrt[3]{36z^2}}$

7. _____

8. _____

9. $\dfrac{6}{\sqrt{7}-2}$

10. $\dfrac{10}{\sqrt{10}+3}$

9. _____

10. _____

11. $\dfrac{\sqrt{3}}{\sqrt{15}-\sqrt{6}}$

12. $\dfrac{2\sqrt{3}+3}{\sqrt{12}-\sqrt{3}}$

11. _____

12. _____

In Problems 13 and 14, perform the indicated operation and simplify.

13. $\sqrt{5}-\dfrac{1}{\sqrt{5}}$

14. $\sqrt{\dfrac{2}{5}}+\sqrt{20}-\sqrt{45}$

13. _____

14. _____

In Problems 15 and 16, simplify each expression so that the denominator does not contain a radical.

15. $\sqrt{\dfrac{9}{5}}$

16. $\dfrac{\sqrt{2}-5}{\sqrt{2}+5}$

15. _____

16. _____

In Problems 17 and 18, rationalize the numerator.

17. $\dfrac{\sqrt{3}+2}{2}$

18. $\dfrac{\sqrt{a}-\sqrt{b}}{\sqrt{2}}$

17. _____

18. _____

Five-Minute Warm-Up 9.7
Functions Involving Radicals

In Problems 1 and 2, simplify each expression.

1. $\sqrt{144}$ **2.** $\sqrt{n^2}, n > 0$

1. _____

2. _____

3. Solve: $-3x - 9 \geq 0$

3. _____

4. Given $f(x) = -2x^2 + 16x$, find $f(-2)$.

4. _____

5. Graph $f(x) = x^2 + 2$ using point plotting.

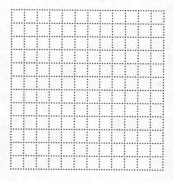

Guided Practice 9.7
Functions Involving Radicals

Objective 1: Evaluate Functions Whose Rule Is a Radical Expression

1. For the functions $f(x) = 2\sqrt{3x-1}$, $g(x) = \sqrt[3]{\dfrac{3x}{x+4}}$, and $h(x) = \sqrt{\dfrac{x+2}{x-2}}$, find each of the following.

(See textbook Example 1)

(a) $f(7)$ **(b)** $g(-3)$ **(c)** $h(6)$

1a. _____

1b. _____

1c. _____

Objective 2: Find the Domain of a Function Whose Rule Contains a Radical

2. If the index on a radical is even, then the radicand must be _____.

3. If the index on a radical is odd, then the radicand can be _____.

4. Find the domain of each of the following functions. *(See textbook Example 2)*

(a) $f(x) = \sqrt{2x-3}$ **(b)** $g(x) = \sqrt[3]{6x-9}$ **(c)** $h(t) = \sqrt[4]{14-7t}$

4a. _____

4b. _____

4c. _____

Objective 3: Graph Functions Involving Square Roots

5. Given the function $f(x) = \sqrt{x+3}$, *(See textbook Example 3)*

(a) find the domain.

5a. _____

(b) graph the function using point-plotting.

(c) Based on the graph, determine the range.

5c. _____

Objective 4: Graph Functions Involving Cube Roots

6. Given the function $g(x) = \sqrt[3]{x} - 3$, *(See textbook Example 4)*

(a) find the domain.

6a. _____

(b) graph the function using point-plotting.

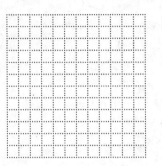

(c) Based on the graph, determine the range.

6c. _____

Do the Math Exercises 9.7
Functions Involving Radicals

In Problems 1 – 3, evaluate each radical function at the indicated values.

1. $f(x) = \sqrt{x + 10}$

    (a) $f(6)$

    (b) $f(2)$

    (c) $f(-6)$

2. $G(t) = \sqrt[3]{t - 6}$

    (a) $G(7)$

    (b) $G(-21)$

    (c) $G(22)$

1a. _____

1b. _____

1c. _____

2a. _____

2b. _____

2c. _____

3. $f(x) = \sqrt{\dfrac{x - 4}{x + 4}}$

    (a) $f(5)$

    (b) $f(8)$

    (c) $f(12)$

3a. _____

3b. _____

3c. _____

In Problems 4 – 8, find the domain of the radical function.

4. $f(x) = \sqrt{x + 4}$

5. $G(x) = \sqrt{5 - 2x}$

4. _____

5. _____

6. $G(z) = \sqrt[3]{5z - 3}$

7. $C(y) = \sqrt[4]{3y - 2}$

6. _____

7. _____

8. $f(x) = \sqrt{\dfrac{3}{x - 3}}$

8. _____

In Problems 9 - 12, (a) determine the domain of the function; (b) determine the range of the function; (c) graph the function using point-plotting.

9. $f(x) = \sqrt{x-1}$

10. $F(x) = \sqrt{4-x}$

9a. _____

9b. _____

10a. _____

10b. _____

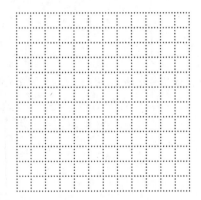

11. $f(x) = \sqrt{x} + 1$

12. $g(x) = \sqrt[3]{x-4}$

11a. _____

11b. _____

12a. _____

12b. _____

Sullivan/Struve/Mazzarella, *Elementary & Intermediate Algebra*, 2e

Five-Minute Warm-Up 9.8
Radical Equations and Their Applications

1. Solve: $4x + 12 = 0$

1. _____

2. Solve: $-4x^2 + 12x - 8 = 0$

2. _____

3. Simplify: $\left(\sqrt{2x}\right)^2$, $x > 0$

3. _____

4. Multiply: $\left(\sqrt{2x} + 5\right)^2$; $x > 0$

4. _____

5. Simplify: $\left[(3x + 8)^{\frac{3}{2}}\right]^{\frac{2}{3}}$; $x > 0$

5. _____

6. Evaluate: $\sqrt{2(-3) + (-3)(-18)}$

6. _____

Guided Practice 9.8
Radical Equations and Their Applications

Objective 1: Solve Radical Equations Containing One Radical

1. Solve: $\sqrt{4x+1} - 2 = 3$ *(See textbook Example 1)*

Step 1: Isolate the radical. $\sqrt{4x+1} - 2 = 3$

Add 2 to both sides:

(a) _____

Step 2: Raise both sides to the power of the index.

The index is 2, so we square both sides:

(b) _____

Simplify:

(c) _____

Step 3: Solve the equation that results.

(d) _____

Step 4: Check

Substitute the value you found in (d) into the original equation. Does this yield a true statement?**(e)** _____

State the solution set:

(f) _____

2. What is meant by *extraneous solutions*?

3. When solving radical equations, what is the key first step? _____

_____

4. Solve: $\sqrt{7x+2} + 5 = 2$ *(See textbook Example 2)*

(a) What value did you find for x?   4a. _____

(b) Does this satisfy the original equation?   4b. _____

(c) State the solution set.   4c. _____

(d) Without solving, how can you tell that this equation has no real solution? 4d. _____

5. Solve: $\sqrt{x+5} + 1 = x$ *(See textbook Example 3)*

(a) What value(s) did you find for x?　　　　　　　　　　　5a. _____

(b) Does this value (or values) satisfy the original equation?　　5b. _____

(c) State the solution set.　　　　　　　　　　　　　　　　5c. _____

6. Solve: $(3x+1)^{\frac{3}{2}} - 2 = 6$ *(See textbook Example 5)*

(a) Isolate the expression containing the rational exponent.　　6a. _____

(b) To what power do we need to raise both sides in order to eliminate the exponent on the variable expression?　　6b. _____

(c) Solve the resulting equation. What value(s) did you find for x?　　6c. _____

(d) Check and then state the solution set.　　　　　　　　　7d. _____

Objective 2: Solve Radical Equations Containing Two Radicals

7. Solve: $\sqrt{2x^2 - 5x - 20} = \sqrt{x^2 - 3x + 15}$ *(See textbook Example 6)*

$$\sqrt{2x^2 - 5x - 20} = \sqrt{x^2 - 3x + 15}$$

Step 1: Isolate one of the radicals.	The radical on the left side of the equation is isolated:	**(a)** _____
Step 2: Raise both sides to the power of the index.	The index is 2, so we square both sides:	**(b)** _____
Step 3: Because there is no radical, we solve the equation that results.		**(c)** _____
Step 4: Check.	Substitute the value(s) you found in (b) into the original equation. Does this yield a true statement? State the solution set:	**(d)** _____ **(e)** _____

Sullivan/Struve/Mazzarella, *Elementary & Intermediate Algebra*, 2e

Do the Math Exercises 9.8
Radical Equations and Their Applications

In Problems 1 – 16, solve each equation.

1. $\sqrt{y-5}=3$

2. $\sqrt{6p-5}=-5$

1. _____

2. _____

3. $\sqrt[3]{9w}=3$

4. $\sqrt{q}-5=2$

3. _____

4. _____

5. $\sqrt{x-4}+4=7$

6. $4\sqrt{t}-2=10$

5. _____

6. _____

7. $\sqrt{w}=w-6$

8. $\sqrt{1-4x}-5=x$

7. _____

8. _____

9. $\sqrt{3x+1}=\sqrt{2x+7}$

10. $\sqrt{2x^2+7x-10}=\sqrt{x^2+4x+8}$

9. _____

10. _____

11. $\sqrt{2x-1}-\sqrt{x-1}=1$ **12.** $\sqrt{4x+1}-\sqrt{2x+1}=2$ 11. _____

12. _____

13. $(6p+3)^{\frac{1}{5}}=(4p-9)^{\frac{1}{5}}$ **14.** $(2x+3)^{\frac{1}{2}}=3$ 13. _____

14. _____

15. $\sqrt[5]{x+23}=2$ **16.** $\sqrt{x-3}+\sqrt{x+4}=7$ 15. _____

16. _____

In Problems 17 and 18, solve for the indicated variable.

17. Solve $v=\sqrt{ar}$ for a.   **18.** Solve $r=\sqrt{\dfrac{S}{4\pi}}$ for S.   17. _____

18. _____

19. Money The annual rate of interest r (expressed as a decimal) required to have A dollars   19. _____
after t years from an initial deposit of P dollars can be calculated with the following
formula:

$$r=\sqrt[t]{\frac{A}{P}}-1$$

Suppose that you deposit \$1,000 in an account that pays 5% annual interest so that
$r=0.05$. How much will you have after $t=2$ years?

Five-Minute Warm-Up 9.9
The Complex Number System

1. List the numbers in the set $\left\{ 8, \dfrac{-6}{3}, \left| -5 \right|, 0.\overline{3}, \dfrac{15}{0}, -\dfrac{2}{5}, \pi, \dfrac{0}{-12} \right\}$ which are:

(a) Natural numbers

1a. _____

(b) Whole numbers

1b. _____

(c) Integers

1c. _____

(d) Rational numbers

1d. _____

(e) Irrational numbers

1e. _____

(f) Real numbers

1f. _____

In Problems 2 – 5, perform the indicated operations and simplify.

2. $\left(x^2 - 1 \right) + \left(2x^2 - 1 \right)$

2. _____

3. $4p^5 \left(-3p + 9 \right)$

3. _____

4. $\left(2x - 7 \right)\left(-3x - 4 \right)$

4. _____

5. $\left(x^2 + 4 \right)\left(x^2 - 4 \right)$

5. _____

Guided Practice 9.9
The Complex Number System

1. The *imaginary unit*, denoted by *i*, is the number whose square is -1. $i^2 =$ _____ or $i =$ _____.

2. *Complex numbers* are numbers of the form _____ where *a* and *b* are _____. When a

number is in a form such as $6 - 2i$, we say that the number is in _____ form. The *real part*

of the complex number is _____ and the *imaginary part* is _____.

Objective 1: Evaluate the Square Root of Negative Real Numbers

3. Write $\sqrt{-81}$ as a pure imaginary number. *(See textbook Example 1)*

3. _____

4. Write $6 + \sqrt{-4}$ in standard form. *(See textbook Example 2)*

4. _____

Objective 2: Add or Subtract Complex Numbers

5. Before beginning any operations with complex numbers, you must write the number in _____
form.

6. In your own words, explain how to add complex numbers _____

_____

Objective 3: Multiply Complex Numbers

7. Use the Distributive Property to multiply $\frac{3}{2}i(6 - 8i)$. *(See textbook Example 5)*

7. _____

8. Multiply $\sqrt{-4} \cdot \sqrt{-9}$. *(See textbook Example 6)*
(a) Explain why the Product Property of Radicals cannot be used to multiply these radicals.

(a)_____

(b) Express the radicals as pure imaginary numbers.

8b._____

(c) Multiply.

8c._____

Objective 4: Divide Complex Numbers

9. Divide: $\dfrac{3+6i}{4+4i}$. *(See textbook Example 8)*

Step 1: Write the numerator and denominator in standard form, $a + bi$.

The numerator and denominator are already in standard form.

Step 2: Multiply the numerator and denominator by the complex conjugate of the denominator.

Identify the conjugate of the denominator:

(a) _____

Multiply the quotient by 1, written with the conjugate:

(b) _____

Step 3: Simplify by writing the quotient in standard form, $a + bi$.

Multiply the numerator; the denominator is of the form $(a+bi)(a-bi) = a^2 + b^2$:

(c) _____

Combine like terms; $i^2 = -1$:

(d) _____

Divide the denominator into each term of the numerator to write in standard form:

(e) _____

Write each fraction in lowest terms:

(f) _____

Objective 5: Evaluate the Powers of i

10. The powers of i are a cyclic function, meaning that the values cycle through a set list. Complete the table to see the only values for the powers of i.

$i = i$

(a) $i^2 = $ _____

(b) $i^3 = $ _____

(c) $i^4 = $ _____

(d) $i^5 = $ _____

(e) $i^6 = $ _____

(f) $i^7 = $ _____

(g) $i^8 = $ _____

Do the Math Exercises 9.9
The Complex Number System

In Problems 1 and 2, write each expression as a pure imaginary number.

1. $-\sqrt{-100}$

2. $\sqrt{-162}$

1. _____

2. _____

In Problems 3 and 4, write each expression as a complex number in standard form.

3. $10 + \sqrt{-32}$

4. $\dfrac{10 - \sqrt{-25}}{5}$

3. _____

4. _____

In Problems 5 – 8, add or subtract as indicated.

5. $(-6 + 2i) + (3 + 12i)$

6. $(-7 + 3i) - (-3 + 2i)$

5. _____

6. _____

7. $\left(-4 + \sqrt{-25}\right) + \left(1 - \sqrt{-16}\right)$

8. $\left(-10 + \sqrt{-20}\right) - \left(-6 + \sqrt{-45}\right)$

7. _____

8. _____

In Problems 9 – 15, multiply.

9. $3i(-2 - 6i)$

10. $(3 - i)(1 + 2i)$

9. _____

10. _____

11. $\left(-\dfrac{2}{3} + \dfrac{4}{3}i\right)\left(\dfrac{1}{2} - \dfrac{3}{2}i\right)$

12. $(2 + 5i)^2$

11. _____

12. _____

13. $(2-7i)^2$

14. $\sqrt{-36} \cdot \sqrt{-4}$

13. _____

14. _____

15. $\left(1-\sqrt{-64}\right)\left(-2+\sqrt{-49}\right)$

15. _____

In Problems 16 – 18, divide.

16. $\dfrac{2-i}{2i}$

17. $\dfrac{2}{4+i}$

16. _____

17. _____

18. $\dfrac{2+5i}{5-2i}$

18. _____

In Problems 19 and 20, simplify.

19. i^{72}

20. i^{131}

19. _____

20. _____

Sullivan/Struve/Mazzarella, *Elementary & Intermediate Algebra*, 2e

Five-Minute Warm-Up 10.1
Solving Quadratic Equations by Completing the Square

1. Multiply: $(3x - 1)^2$

1. _____

2. Factor: $x^2 - 4x + 4$

2. _____

In Problems 3 and 4, solve each polynomial equation.

3. $x^2 - \dfrac{2}{3}x + \dfrac{1}{9} = 0$ **4.** $25n^2 - 49 = 0$

3. _____

4. _____

In Problems 5 and 6, simplify each expression.

5. $\sqrt{\dfrac{81}{25}}$ **6.** $\sqrt{(8x - 3)^2}$

5. _____

6. _____

In Problems 7 and 8, simplify each expression using complex numbers.

7. $\sqrt{-12}$ **8.** $\dfrac{8 + \sqrt{-4}}{4}$

7. _____

8. _____

9. Find the complex conjugate of $-15 + 7i$.

9. _____

Guided Practice 10.1
Solving Quadratic Equations by Completing the Square

Objective 1: Solve Quadratic Equations Using the Square Root Property

1. State the Square Root Property: If $x^2 = p$, where x is any variable expression and p is a real number,

then _____.

2. If the solution to a quadratic equation is $n = -1 \pm 2\sqrt{3}$, write the solution set. _____

3. *True or False:* $\sqrt{x^2 - 16} = \sqrt{81}$ simplifies to $x - 4 = \pm 9$. _____

4. *True or False:* $y^2 = -9$ has no solution. _____

5. Solve: $n^2 - 144 = 0$ *(See textbook Example 1)*

Step 1: Isolate the expression containing the square term.		$n^2 - 144 = 0$
	Add 144 to both sides:	**(a)** _____
Step 2: Use the Square Root Property. Don't forget the $\pm$ symbol.	Take the square root of both sides of the equation:	**(b)** _____
	Simplify the radical:	**(c)** _____
Step 3: Isolate the variable, if necessary.		The variable is already isolated.
Step 4: Verify your solution(s).		
	State the solution set:	**(d)** _____

6. There is no reason that the solution to a quadratic equation must be real. List the possible nature of the solution(s) of a quadratic equation.

(a) Real, which includes: _____, _____, _____

(b) _____ in form _____

Objective 2: *Complete the Square in One Variable*

7. If a polynomial is of the form $x^2 + bx + c$, c must be equal to _____ in order to be a perfect square trinomial.

8. Determine the number that must be added to the expression to make it a perfect square trinomial. Then factor the expression. *(See textbook Example 5)*

(a) $p^2 - 14p$ **(b)** $n^2 + 9n$ **(c)** $z^2 + \dfrac{4}{3}z$

8a. _____

8b. _____

8c. _____

Objective 3: *Solve Quadratic Equations by Completing the Square*

9. Solve: $p^2 - 6p - 18 = 0$ *(See textbook Example 6)*

		$p^2 - 6p - 18 = 0$
Step 1: Rewrite $x^2 + bx + c = 0$ as $x^2 + bx = -c$ by adding or subtracting the constant from both sides of the equation.	Add 18 to both sides:	**(a)** _____
Step 2: Complete the square in the expression $x^2 + bx$ by making it a perfect square trinomial.	What value must be added to both sides to make the expression on the left a perfect square trinomial?	**(b)** _____
	Add this number to both sides of the equation and simplify:	**(c)** _____
Step 3: Factor the perfect square trinomial on the left side of the equation.	Use: $A^2 - 2AB + B^2 = (A - B)^2$	**(d)** _____
Step 4: Solve the equation using the Square Root Property.	Take the square root of both sides of the equation:	**(e)** _____
	Simplify the square root:	**(f)** _____
	Add 3 to both sides:	**(g)** _____
Step 5: Verify your solutions(s).		
	State the solution set:	**(h)** _____

10. To solve the equation $3x^2 - 9x + 12 = 0$ by the completing the square, the first step is_____.

Objective 4: *Solve Problems Using the Pythagorean Theorem*

11. State the Pythagorean Theorem in words. If x and y are the lengths of the legs and z is the length of the hypotenuse, write an equation which uses these variables to state the Pythagorean Theorem.

Do the Math Exercises 10.1
Solving Quadratic Equations by Completing the Square

In Problems 1 – 6, solve each equation using the Square Root Property.

1. $z^2 = 48$

2. $w^2 - 6 = 14$

1. _____

2. _____

3. $(y - 2)^2 = 9$

4. $(2p + 3)^2 = 16$

3. _____

4. _____

5. $\left(y + \dfrac{3}{2}\right)^2 = \dfrac{3}{4}$

6. $q^2 - 6q + 9 = 16$

5. _____

6. _____

In Problems 7 – 9, find the value to complete the square in each expression. Then factor the perfect square trinomial.

7. $p^2 - 4p$

8. $z^2 - \dfrac{1}{3}z$

7. _____
   _____

8. _____
   _____

9. $m^2 + \dfrac{5}{2}m$

9. _____
   _____

In Problems 10 – 15, solve each quadratic equation by completing the square.

10. $y^2 + 3y - 18 = 0$

11. $q^2 + 7q + 7 = 0$

10. _____

11. _____

12. $x^2 - 5x - 3 = 0$

13. $n^2 = 10n + 5$

12. _____

13. _____

14. $3a^2 - 4a - 4 = 0$

15. $2z^2 + 6z + 5 = 0$

14. _____

15. _____

In Problems 16 and 17, the lengths of the legs of a right triangle are given. Find the length of the hypotenuse. Give the exact answers and decimal approximations rounded to two decimal places.

16. $a = 7, b = 24$ **17.** $a = 2, b = \sqrt{5}$ 16. _____

17. _____

18. Right Triangle A right triangle has a leg of length 2 and hypotenuse of length 10.   18. _____
   Find the length of the missing leg. Give the exact answer and a decimal approximation,
   rounded to 2 decimal places.

19. Given that $h(x) = (x + 1)^2$, find all values of x such that $h(x) = 32$.   19. _____

20. Fire Truck Ladder A fire truck has a 75-foot ladder. If the truck can safely park 20   20. _____
   feet from a building, how far up the building can the ladder reach assuming that the top
   of the base of the ladder is resting on top of the truck and the truck is 10 feet tall? Give
   the decimal approximation, rounded to 3 decimal places.

Five-Minute Warm-Up 10.2
Solving Quadratic Equations by the Quadratic Formula

In Problems 1 and 2, simplify each expression.

1. $\sqrt{125}$

2. $\dfrac{15 + \sqrt{72}}{6}$

1. _____

2. _____

In Problems 3 and 4, simplify each expression using complex numbers.

3. $\sqrt{-28}$

4. $\dfrac{6 - 2\sqrt{-4}}{6}$

3. _____

4. _____

5. Divide: $\dfrac{9x^2 - 27x + 3}{3}$

5. _____

6. Evaluate the expression $\sqrt{b^2 - 4ac}$ if $a = 2, b = -4, c = -3$.

6. _____

Guided Practice 10.2
Solving Quadratic Equations by the Quadratic Formula

Objective 1: Solve Quadratic Equations Using the Quadratic Formula

1. If $ax^2 + bx + c = 0$, then $x =$ _____.

2. When using the quadratic formula, the first step is to write the quadratic equation in _____.

3. Write the quadratic equation in standard form and then identify the values assigned to a, b, and c.
    Do not solve the equation.

(a) $x - 2x^2 = -4$ **(b)** $2 - 3x^2 = 8$ **(c)** $3x^2 = 6x$ 3a. _____

3b. _____

3c. _____

4. Solve: $8n^2 - 2n - 3 = 0$ *(See textbook Example 1)*

Step 1: Write the equation in standard form $ax^2 + bx + c = 0$ and identify the values of a, b, and c.

$8n^2 - 2n - 3 = 0$

Since the equation is already in standard form, identify the values for a, b, and c.

(a) $a =$ _____; $b =$ _____; $c =$ _____

Step 2: Substitute the values of a, b, and c into the quadratic formula.

Write the quadratic formula: **(b)** _____

Substitute the values for a, b, and c.   **(c)** _____

Step 3: Simplify the expression found in Step 2.

What is the value of the radicand?   **(d)** _____

Simplify the expression in (c):   **(e)** _____

Write the two expressions using $a \pm b$ means $a - b$ or $a + b$:   **(f)** _____

Step 4: Check

State the solution set: **(g)** _____

Objective 2: Use the Discriminant to Determine the Nature of Solutions in a Quadratic Equation

5. In the quadratic equation $ax^2 + bx + c = 0$, the *discriminant* is used to determine the nature and number of solutions. To find the discriminant, substitute the identified values for a, b, and c into part of the quadratic

formula, _____.

6. Determine the discriminant of each quadratic equation. Use the value of the discriminant to determine whether the quadratic equation has two rational solutions, two irrational solutions, one repeated real solution, or two complex solutions that are not real. *(See textbook Example 5)*

6a. _____

(a) $4x^2 + 5x - 9 = 0$ **(b)** $x^2 + 4x + 9 = 0$ **(c)** $4x^2 = 4x - 1$

_____

6b. _____

_____

6c. _____

_____

Objective 3: Model and Solve Problems Involving Quadratic Equations

7. Advertising Costs Joel has started a catering business for which he buys advertising. He predicts that as time goes by, this expense will decrease because he will have all the business he can handle. A model that predicts the monthly advertising expenditures N (in dollars) x years after he opens his business is given by the equation $N = \dfrac{2000}{x^2 + 5}$. How much did Joel spend on advertising during the third year his catering business was in operation? *(See textbook Example 6)*

(a) Step 1: Identify Here we want to know the value N when $x = ?$ _____

    Step 2: Name The variables are named in the problem. N is monthly advertising expenditures and x is years of operation.

(b) Step 3: Translate Use the information from (a) and the given formula to write a model for this problem.

_____

(c) Step 4: Solve Simplify your expression in (b). What value did you find for N?

_____

(d) Since N represents the monthly cost, what was Joel's annual expenditure? _____

    Step 5: Check

(e) Step 6: Answer the Question _____

     Sullivan/Struve/Mazzarella, *Elementary & Intermediate Algebra, 2e*

Do the Math Exercises 10.2
Solving Quadratic Equations by the Quadratic Formula

In Problems 1 – 6, solve each equation using the quadratic formula.

1. $p^2 - 4p - 32 = 0$ **2.** $10x^2 + x - 2 = 0$

1. _____

2. _____

3. $2q^2 - 4q + 1 = 0$ **4.** $x + \dfrac{1}{x} = 3$

3. _____

4. _____

5. $2z^2 + 7 = 4z$ **6.** $1 = 5w^2 + 6w$

5. _____

6. _____

In Problems 7 – 9, determine the discriminant of each quadratic equation. Use the value of the discriminant to determine whether the quadratic equation has two rational solutions, two irrational solutions, one repeated real solution, or two complex solutions that are not real.

7. $p^2 + 4p - 2 = 0$ **8.** $16x^2 + 24x + 9 = 0$

7. _____

8. _____

9. $6x^2 - x = -4$

9. _____

In Problems 10 – 15, solve each equation using any method you wish.

10. $q^2 - 7q + 7 = 0$ **11.** $3x^2 + 5x = 2$

10. _____

11. _____

12. $5m - 4 = \dfrac{5}{m}$

13. $8p^2 - 40p + 50 = 0$

12. _____

13. _____

14. $(a - 3)(a + 1) = 2$

15. $\dfrac{x-1}{x^2 + 4} = 1$

14. _____

15. _____

In Problem 16, suppose that $f(x) = x^2 + 2x - 8$.

16a. Solve for x, if $f(x) = 0$

16b. Solve for x, if $f(x) = -8$

16a. _____

16b. _____

17. Area The area of a rectangle is 60 square inches. The length of the rectangle is 6 inches more than the width. What are the dimensions of the rectangle?

17. _____

18. Area The area of a triangle is 35 square inches. The height of the rectangle is 2 inches less than the base. What are the base and height of the triangle?

18. _____

19. Roundtrip A Cessna aircraft flies 200 miles due west into the jet stream and flies back home on the same route. The total time of the trip (excluding the time on the ground) takes 4 hours. The Cessna aircraft can fly 120 miles per hour in still air. What is the net effect of the jet stream on the aircraft?

19. _____

Five-Minute Warm-Up 10.3
Solving Equations Quadratic in Form

In Problems 1 and 2, factor completely.

1. $a^4 - 7a^2 - 18$

2. $6(x-1)^2 - 13(x-1) + 6$

1. _____

2. _____

In Problems 3 and 4, simplify each expression.

3. $\left(5x^{-1}\right)^2$

4. $\left(-\dfrac{2}{3}x^3\right)^2$

3. _____

4. _____

5. Solve: $2x^2 + x - 6 = 0$

5. _____

Guided Practice 10.3
Solving Equations Quadratic in Form

Objective 1: Solve Equations That Are Quadratic in Form

1. In general, if a substitution u transforms an equation into one of the form $au^2 + bu + c = 0$, then the original equation is call an **equation quadratic in form.** Here u represents any variable expression and we solve the equation by substituting u for the variable expression written with the coefficient b. For these equations quadratic in form, identify the substitution for u and then write a new equation using your substitution.

(a) $2y - 11\sqrt{y} + 15 = 0$ $u = \underline{\hspace{2cm}}$ $\underline{\hspace{4cm}}$

(b) $v^4 + 10v^2 + 1 = 0$ $u = \underline{\hspace{2cm}}$ $\underline{\hspace{4cm}}$

(c) $(x-1)^2 - 5(x-1) + 6 = 0$ $u = \underline{\hspace{2cm}}$ $\underline{\hspace{4cm}}$

(d) $x^{2/3} - x^{1/3} - 3 = 0$ $u = \underline{\hspace{2cm}}$ $\underline{\hspace{4cm}}$

(e) $4x^{-2} + x^{-1} - 3 = 0$ $u = \underline{\hspace{2cm}}$ $\underline{\hspace{4cm}}$

2. Solve: $x^4 - 6x^2 - 16 = 0$ *(See textbook Example 1)*

Step 1: Determine the appropriate substitution and write the equation in the form $au^2 + bu + c = 0$.	Here we let $u = ?$	**(a)** _____
	Rewrite the equation using your substitution from (a):	$x^4 - 6x^2 - 16 = 0$ **(b)** _____
Step 2: Solve the equation $au^2 + bu + c = 0$.	Factor:	**(c)** _____
	Set each factor to 0 and solve:	**(d)** _____
Step 3: Solve for the variable in the original equation using the value of u from (a).	Substitute from (a) into your solution from (d):	**(e)** _____
	Solve the equations. In this case we use the Square Root Property:	**(f)** _____
	Simplify the radicals:	**(g)** _____
Step 4: Verify your solution(s).	State the solution set:	**(h)** _____

3. Solve: $\left(x^2 + 3\right)^2 - 6\left(x^2 + 3\right) + 8 = 0$ *(See textbook Example 2)*

(a) Here we let $u =$ _____.

(b) In this problem, $u = 4$ or $u = 2$. Replace u and solve for x. State the solution set. _____

4. Solve: $2x + \sqrt{x} - 10 = 0$ *(See textbook Example 3)*

(a) Here we let $u =$ _____.

(b) In this problem, $u = -\dfrac{5}{2}$ or $u = 2$. Replace u and solve for x. State the solution set. _____

5. Solve: $n^{2/3} - 2n^{1/3} - 3 = 0$ *(See textbook Example 5)*

(a) Here we let $u =$ _____.

(b) In this problem, $u = 3$ or $u = -1$. Replace u and solve for x. State the solution set. _____

6. As always, it is important to check for extraneous solutions. List two cases when extraneous solutions might appear.

(a) _____   **(b)** _____

Do the Math Exercises 10.3
Solving Equations Quadratic in Form

In Problems 1 – 14, solve each equation.

1. $x^4 - 10x^2 + 9 = 0$

2. $4b^4 - 5b^2 + 1 = 0$

1. _____

2. _____

3. $(x + 2)^2 - 3(x + 2) - 10 = 0$

4. $x - 5\sqrt{x} - 6 = 0$

3. _____

4. _____

5. $z + 7\sqrt{z} + 6 = 0$

6. $q^{-2} + 2q^{-1} = 15$

5. _____

6. _____

7. $10a^{-2} + 23a^{-1} = 5$

8. $y^{2/3} - 2y^{1/3} - 3 = 0$

7. _____

8. _____

9. $\dfrac{1}{x^2} - \dfrac{7}{x} + 12 = 0$

10. $y^6 - 7y^3 - 8 = 0$

9. _____

10. _____

11. $6b^{-2} - b^{-1} = 1$

12. $x^4 + 3x^2 = 4$

11. _____

12. _____

13. $c^{\frac{1}{2}} + c^{\frac{1}{4}} - 12 = 0$

14. $\left(\dfrac{1}{x-1}\right)^2 + \dfrac{7}{x-1} = 8$

13. _____

14. _____

In Problems 15 and 16, suppose that $f(x) = x^4 + 5x^2 + 3$. *Find the values of x such that*

15. $f(x) = 3$

16. $f(x) = 17$

15. _____

16. _____

In Problems 17 and 18, suppose that $h(x) = 3x^4 - 9x^2 - 8$. *Find the values of x such that*

17. $h(x) = -8$

18. $h(x) = 22$

17. _____

18. _____

In Problems 19 and 20, find the zeros of the function.

19. $f(x) = x^4 - 13x^2 + 42$

20. $h(p) = 8p - 18\sqrt{p} - 35$

19. _____

20. _____

Five-Minute Warm-Up 10.4
Graphing Quadratic Functions Using Transformations

In Problems 1 and 2, graph using the point-plotting method.

1. $y = -x^2$

2. $y = x^2 + 2$

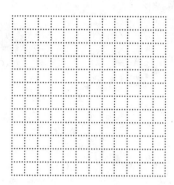

In Problems 3 and 4, find the function value.

3. $f(x) = -x^2 + 6x - 2; f(-3)$

4. $f(x) = 2x^2 + x + 5; f(-4)$

3._____

4._____

5. What is the domain of $f(x) = \dfrac{1}{2}x^2 + \dfrac{4}{3}x - 6$?

5._____

Guided Practice 10.4
Graphing Quadratic Functions Using Transformations

Objective 1: Graph Quadratic Functions of the Form $f(x) = x^2 + k$

In Problems 1 and 2, match the function to either graph (a) *or graph* (b).

1. $f(x) = x^2$ **(a)**   **(b)**   1. _____

2. $f(x) = -x^2$ 2. _____

3. To obtain the graph of $f(x) = x^2 - 2$, shift the graph of $f(x) = x^2$

(a) horizontally or vertically? *(See textbook Example 1 and Example 2)*   3a. _____

(b) How many units will the graph shift?   3b. _____

(c) Does the graph shift right, left, up, or down?   3c. _____

Objective 2: Graph Quadratic Functions of the Form $f(x) = (x - h)^2$

4. To obtain the graph of $f(x) = -(x - 1)^2$, shift the graph of $f(x) = -x^2$

(a) horizontally or vertically? *(See textbook Example 3 and Example 4)*   4a. _____

(b) How many units will the graph shift?   4b. _____

(c) Does the graph shift right, left, up, or down?   4c. _____

Objective 3: Graph Quadratic Functions of the Form $f(x) = ax^2$

5. The graph of $f(x) = ax^2 + bx + c$ is a parabola that opens either up or down. This is determined by the coefficient *a*. *(See textbook Example 6)*
(a) If $a > 0$, the parabola opens   5a. _____

(b) If $a < 0$, the parabola opens   5b. _____

6. The value of *a* will also determine the breadth of the parabola.

(a) If $|a|$ _____ we say the graph is vertically stretched (taller, thinner, steeper).

(b) If _____ $|a|$ _____ we say the graph is vertically compressed (shorter, fatter, flatter).

Objective 4: Graph Quadratic Functions of the Form $f(x) = ax^2 + bx + c$

7. Graph $f(x) = 3x^2 - 12x + 7$. *(See textbook Example 7 and Example 8)*

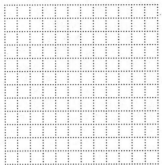

Step 1: Write the function $f(x) = ax^2 + bx + c$ as $f(x) = a(x-h)^2 + k$ by completing the square.

$$f(x) = 3x^2 - 12x + 7$$

Group the terms involving x: **(a)** _____

Factor out the coefficient of the square term, 3, from the parentheses: **(b)** _____

Identify the number required to complete the square: **(c)** _____

When this added to the right side of the equation, what must be done to maintain the equality? **(d)** _____

Write the amended equation: **(e)** _____

Factor the perfect square trinomial: **(f)** _____

Step 2: Graph the function $f(x) = a(x-h)^2 + k$ using transformations.

Identify the vertex: **(g)** _____

Opening direction: **(h)** _____

Axis of symmetry: **(i)** _____

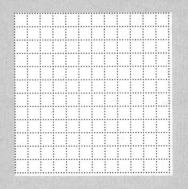

Do the Math Exercises 10.4
Graphing Quadratic Functions Using Transformations

In Problems 1 – 6, use the graph of $y = x^2$ to graph the quadratic function.

1. $f(x) = x^2 - 1$

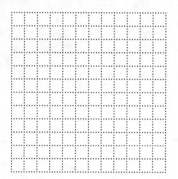

2. $f(x) = (x + 4)^2$

3. $G(x) = 5x^2$

4. $P(x) = -3x^2$

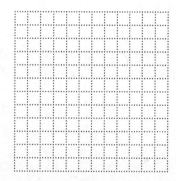

5. $g(x) = (x + 2)^2 - 1$

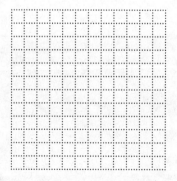

6. $G(x) = (x - 4)^2 + 2$

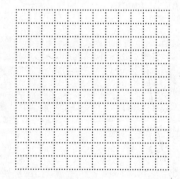

In Problems 7 – 10, write each function in the form $f(x) = a(x - h)^2 + k$. *Then determine the vertex and the axis of symmetry.*

7. $h(x) = x^2 - 7x + 10$

8. $f(x) = 3x^2 + 18x + 25$

7. _____

8. _____

9. $g(x) = -x^2 - 8x - 14$

10. $h(x) = -4x^2 + 4x$

9. _____

10. _____

11. Write a quadratic function in the form $f(x) = a(x - h)^2 + k$ with the properties: opens up; vertically compressed by a factor of ½ ; vertex at $(-5, 0)$

11. _____

12. Determine the quadratic function whose graph is shown below. Each tick mark represents one unit of length.

14. _____

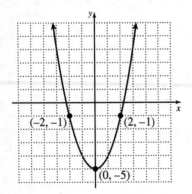

Sullivan/Struve/Mazzarella, *Elementary & Intermediate Algebra*, 2e

Five-Minute Warm-Up 10.5
Graphing Quadratic Functions Using Properties

1. Find the intercepts of the graph of $3x - 4y = -12$.

1. _____

   _____

2. Solve: $2x^2 - 13x - 24 = 0$

2. _____

3. Find the zeros of $f(x) = -2x^2 + 10x + 12$

3. _____

4. If $f(x) = -x^2 - 3x - 2$, find $f(-5)$.

4. _____

Guided Practice 10.5
Graphing Quadratic Functions Using Properties

Objective 1: **Graph Quadratic Functions of the Form** $f(x) = ax^2 + bx + c$

1. The vertex is the turning point of the parabola. If $f(x) = ax^2 + bx + c$, the x-coordinate of the vertex is at

$x =$ _____.

2. The x-intercepts of the parabola can be found by _____.

3. Graph $f(x) = x^2 + 2x - 8$ using its properties. *(See textbook Example 1)*

Step 1: Determine whether the parabola opens up or down.

Determine the values using $f(x) = ax^2 + bx + c$:

(a) $a =$ _____; $b =$ _____; $c =$ _____

Does the parabola open up or down?

(b) _____

Step 2: Determine the vertex and axis of symmetry.

Calculate the x-coordinate of the vertex $\left(x = -\dfrac{b}{2a} \right)$:

(c) _____

Calculate the y-coordinate of the vertex:

(d) _____

Identify the vertex:

(e) _____

Identify the axis of symmetry:

(f) _____

Step 3: Determine the y-intercept.

Evaluate $f(0)$:

(g) _____

Step 4: Find the discriminant, $b^2 - 4ac$, to determine the number of the x-intercepts. Then determine the x-intercepts, if any.

Evaluate the discriminant:

(h) _____

Number of x-intercepts:

(i) _____

Factor $0 = x^2 + 2x - 8$ and use the Zero-Product Property to identify the x-intercepts:

(j) _____

Step 5: Plot the vertex, y-intercept, and x-intercepts. Use the axis of symmetry to find an additional point. Draw the graph of the quadratic function.

Graph:

(k)

Objective 2: Find the Maximum or Minimum Value of a Quadratic Function

4. The maximum or minimum value of a quadratic function is the _____ of the vertex.

In Problems 5 and 6, determine whether the function has a maximum or a minimum value. (See textbook Example 5)

5. $f(x) = -2x^2 + 4x + 3$
6. $f(x) = 3x^2 + 12x - 1$

5. _____

6. _____

Objective 3: Model and Solve Optimization Problem Involving Quadratic Functions

7. Martin is making a dog run in which he will keep his show dogs and decides to enclose an area of his backyard. He uses one side of his house for the pen and encloses the other three sides with fencing. If he has 50 feet of fencing he plans to use, what are the dimensions of the pen that encloses the most area? *(See textbook Example 7)*

Step 1: Identify We wish to determine the dimensions of the rectangle that maximize the area.

Step 2: Name We let x represent one side of the rectangle and y represent the other side.

Step 3: Translate Since we are looking for the maximum area, we use the formula $A = lw$. Our goal is to have A written in terms of one variable. In this case we will choose x, but y will work as well.

(a) Our rectangle has sides x and y. Write an equation for the area using x and y . _____

(b) There is 50 feet of fencing for three sides. Write this equation: _____

(c) Solve for y: _____

(d) Substitute this expression into your equation from (a): _____

(e) Step 4: Solve The maximum occurs at the y-coordinate of the vertex: _____

(f) Substitute your value for x into (b) to find the value for y: _____
   Step 5: Check

(g) Step 6: Answer the Question _____

(h) What is the maximum area Martin can enclose? _____

Do the Math Exercises 10.5
Graphing Quadratic Functions Using Properties

In Problems 1 – 3, use the discriminant to determine the number of x-intercepts the graph of each function will have. Then determine the x-intercepts.

1. $g(x) = 2x^2 - 7x - 4$ **2.** $f(x) = x^2 - 6x + 9$

1. _____

2. _____

3. $P(x) = -2x^2 + 3x + 1$

3. _____

In Problems 4 – 9, graph each quadratic function.

4. $f(x) = x^2 - 2x - 8$

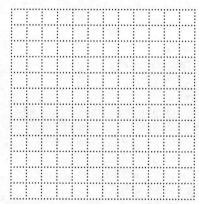

5. $g(x) = -x^2 + 2x + 15$

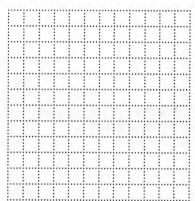

6. $f(x) = x^2 - 4x + 7$

7. $P(x) = -x^2 - 12x - 36$

8. $g(x) = (x + 2)^2 - 1$

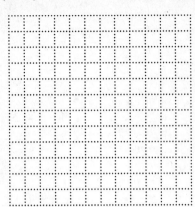

9. $G(x) = (x - 4)^2 + 2$

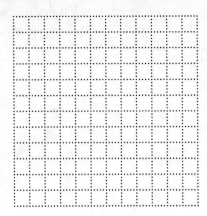

In Problems 10 and 11, determine whether the quadratic function has a maximum or minimum. Then find the maximum or minimum value.

10. $H(x) = -3x^2 + 12x - 1$ **11.** $G(x) = 5x^2 + 10x - 1$

10. _____

11. _____

12. Fun with Numbers The sum of two numbers is 50. Find the numbers such that their product is a maximum.

12. _____

13. Fun with Numbers The difference of two numbers is 10. Find the numbers such that their product is a minimum.

13. _____

14. Punkin Chunkin Suppose that catapult in the Punkin Chunkin contest releases a pumpkin 8 feet above the ground at an angle of $45°$ to the horizontal with an initial speed 220 feet per second. The model $s(t) = -16t^2 + 155t + 8$ can be used to estimate the height s of an object after t seconds.

(a) Determine the time at which the pumpkin is at a maximum height.

14a. _____

(b) Determine the maximum height of the pumpkin.

14b. _____

(c) After how long will the pumpkin strike the ground?

14c. _____

Five-Minute Warm-Up 10.6
Quadratic Inequalities

In Problems 1 – 4, write in interval notation.

1. $-4 \leq x < -2$

2. $-3 < x \leq 1$

1. _____

2. _____

3. $x > -2$

4. $x \leq 5$

3. _____

4. _____

5. Solve: $6x + 3 \leq 11x - 7$

5. _____

6. Solve: $(x - 3)(x + 1) = 2$

6. _____

Guided Practice 10.6
Quadratic Inequalities

Objective 1: Solve Quadratic Inequalities

1. A quadratic inequality is an inequality written in one of the following forms:

$ax^2 + bx + c > 0$; $ax^2 + bx + c \geq 0$; $ax^2 + bx + c < 0$; $ax^2 + bx + c \leq 0$.

(a) If $f(x)$ is a quadratic function and $f(x) > 0$, we are interested in finding x values for which the function is _____(above or below) the x-axis.

1a. _____

(b) If $f(x)$ is a quadratic function and $f(x) < 0$, we are interested in finding x values for which the function is _____(above or below) the x-axis.

1b. _____

2. We will present two methods for solving quadratic inequalities. These methods are:

2a. _____

2b. _____

3. Solve $x^2 + 2x - 3 \leq 0$ using the graphical method. *(See textbook Example 1)*

Step 1: Write the inequality so that $ax^2 + bx + c$ is on one side of the inequality and 0 is on the other.

The inequality is already in this form:

$$x^2 + 2x - 3 \leq 0$$

Step 2: Graph the function $f(x) = ax^2 + bx + c$. Be sure to label the x-intercepts on the graph.

Function to be graphed: **(a)** _____

x-intercepts: **(b)** _____

Vertex: **(c)** _____

(d) Graph:

Step 3: From the graph, determine where the function is positive and where the function is negative. Use the graph to determine the solution set to the inequality.

Are we looking for positive or negative function values in this problem?

(e) _____

State the solution set: **(f)** _____

4a. If $f(x)$ is a quadratic function in factored form and $f(x) > 0$, we are interested in finding the product of the factors for which the function is _____(positive or negative).

4a. _____

4b. If $f(x)$ is a quadratic function in factored form and $f(x) < 0$, we are interested in finding the product of the factors for which the function is _____(positive or negative).

4b. _____

5. Solve $x^2 + 2x - 35 > 0$ using the algebraic method. *(See textbook Example 2)*

Step 1: Write the inequality so that $ax^2 + bx + c$ is on one side of the inequality and 0 is on the other.

The inequality is already in this form:

$$x^2 + 2x - 35 > 0$$

Step 2: Determine the solutions to the equation $ax^2 + bx + c = 0$. Factor:

(a) _____

Use Zero-Product Property: **(b)** _____

Step 3: Use the solutions to the equation solved in Step 2 to separate the real number line into intervals.

List the intervals: **(c)** _____

Step 4: Write the expression in factored form. Within each interval formed in Step 3, choose a test point and determine the sign of each factor. Then determine the sign of the product. Also determine the value of the expression at each solution found in Step 2.

(d) Complete the chart below:

Interval	$(-\infty, \underline{\quad})$	$x = \underline{\quad}$	$(\underline{\quad}, \underline{\quad})$	$x = \underline{\quad}$	$(\underline{\quad}, \infty)$
Test Point					
Sign of ___					
Sign of ___					
Sign of Product					
Conclusion					

To find the solution, select the intervals where the product is (positive or negative)? **(e)** _____

Is 0 included in the solution set? **(f)** _____

State the solution set: **(g)** _____

Do the Math Exercises 10.6
Quadratic Inequalities

In Problems 1 – 10, solve each inequality. Write the solution set in interval notation.

1. $(x-8)(x+1) \leq 0$

2. $(x-4)(x-10) > 0$

1. _____

2. _____

3. $p^2 + 5p + 4 < 0$

4. $2b^2 + 5b < 7$

3. _____

4. _____

5. $x + 6 < x^2$

6. $x^2 - 3x - 5 \geq 0$

5. _____

6. _____

7. $-3p^2 < 3p - 5$

8. $y^2 + 3y + 5 \geq 0$

7. _____

8. _____

9. $3w^2 + w < -2$

10. $p^2 - 8p + 16 \leq 0$

9. _____

10. _____

In Problems 11 and 12, for each function find the values of x that satisfy the given condition.

11. Solve $f(x) > 0$ if $f(x) = x^2 + 4x$ **12.** Solve $f(x) \le 0$ if $f(x) = x^2 + 2x - 48$ 11. _____

12. _____

In Problems 13 and 14, find the domain of the given function.

13. $f(x) = \sqrt{x^2 - 5x}$ **14.** $G(x) = \sqrt{x^2 + 2x - 63}$ 13. _____

14. _____

15. Revenue Function Suppose that the marketing department of Samsung has found that,   15. _____
when a certain model of cellular telephone is sold a price of p dollars, the daily revenue
R (in dollars) as a function of the price p is $R(p) = -5p^2 + 600p$. Determine the prices
for which revenue will exceed $17,500. That is, solve $R(p) > 17,500$.

Sullivan/Struve/Mazzarella, *Elementary & Intermediate Algebra*, 2e

Five-Minute Warm-Up 10.7
Rational Inequalities

1. Write in interval notation: $-3 \le x < 2$

1. _____

2. Solve and graph the solution set: $-5x + 1 > 9 + 3(2x + 1)$

2. _____

3. Solve and write the solution set in interval notation: $\dfrac{3z - 1}{4} - 1 \le \dfrac{6z + 5}{2}$

3. _____

4. Determine whether $x = -2$ satisfies the inequality $5x + 17 \ge 7$.

4. _____

Guided Practice 10.7
Rational Inequalities

Objective 1: Solve a Rational Inequality

1. Solving rational inequalities depends on finding intervals where the polynomials in the rational expression are positive or negative. This means that the inequality must be of the form:

(a) $\dfrac{p(x)}{q(x)} > $ _____ or $\dfrac{p(x)}{q(x)} \geq$ _____ when the quotient is positive and

(b) $\dfrac{p(x)}{q(x)} < $ _____ or $\dfrac{p(x)}{q(x)} \leq$ _____ when the quotient is negative.

2. The quotient is positive when both $p(x)$ and $q(x)$ are _____ or when both $p(x)$ and $q(x)$ are _____.

3. The quotient is negative when $p(x)$ is _____ and $q(x)$ is _____ or when $p(x)$ is _____ and $q(x)$ is _____.

4. We always exclude the values that cause _____.

5. Solve $\dfrac{x+2}{x-4} \leq 0$. Graph the solution set. *(See textbook Example 1)*

Step 1: Write the inequality so that a rational expression is on one side of the inequality and zero is on the other. Be sure to write the rational expression as a single quotient.	$\dfrac{x+2}{x-4} \leq 0$ is already in the required form.

Step 2: Determine the numbers for which the rational expression equals 0 or is undefined.

Value(s) when the rational expression $= 0$: (a) _____

Value(s) when the rational expression is undefined: (b) _____

Step 3: Use the numbers found in Step 2 to separate the real number line into intervals.

Step 4: Choose a test point within each interval formed in Step 3 to determine the sign of $x+2$ and $x-4$. Then determine the sign of the quotient.

Select a test point in the interval $(-\infty, -2)$: (c) _____

Sign of $x+2$: (d) _____

Sign of $x-4$:

(e) _____

Sign of the quotient: (f) _____

continued next page

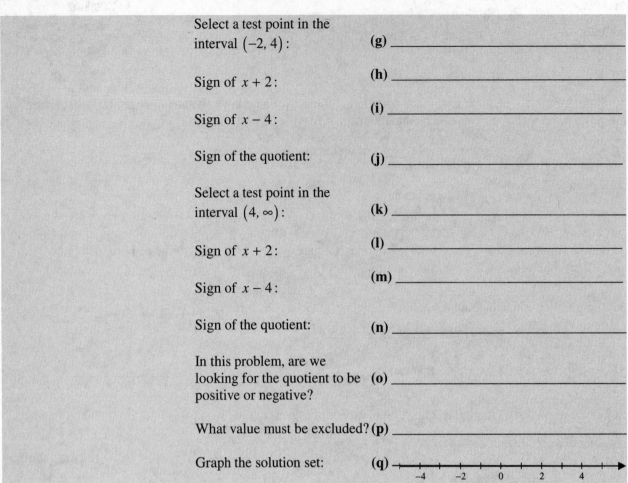

Select a test point in the
interval $(-2, 4)$: **(g)** _____

Sign of $x + 2$: **(h)** _____

(i) _____

Sign of $x - 4$:

Sign of the quotient: **(j)** _____

Select a test point in the
interval $(4, \infty)$: **(k)** _____

Sign of $x + 2$: **(l)** _____

(m) _____

Sign of $x - 4$:

Sign of the quotient: **(n)** _____

In this problem, are we
looking for the quotient to be **(o)** _____
positive or negative?

What value must be excluded? **(p)** _____

Graph the solution set: **(q)**

6. Rewrite the rational expression $\dfrac{5}{x-1} - \dfrac{7}{x+1} > 0$ as single rational expression which

is positive.

6. _____

7. Rewrite the rational expression $\dfrac{3x-7}{x+2} < 2$ as single rational expression which is

negative.

7. _____

8. Complete the following chart used to solve $\dfrac{(x+4)(x-3)}{x-2} \geq 0$. *(See textbook Example 2)*

Interval	$(-\infty, -4)$	-4	$(-4, 2)$	2	$(2, 3)$	3	$(3, \infty)$
Test Point							
Sign of $x + 4$							
Sign of $x - 3$							
Sign of $x - 2$							
Sign of quotient							
Conclusion							

9. Graph the solution set to Problem 8.

Sullivan/Struve/Mazzarella, *Elementary & Intermediate Algebra,* 2e

Do the Math Exercises 10.7
Rational Inequalities

In Problems 1 – 10, solve each rational inequality. *Express your answer in interval notation.*

1. $\dfrac{x+8}{x+2} < 0$

2. $\dfrac{x+12}{x-2} \geq 0$

1. _____

2. _____

3. $\dfrac{x-10}{x+5} \leq 0$

4. $\dfrac{(5x-2)(x+4)}{x-5} < 0$

3. _____

4. _____

5. $\dfrac{(3x-2)(x-6)}{x+1} \geq 0$

6. $\dfrac{x+3}{x-4} > 1$

5. _____

6. _____

7. $\dfrac{3x-7}{x+2} \leq 2$

8. $\dfrac{3x+20}{x+6} < 5$

7. _____

8. _____

9. $\dfrac{2}{x+3} + \dfrac{2}{x} \leq 0$

10. $\dfrac{1}{x-4} \geq \dfrac{3}{2x+1}$

9. _____

10. _____

In Problems 11 and 12, for each function find the values of x that satisfy the given condition.

11. Solve $R(x) \geq 0$ if $R(x) = \dfrac{x+3}{x-8}$

12. Solve $R(x) < 0$ if $R(x) = \dfrac{3x+2}{x-4}$

11. _____

12. _____

In Problems 13 and 14, find the x-intercept of the graph of each function.

13. $h(x) = -3x^2 - 7x + 20$

14. $R(x) = \dfrac{x^2 + 5x + 6}{x+2}$

13. _____

14. _____

15. Average Cost Suppose that the daily cost C of manufacturing x bicycles is given by $C(x) = 90x + 5000$. Then the average daily cost $\overline{C}$ is given by $\overline{C}(x) = \dfrac{90x + 5000}{x}$.

How many bicycles must be produced each day in order for the average cost to be no more than $130?

15. _____

Five-Minute Warm-Up 11.1
Composite Functions and Inverse Functions

1. Determine the domain: $R(x) = \dfrac{4}{x^2 - 3x + 2}$.

1. _____

2. Use the function $f(x) = -3x^2 + 1$ to find the following.

(a) $f(-4)$ **(b)** $f(a-2)$

2a. _____

2b. _____

(c) $f(x+h)$

2c. _____

In Problem 3, use the Vertical Line Test to determine whether the following is the graph of a function.

3a.

3b.

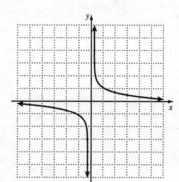

3a. _____

3b. _____

Guided Practice 11.1
Composite Functions and Inverse Functions

Objective 1: Form the Composite Function

1. Function composition is the process of evaluating one function and then carrying the result forward to be evaluated in a second function. The notation $f(g(x))$ means evaluate the inner function, $g(x)$, and then evaluate the result in the outer function, $f(x)$. This function composition is written with the notation

_____. This notation is read "f composed with g". The mathematical notation "$\circ$" is called small circle, so we can also say "f small circle g of x".

In Problems 2 – 3, suppose that $f(x) = 2x^2 + 7$ and $g(x) = x - 1$.
(See textbook Example 1)

2. Find $(f \circ g)(-2)$.

    (a) Evaluate $g(-2)$.

    (b) Use this result to find $f(g(-2))$.

    (c) What is $(f \circ g)(-2)$?

3. Find $(g \circ f)(4)$.

    (a) Evaluate $f(4)$.

    (b) Use this result to find $g(f(4))$.

    (c) What is $(g \circ f)(4)$?

2a. _____

2b. _____

2c. _____

3a. _____

3b. _____

3c. _____

Objective 2: Determine Whether or Not a Function is One-to-One

4. In your own words, what does it mean for a function to be one-to-one?

5. Determine whether or not the function is one-to-one. *(See textbook Example 3)*
    (a) $\{(1, -3), (-3, 1), (2, -4), (-2, 4)\}$
    (b) $\{(0, 1), (1, 2), (2, 3), (3, 1)\}$

6. Graphically, how can you test whether a function is one-to-one?

5a. _____

5b. _____

6. _____

Objective 3: Determine the Inverse of a Function Defined by a Map or Set of Ordered Pairs

7. In order for the inverse of a function to also be a function, the function must be _____.

8. If $f(x)$ is a one-to-one function, then its inverse function is written with the notation _____.

This means that if the ordered pair (a, b) satisfies $f(x)$, then the ordered pair _____ satisfies the inverse function.

9. Given the function $\{(-3, 15), (-1, -5), (0, 0), (2, 10)\}$, find

    (a) the inverse function *(See textbook Example 6)*

    (b) the domain of the function

    (c) the range of the function

    (d) the domain of the inverse function

    (e) the range of the inverse function

9a. _____

9b. _____

9c. _____

9d. _____

9e. _____

Objective 4: Obtain the Graph of the Inverse Function from the Graph of the Function

10. Graphs can be transformed in several different ways: translation (slide), reflection (flip), and rotation (turn). A graph is symmetric if it is a reflection across an axis of symmetry. For instance, $y = x^2$ is symmetric about the y-axis. The graph of a function and its inverse are symmetric about the line _____.

Objective 5: Find the Inverse of a Function Defined by an Equation

11. Find the inverse of $f(x) = 4x - 8$. *(See textbook Example 8)*

Step 1: Replace *f(x)* with *y* in the equation for *f(x)*.

$$f(x) = 4x - 8$$

    Replace $f(x)$ with y.   **(a)** _____

Step 2: Interchange the variables to write in inverse.

    Rewrite equation (a) exchanging the variables x and y.   **(b)** _____

Step 3: Solve the equation found in Step 2 for *y* in terms of *x*.

    Add 8 to both sides: **(c)** _____

    Divide both sides by 4:   **(d)** _____

Step 4: Replace y with $f^{-1}(x)$.   **(e)** _____

Step 5: Verify your result by showing that
$$f^{-1}(f(x)) = x \text{ and}$$
$$f(f^{-1}(x)) = x.$$

Do the Math Exercises 11.1
Composite Functions and Inverse Functions

In Problems 1 – 4, use the functions $f(x) = x^2 - 3$ and $g(x) = 5x + 1$ to find each of the following.

1. $(f \circ g)(3)$ **2.** $(g \circ f)(-2)$

1. _____

2. _____

3. $(f \circ f)(1)$ **4.** $(g \circ g)(-4)$

3. _____

4. _____

5. Given the functions $f(x) = x - 3$ and $g(x) = 4x$, find $(f \circ g)(x)$.

5. _____

6. Given the functions $f(x) = \sqrt{x+2}$ and $g(x) = x - 2$, find $(g \circ f)(x)$.

6. _____

7. Given the functions $f(x) = \dfrac{2}{x-1}$ and $g(x) = \dfrac{4}{x}$, find $(f \circ f)(x)$.

7. _____

In Problems 8 – 10, determine whether the function is one-to-one.

8. $\{(-2, -8), (-1, -1), (0, 0), (1, 1), (2, 8)\}$

8. _____

9. $\{(-3, 0), (-2, 3), (-1, 0), (0, -3)\}$

9. _____

10.

10. _____

11. Find the inverse of the function $\{(-10, 1), (-5, 4), (0, 3), (-5, 2)\}$.

11. _____

In Problems 12 and 13, verify that the functions f and g are inverses of each other.

12. $f(x) = 10x$; $g(x) = \dfrac{x}{10}$

13. $f(x) = \dfrac{2}{x+4}$; $g(x) = \dfrac{2}{x} - 4$

12. _____

13. _____

In Problems 14 – 19, find the inverse function of the given one-to-one function.

14. $g(x) = x + 6$

15. $H(x) = 3x + 8$

14. _____

15. _____

16. $f(x) = x^3 - 2$

17. $G(x) = \dfrac{2}{3-x}$

16. _____

17. _____

18. $R(x) = \dfrac{2x}{x+4}$

19. $g(x) = \sqrt[3]{x+2} - 3$

18. _____

19. _____

20. Volume of a Balloon The volume V of a hot-air balloon (in cubic meters) as a function of its radius r is given by $V(r) = \dfrac{4}{3}\pi r^3$. If the radius r of the balloon is increasing as a function of time t (in minutes) according to $r(t) = 3\sqrt[3]{t}$, for $t \geq 0$, find the volume of the balloon as a function of time t. What will be the volume of the balloon after 30 minutes?

20. _____

Five-Minute Warm-Up 11.2
Exponential Functions

In Problems 1 – 4, evaluate each expression.

1. 2^4

2. 2^{-2}

1._____

2._____

3. 3^0

4. 10^{-1}

3._____

4._____

5. Write 6.023455 as a decimal
(a) rounded to 4 decimal places.

(b) truncated to 4 decimal places.

5a._____

5b._____

In Problems 6 – 8, simplify each expression.

6. $5x^3 \bullet 2x^{-5}$

7. $\dfrac{4a^2}{10a^{-4}}$

6._____

7._____

8. $\left(4p^5\right)^3$

8._____

9. Solve: $6x^2 = 7x + 5$

9._____

Guided Practice 11.2
Exponential Functions

Objective 1: Evaluate Exponential Expressions

1. An exponential function is a function of the form $f(x) = a^x$ where a is _____ and $a \neq$ ____.

In Problems 2 and 3, evaluate each expression to 5 decimal places. (See textbook Example 1)

2. $2^{1.4}$

3. $2^{\sqrt{2}}$

2. _____

3. _____

Objective 2: Graph Exponential Functions

In Problems 4 and 5, match the function to the graph. (See textbook Examples 2 and 3)

4. $f(x) = a^x; a > 1$

(a)

4. _____

5. $f(x) = a^x; 0 < a < 1$

5. _____

(b)

Objective 3: Define the Number e

6. What is an approximate value of e to the nearest thousandth?

6. _____

7. Evaluate each of the following to two decimal places.

(a) e^3

(b) e^{-2}

7a. _____

7b. _____

Objective 4: Solve Exponential Equations

8. The Property for Solving Exponential Equations states that if two exponential functions have the same base and the exponential functions are equal, then it must be true that _____.

9. Solve: $3^{2x+1} = 27$ *(See textbook Example 5)*

Step 1: Use the Laws of Exponents to write both sides of the equation with the same base.	Prime factor 27 and write in exponential form:	$3^{2x+1} = 27$ **(a)** _____
Step 2: Set the exponents on each side of the equation equal to each other.		**(b)** _____
Step 3: Solve the equation resulting from Step 2.	Subtract 1 from both sides:	**(c)** _____
	Divide both sides by 2:	**(d)** _____
Step 4: Verify your solution(s).	Substitute your value into the original equation.	We leave it to you to verify your solution.
	State the solution set:	**(e)** _____

Objective 5: Study Exponential Models that Describe Our World

10. Strontium 90 is a radioactive material that decays according to the function $A(t) = A_0 e^{-0.087t}$, where A_0 is the initial amount present and A is the amount present at time t (in days). If you begin with 100 grams of Strontium 90, how much will be present after 5 days?

10. _____

11. What is the compound interest formula? Identify each of the variables in the formula.

12. Suppose that you deposit $100 into a savings account that earns 7% compounded quarterly for a period of 5 years.

(a) Identify the value of each variable in the compound interest formula.

12a. _____

(b) How much is in the account 5 years after the $100 deposit?

12b. _____

(c) You also deposit $100 in another bank because you believe you are getting a better deal when you receive 7% compounded daily. Assuming there are 360 days per business year, identify the value of each variable in the compound interest formula.

12c. _____

(d) How much is in the account after 5 years?

12d. _____

Do the Math Exercises 11.2
Exponential Functions

In Problem 1 and 2, approximate each number using a calculator. Round your answer to three decimal places.

1a. $5^{1.4}$

1b. $5^{1.41}$

1a. _____

1b. _____

1c. $5^{1.414}$

1d. $5^{1.4142}$

1c. _____

1d. _____

1e. $5^{\sqrt{2}}$

1e. _____

2a. e^3

2b. $e^{1.5}$

2a. _____

2b. _____

In Problems 3 – 5, graph each function.

3. $g(x) = 10^x$

4. $H(x) = 2^{x-2}$

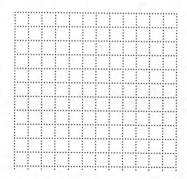

5. $f(x) = e^x - 1$

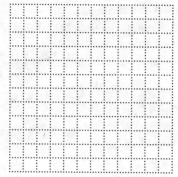

In Problems 6 –11, solve each equation.

6. $3^x = 3^{-2}$

7. $2^{x+3} = 128$

6. _____

7. _____

8. $3^{-x+4} = 27^x$

9. $9^{2x} \cdot 27^{x^2} = 3^{-1}$

8. _____

9. _____

10. $\left(\dfrac{1}{6}\right)^x - 36 = 0$

11. $e^{3x} = e^2$

10. _____

11. _____

In Problem 12 and 13, suppose that $f(x) = 3^x$.

12. What is $f(2)$? What point is on the graph of f?

13. If $f(x) = \dfrac{1}{81}$, what is x? What point is on the graph of f?

12. _____

13. _____

14. A Population Model According to the Statistical Abstract of the United States, the population of the world in 2005 was 6,448 million people. In addition, the population of the world was growing at a rate of 1.26% per year. Assuming that this growth rate continues, the model $P(t) = 6,448(1.0126)^{t-2005}$ represents the population P (in millions of people) in year t.

(a) According to this model, what will be the population of the world in 2008?

14a. _____

(b) According to this model, what will be the population of the world in 2015?

14b. _____

Five-Minute Warm-Up 11.3
Logarithmic Functions

1. Solve: $4x + 6 > 0$

1. _____

2. Solve: $\sqrt{2x + 3} = x$

2. _____

3. Solve: $x^2 = -7x - 12$

3. _____

In Problems 4 and 5, evaluate each expression.

4. 4^{-2} **5.** $\left(\dfrac{1}{2}\right)^{-3}$

4. _____

5. _____

In Problems 6 and 7, find the function value.

6. $f(x) = x^2$; $f(-2)$ **7.** $f(x) = 2^x$; $f(-2)$

6. _____

7. _____

Guided Practice 11.3
Logarithmic Functions

1. The logarithmic function to the base a, where $a > 0$ and $a \neq 1$, is denoted by $y = \log_a x$ and is read as "y is the logarithm to the base a of x". This is defined as

$$y = \log_a x \text{ is equivalent to } \underline{\hspace{3cm}}$$

Objective 1: Change Exponential Expression to Logarithmic Expressions

In Problems 2 and 3, rewrite each exponential expression as an equivalent expression involving a logarithm. (See textbook Example 1)

2. $2^{-3} = \dfrac{1}{8}$ **3.** $a^4 = 3$

2. _____

3. _____

Objective 2: Change Logarithmic Expressions to Exponential Expressions

In Problems 4 and 5, rewrite each logarithmic expression as an equivalent expression involving an exponent. (See textbook Example 2)

4. $p = \log_4 30$ **5.** $\log_n 3 = -5$

4. _____

5. _____

Objective 4: Determine the Domain of a Logarithmic Function
(See textbook Example 5)

6a. _____

6a. The domain of the logarithmic function is

6b. _____

6b. The range of the logarithmic function is

6c. _____

6c. Determine the domain of the function $f(x) = \log_3(10 - 2x)$.

Objective 5: Graph Logarithmic Functions

7. Because exponential functions and logarithmic functions are inverses of each other, we know that the

graph of $y = \log_5 x$ is a reflection of _____ across the line $y = x$. Graph both of these functions in the same coordinate plane. *(See textbook Example 6)*

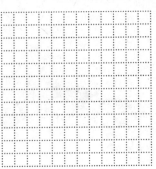

Objective 6: Work with Natural and Common Logarithms

8. The natural logarithm: $y = \ln x$ is written in exponential form as   8. _____

9. The common logarithm: $y = \log x$ is written in exponential form as: 9. _____

Objective 7: Solve Logarithmic Equations

In Problems 10 and 11, solve the logarithmic equation. Be sure to check your answers as extraneous solutions may appear. (See textbook Example 9 and Example 10)

10. $\log_3 (5 - 2x) = 2$ **11.** $\ln x = -2$ 10. _____

11. _____

Objective 8: Study Logarithmic Models That Describe Our World

12. List 3 applications of logarithmic functions that are used in the world today.   12a. _____

12b. _____

12c. _____

Do the Math Exercises 11.3
Logarithmic Functions

In Problems 1 – 3, change each exponential expression to an equivalent expression involving a logarithm.

1. $64 = 8^2$ **2.** $b^4 = 23$

1. _____

2. _____

3. $10^{-3} = z$

3. _____

In Problems 4 – 6, change each logarithmic expression to an equivalent expression involving an exponent.

4. $\log_3 81 = 4$ **5.** $\log_6 x = -4$

4. _____

5. _____

6. $\log_a 16 = 2$

6. _____

In Problems 7 – 8, find the exact value of each logarithm without using a calculator.

7. $\log_4 16$ **8.** $\log_{\sqrt{3}} 3$

7. _____

8. _____

In Problems 9 – 10, find the domain of each function.

9. $f(x) = \log_3(x - 2)$ **10.** $G(x) = \log_4(3 - 5x)$

9. _____

10. _____

In Problems 11 and 12, use a calculator to evaluate each expression. Round your answer to three decimal places.

11. log 0.78

12. ln $\dfrac{1}{2}$

11. _____

12. _____

In Problems 13 – 18, solve each logarithmic equation.

13. $\log_3(5x - 3) = 3$

14. $\log_4(8x + 10) = 3$

13. _____

14. _____

15. $\log_a 81 = 2$

16. $\log (2x + 3) = 1$

15. _____

16. _____

17. $\ln e^{2x} = 8$

18. $\log_3(x^2 + 1) = 2$

17. _____

18. _____

19. Alaska, 1964 According to the United States Geological Survey, an earthquake on March 28, 1964 in Prince William Sound, Alaska resulted in a seismographic reading of 1,584,893 millimeters 100 kilometers from its epicenter. What was the magnitude of this earthquake? This earthquake was the second largest ever recorded, with the largest being the Great Chilean Earthquake of 1960, whose magnitude was 9.5 on the Richter scale.

19. _____

Five-Minute Warm-Up 11.4
Properties of Logarithms

1. Write 1.13985 as a decimal

(a) rounded to 3 decimals places

(b) truncated to 3 decimal places.

1a. _____

1b. _____

In Problems 2 and 3, write each expression with a rational exponent.

2. $\sqrt{x}$

3. $\sqrt[4]{a^3}$

2. _____

3. _____

In Problems 4 and 5, write in exponential form using prime numbers in the base.

4. $\dfrac{1}{16}$

5. $\dfrac{27}{8}$

4. _____

5. _____

In Problems 6 and 7, simplify each expression.

6. $x^0, x \neq 0$

7. $6a^0, a \neq 0$

6. _____

7. _____

8. Find the inverse function of $y = \log_3 x$. Write the equation in exponential form.

8. _____

Guided Practice 11.4
Properties of Logarithms

Objective 1: Understand the Properties of Logarithms

1. There are four useful properties that can be quickly derived from the definition of a logarithm. While it is not essential, it will make your work with logarithms faster and easier if you memorize them.

For any real number a, for which the logarithm is defined:

$$\log_a 1 = 0 \qquad \log_a a = 1 \qquad \log_a a^r = r \qquad a^{\log_a M} = M$$

Use these properties to simplify the following. *(See textbook Example 1 and Example 2)*

(a) $3^{\log_3 \sqrt{2}}$ **(b)** $\log_4 1$ **(c)** $\ln e$ **(d)** $\log_x x^7$

1a. _____

1b. _____

1c. _____

1d. _____

Objective 2: Write a Logarithmic Expression as a Sum or Difference of Logarithms

2. There are three important rules that you will need as well. These should be easy to remember because they are very similar to rules you already know, Laws of Exponents. For each of these, M, N, and a are positive real numbers with $a \neq 1$.

(a) The Product Rule: $\log_a (M \cdot N) = $ _____

(b) The Quotient Rule: $\log_a \left(\dfrac{M}{N} \right) = $ _____

(c) The Power Rule: $\log_a M^r = $ _____

3. Use the Product Rule of Logarithms to write $\log(9x)$ as the sum of logarithms. *(See textbook Example 4)*

3. _____

4. Use the Quotient Rule of Logarithms to write $\ln\left(\dfrac{2}{x}\right)$ as the difference of logarithms. *(See textbook Example 5)*

4. _____

Objective 3: Write a Logarithmic Expression as a Single Logarithm

5. Now we will reverse the process and write an expanded logarithmic expression as a single logarithm. This will be an important skill in the next section.

Use the Quotient Rule of Logarithms to write $\log_4 (x + 1) - \log_4 (x^2 - 1)$ as a single logarithm.
(See textbook Example 9)

5. _____

Objective 4: Evaluate Logarithms Whose Base is Neither 10 Nor e

6. Calculators only have keys for the common logarithm, log, and the natural logarithm, ln. When we need to find the logarithmic value of an expression that uses a base other than 10 or e, we use the Change-of-Base Formula. If *M, a* and *b* are positive real numbers with $a \neq 1$, $b \neq 1$, then

Change-of-Base Formula: $\log_a M = $

_____

7. Approximate $\log_2 9$ using the Change-of-Base Formula. Round you answer to three decimal places.
(See textbook Example 12)

7. _____

Do the Math Exercises 11.4
Properties of Logarithms

In Problem 1, use properties of logarithms to find the exact value of each expression.
Do not use a calculator.

1a. $\log_5 5^{-3}$

1b. $5^{\log_5 \sqrt{2}}$

1c. $e^{\ln 10}$

1a. _____

1b. _____

1c. _____

In Problem 2, suppose that $\ln 2 = a$ *and* $\ln 3 = b$. *Use properties of logarithms to write*
each logarithm in terms of a and b.

2a. $\ln 4$

2b. $\ln 18$

2a. _____

2b. _____

In Problems 3 – 10, write each expression as a sum and/or difference of logarithms.
Express exponents as factors.

3. $\log_4\left(\dfrac{a}{b}\right)$

4. $\log_3 (a^3 b)$

3. _____

4. _____

5. $\log_2 (8z)$

6. $\log_2\left(\dfrac{16}{p}\right)$

5. _____

6. _____

7. $\log_2\left(32\sqrt[4]{z}\right)$

8. $\ln\left(\dfrac{\sqrt[5]{x}}{(x+2)^2}\right)$

7. _____

8. _____

9. $\log_6 \sqrt[3]{\dfrac{x-2}{x+1}}$

10. $\log_4\left[\dfrac{x^3(x-3)}{\sqrt[3]{x+1}}\right]$

9. _____

10. _____

In Problems 11 – 19, write each expression as a single logarithm.

11. $\log_4 32 + \log_4 2$

12. $\log_2 48 - \log_2 3$

11. _____

12. _____

13. $8\log_2 z$

14. $4\log_2 a + 2\log_2 b$

13. _____

14. _____

15. $\dfrac{1}{3}\log_4 z + 2\log_4(2z+1)$

16. $\log_7 x^4 - 2\log_7 x$

15. _____

16. _____

17. $\dfrac{1}{3}\left[\ln(x-1) + \ln(x+1)\right]$

18. $\log_5\left(x^2 + 3x + 2\right) - \log_5\left(x+2\right)$

17. _____

18. _____

19. $10\log_4 \sqrt[5]{x} + 4\log_4 \sqrt{x} - \log_4 16$

19. _____

In Problem 20, use the Change-of-Base Formula and a calculator to evaluate each logarithm. Round your answer to three decimal places.

20a. $\log_7 5$

20b. $\log_{\sqrt{3}} \sqrt{6}$

20a. _____

20b. _____

Five-Minute Warm-Up 11.5
Exponential and Logarithmic Equations

In Problems 1 – 4, solve each equation.

1. $\dfrac{2}{3}x - 7 = -1$

2. $x^2 + 5x = 24$

1. _____

2. _____

3. $4n^2 = 2 - 7n$

4. $(x-1)^2 - 5(x-1) - 6 = 0$

3. _____

4. _____

5. Find the domain: $f(x) = \log_2(-2x + 6)$

5. _____

Guided Practice 11.5
Exponential and Logarithmic Equations

Objective 1: Solve Logarithmic Equations Using the Properties of Logarithms

1. We use the following property where M, N, and a are positive real numbers with $a \neq 1$ to solve logarithmic equations where the log function appears on both sides of the equation.

$$\text{If } \log_a M = \log_a N, \text{ then } M = N.$$

M and N are called arguments so we say, "if there is equality between two logarithmic expressions which have the same base, set the arguments equal." Note that each log function has to be completely simplified to a single logarithm. Also, be careful to check for extraneous solutions.

Use this property to solve the following equations. *(See textbook Example 1 and Example 2)*

(a) $\log_2 x = \log_2(3x - 5)$ **(b)** $\log_4(x + 3) - \log_4 x = \log_4 10$ 1a. _____

1b. _____

(c) $\dfrac{1}{2}\ln x = 3\ln 2$ 1c. _____

Objective 2: Solve Exponential Equations

2. In Section 8.2, we were able to solve exponential equations of the form $a^u = a^v$ by using the Property for Solving Exponential Equations. This states that if two exponential functions have the same base and the exponential functions are equal, it must be true that the exponents are equal.

Now we will encounter exponential equations which cannot be written on a common base. For this circumstance, we use the definition of a logarithm to convert from exponential form to logarithmic form. Use this approach to solve each of the following. Give both the exact and approximate solution. *(See textbook Example 3 and Example 4)*

(a) $3^x = 12$ **(b)** $\dfrac{1}{2}e^{3x} = 9$ 2a. _____

2b. _____

Objective 3: Solve Equations Involving Exponential Models

3. Radioactive Decay The half-life of carbon 10 is 19.255 seconds. Suppose that a researcher possesses a 200-gram sample of carbon 10. The amount A (in grams) of carbon 10 after t seconds is given by

$$A(t) = 100 \cdot \left(\frac{1}{2}\right)^{\frac{t}{19.255}}$$

(See textbook Example 5)

(a) Write a model to find when there will be 90 grams of carbon 10 left in the sample.   3a. _____

(b) Use logarithms to solve the equation from part (a).   3b. _____

4. The population of a small town is growing at a rate of 3% per year. The population of the town can be calculated by the exponential function $P(t) = 2500e^{0.03t}$ where t is the number of years after 1950. *(See textbook Example 5 and Example 6)*

(a) What was the population in 1965?   4a. _____

(b) Write a model to find when the population reached 7500 people.   4b. _____

(c) Use logarithms to solve the equation from (b) and find when the population reached 7500 people.   4c. _____

(d) How long will it take for the population to double? (That is, for the town to have a population of 5000 people.)   4d. _____

Do the Math Exercises 11.5
Exponential and Logarithmic Equations

In Problems 1 – 18, solve each equation. Express irrational solutions in exact form and as a decimal rounded to 3 decimal places.

1. $\log_5 x = \log_5 13$

2. $\frac{1}{2}\log_2 x = 2\log_2 2$

1. _____

2. _____

3. $\log_2 (x - 7) + \log_2 x = 3$

4. $\log_3 (x + 5) - \log_3 x = 2$

3. _____

4. _____

5. $\log_5 (x + 3) + \log_5 (x - 4) = \log_5 8$

6. $3^x = 8$

5. _____

6. _____

7. $4^x = 20$

8. $e^x = 3$

7. _____

8. _____

9. $10^x = 0.2$

10. $2^{2x} = 5$

9. _____

10. _____

11. $3 \cdot 4^x = 15$

12. $\log_6 x + \log_6 (x + 5) = 2$

11. _____

12. _____

13. $3 \log_2 x = \log_2 8$

14. $5 \log_4 x = \log_4 32$

13. _____

14. _____

15. $-4e^x = -16$

16. $9^x = 27^{x-4}$

15. _____

16. _____

17. $\log_7 x = \log_7 8$

18. $\log_3 (x - 5) + \log_3 (x + 1) = \log_3 7$

17. _____

18. _____

19. A Population Model According to the Statistical Abstract of the United States, the population of the world in 2005 was 6,448 million people. In addition, the population of the world was growing at a rate of 1.26% per year. Assuming that this growth rate continues, the model $P(t) = 6,448(1.0126)^{t - 2005}$ represents the population P (in millions of people) in year t. According to this model, when will the population of the world be 9.65 billion people?

19. _____

20. Depreciation Based on data obtained from the Kelley Blue Book, the value V of a Dodge Stratus that is t years old can be modeled by $V(t) = 19,282(0.84)^t$. According to the model, when will the car be worth $10,000?

20. _____

Sullivan/Struve/Mazzarella, *Elementary & Intermediate Algebra*, 2e

Five-Minute Warm-Up 12.1
Distance and Midpoint Formulas

In Problems 1 – 3, simplify each expression.

1. $\sqrt{40}$ **2.** $\sqrt{108}$ **3.** $\sqrt{32p^4}$ 1. _____

2. _____

3. _____

4. Simplify the expression: $\sqrt{(2x-5)^2}$ 4. _____

In Problems 5 and 6, simplify each expression.

5. $-2\sqrt{25}$ **6.** $\sqrt{(-5-2)^2 + (16-(-8))^2}$ 5. _____

6. _____

7. Find the area of a triangle whose base has length of $\sqrt{18}$ cm and whose height has length
of $\sqrt{8}$ cm.   7. _____

8. Find the length of the hypotenuse of a right triangle whose legs are 6 and $6\sqrt{3}$.   8. _____

Guided Practice 12.1
Distance and Midpoint Formulas

Objective 1: Use the Distance Formula

1. We can find the distance between two points in the Cartesian plane using the Pythagorean Theorem. This can be accomplished by plotting the points, drawing a right triangle, and applying $a^2 + b^2 = c^2$ where c is the length of the hypotenuse or, in this case, the distance between the points. If you get stuck or forget the distance formula, you can always use this approach.

We use the Distance Formula to find the length of a line segment quickly and easily. If the two points in the Cartesian plane are $P_1 = (x_1, y_1)$ and $P_2 = (x_2, y_2)$, the distance between P_1 and P_2, denoted $d(P_1, P_2)$, is

_____

2. Be sure to use the Rule for Order of Operations when finding the distance between two points. If we want to find the distance between (a, b) and (c, d), the steps are:

(a) subtract _____; **(b)** subtract _____; **(c)** square the value from part _____;

(d) square the value from part _____; **(e)** _____; **(f)** _____; **(g)** _____.

3. Find the distance between $(9, 3)$ and $(1, -1)$. Find both the exact value and the approximate distance to two decimal places. *(See textbook Example 1)*

3. _____

Objective 2: Use the Midpoint Formula

4. A *midpoint* is a point (in this case an ordered pair) which divides a line segment into _____.

5. To find the coordinates of the midpoint, we use the Midpoint Formula. This states that if a line segment has endpoints at $P_1 = (x_1, y_1)$ and $P_2 = (x_2, y_2)$, the midpoint, M, is an ordered pair such that

$$M = \left(\frac{}{2}, \frac{}{2} \right).$$

You can see that the Midpoint Formula averages the x values to find a coordinate in the middle and averages the y values to find a coordinate in the middle. You can verify that the midpoint divides the segment into two segments of equal length by finding the distance from P_1 to M and the finding the distance from M to P_2. These distances will be equal. This step is not necessary, but it is a good check.

6. Find the midpoint of the line segment joining $P_1 = (-3, 2)$ and $P_2(-5, -8)$. *(See textbook Example 4)*

6. _____

Sullivan/Struve/Mazzarella, *Elementary & Intermediate Algebra*, 2e

Do the Math Exercises 12.1
Distance and Midpoint Formulas

In Problems 1 – 6, find the distance $d(P_1, P_2)$ between points P_1 and P_2.

1. $P_1 = (1, 3)$; $P_2 = (4, 7)$ **2.** $P_1 = (-10, -3)$; $P_2 = (14, 4)$ 1. _____

2. _____

3. $P_1 = (-1, 2)$; $P_2 = (-1, 0)$ **4.** $P_1 = (5, 0)$; $P_2 = (-1, -4)$ 3. _____

4. _____

5. $P_1 = \left(\sqrt{6}, -2\sqrt{2}\right); P_2 = \left(3\sqrt{6}, 10\sqrt{2}\right)$ **6.** $P_1 = (-1.7, 1.3)$; $P_2 = (0.3, 2.6)$ 5. _____

6. _____

In Problems 7 – 12, find the midpoint of the line segment formed by joining points P_1 and P_2.

7. $P_1 = (1, 3)$; $P_2 = (5, 7)$ **8.** $P_1 = (-10, -3)$; $P_2 = (14, 7)$ 7. _____

8. _____

9. $P_1 = (-1, 2)$; $P_2 = (3, 9)$ **10.** $P_1 = (5, 0)$; $P_2 = (-1, -4)$ 9. _____

10. _____

11. $P_1 = \left(\sqrt{6}, -2\sqrt{2}\right); P_2 = \left(3\sqrt{6}, 10\sqrt{2}\right)$ **12.** $P_1 = (-1.7, 1.3)$; $P_2 = (0.3, 2.6)$ 11. _____

12. _____

13. Consider the three points $A = (-2, 3)$, $B = (2, 0)$, and $C = (5, 6)$.

    (a) Plot each point in the Cartesian plane and form the triangle ABC.

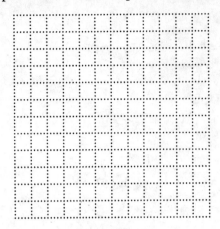

    (b) Find the length of each side of the triangle.

13b. _____

14. Find all points having a y-coordinate of -3 whose distance from the point $(-4, 2)$ is 13.　　14. _____

Five-Minute Warm-Up 12.2
Circles

In Problems 1 and 2, complete the square. Determine the number that must be added to the expression to make it a perfect square trinomial. Then factor the expression.

1. $x^2 - 14x$

2. $y^2 - 5y$

1. _____

2. _____

In Problems 3 and 4, factor completely.

3. $y^2 + 16y + 64$

4. $2x^2 - 12x + 18$

3. _____

4. _____

5. Find **(a)** the area and **(b)** the circumference of a circle whose diameter is 15 inches. Give both the exact answer and then the answer rounded to 2 decimal places.

5a. _____

_____

5b. _____

_____

Guided Practice 12.2
Circles

Objective 1: Write the Standard Form of the Equation of a Circle

1. A *circle* is the set of all points in the Cartesian plane that are a fixed distance r from a fixed point (h, k).

   (a) The point (h, k) is called the _____.

   (b) The fixed distance r is called the _____.

   (c) We also know that if d is the length of the diameter of the circle, then _____.

2. The *standard form of an equation of a circle* with radius r and center (h, k) is _____.

3. Write the standard form of the equation of the circle with radius 5 and center $(-1, 3)$. *(See textbook Example 1)*

3. _____ _____

Objective 2: Graph a Circle

4. Graph the equation: $(x - 2)^2 + (x + 3)^2 = 4$ *(See textbook Example 2)*

(a) Identify the center: _____ (b) Length of radius: _____ (c) Graph:

Objective 3: *Find the Center and Radius of a Circle from an Equation in General Form*

5. General form expands (multiplies) the binomials, regroups like terms, and has all the terms on one side of the equation and zero on the other side of the equation. What is the general form of the equation of a circle?

_____

6. Graph the equation: $x^2 + y^2 + 6x - 2y + 1 = 0$ *(See textbook Example 3)*

(a) Complete the square for the x terms and complete the square for the y terms:

$$x^2 + 6x + \underline{\quad} + y^2 - 2y + \underline{\quad} = -1 + \underline{\quad} + \underline{\quad}$$

(b) Factor:

$$(x + \underline{\quad})^2 + (y - \underline{\quad})^2 = \underline{\quad}$$

(c) Identify the center: _____ and the length of radius: _____

(d) Graph:

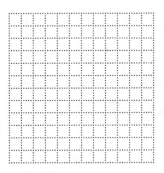

Sullivan/Struve/Mazzarella, *Elementary & Intermediate Algebra, 2e*

Do the Math Exercises 12.2
Circles

In Problems 1 – 4, write the standard form of the equation of each circle whose radius is r and center is (h, k). Graph each circle.

1. $r = 5$; $(h, k) = (0, 0)$

2. $r = 2$; $(h, k) = (1, 0)$

1. _____

2. _____

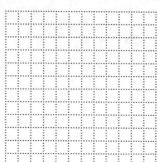

3. $r = 4$; $(h, k) = (-4, 4)$

4. $r = \sqrt{7}$; $(h, k) = (5, 2)$

3. _____

4. _____

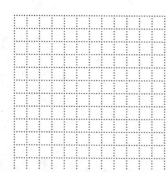

In Problems 5 – 8, identify the center (h, k) and radius r of each circle. Graph each circle.

5. $x^2 + y^2 = 25$

6. $(x - 5)^2 + (y + 2)^2 = 49$

5. _____

6. _____

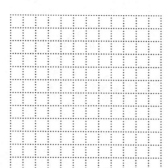

7. $(x - 6)^2 + y^2 = 36$

8. $(x - 2)^2 + (y + 2)^2 = \dfrac{1}{4}$

7. _____

8. _____

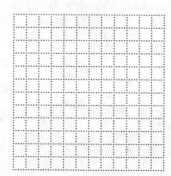

In Problems 9 – 11, find the center (h, k) and radius r of each circle.

9. $x^2 + y^2 + 2x - 8y + 8 = 0$

10. $x^2 + y^2 + 4x - 12y + 36 = 0$

9. _____

10. _____

11. $2x^2 + 2y^2 - 28x + 20y + 20 = 0$

11. _____

In Problems 12 – 14, find the standard form of the equation of each circle.

12. Center at (0, 3) and containing the point (3, 7).

12. _____

13. Center at (2, –3) and tangent to the *x*-axis.

13. _____

14. With endpoints of a diameter at (–5, –3) and (7, 2).

14. _____

15. Find the area and circumference of the circle $(x - 3)^2 + (y - 8)^2 = 64$.

15. _____

Five-Minute Warm-Up 12.3
Parabolas

In Problems 1 – 3, use the function $f(x) = 2(x-2)^2 + 1$.

1. Identify the vertex.

2. Does the parabola open up or down?

1. _____

2. _____

3. Name the axis of symmetry.

3. _____

In Problems 4 and 5, complete the square. Determine the number that must be added to the expression to make it a perfect square trinomial. Then factor the expression.

4. $x^2 + 10x$

5. $-3x^2 + 12x$

4. _____

5. _____

6. Solve: $(x-4)^2 = 16$

6. _____

Guided Practice 12.3
Parabolas

Objective 1: Graph Parabolas in Which the Vertex Is the Origin

1. In this course, the axis of symmetry is parallel to either the x-axis or y-axis. This means that the parabola opens up, down, left, or right. In the equation of the parabola, the coefficient of the linear variable $\left(x^1 \text{ or } y^1\right)$ will determine the direction that the parabola opens. If k is a real number (in the text $k = 4a$ as this coefficient can be used to determine the breadth of the parabola):

    (a) $y^2 = kx$ opens either

1a. _____

    (b) If $k > 0$, the parabola opens

1b. _____

    (c) If $k < 0$, the parabola opens

1c. _____

Notice that in (b), the positive x-axis has an arrow which points to the right and the parabola opens right.

    (d) $x^2 = ky$ opens either

1d. _____

    (e) If $k > 0$, the parabola opens

1e. _____

    (f) If $k < 0$, the parabola opens

1f. _____

Notice that in (e), the positive y-axis has an arrow which points up and the parabola opens up.

2. Determine which direction each parabola opens. *(See textbook Example 1 and Example 2)*

    (a) $x^2 = -4y$

2a. _____

    (b) $y^2 = 4x$

2b. _____

Objective 2: Find the Equation of a Parabola

3. Find the equation of a parabola with vertex at $(0, 0)$ if its axis of symmetry is the x-axis and its graph contains the point $(-2, -1)$. *(See textbook Example 3 and Example 4)*

    (a) Which direction does the parabola open?

3a. _____

    (b) Review the equations in your text. Which matches the given information?

3b. _____

    (c) Substitute the given information to find the equation for the parabola.

3c. _____

Objective 3: *Graph Parabolas in Which the Vertex Is Not the Origin*

4. Graph the parabola $x^2 - 8x + 4y + 20 = 0$. *(See textbook Example 5)*

    (a) Isolate the terms involving the second-degree variable: 4a. _____

    (b) Complete the square: 4b. _____

    (c) Simplify: 4c. _____

    (d) Factor: 4d. _____

    (e) Which direction does the parabola open?   4e. _____

    (f) Identify the vertex.   4f. _____

    (g) Find two more points on the parabola and then graph.

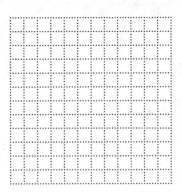

Do the Math Exercises 12.3
Parabolas

In Problems 1 – 5, find the equation of the parabola described.

1. vertex at $(0, 0)$; focus at $(0, 5)$

1. _____

2. vertex at $(0, 0)$; focus at $(-8, 0)$

2. _____

3. vertex at $(0, 0)$; contains the point $(2, 2)$; axis of symmetry the x-axis

3. _____

4. vertex at $(0, 0)$; directrix $x = -4$

4. _____

5. focus at $(0, -2)$; directrix $y = 2$

5. _____

In Problems 6 – 13, graph the parabola. Find (a) the vertex, (b) the focus, and (c) the directrix.

6. $x^2 = 28y$ **7.** $y^2 = 10x$

6a. _____

6b. _____

6c. _____

                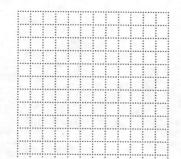

7a. _____

7b. _____

7c. _____

8. $x^2 = -16y$

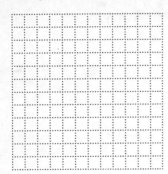

9. $(x + 4)^2 = -4(y - 1)$

8a. _____

8b. _____

8c. _____

9a. _____

9b. _____

9c. _____

10. $(y - 2)^2 = 12(x + 5)$

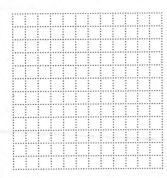

11. $x^2 + 2x - 8y + 25 = 0$

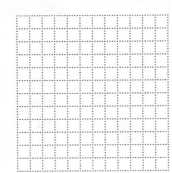

10a. _____

10b. _____

10c. _____

11a. _____

11b. _____

11c. _____

12. $y^2 - 8y + 16x - 16 = 0$

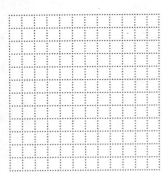

13. $x^2 - 4x + 10y + 4 = 0$

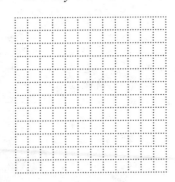

12a. _____

12b. _____

12c. _____

13a. _____

13b. _____

13c. _____

14. Suspension Bridge   The cables of a suspension bridge are in the shape of a parabola. The towers supporting the cable are 400 feet apart and 80 feet high. If the cables touch the road surface midway between the towers, what is the height of the cable at a point 100 feet from the center of the bridge?

14.

Sullivan/Struve/Mazzarella, *Elementary & Intermediate Algebra*, 2e

Five-Minute Warm-Up 12.4
Ellipses

In Problems 1 – 3, complete the square. Determine the number that must be added to the expression to make it a perfect square trinomial. Then factor the expression.

1. $y^2 - 9y$

2. $x^2 + 12x$

1. _____

2. _____

3. $4y^2 - 2y$

3. _____

In Problems 4 – 7, use the function $y = 9x^2 + 54x - 87$.

4. Write the equation in standard form by completing the square.

5. Identify the vertex.

4. _____

5. _____

6. _____

6. Does the parabola open up or down?

7. Name the axis of symmetry.

7. _____

Guided Practice 12.4
Ellipses

Objective 1: Graph Ellipses in Which the Center Is the Origin

1. An *ellipse* is the set of all points in the plane such that the sum of the distances from two fixed points is a constant.

   (a) The fixed points are called the _____.

   (b) The long axis contains the fixed points and is called the _____.

   (c) The other axis is perpendicular to long axis and is called the _____.

   (d) The point where the two axes intersect is the _____ of the ellipse.

   (e) The major axis contains turning points of the ellipse called _____.

2. The standard form of an ellipse is either $\dfrac{x^2}{a^2} + \dfrac{y^2}{b^2} = 1$ or $\dfrac{x^2}{b^2} + \dfrac{y^2}{a^2} = 1$. *(See textbook Example 1 and Example 2)*

(a) In either of these equations, the larger of the two denominators is _____.

(b) The distance from the center to the vertex is _____ units of length.

(c) Therefore, the length of the major axis is _____.

(d) The length of the minor axis is _____.

(e) The term with larger denominator tell us which axis is the _____ axis.

(f) The foci are c units from the center, on the major axis, where $c^2 = $ _____.

(g) For these two equations, the center of the ellipse is _____.

3. Find the intercepts to graph each ellipse: *(See textbook Example 1 and Example 2)*

(a) $\dfrac{x^2}{9} + \dfrac{y^2}{25} = 1$

(b) $4x^2 + 16y^2 = 64$

Objective 2: Find the Equation of an Ellipse in Which the Center Is the Origin

4. Find the equation, in standard form, of the ellipse whose center is at $(0, 0)$, one focus is at $(0, 5)$ and one vertex is at $(0, 13)$. *(See textbook Example 3)*

4. _____

Objective 3: Graph Ellipses in Which the Center Is Not the Origin

In Problems 5 – 7, **(a)** write the equation in the form $\dfrac{(x-h)^2}{a^2} + \dfrac{(y-k)^2}{b^2} = 1$ or

$\dfrac{(x-h)^2}{b^2} + \dfrac{(y-k)^2}{a^2} = 1$, then identify **(b)** the center, **(c)** the vertices and **(d)** the foci.

(See textbook Example 4)

5. $\dfrac{(x+5)^2}{9} + \dfrac{(y-2)^2}{25} = 1$

6. $4(x-1)^2 + 9(y-3)^2 = 36$

7. $16x^2 + 9y^2 - 128x + 54y - 239 = 0$

5a. _____

5b. _____

5c. _____

5d. _____

6a. _____

6b. _____

6c. _____

6d. _____

7a. _____

7b. _____

7c. _____

7d. _____

Sullivan/Struve/Mazzarella, *Elementary & Intermediate Algebra*, 2e

Do the Math Exercises 12.4
Ellipses

In Problems 1 – 4, graph the ellipse. Find (a) the vertices and (b) the foci of each ellipse.

1. $\dfrac{x^2}{25} + \dfrac{y^2}{4} = 1$

2. $\dfrac{x^2}{16} + \dfrac{y^2}{36} = 1$

1a. _____

1b. _____

2a. _____

2b. _____

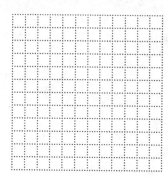

3. $\dfrac{x^2}{64} + y^2 = 1$

4. $9x^2 + y^2 = 81$

3a. _____

3b. _____

4a. _____

4b. _____

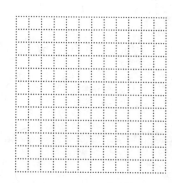

In Problems 5 – 8, find an equation for each ellipse.

5. center at (0, 0); focus at (2, 0); vertex at (5, 0)

5. _____

6. center at (0, 0); focus at (0, –1); vertex at (0, 5)

6. _____

7. foci at (0, ±2); vertices at (0, ±7)

7. _____

8. foci at (±6); length of the major axis is 20

8. _____

In Problems 9 and 10, graph each ellipse.

9. $\dfrac{(x+8)^2}{81}+(y-3)^2=1$

10. $9(x-3)^2+(y-4)^2=81$

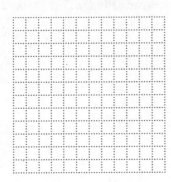

11. Consider the graph of the ellipse: $25x^2+150x+9y^2-72y+144=0$.
   (a) Write the equation of the ellipse in standard form.   11a. _____

   (b) Find the center.   11b. _____

   (c) Find the vertices.   11c. _____

   (d) Find the foci.   11d. _____

12. **Bridge Arch** An arch in the shape of the upper half of an ellipse is used to support a bridge that is to span a river 60 feet side. The center of the arch is 16 feet above the center of the river.

   (a) Write the equation for the ellipse in which the x-axis coincides with the water and the y-axis passes though the center of the arch.   12a. _____

   (b) Can a rectangular barge that is 25 feet wide and sits 12 feet above the surface of the water fit through the opening of the bridge?   12b. _____

Five-Minute Warm-Up 12.5
Hyperbolas

In Problems 1 and 2, solve the equation.

1. $y^2 = 16$ **2.** $(y+3)^2 = 4$

1. _____

2. _____

In Problems 3 and 4, complete the square. Determine the number that must be added to the expression to make it a perfect square trinomial. Then factor the expression.

3. $x^2 + 8x$ **4.** $y^2 - \dfrac{4}{3}y$

3. _____

4. _____

5. Graph $y = \pm\dfrac{2}{3}x$. That is, graph $y = \dfrac{2}{3}x$ and $y = -\dfrac{2}{3}x$ on the same coordinate plane.   5. _____

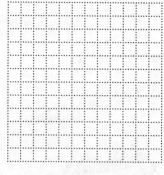

Guided Practice 12.5
Hyperbolas

Objective 1: Graph Hyperbolas in Which the Center Is the Origin

1. A *hyperbola* is the collection all points in the plane the difference of whose distances from two fixed points is a positive constant.

(a) The two fixed points are called _____.

(b) The line containing these points, as well as the center and the vertices, is called the _____.

(c) The midpoints of the line segment joining the foci is the _____.

(d) The line through the center, perpendicular to the transverse axis, is called the _____.

(e) The branches of the hyperbola have turning points called _____.

2. The standard form of a hyperbola is either $\dfrac{x^2}{a^2} - \dfrac{y^2}{b^2} = 1$ or $\dfrac{y^2}{a^2} - \dfrac{x^2}{b^2} = 1$. *(See textbook Example 1 and Example 2)*

(a) In either of these equations, the first denominator is _____, whether it is larger or smaller.

(b) The distance from the center to the vertex is _____ units of length.

(c) Therefore, the length of the transverse axis is _____.

(d) The length of the conjugate axis is _____.

(e) If the first, or positive, term is $\dfrac{x^2}{a^2}$, the hyperbola opens _____.

(f) If the first, or positive, term is $\dfrac{y^2}{a^2}$, the hyperbola opens _____.

(g) The foci are c units from the center, on the transverse axis, where $c^2 =$ _____.

(h) For these two equations, the center of the hyperbola is _____.

3. Graph the hyperbola $\dfrac{x^2}{16} - \dfrac{y^2}{9} = 1$. *(See textbook Example 1)*

(a) Find the center.

3a. _____

(b) The equation is of the form $\dfrac{x^2}{a^2} - \dfrac{y^2}{b^2} = 1$, where $c^2 = a^2 + b^2$.   3b. _____
Find the values of a and b.

(c) Find the value of c.

3c. _____

(d) Find the vertices and foci.

3d. _____

(e) Let $x = \pm c$ to locate points above and below the foci.

3e. _____

(f) Plot the vertices, foci, and the four points found in **(e)** to graph the hyperbola.

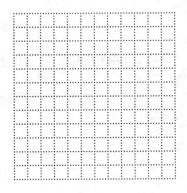

Objective 3: *Find the Asymptotes of a Hyperbola in Which the Center Is the Origin*

4. In your own words, what is an *asymptote*?

5. The equations of the two asymptotes of the hyperbola can be found using the values of a and b as determined from the standard form. The equations for the asymptotes changes when the direction the hyperbola opening changes. Determine the equations of the asymptotes for each hyperbola:

Hyperbola	Equation of Asymptotes
$\dfrac{x^2}{a^2} - \dfrac{y^2}{b^2} = 1$	**(a)** $y = \pm$
$\dfrac{y^2}{a^2} - \dfrac{x^2}{b^2} = 1$	**(b)** $y = \pm$

Do the Math Exercises 12.5
Hyperbolas

In Problems 1 – 4, graph each hyperbola. Find (a) the vertices and (b) the foci.

1. $\dfrac{x^2}{9} - \dfrac{y^2}{16} = 1$

2. $\dfrac{y^2}{81} - \dfrac{x^2}{9} = 1$

1a. _____

1b. _____

2a. _____

2b. _____

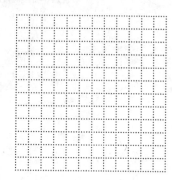

3. $x^2 - 9y^2 = 36$

4. $4y^2 - 9x^2 = 36$

3a. _____

3b. _____

4a. _____

4b. _____

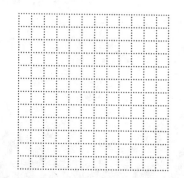

In Problems 5 – 8, find the equation for the hyperbola described.

5. center at (0, 0); focus at (–4, 0); and vertex (–1, 0)

5. _____

6. vertices at (0, 6) and (0, –6); focus at (0, 8)

6. _____

7. vertices at (0, –4) and (0, 4); asymptote the line $y = 2x$

7. _____

8. foci at (–9, 0) and (9, 0); asymptote the line $y = -3x$

8. _____

Do the Math Exercises 12.5

In Problems 9 – 14, identify the graph of each equation as a circle, parabola, ellipse, or hyperbola.

9. $x^2 + 4y = 4$

10. $3y^2 - x^2 = 9$

9. _____

10. _____

11. $y^2 - 4y - 4x^2 + 8x = 4$

12. $4x^2 + 8x + 4y^2 - 4y - 12 = 0$

11. _____

12. _____

13. $4y^2 + 3x - 16y + 19 = 0$

14. $9x^2 + 4y^2 - 18x + 8y - 23 = 0$

13. _____

14. _____

15. Consider the hyperbola $\dfrac{y^2}{25} - \dfrac{x^2}{4} = 1$.

   (a) Find the vertices.

15a. _____

   (b) Find the foci.

15b. _____

16. Consider the hyperbola $\dfrac{x^2}{36} - \dfrac{y^2}{36} = 1$. Find the equation of the asymptotes.

16. _____

Five-Minute Warm-Up 13.1
Sequences

1. If $f(x) = -2x^2 - 3x$, find the function value.

   (a) $f(1)$ **(b)** $f(-3)$

   1a. _____

   1b. _____

2. Evaluate the expression $(-1)^n (2n - 3)$ for each of the following.

   (a) $n = 1$ **(b)** $n = 2$ **(c)** $n = 3$ **(d)** $n = 4$

   2a. _____

   2b. _____

   2c. _____

   2d. _____

3. Evaluate the expression $\left(-\dfrac{1}{3}\right)^{n+1}$ for each of the following.

   (a) $n = 1$ **(b)** $n = 2$ **(c)** $n = 3$

   3a. _____

   3b. _____

   3c. _____

4. If $f(x) = \dfrac{1}{2x}$, find $f(1) + f(2) + f(3) + f(4)$.

   4. _____

Guided Practice 13.1
Sequences

1. A *sequence* is a function whose domain is the set of positive integers.

(a) The numbers in the ordered list are called _____ of the sequence and we separate each entry on the list from the next entry by a comma.

(b) Sequences can be either infinite or finite. If the list does not end, it is called *infinite* and we use three dots, called _____ , to indicate that the pattern continues indefinitely.

(c) By contrast, a _____ sequence has a countable number of terms.

Objective 1: Write the First Several Terms of a Sequence

2. We use the notation a_6 to mean the sixth term of the sequence. The formula for the nth term, or *general term*, of the sequence is denoted

2. _____

3. Write the first five terms of the sequence $\{a_n\} = \left\{\dfrac{2^n - 1}{n}\right\}$. *(See textbook Example 1)*

3. _____

Objective 2: Find a Formula for the nth Term of a Sequence

4. Sometimes a sequence is indicated by an observed pattern and it is our job to find the pattern. Try subtracting successive terms to find a constant difference or dividing successive terms to find a constant ratio. Sometimes the pattern is neither of these, but rather something you can recognize such as perfect squares.

Find the formula for the *n*th term of the sequence: *(See textbook Example 3)*

(a) 3, 6, 9, 12, ...

(b) $\dfrac{1}{6}, -\dfrac{1}{36}, \dfrac{1}{216}, -\dfrac{1}{1296}, ...$

4a. _____

4b. _____

Objective 3: Use Summation Notation

5. We use *summation notation* to indicate that the terms of the sequence should be added. The *index* of summation can be any variable, but typically we use *i*. This tells you where to start the sum and where to end. When there are a finite number of terms to be added, the sum is called a *partial sum*.

Consider the partial sum: $\displaystyle\sum_{i=1}^{4}\left(i^2 + 3\right)$. We substitute the values $i =$ ___, $i =$ ___, $i =$ ___, $i =$ ___ into the

formula $i^2 + 3$ to get the terms _____, _____, _____, _____. The sum is _____. *(See textbook Example 4)*

6. Write out the sum and determine its value: $\displaystyle\sum_{k=0}^{5}\left(2k - 5\right)$ _____

7. Express the sum using summation notation: $0 + 2 + 4 + 6 + 8 + 10 + 12$ *(See textbook Example 5)*

7. _____

Do the Math Exercises 13.1
Sequences

In Problems 1 – 4, write down the first five terms of each sequence.

1. $\{n-4\}$

2. $\left\{\dfrac{n+4}{n}\right\}$

1._____

2._____

3. $\{3^n - 1\}$

4. $\left\{\dfrac{n^2}{2}\right\}$

3._____

4._____

In Problems 5 – 8, find the nth term of each sequence suggested by the pattern.

5. 5, 10, 15, 20, …

6. $\dfrac{1}{2}, 1, \dfrac{3}{2}, 2, \dfrac{5}{2}, \dots$

5._____

6._____

7. 0, 7, 26, 63, …

8. $1, -\dfrac{1}{2}, \dfrac{1}{4}, -\dfrac{1}{8}, \dots$

7._____

8._____

In Problems 9 - 14, determine the value of the sum.

9. $\displaystyle\sum_{i=1}^{5}(3i+2)$

10. $\displaystyle\sum_{i=1}^{4}\dfrac{i^3}{2}$

9._____

10._____

11. $\displaystyle\sum_{k=1}^{4}3^k$

12. $\displaystyle\sum_{k=1}^{8}\left[(-1)^k \cdot k\right]$

11._____

12._____

13. $\displaystyle\sum_{j=1}^{8}2$

14. $\displaystyle\sum_{j=5}^{10}(k+4)$

13._____

14._____

In Problems 15 – 18, express each sum using summation notation.

15. $1 + 3 + 5 + \ldots + 17$

16. $1 + \dfrac{1}{2} + \dfrac{1}{4} + \ldots + \dfrac{1}{2^{15}}$

15. _____

16. _____

17. $\dfrac{2}{3} - \dfrac{4}{9} + \dfrac{8}{27} + \ldots + (-1)^{15+1}\left(\dfrac{2}{3}\right)^{15}$

18. $3 + 3 \cdot \dfrac{1}{2} + 3 \cdot \dfrac{1}{4} + \ldots + 3 \cdot \left(\dfrac{1}{2}\right)^{11}$

17. _____

18. _____

19. The Future Value of Money Suppose that you place \$5,000 into a company 401(k) plan that pays 8% interest compounded monthly. The balance in the account after n quarters is given by $a_n = 5{,}000\left(1 + \dfrac{0.08}{12}\right)^n$.

(a) Find the value in the account after 1 quarter.

19a. _____

(b) Find the value in the account after 1 year.

19b. _____

(c) Find the value in the account after 10 years.

19c. _____

Five-Minute Warm-Up 13.2
Arithmetic Sequences

1. Determine the slope of $y = 4x + 5$.

1.

2. If $g(x) = \dfrac{2}{3}x - 1$, find $g\left(-\dfrac{6}{5}\right)$.

2. _____

3. Solve the following systems of linear equations:

(a) $\begin{cases} 3x - 5y = 22 \\ x - y = 10 \end{cases}$

(b) $\begin{cases} x - 2y = 9 \\ 2x + y = -2 \end{cases}$

3a. _____

3b. _____

4. Evaluate the expression: $\dfrac{9}{2}\left(-\dfrac{4}{3} + \left(-\dfrac{20}{3}\right)\right)$

4.

Guided Practice 13.2
Arithmetic Sequences

Objective 1: Determine If a Sequence Is Arithmetic

1. If there is a constant difference between the successive terms, the sequence is called an *arithmetic sequence*.

(a) In formulas for arithmetic sequences, we label the common difference _____.

(b) We label the first term _____.

2. Determine if the sequence 5, 8, 11, 14, ... is arithmetic. If it is, determine the first term and the common difference. *(See textbook Example 1)*

2._____ _____

3. Show that the sequence $\{a_n\} = \{2 + n^2\}$ is not arithmetic by listing the first six terms and calculating the difference between successive terms. *(See textbook Example 3)*

3. _____

Objective 2: Find a Formula for the nth Term of an Arithmetic Sequence

4. The *n*th term of an arithmetic sequence whose first term is *a* and whose common difference is *d*, is determined by the formula: $a_n = a + (n-1)d$.

(a) Find a formula for the *n*th term of the arithmetic sequence whose first term is -3 and whose common difference is 5. *(See textbook Example 4)*

4a. _____

(b) Find the 8th term of this sequence.

4b. _____

5. The 5th term of an arithmetic sequence is 24, and the 11th term is 42. *(See textbook Example 5)*

(a) Write and solve a system of linear equations to find the first term and the common difference.

5a. _____

(b) Give a formula for the *n*th term.

5b. _____

Objective 3: Find the Sum of an Arithmetic Sequence

6. Let $\{a_n\}$ be an arithmetic sequence with first term a and common difference d. The sum

S_n of the first n terms of $\{a_n\}$ is $S_n = \dfrac{n}{2}(a + a_n)$.

Find the sum of the first 10 terms of the arithmetic sequence 12, 16, 20, 24, ... *(See textbook Example 6)*

(a) Write a formula for the *n*th term.   6a. _____

(b) Use the formula to find the 10th term of the sequence.   6b. _____

(c) Find the sum of the first 10 terms of the arithmetic sequence.   6c. _____

7. Find the sum of the first 10 terms of the arithmetic sequence $\{-10n + 13\}$. *(See textbook Example 7)*

(a) Use the formula to find the 1st and 10th term of the sequence.   7a. _____

(b) Find the sum of the first 10 terms of the arithmetic sequence.   7b. _____

Do the Math Exercises 13.2
Arithmetic Sequences

In Problems 1 – 2, find the common difference and write out the first four terms.

1. $\{10n + 1\}$

2. $\left\{\dfrac{1}{4}n + \dfrac{3}{4}\right\}$

1. _____

2. _____

In Problems 3 – 5, find a formula for the nth term of the arithmetic sequence whose first term is $\underline{a}$ and common difference $\underline{d}$ is given. What is the fifth term?

3. $a = 8, d = 3$

4. $a = 12, d = -3$

3. _____

4. _____

5. $a = -3; d = \dfrac{1}{2}$

5. _____

In Problems 6 – 8, write a formula for the nth term of each arithmetic sequence. Use the formula to find the 20th term of the sequence.

6. $-5, -1, 3, 7, \ldots$

7. $20, 14, 8, 2, \ldots$

6. _____

7. _____

8. $10, \dfrac{19}{2}, 9, \dfrac{17}{2}, \ldots$

8. _____

In Problems 9 – 12, find the formula for the nth term of an arithmetic sequence using the given information.

9. 5th term is 7; 9th term is 19

10. 2nd term is –9; 8th term is 15

9. _____

10. _____

11. 6th term is –8; 12th term is –38

12. 5th term is 5; 13th term is 7

11. _____

12. _____

13. Find the sum of the first 40 terms of the sequence 1, 8, 15, 22, ...

13. _____

14. Find the sum of the first 75 terms of the sequence –9, –5, –1, 3 ...

14. _____

15. Find the sum of the first 50 terms of the sequence 12, 4, –4, –12, ...

15. _____

16. Find the sum of the first 80 terms of the arithmetic sequence $\{2n - 13\}$.

16. _____

17. Find the sum of the first 35 terms of the arithmetic sequence $\{-6n + 25\}$.

17. _____

18. Find the sum of the first 28 terms of the arithmetic sequence $\left\{7 - \dfrac{3}{2}n\right\}$.

18. _____

19. Find x so that $2x$, $3x + 2$, and $5x + 3$ are consecutive terms of an arithmetic sequence.

19. _____

20. The Theater An auditorium has 40 seats in the first row and 25 rows in all. Each successive row contains 2 additional seats. How many seats are in the auditorium?

20. _____

Five-Minute Warm-Up 13.3
Geometric Sequences and Series

1. If $f(x) = \left(\dfrac{2}{3}\right)^x$, find each of the following.

   (a) $f(1)$ **(b)** $f(2)$ **(c)** $f(3)$

1a. _____

1b. _____

1c. _____

2. If $g(n) = 3n^2$, find each of the following.

   (a) $g(1)$ **(b)** $g(2)$ **(c)** $g(3)$

2a. _____

2b. _____

2c. _____

3. Simplify each expression.

   (a) $\dfrac{24x^5}{15x^2}$ **(b)** $\left(-3r^4\right)^2$

3a. _____

3b. _____

4. Evaluate the expression: $\dfrac{\frac{3}{2}}{1 - \frac{1}{4}}$

4. _____

Guided Practice 13.3
Geometric Sequences and Series

Objective 1: Determine If a Sequence Is Geometric

1. If there is a constant ratio between the successive terms, the sequence is called a *geometric sequence*.

(a) In formulas for geometric sequences, we label the common ratio _____.

(b) We label the first term _____.

2. Determine if the sequence $36, 18, 9, \dfrac{9}{2}, \ldots$ is geometric. If it is, determine the first term and the common ratio. *(See textbook Example 1)*

2. _____

3. Show that the sequence $\{b_n\} = \left\{\left(\dfrac{2}{5}\right)^{n-1}\right\}$ is geometric by listing the first four terms and calculating the ratio between successive terms. *(See textbook Example 3)*

3. _____

Objective 2: Find a Formula for the nth Term of a Geometric Sequence

4. The *n*th term of a geometric sequence whose first term is a and whose common ratio is r, is determined by the formula: $a_n = ar^{n-1}; r \neq 0$.

(a) Find a formula for the *n*th term of the geometric sequence: $2, -\dfrac{2}{3}, \dfrac{2}{9}, -\dfrac{2}{27}, \ldots$.
(See textbook Example 4)

4a. _____

(b) Find the 8th term of this sequence.

4b. _____

Objective 3: Find the Sum of a Geometric Sequence

5. Let $\{a_n\}$ be a geometric sequence with first term a and common ratio r, where $r \neq 0, r \neq 1$.

The sum S_n of the first n terms of $\{a_n\}$ is $S_n = a \cdot \dfrac{1 - r^n}{1 - r}$; $r \neq 0, r \neq 1$.

(a) Find the first term and the common ratio, r, of the geometric sequence 6, 24, 96, 384, ... *(See textbook Example 5)*

5a. _____

(b) Find the sum of the first 10 terms of this sequence.

5b. _____

Objective 4: Find the Sum of a Geometric Series

6. An infinite sum of the terms of a geometric sequence is called a *geometric series*. We can find the sum of the series with the formula: $\displaystyle\sum_{n=1}^{\infty} ar^{n-1} = \dfrac{a}{1 - r}$ provided that $-1 < r < 1$.

(a) Find the first term and the common ratio, r, of the geometric series: $6 - 2 + \dfrac{2}{3} - \dfrac{2}{9} + ...$

(See textbook Example 7)

6a. _____

(b) Find the sum of this series.

6b. _____

Objective 5: Solve Annuity Problems

7. If P represents the deposit in dollars made at each payment period for an annuity at i percent interest per payment period, the amount A of the annuity after n payment periods is: $A = P \cdot \dfrac{(1 + i)^n - 1}{i}$.

Retirement Raymond is planning on retiring in 15 years, so he contributes $1,500 into his IRA every 6 months (semiannually). What will be the value of the IRA when Raymond retires if the per annum interest rate is 10% compounded semiannually? *(See textbook Example 10)*

7. _____

Sullivan/Struve/Mazzarella, *Elementary & Intermediate Algebra*, 2e

Do the Math Exercises 13.3
Geometric Sequences and Series

In Problems 1 – 3, find the common ratio and write out the first four terms of each geometric sequence.

1. $\{(-2)^n\}$

2. $\left\{\dfrac{2^n}{3}\right\}$

1. _____

2. _____

3. $\left\{\dfrac{3^{-n}}{2^{n-1}}\right\}$

3. _____

In Problems 4 – 7, determine whether the given sequence is arithmetic, geometric, or neither.

4. $\{8-3n\}$

5. $\{n^2-2\}$

4. _____

5. _____

6. $100, 20, 4, \dfrac{4}{5}, \ldots$

7. $5, -2, 3, -1, 2, \ldots$

6. _____

7. _____

In Problems 8 and 9, find a formula for the nth term of the geometric sequence whose first term and common ratio are given. Use the formula to find the 8th term.

8. $a=30, r=\dfrac{1}{3}$

9. $a=1, r=-4$

8. _____

9. _____

In Problems 10 – 12, find the indicated term of each geometric sequence.

10. 12th term of $1, 3, 9, 27, \ldots$

11. 8th term of $10, -20, 40, -80, \ldots$

10. _____

11. _____

12. 10th term of $0.4, 0.04, 0.004, 0.0004, \ldots$

12. _____

In Problems 13 and 14, find the sum of each geometric series.

13. $3 + 9 + 27 + \ldots + 3^{10}$

14. $\sum_{n=1}^{12}\left[5 \cdot 2^n\right]$

13. _____

14. _____

In Problems 15 – 17, find the sum of each infinite geometric series.

15. $1 + \dfrac{1}{3} + \dfrac{1}{9} + \ldots$

16. $12 - 3 + \dfrac{3}{4} - \dfrac{3}{16} + \ldots$

15. _____

16. _____

17. $\sum_{n=1}^{\infty}\left(10 \cdot \left(\dfrac{1}{3}\right)^n\right)$

17. _____

In Problems 18 and 19, express each repeating decimal as a fraction in lowest terms.

18. $0.\overline{3}$

19. $0.\overline{45}$

18. _____

19. _____

20. Depreciation of a Car Suppose that you have just purchased a Chevy Cavalier for $16,000. Historically, the car depreciates by 10% each year, so that next year the car is worth $16,000(0.9). What will the value of the car be after you have owned it for four years?

20. _____

Five-Minute Warm-Up 13.4
The Binomial Theorem

In Problems 1 – 4, find the product.

1. $(x+2)^2$

2. $(y-3)^2$

1. _____

2. _____

3. $(4x-5y)^2$

4. $\left(3n+\dfrac{2}{3}\right)^2$

3. _____

4. _____

5. Simplify: $\dfrac{7\cdot 6\cdot 5\cdot 4\cdot 3\cdot 2}{3\cdot 2\cdot 4\cdot 3\cdot 2}$

5. _____

Guided Practice 13.4
The Binomial Theorem

Objective 1: Compute Factorials

1. If $n \geq 0$ is an integer, the factorial symbol $n!$ (read "n factorial") is defined as:

$$0! = 1; \ 1! = 1; \ n! = n(n-1)(n-2) \cdot \ldots \cdot 3 \cdot 2 \cdot 1 \text{ for } n \geq 2.$$

Evaluate each of the following. *(See textbook Example 1)*

(a) $\dfrac{10!}{4!}$

(b) $\dfrac{6!}{2!(6-2)!}$

1a. _____

1b. _____

Objective 2: Evaluate a Binomial Coefficient

2. If j and n are integers with $0 \leq j \leq n$, the symbol $\dbinom{n}{j}$ (read "n choose j") is defined as

$$\binom{n}{j} = \frac{n!}{j!(n-j)!}.$$

Evaluate each of the following. *(See textbook Example 2)*

(a) $\dbinom{5}{3}$

(b) $\dbinom{13}{7}$

2a. _____

2b. _____

Objective 3: Expand a Binomial

3. Multiplying binomials can become unwieldy when the exponents become large. We now introduce techniques for binomial expansion. We can find the binomial coefficients in a binomial expansion using Pascal's Triangle or the Binominal Theorem, which states that for any positive integer n,

$$(x+a)^n = \binom{n}{0}x^n + \binom{n}{1}ax^{n-1} + \binom{n}{2}a^2 x^{n-2} + \ldots + \binom{n}{j}a^j x^{n-j} + \ldots + \binom{n}{n}a^n.$$

Expand $(p+2)^4$ using the Binomial Theorem. *(See textbook Example 3)*

Do the Math Exercises 13.4
The Binomial Theorem

In Problems 1 – 4, evaluate each expression.

1. $5!$

2. $\dfrac{6!}{2!}$

1. _____

2. _____

3. $\dfrac{10!}{2! \cdot 8!}$

4. $0!$

3. _____

4. _____

In Problems 5 – 8, evaluate each expression.

5. $\dbinom{5}{3}$

6. $\dbinom{7}{5}$

5. _____

6. _____

7. $\dbinom{50}{49}$

8. $\dbinom{1000}{1000}$

7. _____

8. _____

In Problems 9 – 16, expand each expression using the Binomial Theorem.

9. $(x-1)^4$

10. $(x+5)^5$

9. _____

10. _____

11. $(2q + 3)^4$

12. $(3w - 4)^4$

11. _____

12. _____

13. $(y^2 - 3)^4$

14. $(3b^2 + 2)^5$

13. _____

14. _____

15. $(p - 3)^6$

16. $(3x^2 + y^3)^4$

15. _____

16. _____

17. Use the Binomial Theorem to find the numerical value of $(1.001)^4$ correct to five decimal 17. _____
places. [Hint: $(1.001)^5 = (1 + 10^{-3})^5$].

Chapter 1 Answers
Section 1.2

Five-Minute Warm-Up **1.** Counting numbers such as $1, 2, 3...$ **2.** Numbers whose only factors are 1 and itself. **3.** Natural numbers which are not prime. 1 is neither prime nor composite. **4.** The LCM of two or more numbers is the smallest number that is a multiple of each of the numbers. **5a.** 4, 9 **5b.** 36 **6.** 24, 48, 72 **7.** 1, 2, 4 **8.** 1, 2, 3, 4, 6, 18 **9.** $2 \cdot 3 \cdot 3$

Guided Practice **1a.** $2 \cdot 3 \cdot 5$ **1b.** $2 \cdot 2 \cdot 2 \cdot 3 \cdot 5$ **2a.** $2 \cdot 2 \cdot 2$ **2b.** $2 \cdot 2 \cdot 3$ **2c.** $2 \cdot 2$ **2d.** $2 \cdot 3$ **2e.** 24 **3a.** $\frac{3}{3}$ **3b.** $\frac{15}{24}$ **4a.** $2 \cdot 2 \cdot 3 \cdot 3$ **4b.** $2 \cdot 2 \cdot 2 \cdot 3$ **4c.** $2 \cdot 2 \cdot 2 \cdot 3 \cdot 3$ **4d.** 72 **4e.** $\frac{2}{2}$ **4f.** $\frac{3}{3}$ **4g.** $\frac{7}{36} = \frac{14}{72}; \frac{11}{24} = \frac{33}{72}$ **5a.** 94,000 **5b.** 94,200 **5c.** 94,205 **5d.** 94,204.6 **5e.** 94,200 **5f.** 94,204.64 **6.** 0.75 **7.** 0.5%

Do the Math **1.** $2 \cdot 3 \cdot 3 \cdot 3$ **2.** $3 \cdot 3 \cdot 7$ **3.** 280 **4.** 180 **5.** $\frac{12}{15}$ **6.** $\frac{10}{28}$ **7.** $\frac{3}{36}$ and $\frac{10}{36}$ **8.** $\frac{25}{60}$ and $\frac{28}{60}$ **9.** $\frac{3}{5}$ **10.** $\frac{8}{9}$ **11.** tenths place **12.** ones place **13.** 7300 **14.** 37.4 **15.** $0.\overline{2}$ **16.** 0.34375 **17.** $\frac{2}{5}$ **18.** $\frac{179}{500}$ **19.** 0.59 **20.** 34.9%

Section 1.3

Five-Minute Warm-Up **1.** 0 **2.** undefined **3.** 1 **4.** 3 **5a.** 3 **5b.** 7 **6.** $\frac{3}{6}$, 0.001, $\frac{0}{1}$, $\frac{4}{2}$ **7.** $\frac{3}{6}$, 0.001, $\frac{4}{2}$ **8.** $\frac{3}{6}$, 0.001 **9.** $\frac{0}{1}$ **10.** $0.8\overline{3}$ **11.** 0.8

Guided Practice **1a.** $B = \{0, 2, 4, 6, 8\}$ **1b.** $C = \{1, 3, 5, 7, 9\}$ **2a.** $\{14\}$ **2b.** $\left\{14, \frac{0}{3}\right\}$ **2c.** $\left\{14, \frac{0}{3}, \frac{-8}{2}, -10\right\}$ **2d.** $\left\{14, \frac{0}{3}, \frac{-8}{2}, -10, 2.\overline{6}\right\}$ **2e.** $\{-1.050050005...\}$ **2f.** $\left\{14, \frac{0}{3}, \frac{-8}{2}, -10, 2.\overline{6}, -1.050050005...\right\}$ **3a.** Ir, $\mathbb{R}$ **3b.** $\mathbb{Z}$, $\mathbb{Q}$, $\mathbb{R}$ **3c.** $\mathbb{Q}$, $\mathbb{R}$ **3d.** $\mathbb{N}$, W, $\mathbb{Z}$, $\mathbb{Q}$, $\mathbb{R}$ **4.** See Graphing Answer Section **5a.** > **5b.** = **5c.** > **6a.** True **6b.** True **6c.** False **7a.** $x > 0$ **7b.** $x < 0$ **8.** positive **9a.** 0 **9b.** 4.2 **9c.** 120

Do the Math **1.** $B = \{1, 2, 3, 4, ..., 24\}$ **2.** $C = \{-5, -4, -3, -2, -1, 0, 1, 2, 3\}$ **3.** $F = \{ \ \}$ or $\varnothing$ **4.** 3, 0 **5.** $-4, 3, -\frac{13}{2}, 0$ **6.** All numbers listed **7.** See Graphing Answer Section **8.** False **9.** True **10.** > **11.** < **12.** = **13.** 8 **14.** 7 **15.** $\frac{13}{9}$

Section 1.4

Five-Minute Warm-Up **1.** division **2.** subtraction **3.** addition **4.** multiplication **5a.** $\frac{9}{18}$ **5b.** 9/18 **5c.** $9 \div 18$ **5d.** $18\overline{)9}$ **6a.** 13 **6b.** $\frac{15}{4}$ **6c.** 0 **7.** $\frac{5}{2}$

Guided Practice **1a.** positive **1b.** negative **2.** the same as the sign of the integer having the larger absolute value. **3a.** 45 **3b.** 22 **3c.** 67 **3d.** negative **3e.** -67 **4a.** 73 **4b.** 81 **4c.** 8 **4d.** -81 **4e.** negative **4f.** negative **4g.** -8 **5a.** $-\frac{9}{2}$ **5b.** 10.3 **6a.** $-32 + 61$ **6b.** 29 **7a.** positive **7b.** negative **7c.** zero **8a.** -72 **8b.** 60 **8c.** -117 **9a.** 36 **9b.** 12 **9c.** 3 **10a.** -72 **10b.** 72 **10c.** -1 **11.** $-\frac{1}{3}$

Do the Math 1. 8 2. –18 3. –213 4. 2 5. 34 6. –7 7. –7 8. –24 9. 71 10. 63 11. 110 12. –896 13. –192

14. $\dfrac{1}{10}$ 15. $-\dfrac{1}{3}$ 16. 4 17. –24 18. $\dfrac{20}{3}$ 19. $32 + (-64) = -32$ 20. $-40 \div 100$ or $\dfrac{-40}{100} = -\dfrac{2}{5}$

Section 1.5

Five-Minute Warm-Up 1. 90 2. –25 3. –78 4. –136 5. $\dfrac{1}{4}$ 6. 120 7. $\dfrac{25}{60}$

Guided Practice 1a. $-\dfrac{4}{5}$ 1b. –8 1c. $\dfrac{1}{5}$ 2. $-\dfrac{9}{40}$ 3a. $\dfrac{8}{15} \bullet \dfrac{45}{4}$ 3b. $\dfrac{2 \bullet 2 \bullet 2 \bullet 3 \bullet 3 \bullet 5}{2 \bullet 2 \bullet 3 \bullet 5}$

3c. $\dfrac{2 \bullet \cancel{2} \bullet \cancel{2} \bullet \cancel{3} \bullet 3 \bullet \cancel{5}}{\cancel{2} \bullet \cancel{2} \bullet \cancel{3} \bullet \cancel{5}}$ 3d. $\dfrac{6}{1} = 6$ 4a. $\dfrac{7-11}{12}$ 4b. $\dfrac{7+(-11)}{12}$ 4c. $\dfrac{-4}{12}$ 4d. $-\dfrac{1}{3}$ 5a. $2 \bullet 2 \bullet 3$

5b. $3 \bullet 3$ 5c. $2 \bullet 2 \bullet 3 \bullet 3$ 5d. 36 5e. $\dfrac{3}{3}$ 5f. $\dfrac{4}{4}$ 5g. $\dfrac{5}{12} = \dfrac{15}{36}; \dfrac{4}{9} = \dfrac{16}{36}$ 5h. $\dfrac{15+16}{36}$ 5i. $\dfrac{31}{36}$ 6a. $\dfrac{-3}{1}$

6b. $\dfrac{-24}{8} + \dfrac{5}{8}$ 6c. $\dfrac{-19}{8}$ 6d. $-\dfrac{19}{8}$ 7. at the right end of the integer. 8. sum

Do the Math 1. $\dfrac{5}{12}$ 2. –27 3. $-\dfrac{8}{5}$ 4. $\dfrac{5}{9}$ 5. $\dfrac{4}{9}$ 6. $-\dfrac{1}{8}$ 7. 1 8. $-\dfrac{1}{16}$ 9. $-\dfrac{40}{27}$ 10. $\dfrac{4}{3}$ 11. 2 12. $\dfrac{25}{8}$

13. $-\dfrac{16}{15}$ 14. $-\dfrac{203}{60}$ 15. 43.2 16. 26.32 17. 33.79 18. 22.1 19. 42.1 20. 1600

Section 1.6

Five-Minute Warm-Up 1. –2 2. –12 3. $\dfrac{2}{3}$ 4. 45 5. 5

Guided Practice 1a. $\dfrac{4}{7}$ 1b. $-\dfrac{1}{4}$ 2a. $16\dfrac{1}{2}$ feet 2b. 900 seconds 3. order 4. division; subtraction

5a. $6 + (-12)$ 5b. $\dfrac{1}{2} \bullet (4 + 20)$ 6a. 4 6b. 90 7. grouping 8a. $-9 + (12 + 2)$ 8b. $\left(3 \bullet \dfrac{2}{3}\right) \bullet 15$ 9a. 20

9b. 50 10a. 0 10b. 0 10c. undefined

Do the Math 1. 43 and $\dfrac{1}{3}$ yards = 43 yards, 1 foot 2. 59 meters 3. 14 gallons, 2 quarts

4. 7 pounds, 8 ounces 5. Commutative Property of Multiplication 6. Associative Property of Multiplication

7. $\dfrac{a}{0}$ is undefined 8. Multiplicative Inverse Property 9. 59 10. 28 11. –72 12. 13 13. 0 14. 2 15. 1 16. 30

17. $-\dfrac{21}{16}$

Section 1.7

Five-Minute Warm-Up 1. –81 2. –48 3. –32 4. –45 5. 70 6. 81

Guided Practice 1a. base 1b. exponent 1c. $2 \bullet 2 \bullet 2 \bullet 2 \bullet 2 = 32$ 2a. 9 2b. –9 3a. squared

3b. $(-6)^2$ 3c. $(-6)(-6) = 36$ 4a. cubed 4b. $(-5)^3$ 4c. $(-5)(-5)(-5) = -125$ 5a. Parentheses

5b. Exponents 5c. Multiply or Divide 5d. Add or Subtract 6. $[\ ], \{\ \}, |\ |$ 7. –31 8a. $\dfrac{4 \bullet 2^3 + (-16)}{3(-2)^2}$

8b. $\dfrac{4 \bullet 8 + (-16)}{3(4)}$ 8c. $\dfrac{32 + (-16)}{12}$ 8d. $\dfrac{16}{12}$ 8e. $\dfrac{4}{3}$

Do the Math 1. 4^5 2. $(-8)^3$ 3. 32 4. $\dfrac{625}{16}$ 5. 0.0016 6. –625 7. 1 8. $-\dfrac{243}{32}$ 9. 36 10. 40 11. 5 12. $\dfrac{4}{9}$

13. 23 14. 13.5 15. –26 16. $-\dfrac{49}{2}$ 17. $\dfrac{81}{64}$ 18. 24 19. $\dfrac{5}{24}$

Section 1.8

Five-Minute Warm-Up **1.** 23 **2.** −10 **3.** −45 **4.** 7 **5a.** 16 **5b.** −16 **6.** 225

Guided Practice **1.** variable **2.** constant **3.** algebraic expression **4.** evaluating **5.** 21 **6.** term

7. coefficient **8.** like terms **9.** x^2; $-2xy$; $-y^2$ **10a.** $\dfrac{1}{2}$ **10b.** −1 **10c.** 14 **10d.** $-\dfrac{2}{5}$ **11a.** unlike **11b.** like

12a. $6x - 2$ **12b.** $-2y - 1$ **13a.** $4x$ **13b.** $6x + 3$ **14.** $9x + 12$

Do the Math **1.** −1 **2.** −32 **3.** $3m^4$, $-m^3n^2$, $4n$, −1; 3, −1, 4, −1 **4.** t^3, $-\dfrac{t}{4}$; 1, $-\dfrac{1}{4}$ **5.** like **6.** unlike

7. $12s + 6$ **8.** $-5k + 5n$ **9.** $6x + 9y$ **10.** $-5p^5$ **11.** $6m - 9n + 8p$ **12.** $9m - 6$ **13.** $\dfrac{13}{10}y$ **14.** $-21x + 21$ **15.** $884

Chapter 2 Answers
Section 2.1

Five-Minute Warm-Up **1.** $\dfrac{2}{3}$ **2.** $\dfrac{1}{14}$ **3.** 1 **4.** $-18x - 15$ **5.** $11 - 6x$ **6.** −26

Guided Practice **1.** Substitute the value into the original equation. If this results in a true statement, then the value for the variable is a solution to the equation. **2a.** Yes **2b.** No **3.** Whatever you add to one side of the equation, you must add to the other side of the equation to form an equivalent equation. **4.** Yes. Since $a - b = a + (-b)$, subtraction is an alternate way of writing addition. Subtraction means to add the opposite.

5. isolating the variable **6a.** $x + 13 - 13 = -11 - 13$ **6b.** $x + 0 = -24$ **6c.** $x = -24$ **6d.** $\{-24\}$

7. When you multiply one side of an equation by a non-zero quantity, you must also multiply the other side by the same non-zero quantity to form an equivalent equation. Yes, this property applies to division. Division means to multiply by the reciprocal. **8a.** $-\dfrac{1}{9} \bullet (-9x) = -\dfrac{1}{9} \bullet (324)$ **8b.** $\left(-\dfrac{1}{9} \bullet (-9)\right)x = -\dfrac{1}{9} \bullet 324$

8c. $1 \bullet x = -36$ **8d.** $x = -36$ **8e.** $\{-36\}$ **9a.** Divide both sides by 3; which is the same as multiply both sides by $\dfrac{1}{3}$. **9b.** Multiply both sides by 15 **9c.** Multiply both sides by $-\dfrac{3}{2}$ **9d.** Multiply both sides by $\dfrac{9}{4}$

Do the Math **1.** no **2.** no **3.** yes **4.** no **5.** 19 **6.** −15 **7.** $\dfrac{1}{2}$ **8.** $\dfrac{13}{24}$ **9.** $\dfrac{15}{2}$ **10.** $\dfrac{-5}{2}$ **11.** 12 **12.** 30 **13.** 14

14. $-\dfrac{5}{9}$ **15.** $799

Section 2.2

Five-Minute Warm-Up **1.** $-11x - 8$ **2.** 93 **3.** x **4.** $2x - 9$ **5.** $\dfrac{3}{7}$ **6.** 132.5

Guided Practice **1a.** 9 **1b.** $6x - 9 + 9 = -27 + 9$ **1c.** $6x = -18$ **1d.** 6; $\dfrac{1}{6}$ **1e.** $\dfrac{6x}{6} = \dfrac{-18}{6}$ **1f.** $x = -3$

1g. $\{-3\}$ **2a.** $\dfrac{5}{4}n + 3 - 3 = -12 - 3$ **2b.** $\dfrac{5}{4}n = -15$ **2c.** $\dfrac{4}{5}\left(\dfrac{5}{4}n\right) = \dfrac{4}{5}(-15)$ **2d.** $n = -12$ **2e.** $\{-12\}$

3. combining like terms on each side of the equation. **4.** Distributive **5a.** $-2x + 5 = -4$
5b. $24n + 36 = -2n - 1$ **6.** Add $5x$ to each side of the equation, and then subtract 4 from each side. Answers may vary. **7a.** $3z + 15 - 16z = 2 - z - 3$ **7b.** $-13z + 15 = -z - 1$
7c. $-13z + z + 15 = -z + z - 1$ **7d.** $-12z + 15 = -1$ **7e.** $-12z + 15 - 15 = -1 - 15$ **7f.** $-12z = -16$

7g. $\dfrac{-12z}{-12} = \dfrac{-16}{-12}$ **7h.** $z = \dfrac{4}{3}$ **7i.** $\left\{\dfrac{4}{3}\right\}$

Do the Math **1.** −3 **2.** $\dfrac{5}{3}$ **3.** 8 **4.** 25 **5.** −8 **6.** −3 **7.** −2 **8.** −2 **9.** 2 **10.** $\dfrac{1}{3}$ **11.** 2 **12.** $\dfrac{8}{3}$ **13.** 35 g **14.** $8.75

15. 68 inches, 70 inches, 72 inches

Section 2.3

Five-Minute Warm-Up **1.** 35 **2.** 225 **3.** $-3x + 4$ **4.** $43x - 270$ **5.** $x + 28$ **6.** $4x - 8$ **7.** $10x - 10$

Guided Practice **1a.** 12 **1b.** $12 \cdot \left(\frac{3}{2}x - \frac{4}{3}x\right) = 12 \cdot \left(-\frac{9}{4}\right)$ **1c.** $12 \cdot \left(\frac{3}{2}x\right) - 12 \cdot \left(\frac{4}{3}x\right) = 12 \cdot \left(-\frac{9}{4}\right)$

1d. $18x - 16x = -27$ **1e.** $2x = -27$ **1f.** $\frac{2x}{2} = \frac{-27}{2}$ **1g.** $x = -\frac{27}{2}$ **1h.** $\left\{-\frac{27}{2}\right\}$ **2a.** 18

2b. $18\left(\frac{4x+3}{9} + 1\right) = 18\left(\frac{2x+1}{2}\right)$ **2c.** $2(4x + 3) + 18 \cdot 1 = 9(2x + 1)$ **2d.** $8x + 6 + 18 = 18x + 9$

2e. $8x + 24 = 18x + 9$ **3.** $\{3000\}$ **4a.** false **4b.** $\varnothing$ **4c.** contradiction **5a.** 81 **5b.** yes; yes **5c.** 46; 81

Do the Math **1.** 3 **2.** $\frac{44}{9}$ **3.** 8 **4.** $\frac{8}{3}$ **5.** 20 **6.** 250 **7.** 8 **8.** 1 **9.** $\varnothing$ or $\{\ \}$; contradiction

10. all real numbers; identity **11.** $\left\{\frac{3}{2}\right\}$; conditional equation **12.** $\varnothing$ or $\{\ \}$; contradiction **13.** \$48

14. 10 nickels **15.** \$86,200

Section 2.4

Five-Minute Warm-Up **1.** 28 **2.** 12.38 **3.** 0.0725 **4.** 78.5 **5.** $\{4\}$

Guided Practice **1.** $68°F$ **2.** *I*: interest earned; *r*: annual interest rate, as a decimal;
P: Principal (amount borrowed or amount deposited); *t* time of deposit, typically in years **3a.** $A = s^2$; $P = 4s$

3b. $A = lw$; $P = 2l + 2w$ **3c.** $A = \frac{1}{2}bh$; $P = a + b + c$ **3d.** $A = \frac{1}{2}h(B + b)$; $P = a + b + c + B$

3e. $A = ah$; $P = 2a + 2b$ **3f.** $A = \pi r^2$; $C = 2\pi r = \pi d$ **3g.** $V = s^3$; $S = 6s^2$

3h. $V = lwh$; $S = 2lw + 2lh + 2wh$ **3i.** $V = \frac{4}{3}\pi r^3$; $S = 4\pi r^2$ **3j.** $V = \pi r^2 h$; $S = 2\pi r^2 + 2\pi rh$

3k. $V = \frac{1}{3}\pi r^2 h$ **4a.** $P = 2l + 2w$ **4b.** 30.5 m **4c.** \$457.50 **5a.** $6x - 6x - 12y = -6x - 24$

5b. $-12y = -6x - 24$ **5c.** $\frac{-12y}{-12} = \frac{-6x - 24}{-12}$ **5d.** $y = \frac{1}{2}x + 2$ **6a.** $C = R - P$ **6b.** $C = \$2100$

Do the Math **1.** 1066.8 meters **2.** \$834 **3.** \$150 **4a.** 104 units **4b.** 640 units^2 **5a.** 17.58 units

5b. 24.62 units^2 **6.** $m = \frac{F}{v^2}$ **7.** $B = \frac{3V}{h}$ **8.** $b = S - a - c$ **9.** $l = \frac{P - 2w}{2}$ **10.** $y = 2x + 18$ **11.** $y = 2x - 3$

12. $y = -\frac{5}{6}x + 3$ **13.** $y = \frac{4}{15}x - 2$ **14a.** $R = P + C$ **14b.** \$6000 **15a.** $t = \frac{I}{Pr}$ **15b.** 2 years

Section 2.5

Five-Minute Warm-Up **1.** $\{-54.72\}$ **2.** $\{32\}$ **3a.** $\times$ **3b.** $-$ **3c.** $\times$ **3d.** $+$ **3e.** $\div$ **3f.** $+$ **3g.** $-$
3h. $\div$ **3i.** $-$ **3j.** $+$ **3k.** $\div$ **3l.** $-$ **3m.** $\times$ **3n.** $+$ **3o.** $+$ **3p.** $\times$ **3q.** $-$ **3r.** $\times$ **3s.** $\times$ **3t.** $+$

Guided Practice **1a.** $-5 + 3x$ or $3x - 5$ **1b.** $5(r + 25)$ **1c.** $3x + 12$ **1d.** $\frac{2p}{7}$ **1e.** $\frac{z}{2} - 18$ or $\frac{1}{2}z - 18$

1f. $w - 900$ **2a.** $b - a$ **2b.** $a - b$ **2c.** $b - a$ **2d.** $\frac{a}{b}$ **2e.** $\frac{b}{a}$ **3a.** $x + 5 = 19$ **3b.** $2y - 14 = 30$

3c. $z - 9 = 6 + \frac{2}{5}z$ **4.** Identify what you are looking for; Give names to the unknowns; Translate the problem
into the language of mathematics; Solve the equation(s) found in Step 3; Check the reasonableness of your
answer; Answer the question **5a.** $n + 1$ **5b.** $n + 2$ **6a.** $x + 2$ **6b.** $x + 4$ **6c.** $x + 6$ **7a.** $p + 2$ **7b.** $p + 4$
7c. $p + 6$ **8a.** $n + 2$; $n + 4$ **8b.** $n + (n + 2) + (n + 4) = 453$ **8c.** $n = 149$ **8d.** 149, 151, 153 are the three
odd integers **9a.** $x - 5000$ **9b.** $x + (x - 5000) = 20,000$ **9c.** $x = 12,500$ **9d.** \$12,500 in stocks and \$7500 in
bonds

Do the Math 1. $2x$ 2. $x - 8$ 3. $\dfrac{-14}{x}$ 4. $4x + 21$ 5. Indians: r; Blue Jays: $r - 3$ 6. Ralph's amount: R; Beryl's amount: $3R + 0.25$ 7. number paid tickets: p; number promotion tickets: $12{,}765 - p$ 8. $43 + x = -72$ 9. $49 = 2x - 3$ 10. $\dfrac{x}{-6} - 15 = 30$ 11. $2(x + 5) = x + 7$ 12. 25, 27, 29 13. Ryugyong Hotel: 105 stories; Sears Tower: 110 stories 14. Stocks: \$24,000; bonds: \$16,000 15. 240 minutes

Section 2.6

Five-Minute Warm-Up 1a. 0.62 1b. 0.0175 2a. 5.5% 2b. 150% 3. $1.75p$ 4. $\{13.25\}$

Guided Practice 1a. $\dfrac{3}{4}$ 1b. 1 1c. $\dfrac{21}{400}$ 2a. 0.68 2b. 0.025 2c. 1.5 3a. 8% 3b. 70% 3c. 30%

4a. $n = 0.72(30)$ 4b. 21.6 5a. $150 = x \bullet (120)$ 5b. 125% 6a. $0.075p$
6b. $p + 0.075p = 1343.75$ or $1.075p = 1343.75$ 6c. $p = 1250$ 6d. The computer was \$1250 before sales tax.
7a. $0.60p$ 7b. $p - 0.6p = 224$ or $0.4p = 224$ 7c. $p = 560$ 7d. The price of the skis, before the discount, was \$560.

Do the Math 1. 42.5 2. 15 3. 13.5 4. 305 5. 2000 6. 200 7. 16% 8. 75% 9. \$8000 10. \$22.57
11. \$200,000 12. \$15,550 13. \$41.48 14. \$1627 15. 24.86 million

Section 2.7

Five-Minute Warm-Up 1. $\{50\}$ 2. $\left\{\dfrac{7}{2}\right\}$ 3a. $12 + 2x$ 3b. $\dfrac{x}{2} - 25$ 3c. $2(45 - x)$ 3d. $15 + 2x$
3e. $2(x + 30)$ 4. $8 - p$

Guided Practice 1. $90°$ 2. $180°$ 3a. $x - 20$ 3b. $x + x - 20 = 180$ 3c. $x = 100$ 3d. The large angle is $100°$ and the smaller angle is $80°$. 4. $180°$ 5a. $2x$ 5b. $30 + 2x$ 5c. $x + 2x + 2x + 30 = 180$ 5d. $x = 30$
5e. The first angle measures $30°$, the second angle measures $60°$, and the third angles measures $90°$.
6a. $x + 20$ 6b. $P = 2l + 2w$ 6c. $200 = 2(x + 20) + 2x$ 6d. $x = 40$; The dimensions of the tablecloth are 40" by 60". 7a. The distances add to 50 miles. 7b. See Graphing Answer Section
7c. $2.5r + 2.5(r + 4) = 50$; $r = 8$ 7d. The slower boat is traveling at 8 mph and the faster boat is traveling at 12 mph.
Do the Math 1. $x = 57.5$; $57.5°$ and $32.5°$ 2. $18°$, $72°$, $90°$ 3. length = 24 meters; width = 2 meters
4. 7.5 hr 4a. $72t$ 4b. $66t$ 4c. $72t - 66t$ 4d. $72t - 66t = 45$ 5. See Graphing Answer Section;
$2r + 3(r - 10) = 580$ 6. 4 feet 7. 12 feet 8. length = 54 inches; width = 36 inches 9. eastbound: 18 mph
10. $2\dfrac{1}{2}$ hours

Section 2.8

Five-Minute Warm-Up 1. $<$ 2. $<$ 3. $>$ 4. $=$ 5. $>$ 6. $<$ 7. See Graphing Answer Section
Guided Practice 1. square bracket; parenthesis 2. See Graphing Answer Section 3a. $(-\infty, -5)$
3b. $[10, \infty)$ 4. true 5. true 6. false 7a. $3x + 10 - 10 > 1 - 10$ 7b. $3x > -9$ 7c. $x > -3$ 7d. $\{x \mid x > -3\}$
7e. $(-3, \infty)$ 7f. See Graphing Answer Section 8a. $(12, \infty)$ 8b. $(-\infty, -25]$
9a. $6 \bullet \dfrac{1}{6}(4x - 5) \le 6 \bullet \dfrac{1}{2}(2x + 3)$ 9b. $1 \bullet (4x - 5) \le 3 \bullet (2x + 3)$ 9c. $4x - 5 \le 6x + 9$ 9d. $-2x - 5 \le 9$
9e. $-2x \le 14$ 9f. $x \ge -7$ 9g. $\{x \mid x \ge -7\}$ 9h. $[-7, \infty)$ 10a. $\ge$ 10b. $\ge$ 10c. $>$ 10d. $>$ 10e. $\le$ 10f. $\le$
10g. $<$ 10h. $<$
Do the Math 1. See Graphing Answer Section; $(5, \infty)$ 2. See Graphing Answer Section; $(-\infty, 6]$
3. See Graphing Answer Section; $[-2, \infty)$ 4. See Graphing Answer Section; $(-\infty, -3)$ 5. $(-\infty, 3]$ 6. $(-2, \infty)$
7. $>$; Addition Property of Inequality 8. $\ge$; Multiplication Property of Inequality 9. $\{x \mid x < 3\}$; $(-\infty, 3)$; See
Graphing Answer Section 10. $\{x \mid x > 3\}$; $(3, \infty)$; See Graphing Answer Section 11. $\{x \mid x \le -4\}$; $(-\infty, -4]$; See
Graphing Answer Section 12. $\{x \mid x > -2\}$; $(-2, \infty)$; See Graphing Answer Section 13. $\{x \mid x \ge 5\}$; $[5, \infty)$; See
Graphing Answer Section 14. $\{x \mid x \ge -1\}$; $[-1, \infty)$; See Graphing Answer Section

15. $\left\{x \mid x > \dfrac{11}{2}\right\}; \left(\dfrac{11}{2}, \infty\right)$; See Graphing Answer Section **16.** $\varnothing$ or $\{\ \}$; See Graphing Answer Section

17. $\{p \mid p \text{ is any real number}\}; (-\infty, \infty)$; See Graphing Answer Section **18.** $x \geq 250$ **19.** $x < 25$
20. at most 71 miles

Chapter 3 Answers
Section 3.1

Five-Minute Warm-Up **1.** See Graphing Answer Section **2a.** 7 **2b.** -3 **3a.** -25 **3b.** 9 **4.** $\{5\}$ **5.** $\{3\}$

Guided Practice **1.** See Graphing Answer Section **2.** the origin **3.** left **4A** $(4, -3)$ **4B** $(-3, -1)$

4C $(-2, 1)$ **5a.** No **5b.** Yes **6a.** $7 - 12 = -5$ **6b.** $-\dfrac{5}{2}$ **6c.** $\left(3, -\dfrac{5}{2}\right)$ **7a.** $-2; -7; (-2, -7)$

7b. $-1; -4; (-1, -4)$ **7c.** $0; -1; (0, -1)$ **7d.** $1; 2; (1, 2)$ **7e.** $2; 5; (2, 5)$

Do the Math **1.** See Graphing Answer Section; Quadrant I: R; Quadrant II: S; Quadrant III: P, T; Quadrant IV: Q, U **2.** See Graphing Answer Section; Quadrant I: U; Quadrant III: T; Quadrant IV: P, V; x-axis: R, S; y-axis: Q, S **3.** $P(0, 2)$: y-axis; $Q(-3, -1)$: Quadrant III; $R(-2, 4)$: Quadrant II; $S(2, 2)$: Quadrant I; $T(3, -2)$: Quadrant IV; $U(-5, 0)$: x-axis **4.** A Yes B No C Yes **5.** A No B No C Yes **6.** $(2, 5)$ **7.** $(4, 3)$

8.–9. See Graphing Answer Section **10.** A -9 B 7 C -6 **11.** A $\dfrac{1}{6}$ B $\dfrac{3}{2}$ C $-\dfrac{1}{2}$ **12a.** $\$11.70$ **12b.** $\$41.70$ **12c.**

15.5 mi **12d.** It costs $\$29.70$ to take a taxi 14 miles.

Section 3.2

Five-Minute Warm-Up **1.** $\{-9\}$ **2.** $\left\{-\dfrac{10}{3}\right\}$ **3.** $\{-2\}$ **4a.** 22 **4b.** 12 **5a.** $y = -1$ **5b.** $x = -4$

6. See Graphing Answer Section
Guided Practice **1.** See Graphing Answer Section **2.** standard **3.** $y = 0$ **4.** $x = 0$ **5a.** -2 **5b.** 3

5c.–7. See Graphing Answer Section
Do the Math **1.** Not linear **2.** Linear **3.–4.** See Graphing Answer Section **5.** $(0, 2), (2, 0)$ **6.** $(0, -3), (6, 0)$
7. $(0, 6)$ **8.** $(7, 0)$ **9.** $(0, -6), (10, 0)$ **10.** $(0, -8), (2, 0)$ **11.–14.** See Graphing Answer Section

Section 3.3

Five-Minute Warm-Up **1.** $\dfrac{1}{2}$ **2.** 3 **3.** $-\dfrac{5}{3}$ **4.** -2 **5.** undefined **6.** 0 **7.** $-\dfrac{5}{6}$

Guided Practice **1.** slope **2.** $m = \dfrac{y_2 - y_1}{x_2 - x_1}$ **3.** -5 **4.** undefined **5.** vertical **6.** 0 **7.** horizontal **8a.** slants

upward from left to right **8b.** slants downward from left to right **8c.** horizontal **8d.** vertical
9. See Graphing Answer Section

Do the Math **1.** $\dfrac{3}{4}$ **2.** $-\dfrac{7}{4}$ **3a., 3b.** See Graphing Answer Section **3c.** $m = \dfrac{5}{2}$; the value of y increases by 5

units when x increases by 2 units. **4a., 4b.** See Graphing Answer Section **4c.** $m = -\dfrac{1}{6}$; the value of y decreases

by 1 unit when x increases by 6 units. **5.** $m = 0$ **6.** m is undefined **7.–8.** See Graphing Answer Section **9.** $\dfrac{4}{45}$

10. $m = 0.225$ million; the income increases by 0.225 million dollars or $\$225,000$ for each year of college

Section 3.4

Five-Minute Warm-Up **1.** $y = -\dfrac{7}{5}x - 7$ **2.** $y = \dfrac{3}{8}x - \dfrac{3}{2}$ **3.** $\left\{-\dfrac{4}{3}\right\}$ **4a.** $-\dfrac{5}{3}$ **4b.** $-\dfrac{1}{2}$

Guided Practice **1.** $m; b$ **2.** $-\dfrac{1}{2}; 6$ **3.** $-2; 5$ **4a.** $\dfrac{2}{5}$ **4b.** -1 **4c.** See Graphing Answer Section

5a. $y = -\dfrac{2}{3}x + 2$ **5b.** $-\dfrac{2}{3}$ **5c.** 2 **5d.** See Graphing Answer Section **6.** $y = -\dfrac{1}{4}x + 3$ **7a.** $y = 0.07x + 22$

7b. $\$29$
Sullivan/Struve/Mazzarella, *Elementary & Intermediate Algebra*, 2e

Do the Math **1.** $m = -6$; $b = 2$ **2.** $m = -1$; $b = -12$ **3.** $m = \dfrac{3}{4}$; $b = 3$ **4.** $m = -\dfrac{5}{3}$; $b = 4$ **5.–8.** See Graphing

Answer Section **9.** $y = x + 10$ **10.** $y = \dfrac{4}{7}x - 9$ **11.** $y = \dfrac{1}{4}x + \dfrac{3}{8}$ **12.** $y = -2$ **13.** $x = 4$ **14.** $y = -3x$

15a. 2625 calories **15b.** 9 years old **15c.** The recommended caloric intake increases 125 calories per year.
15d. Age 3 is outside the given range this equation applies to. **15e.** See Graphing Answer Section

Section 3.5

Five-Minute Warm-Up **1.** $y = -4x + 10$ **2.** $y = 3x + 4$ **3.** $-\dfrac{1}{3}$ **4.** -2 **5.** $-7x + 21$ **6.** -1

Guided Practice **1.** $y - y_1 = m(x - x_1)$ **2a.** 9; -2; -1 **2b.** $y - y_1 = m(x - x_1)$

2c. $y - (-1) = 9(x - (-2))$ **2d.** $y + 1 = 9(x + 2)$ **2e.** $y + 1 = 9x + 18$ **2f.** $y = 9x + 17$ **3a.** $-\dfrac{5}{6}$; 0; 12

3b. $y - y_1 = m(x - x_1)$ **3c.** $y - (12) = -\dfrac{5}{6}(x - 0)$ **3d.** $y = -\dfrac{5}{6}x + 12$ **4a.** 0; 5; -11

4b. $y - y_1 = m(x - x_1)$ **4c.** $y - (-11) = 0(x - 5)$ **4d.** $y + 11 = 0$; $y = -11$ **5.** the slope **6a.** $m = \dfrac{y_2 - y_1}{x_2 - x_1}$

6b. $x_1 = 1$, $y_1 = 5$, $x_2 = -1$, $y_2 = -1$ **14c.** $m = \dfrac{-1 - 5}{-1 - 1} = \dfrac{-6}{-2} = 3$ **6d.** $y - y_1 = m(x - x_1)$

6e. $m = 3$, $x_1 = 1$, $y_1 = 5$ **6f.** $y - 5 = 3(x - 1)$ **6g.** $y - 5 = 3x - 3$ **6h.** 5; $y = 3x + 2$ **6i.** yes **6j.** no

6k. 3 **6l.** 2 **7a.** $\dfrac{3 + 1}{-5 + 5} = \dfrac{4}{0} =$ undefined **7b.** vertical **7c.** -5 **7d.** $x = -5$

Do the Math **1.** $y = 6x - 23$; See Graphing Answer Section **2.** $y = -5x + 27$; See Graphing Answer Section

3. $y = -\dfrac{1}{2}x - 2$; See Graphing Answer Section **4.** $y = -1$; See Graphing Answer Section **5.** $y = -1$ **6.** $x = 4$

7. $y = -\dfrac{3}{2}x + 1$ **8.** $y = 3x + 6$ **9.** $y = 5$ **10.** $x = -3$ **11a.** After 30 years, monthly income is $3600.

11b. See Graphing Answer Section **11c.** $y = 45x + 2250$ **11d.** $2925 **11e.** Monthly income increases by $45
for each additional year of service.

Section 3.6

Five-Minute Warm-Up **1.** $-\dfrac{1}{5}$ **2.** 3 **3.** $-\dfrac{4}{9}$ **4.** $y = 4x - 12$ **5a.** $\dfrac{1}{4}$ **5b.** $-\dfrac{1}{2}$ **6.** $y = -\dfrac{3}{2}x + \dfrac{11}{2}$

Guided Practice **1.** Two lines are parallel if they never intersect. **2.** slope; y-intercept **3.** $=$; $\neq$

4a. $y = 4x - 1$ **4b.** 4; -1 **4c.** $y = 4x + 5$ **4d.** 4; 5 **4e.** Since the slopes are equal and the y-intercepts are

different, we know that L_1 is parallel to L_2 **5a.** $y = \dfrac{5}{2}x + \dfrac{1}{2}$ **5b.** $\dfrac{5}{2}$ **5c.** $\dfrac{5}{2}$ **5d.** $\dfrac{5}{2}$; -3; -4

5e. $y - y_1 = m(x - x_1)$ **5f.** $y - (-4) = \dfrac{5}{2}(x - (-3))$ **5g.** $y + 4 = \dfrac{5}{2}x + \dfrac{15}{2}$; $y = \dfrac{5}{2}x + \dfrac{7}{2}$

6. Two lines are perpendicular if they intersect at right angles $(90°)$. **7.** -1 **8.** -1; $m_1 = -\dfrac{1}{m_2}$ **9a.** $\dfrac{3}{4}$; 6

9b. $\dfrac{4}{3}$; -2 **9c.** $\dfrac{3}{4} \cdot \dfrac{4}{3} = 1$ **9d.** Since the product of the slopes is not -1, L_1 is not perpendicular to L_2.

10a. $y = 2x + 7$ **10b.** 2 **10c.** $-\dfrac{1}{2}$ **10d.** $-\dfrac{1}{2}$; 3; -12 **10e.** $y - y_1 = m(x - x_1)$

10f. $y - (-12) = -\dfrac{1}{2}(x - (3))$ **10g.** $y + 12 = -\dfrac{1}{2}x + \dfrac{3}{2}$; $y = -\dfrac{1}{2}x - \dfrac{21}{2}$

Do the Math 1-3. See Graphing Answer Section **4.** neither **5.** perpendicular **6.** parallel **7.** neither

8. $y = 2x - 19$ **9.** $x = -4$ **10.** $y = -8$ **11.** $y = -\frac{2}{3}x + 11$ **12.** $y = -3x + 19$ **13.** $y = \frac{1}{2}x - 4$ **14.** $y = -6$

15. $x = 11$

Section 3.7

Five-Minute Warm-Up **1.** $\{x \mid x < -8\}$ **2.** $\{x \mid x \geq -3\}$ **3.** $\{x \mid x \leq -5\}$ **4.** See Graphing Answer Section

Guided Practice **1.** True **2.** yes **3.** dashed; solid **4.** half-planes **5.** shade **6a.** $y = x + 2$ **6b.** 1 **6c.** 2

6d. solid **6e.** $(0, 0)$ **6f.** false **6g.** opposite **6h.** See Graphing Answer Section **7a.** dashed **7b.** no

7c. See Graphing Answer Section **8a.** $4.32x + 2.50y \geq 5000$ **8b.** no

Do the Math **1.** A No B Yes C No **2.** A No B No C Yes **3.** A Yes B Yes C Yes **4.** A No B Yes C No

5.–12. See Graphing Answer Section **13a.** $160a + 75c \leq 500$ **13b.** Yes **13c.** Yes

Chapter 4 Answers
Section 4.1

Five-Minute Warm-Up **1a.–b.** See Graphing Answer Section **2.** Yes **3.** No

Guided Practice **1a.** No **1b.** Yes **2a.** -5 **2b.** 5 **2c.** $y = -2x - 1$ **2d.** -2 **2e.** -1 **2f.** $(-2, 3)$

2g. See Graphing Answer Section **2h.** $(-2, 3)$ **3.** See Graphing Answer Section; $\varnothing$ **4a.** inconsistent; the lines are parallel **4b.** consistent and dependent; the lines are coincident **4c.** consistent and independent; the lines intersect **5a.** infinitely many **5b.** consistent **5c.** dependent

Do the Math **1a.** Yes **1b.** No **1c.** No **2a.** No **2b.** No **2c.** Yes **3.** See Graphing Answer Section **4.** See Graphing Answer Section; no solution; $\{\ \}$ or $\varnothing$ **5.** See Graphing Answer Section **6.** See Graphing Answer Section; infinitely many solutions **7.** no solution; inconsistent **8.** infinitely many solutions; consistent; dependent **9.** one solution; consistent; independent **10.** infinitely many solutions; consistent; dependent

11. See Graphing Answer Section; $\begin{cases} y = 60 + 0.14x \\ y = 30 + 0.2x \end{cases}$ The cost for driving 500 miles is the same for both companies ($130). Choose Slow-but-Cheap to drive 400 miles.

Section 4.2

Five-Minute Warm-Up **1.** $y = \frac{5}{3}x + 6$ **2.** $x = -\frac{8}{3}y - 4$ **3.** $\{-7\}$ **4.** $\{3\}$

Guided Practice **1a.** $4x + 3y = -23$ **1b.** $4x + 3(-x - 7) = -23$ **1c.** $4x - 3x - 21 = -23$

1d. $x - 21 = -23$ **1e.** $x = -2$ **1f.** $y = -x - 7$ **1g.** $y = -(-2) - 7$ **1h.** $y = -5$ **1i.** $(-2, -5)$ **2.** $(4, 10)$

3. infinitely many solutions; consistent/dependent **4a.** $x + y = -11$ **4b.** $x - y = -101$ **4c.** $\begin{cases} x + y = -11 \\ x - y = -101 \end{cases}$

4d. $(-56, 45)$ **4e.** The two numbers are -56 and 45.

Do the Math **1.** $(-3, 5)$ **2.** $(18, 13)$ **3.** $\left(-\frac{2}{5}, -5\right)$ **4.** $\left(-\frac{1}{2}, -2\right)$ **5.** no solution; $\varnothing$ or $\{\ \}$; inconsistent

6. infinitely many solutions; consistent and dependent **7.** no solution; $\varnothing$ or $\{\ \}$; inconsistent

8. no solution; $\varnothing$ or $\{\ \}$; inconsistent **9.** $\left(2, \frac{3}{2}\right)$ **10.** infinitely many solutions **11.** $\left(\frac{19}{21}, -\frac{6}{7}\right)$

12. no solution; $\varnothing$ or $\{\ \}$ **13.** $\left(-\frac{1}{3}, \frac{1}{6}\right)$ **14.** infinitely many solutions

15. $8000 in international stock fund; $16,000 in domestic growth fund

Section 4.3

Five-Minute Warm-Up **1.** $-\frac{5}{4}$ **2.** 6 **3.** $21x - 14y$ **4.** $\varnothing$ **5.** $-9y - 9$ **6a.** 24 **6b.** 3 **6c.** 2

Guided Practice 1. $(-5, 7)$ 2a. $(1) -10x - 5y = 20$; $(2) 3x + 5y = 29$ 2b. $-7x = 49$ 2c. $x = -7$
2d. $2(-7) + y = -4;$ $y = 10$ 2e. $(-7, 10)$ 3a. $5x - 2y = 4$ 3b. $-3x + 10y = -20$ 3c. $(0, -2)$ 4. $\varnothing$
5. infinitely many solutions 6a. $a + c = 525$ 6b. $7.50a + 4.50c = 3337.50$ 6c. $(325, 200)$ 6d. 325 adult
tickets and 200 children's tickets were sold.

Do the Math 1. $(-3, 2)$ 2. $\left(\dfrac{4}{3}, \dfrac{3}{2}\right)$ 3. no solution; $\{\ \}$ or $\varnothing$; inconsistent

4. infinitely many solutions; dependent 5. no solution; $\{\ \}$ or $\varnothing$ 6. $(-14, 10)$ 7. infinitely many solutions
8. $\left(\dfrac{95}{29}, -\dfrac{43}{29}\right)$ 9. $\left(5, -\dfrac{1}{3}\right)$ 10. $(-0.1, -0.2)$ 11. $(1, 4)$ 12. $(8, 17)$ 13. biscuit 28 g; orange juice 42 g

Section 4.4

Five-Minute Warm-Up 1a. 325 miles 1b. 3 hours 2a. $945 2b. $52.50

3a. $2x - 7 = 45$ 3b. $5(x + 3) = \dfrac{x}{2}$ 3c. $\dfrac{x}{3} = 20 - x$

Guided Practice 1a. $4x + y = 68$ 1b. $x - 2y = -1$ 1c. $(15, 8)$ 1d. The numbers are 15 and 8.
2. $180°$ 3a. $x + y = 180$ 3b. $x = 30 + y$ 3c. $(105, 75)$ 3d. The two supplementary angles are

$105°$ and $75°$. 4a. $a + w$ 4b. $a - w$ 4c–d. See Graphing Answer Section 4e. $\begin{cases} 6a + 6w = 2400 \\ 8a - 8w = 2400 \end{cases}$

4f. $(350, 50)$ 4g. The speed the wind is moving at is 50 mph, and the air speed of the plane is 350 mph
Do the Math 1. $20 + 3a = 2b + 50$ 2. $l = 3w - 8$ 3. $4(a - w) = 1200$ 4. 19, 36 5. 18, 14
6. length 36.25 ft; width 26.25 ft 7. $25°, 65°$ 8. $96°, 84°$ 9. airplane 485 mph; wind 30 mph
10. still water rate 5 mph; current speed 1 mph 11. Gabriella's horse 2 mph; Monica's horse 6 mph

Section 4.5

Five-Minute Warm-Up 1a. $30 1b. $2030 2a. 0.4 2b. 0.0015 3. $(7, -5)$

Guided Practice 1a–c. See Graphing Answer Section 1d. $\begin{cases} a + s = 40 \\ 7.5a + 4s = 202 \end{cases}$ 2a–c. See Graphing

Answer Section 2d. $\begin{cases} d + q = 42 \\ 0.1d + 0.25q = 6.75 \end{cases}$ 2e. There are 25 dimes and 17 quarters. 3a–c. See Graphing

Answer Section 3d. $\begin{cases} a + p = 50 \\ 6.5a + 4p = 300 \end{cases}$ 4a–c. See Graphing Answer Section 4d. $\begin{cases} x + y = 90 \\ 0.25x + 0.4y = 27 \end{cases}$

Do the Math 1. See Graphing Answer Section $\begin{cases} b + n = 69 \\ 10b + 15n = 895 \end{cases}$ 2. See Graphing Answer Section

3. $\begin{cases} s + c = 1700 \\ 0.0275s + 0.02c = 37.75 \end{cases}$ 3. See Graphing Answer Section $\begin{cases} p + t = 40 \\ 5p + 2t = 3(40) \end{cases}$ 4. $\begin{cases} a + c = 22 \\ 15a + 7c = 274 \end{cases}$

5. $\begin{cases} A + B = 2650 \\ 0.05A + 0.065B = 155 \end{cases}$ 6. $\begin{cases} 8.60B + 5.75W = 143.45 \\ B = 2W - 2 \end{cases}$ 7. adult $4.50; child $3.25
8. $1500 in 4.5% account; $3500 in 9% account 9. 14 liters

Section 4.6

Five-Minute Warm-Up 1. $(-\infty, -2]$ 2. $(-1, \infty)$ 3a. See Graphing Answer Section
3b. See Graphing Answer Section
Guided Practice 1. (c) 2. graphing 3. dashed 4. solid 5. the opposite half-plane
6. intersection 7. See Graphing Answer Section 8a. $5x + 8y \le 40$ 8b. $y \ge 2x$ 8c. $x \ge 0$; $y \ge 0$
8d. See Graphing Answer Section 8e. No
Do the Math 1a. Yes 1b. No 1c. No 2a. No 2b. No 2c. Yes 3.–7a. See Graphing Answer Section
7b. Yes 7c. No

Chapter 5 Answers
Section 5.1

Five-Minute Warm-Up 1. -1 **2.** $-2x^2 + 4$ **3.** $-10x - 6y + 9$ **4.** $-15x + 10$ **5.** $-x^2 y + 3xy^2$ **6.** 7

Guided Practice 1a. A single term which is the product of a constant and a variable with whole number exponents. **1b.** The constant multiplied with the variable. **1c.** The degree is the same as the exponent on the variable. **1d.** The degree is the sum of the exponents on the variables. **2a.** A polynomial is the sum of two or more monomials. **2b.** The degrees of the terms are in descending order. **2c.** The degree of the polynomial is the same as the highest degree of any of the terms in the polynomial. **3a.** monomial **3b.** binomial **3c.** trinomial **3d.** polynomial **4.** Like terms have the same variables, raised to the same powers.

5. $7x^3 - x^2 - 5x + 5$ **6.** $-x^2 y - 14x^2 y^2 + xy^2$ **7.** $9z^3 - 7z^2 + z - 6$ **8.** $-n^2 + 2n$ **9a.** 5 **9b.** 41 **10.** -7

Do the Math 1. Yes; coefficient-1; degree 7 **2.** No **3.** No **4.** Yes; $p^5 - 3p^4 + 7p + 8$; degree 5; polynomial **5.** $7x^2 - x - 3$ **6.** $-10w^2 + 6w - 2$ **7.** $\dfrac{29}{24}b^2 - \dfrac{7}{15}b$ **8.** $-2a^2 - 3ab - 8b^2$ **9.** $2x^2 + 3x - 7$

10. $-2m^4 + 2m^2 + 7$ **11.** $\dfrac{7}{12}x^2 - \dfrac{25}{24}x - 6$ **12.** $-6m^2 n + 4mn - 1$ **13.** 10; 9; 9 **14.** 10; 2.125; $\dfrac{65}{32}$ **15.** 4

16. $-\dfrac{3}{2}$

Section 5.2

Five-Minute Warm-Up 1a. $\left(\dfrac{3}{4}\right)^3$ **1b.** $(-5)^4$ **2a.** -9 **2b.** $\dfrac{27}{8}$ **2c.** 16 **2d.** $-\dfrac{64}{27}$ **2e.** -32 **2f.** -36

3. -12 **4.** $20 - 10x$

Guided Practice 1. sum **2a.** r^8 **2b.** $m^3 n^5$ **3.** multiply **4a.** p^{18} **4b.** $\left(-x^{12}\right) = x^{12}$ **5.** positive **6.** negative

7. raised to that power **8a.** $125x^3 y^6$ **8b.** $m^8 n^{12}$ **9a.** $-12x^{11}$ **9b.** q^7 **10a.** $10m^5 n^7$ **10b.** $48p^4 q^{10}$

Do the Math 1. 81 **2.** a^{10} **3.** b^{13} **4.** $(-z)^6$ **5.** 81 **6.** $(-n)^{21}$ **7.** k^{24} **8.** $(-a)^{18}$ **9.** $16y^6$ **10.** $\dfrac{27}{64}n^6$

11. $-64a^3 b^6$ **12.** $81a^{24} b^4 c^{16}$ **13.** $-14b^9$ **14.** $\dfrac{1}{6}y^{11}$ **15.** $12a^7 b^4$ **16.** $\dfrac{20}{3}a^3 b^2$

Section 5.3

Five-Minute Warm-Up 1. x^7 **2.** $20y^8$ **3.** $64z^6$ **4.** $9a^8$ **5.** $\dfrac{25}{4}x^2$ **6.** $-16x^{11} y^{16}$ **7.** $44a - 33b$

8. $\dfrac{4x}{5} + \dfrac{3}{4}$

Guided Practice 1. the Distributive Property **2a.** $-15a^3 b^2 + 6a^2 b^3 - 9ab^4$ **2b.** $42x^7 - 3x^6 - 8x^5$

3a. $x^2 - 6x + 8$ **3b.** $6x^2 - 7x - 5$ **4a.** multiply two binomials **4b.** First, Outer, Inner, Last **4c.** no

5a. $u^2 - 2u - 15$ **5b.** $7x^2 - 23xy + 6y^2$ **6.** $A^2 - B^2$ **7a.** $x^2 - 81$ **7b.** $4a^2 - 25b^2$ **8a.** $A^2 + 2AB + B^2$

8b. $A^2 - 2AB + B^2$ **9a.** $(A - B)^2 = A^2 - 2AB + B^2$ **9b.** x **9c.** 3 **9d.** x^2 **9e.** $6x$ **9f.** 9 **9g.** $x^2 - 6x + 9$

10a. $144 - 24x + x^2$ **10b.** $16x^2 + 40xy + 25y^2$ **11a.** $3x^3 + 5x^2 - 14x + 4$ **11b.** $8x^3 - 14x^2 - 27x - 9$

Do the Math 1. $6m^2 - 21m$ **2.** $9b^2 - 3b$ **3.** $8w^3 + 12w^2 - 20w$ **4.** $14r^3 s + 6r^2 s^2$ **5.** $n^2 - 3n - 28$

6. $10n^2 - 19ny + 6y^2$ **7.** $x^2 + 10x + 21$ **8.** $12z^2 - 5z - 2$ **9.** $x^4 - 7x^2 + 10$ **10.** $18r^2 + 51rs + 35s^2$

11. $36r^2 - 1$ **12.** $64a^2 - 25b^2$ **13.** $x^2 + 8x + 16$ **14.** $36b^2 - 60b + 25$ **15.** $9x^2 + 12xy + 4y^2$

16. $y^2 - \dfrac{2}{3}y + \dfrac{1}{9}$ **17.** $6a^3 - 17a^2 - 4a + 3$ **18.** $-4k^3 - 16k^2 + 84k$ **19.** $-2m^5 + m^4 - 8m^3 - 7m - 4$

20. $2a^3 + 9a^2 + 3a - 4$

Five-Minute Warm-Up **1.** $49x^6y^2$ **2.** $\dfrac{36}{25}$ **3a.** $-\dfrac{1}{3}$ **3b.** $\dfrac{8}{7}$ **4.** $\dfrac{9}{5}$ **5.** $-\dfrac{11}{24}$

Guided Practice **1.** subtract **2a.** x^7 **2b.** $-\dfrac{9}{4}a^2b$ **3.** To raise a quotient to a power, both the numerator and the denominator are raised to the indicated power. The answer is (c) it does not matter which occurs first, although generally it is easier to simplify first. Be sure variables are non-zero. **4a.** $-\dfrac{v^3}{8}$ **4b.** $\dfrac{49a^{10}}{16b^8}$ **5.** 1

6a. 1 **6b.** 1 **6c.** 12 **6d.** –1 **6e.** 1 **6f.** –4 **7a.** $\dfrac{1}{a^n}$ **7b.** a^n **7c.** $\left(\dfrac{b}{a}\right)^{n} = \dfrac{b^n}{a^n}$ **8a.** $-\dfrac{1}{32}$ **8b.** $-\dfrac{1}{12}$ **8c.** $\dfrac{5}{a^2}$

9a. $\left(\dfrac{4}{3} \cdot (-18)\right)\left(x^{-2} \cdot x^5\right)\left(y^4 \cdot y^{-7}\right)$ **9b.** -24 **9c.** x^3 **9d.** y^{-3} **9e.** $-\dfrac{24x^3}{y^3}$

Do the Math **1.** 1000 **2.** x^6 **3.** $\dfrac{-3xy}{2}$ **4.** $3rs$ **5.** $\dfrac{16}{81}$ **6.** $\dfrac{49}{x^4}$ **7.** $-\dfrac{a^{15}}{b^{50}}$ **8.** $\dfrac{16m^4n^8}{q^{12}}$ **9.** -1 **10.** 1 **11.** 1

12. $-11x$ **13.** $-\dfrac{7}{z^5}$ **14.** $\dfrac{p^4}{16}$ **15.** $4b^3$ **16.** $36t$ **17.** 1 **18.** $\dfrac{2a^2}{b^2}$ **19.** $\dfrac{x^8}{25y^6}$ **20.** $20a^5$

Five-Minute Warm-Up **1.** $-27x^4$ **2.** $\dfrac{1}{9n^3}$ **3.** $-27z^3 - 18z^2 + 9z$ **4a.** 3 **4b.** $-7x^3 - 3x^2 + 5x + 13$

5. -1 **6.** $-x - 2$

Guided Practice **1a.** $2x^2 + 9x$ **1b.** $x + 4y^2 - 1$ **2.** Multiply the quotient by the divisor. Add the remainder to this product. The result will be equal to the dividend if the problem was divided correctly.

3a. 71 **3b.** 8047 **3c.** 113 **3d.** 24 **3e.** $113\dfrac{24}{71}$ **4a.** x^2 **4b.** $x^3 + x^2$ **4c.** $-3x^2 + x + 6$

4d. $x^2 - 3x + 4 + \dfrac{2}{x+1}$ **5.** standard **6.** False

Do the Math **1.** $x - 2$ **2.** $2m + 1 - \dfrac{1}{2m^2}$ **3.** $\dfrac{4}{5}a - \dfrac{3}{5} + \dfrac{2}{5a}$ **4.** $-\dfrac{7}{6} - \dfrac{7}{2p} + \dfrac{1}{2p^2}$ **5.** $-1 + 3y^2 - \dfrac{16y^3}{5}$

6. $-7x - 4y$ **7.** $-\dfrac{3y^2}{x^2} - 5$ **8.** $\dfrac{2}{mn} + \dfrac{3m}{n}$ **9.** $x + 8$ **10.** $x^2 - 7x + 2$ **11.** $x^3 - x^2 + 1$ **12.** $x^2 - 4x + 3 - \dfrac{2}{x-3}$

13. $3x - 2 - \dfrac{10}{2+3x}$ **14.** $16x^4 + 12x^2 + 9$

Five-Minute Warm-Up **1.** $19x^5$ **2.** $2.56n^{-6}$ or $\dfrac{2.56}{n^6}$ **3.** $0.2p^4$ **4a.** 4200 **4b.** 0.00305 **4c.** 2.1 **5a.** 10^8

5b. 10^{-9} **5c.** 10^5 **5d.** 10^{-8} **5e.** 10^5

Guided Practice **1a.** $1 \le x < 10$ **1b.** any integer **1c.** positive **1d.** negative **2a.** 7 **2b.** positive

2c. 4.5×10^7 **3a.** 5 **3b.** negative **3c.** 3×10^{-5} **4a.** right **4b.** left **5a.** 4 **5b.** right **5c.** 60,200 **6a.** -3

6b. left **6c.** 0.0091 **7a.** 8×10^{13} **7b.** 5.4×10^{-4} **8a.** 4×10^5 **8b.** 9×10^{36}

Do the Math **1.** 8×10^9 **2.** 1×10^{-7} **3.** 2.83×10^{-5} **4.** 4.01×10^8 **5.** 8×10^0 **6.** 1.2×10^2 **7.** 375

8. 6,000,000 **9.** 0.0005 **10.** 0.49 **11.** 540,000 **12.** 0.005123 **13.** 2.4×10^{-8} **14.** 1×10^4 **15.** 5×10^{-2}

16. 4×10^5 **17.** 1.1×10^{-7} **18.** 2×10^{11}

Chapter 6 Answers
Section 6.1

Five-Minute Warm-Up **1a.** $2 \cdot 2 \cdot 3 \cdot 3$ **1b.** $3 \cdot 3 \cdot 5 \cdot 5$ **2.** $-12x + 27$ **3.** $2x^2 + 5x - 12$

4. $4x^4 - 36x^2$ **5a.** $\frac{1}{2}, 10$ **5b.** 5 **6.** $4x^2y$

Guided Practice **1a.** $3 \cdot 3 \cdot 3$ **1b.** $2 \cdot 2 \cdot 3 \cdot 3$ **1c.** $3 \cdot 3 \cdot 5$ **1d.** $3 \cdot 3$ **1e.** 9 **2a.** $6x^2$ **2b.** $3ab$

3a. $2m^2n^2$ **3b.** $2m^2n^2 \cdot 3m^2 + 2m^2n^2 \cdot 9mn^2 - 2m^2n^2 \cdot 11n^3$ **3c.** $2m^2n^2(3m^2 + 9mn^2 - 11n^3)$

4a. $-3x^3(8x^2 + 3)$ **4b.** $(x + 3)(4x + 7)$ **5.** 4 **6.** True **7a.** $2x$ **7b.** $3y$ **7c.** $2x(x - 2) + 3y(x - 2)$

7d. $(x - 2)(2x + 3y)$ **8.** $(x - 2y)(9 - 4a)$ **9.** $2(2x + 3)(x^2 - 3)$

Do the Math **1.** 7 **2.** $13xy$ **3.** xyz **4.** $x + y$ **5.** $3(a - b)$ **6.** $-3b(3b + 2a)$ **7.** $4a^3b^2(2 + 3a^2)$
8. $5x^2(x^2 + 2x - 5)$ **9.** $-2(y^2 - 5y + 7)$ **10.** $-2n(11n^3 - 9n - 7)$ **11.** $(a - 5)(a + 6)$ **12.** $(x + a)(x + 2)$
13. $(m - 3)(n + 2)$ **14.** $(z + 4)(z^2 + 3)$ **15.** $(x - 1)(x^2 - 5)$

Section 6.2

Five-Minute Warm-Up **1.a.** $-1, 12; -2, 6; -3, 4; 1, -12; 2, -6; 3, -4$ **1b.** $1, 36; 2, 18; 3, 12; 4, 9;$
1b. $-1, -36; -2, -18; -3, -12; -4, -9$ **2a.** -15 **2b.** 36 **3a.** 6 **3b.** -16 **4a.** $4, -9$ **4b.** $-3, -2$
4c. $-5, 1$ **4d.** $3, 6$ **5.** $-1, 7, -2$ **6.** $x^2 - 10x + 24$

Guided Practice **1a.** $19; 11; 9; -19; -11; -9$ **1b.** $2, 9$ **1c.** $(y + 2)(y + 9)$

2a. $37; 20; 15; 13; -37; -20; -15; -13$ **2b.** $(z - 3)(z - 12)$ **3a.** See Graphing Answer Section

3b. $(x - 7)(x + 8)$ **4a.** See Graphing Answer Section **4b.** $(n + 4)(n - 6)$ **5.** Factors of -6 are:
$-1, 6; 1, -6; -2, 3; 2, -3$. The sums are $5, -5, 1, -1$. Since there are no two factors of -6 whose sum is 3,
the polynomial is prime. **6.** $3p(p - 6)(p + 3)$

Do the Math **1.** $(n + 2)(n + 10)$ **2.** $(y + 1)(y - 9)$ **3.** $(y - 4)(y + 10)$ **4.** prime **5.** $(x - 2y)(x - 12y)$
6. $4p^2(p - 2)(p + 1)$ **7.** $-2(x - 10)(x - 5)$ **8.** $-3(x + 1)(x + 5)$ **9.** $x(x + 15)(x - 5)$ **10.** $-2z(z + 4)(z - 3)$
11. $-(r + 6)^2$ **12.** prime **13.** $x(x - 8)(x + 2)$ **14.** $(x + 3y)(x + 4y)$ **15.** $(x + 5)^2$

Section 6.3

Five-Minute Warm-Up **1.** $4, 1, -1$ **2a.** $2 \cdot 3 \cdot 3$ **2b.** $2 \cdot 3 \cdot 5 \cdot 5$ **3.** $6x^2 - x - 2$ **4.** $(x - y)(4 + a)$
5. $3rs(4r^2s + 1 - 2s^3)$ **6.** $(2z + 1)(7z - 4)$

Guided Practice **1a.** $(3x + ?)(x + ?)$ **1b.** $1, 2; -1, -2$ **1c.** $1, 2$ **1d.** $(3x + 1)(x + 2)$
2. $(2a - 3b)(9a - 4b)$ **3.** $-(3x + 2)(2x - 7)$ **4a.** $3; 12$ **4b.** 36 **4c.** $-37; -20; -15; -13; -12$ **4d.** $-4, -9$
4e. $3x^2 - 4x - 9x + 12 = x(3x - 4) - 3(3x - 4)$ **4f.** $(x - 3)(3x - 4)$ **5.** $(13x - 4)(x + 1)$
Do the Math **1.** $(3x - 2)(x + 6)$ **2.** $(5x + 1)(x + 3)$ **3.** $(11p - 2)(p - 4)$ **4.** $(3x + y)(x + 2y)$
5. $2(3x + 2y)(x - 3y)$ **6.** $-3(2x - 5)(x + 3)$ **7.** $(7n + 1)(n - 4)$ **8.** $(5t - 1)(5t + 2)$ **9.** $(5t + 4)(4t + 1)$
10. $(4p - 1)(3p - 5)$ **11.** $2(3x + 2y)(3x - y)$ **12.** $-(10y + 3)(y - 5)$ **13.** $2(x + 5)(9x - 1)$ **14.** $3xy(3x^2 + 2x + 1)$
15. prime

Section 6.4

Five-Minute Warm-Up **1.** 100 **2.** -27 **3.** $64x^6$ **4.** $4p^2 + 20p + 25$ **5.** $16a^2 - 81b^2$
6. $1, 4, 9, 16, 25, 36, 49, 64, 81$ **7.** $1, 8, 27, 64$
Guided Practice **1a.** $A^2 + 2AB + B^2$ **1b.** $A^2 - 2AB + B^2$ **2a.** z^2, z **2b.** $16; 4$ **2c.** $-8z$, yes,
$-8z = -2(z)(4)$ **2d.** $(z - 4)^2$ **3a.** $(p + 11)^2$ **3b.** $3n(2m - 3n)^2$ **4.** $A^2 - B^2$ **5a.** $(x - 7)(x + 7)$
5b. $(5m^3 - 6n^2)(5m^3 + 6n^2)$ **5c.** $(a - 2)(a + 2)(a^2 + 4)(a^4 + 16)$ **5d.** $3y(2x - 5y)(2x + 5y)$
6a. $A^3 + B^3$ **6b.** $A^3 - B^3$ **6c.** $A^3 + 3A^2B + 3AB^2 + B^3$ **7a.** $(p - 4)(p^2 + 4p + 64)$
7b. $(2x^2 + 3y)(4x^4 - 6x^2y + 9y^2)$ **8a.** $3x(2x + 5)(4x^2 - 10x + 25)$
8b. $2xy(5x - 2y)(25x^2 + 10xy + 4y^2)$

Do the Math 1. $(m+6)^2$ 2. $(3a-2)^2$ 3. $(4y-9)^2$ 4. $(2a+5b)^2$ 5. $(6m-5n)(6m+5n)$

6. $(a-2)(a+2)(a^2+4)$ 7. $(4r-5s)(16r^2+20rs+25s^2)$ 8. $(m^3-3n^2)(m^6+3m^3n^2+9n^4)$

9. $(5y+3z^2)(25y^2-15yz^2+9z^4)$ 10. $5(2x+3y^2)(4x^2-6xy^2+9y^4)$ 11. $3n(2n-3)^2$

12. $4(2a+b^2)(4a^2-2ab+b^4)$ 13. $x^2(x-15)(x+15)$ 14. prime 15. $3(x+3)^2$

Section 6.5

Five-Minute Warm-Up 1. $20x^2+7xy-6y^2$ 2. $a^2+8ab+16b^2$ 3. $-9a(3a^2-a+2)$

4. $3(2n-1)(2m-3)$ 5. $(p-2q)(4p+3)$

Guided Practice 1. factor out the GCF 2a. 4 2b. $4(x^2+4x-21)$ 2c. 3 2d. $4(x+7)(x-3)$ 3a. 2

3b. $(8a-9b)(8a+9b)$ 4a. 2 4b. $2(4a^2+12ab+9b^2)$ 4c. 3 4d. $4a^2$; $2a$ 4e. $9b^2$; $3b$

4f. $12ab$; yes, $12ab=2(2a)(3b)$ 4g. $2(2a+3b)^2$ 5. $(3p^2+1)(9p^4-3p^2+1)$ 6. $2(n^2-3)(n-5)$

7. $-3x(y+1)(y+3)$

Do the Math 1. $(x-16)(x+16)$ 2. $(1-y)(1+y+y^2)(1+y^3+y^6)$ 3. $(x+6)(x-1)$

4. $(2x-1)(x-3)(x+3)$ 5. $25(2x-y)(2x+y)$ 6. $(3st-1)(2st+1)$ 7. $(2x^2+5y)(4x^4-10x^2y+25y^2)$

8. $3m(2-m^2)(2+m^2)(4+m^4)$ 9. $4t^2(t^2+4)$ 10. $2n(2n-3)(2n+3)$ 11. prime

12. $3q(2p+3q)(4p^2-6pq+9q^2)$ 13. $(x+y)(x-4)(x+4)$ 14. $-3x(x+3)(x+1)$ 15. $a(2a-b)(3a-b)$

Section 6.6

Five-Minute Warm-Up 1. $\left\{\dfrac{1}{2}\right\}$ 2. $\{7\}$ 3a. 15 3b. 10 4. $(x+9)(x-7)$ 5. $(2p+3)(2p-1)$

6. $(x-9)(x+9)$ 7. $(n-8)^2$

Guided Practice 1. If the product of two numbers is zero, then one of the factors must be zero. That is, if

$a \bullet b = 0$, then $a = 0$ or $b = 0$ or both a and b are zero. 2. $\left\{-1, \dfrac{3}{2}\right\}$ 3. quadratic equation

4. List the terms from the highest power to the lowest power. 5a. $(x+8)(x-3)=0$ 5b. $x+8=0$

5c. $x-3=0$ 5d. $x=-8$ 5e. $x=3$ 5f. $\{-8, 3\}$ 6a. $3t^2+11t-4=0$ 6b. $(3t-1)(t+4)=0$

6c. $\left\{\dfrac{1}{3}, -4\right\}$ 7a. multiply the binomials 7b. standard form 7c. $(x-10)(x+5)=0$ 7d. $\{10, -5\}$

8a. $4x^2-24x+36=0$ 8b. $4(x-3)^2=0$ 8c. $\{3\}$ 9a. no 9b. 4 9c. factor by grouping

9d. $(p+2)(p-3)(p+3)=0$ 9e. $p+2=0$ 9f. $p-3=0$ 9g. $p+3=0$ 9h. $p=-2$ 9i. $p=3$

9j. $p=-3$ 9k. $\{2, 3, -3\}$

Do the Math 1. $\{-9, 0\}$ 2. $\left\{-4, \dfrac{3}{4}\right\}$ 3. linear 4. quadratic 5. $\{-3, 8\}$ 6. $\left\{0, \dfrac{2}{7}\right\}$ 7. $\left\{-\dfrac{7}{3}, 2\right\}$ 8. $\{-6\}$

9. $\{-2, 8\}$ 10. $\{-3, 10\}$ 11. $\left\{-\dfrac{3}{2}, \dfrac{1}{2}\right\}$ 12. $\{-6, 4\}$ 13. $\left\{-\dfrac{7}{3}, 0, 2\right\}$ 14. $\{-3, -2, 3\}$ 15. 1 sec, 3 sec

Section 6.7

Five-Minute Warm-Up 1. $\{-9, 5\}$ 2. $\{-6\}$ 3. $\left\{-\dfrac{5}{2}, -\dfrac{1}{3}\right\}$ 4. 15 in. 5. $x^2-10x+25$

6. $-9h(2h-1)(h-1)$

Guided Practice 1a. 0 sec or 3 sec **1b.** 4 sec **2a.** $n + 2$ **2b.** $A = l \bullet w$ **2c.** $n; n + 2$

2d. $255 = n(n + 2)$ **2e.** $n = 15$ or $n = -17$ **2f.** The rectangle has dimensions $15\ cm \times 17\ cm$ **3.** In a right triangle, the square of the length of the hypotenuse is equal to the sum of the squares of the lengths of the legs. **4.** $z^2 = x^2 + y^2$ **5a.** $30\ cm$ **5b.** $7\ ft$ **6a.** $x = 0$ or $x = 9$ **6b.** leg: $9\ m$; leg: $12\ m$; hypotenuse: $15\ m$

Do the Math 1. 10, 25 **2.** 14, 26 **3.** base = 6; height = 14 **4.** base= 12; height = 14 **5.** base = 11; height = 7 **6.** $B = 17$; $h = 5$; $b = 11$ **7.** 9, 12, 15 **8.** 15, 8, 17 **9.** 3 sec **10.** width = 3 ft; length = 7 ft **11.** base = 8m; height = 6m **12.** length = 13 yd; width = 8yd **13a.** width = 26 in.; height = 36 in. **13b.** No

Chapter 7 Answers
Section 7.1

Five-Minute Warm-Up 1. -2 **2.** $(4x - 3)(x + 1)$ **3.** $\left\{ -\dfrac{5}{2}, 3 \right\}$ **4.** $\dfrac{10}{21}$ **5.** $\dfrac{2x}{3y^2}$

Guided Practice 1a. $\dfrac{3}{10}$ **1b.** 4 **2a.** $-\dfrac{2}{9}$ **2b.** $\dfrac{7}{4}$ **3.** the denominator is equal to zero. **4a.** $x = -8$

4b. $x = 3$ or $x = 6$ **5a.** factor **5b.** divide out **6a.** $\dfrac{6(x - 3)}{(x - 2)(x - 3)}$ **6b.** $\dfrac{6\cancel{(x-3)}}{(x - 2)\cancel{(x-3)}}$ **6c.** $\dfrac{6}{x - 2}$

7. $\dfrac{x+1}{2(x + 2)}$ **8.** $-\dfrac{x - 5}{2(x + 2)}$

Do the Math 1a $\dfrac{2}{3}$ **1b.** undefined **1c.** 0 **2a.** $\dfrac{7}{4}$ **2b.** 1 **2c.** 3 **3a.** 15 **3b.** $-\dfrac{3}{5}$ **3c.** -3 **4a.** -5 **4b.** -9 **4c.** 0

5. -8 **6.** $\dfrac{3}{4}$ **7.** $-2, 1$ **8.** $-4, -1, 0$ **9.** $2p + 1$ **10.** -1 **11.** $\dfrac{x-3}{x+2}$ **12.** $\dfrac{x+2}{x-3}$ **13.** $-\dfrac{1}{b+a}$ **14.** $\dfrac{z^2 + 2}{z + 2}$

15. $\dfrac{x+3}{2x-3}$ **16.** $-\dfrac{x+1}{x+5}$

Section 7.2

Five-Minute Warm-Up 1. $\dfrac{27}{14}$ **2.** $-\dfrac{2}{5}$ **3.** $\dfrac{1}{7}$ **4.** $-5x(x - 5)$ **5.** $\dfrac{x-3}{x-6}$

Guided Practice 1a. $\dfrac{x+3}{8} \bullet \dfrac{4(x-3)}{(x+3)(x-3)}$ **1b.** $\dfrac{4(x+3)(x-3)}{8(x+3)(x-3)}$ **1c.** $\dfrac{14\cancel{(x+3)}\cancel{(x-3)}}{28\cancel{(x+3)}\cancel{(x-3)}}$ **1d.** $\dfrac{1}{2}$

2a. $\dfrac{x(x - 4)}{(x - 2)(x + 2)} \bullet \dfrac{(x - 3)(x + 2)}{(x - 4)}$ **2b.** $\dfrac{x(x - 4)(x - 3)(x + 2)}{(x - 2)(x + 2)(x - 4)}$ **2c.** $\dfrac{x\cancel{(x-4)}(x - 3)\cancel{(x+2)}}{(x - 2)\cancel{(x+2)}\cancel{(x-4)}}$

2d. $\dfrac{x(x - 3)}{(x - 2)}$ **3.** $-\dfrac{2(x - y)}{x(x + y)}$ **4a.** $\dfrac{3x + 15}{36} \bullet \dfrac{24}{5x + 25}$ **4b.** $\dfrac{3(x + 5)}{2\bullet 2\bullet 3\bullet 3} \bullet \dfrac{2\bullet 2\bullet 2\bullet 3}{5(x + 5)}$

4c. $\dfrac{3\bullet(x + 5)\bullet 2\bullet 2\bullet 2\bullet 3}{3\bullet 2\bullet 2\bullet 3\bullet 5\bullet(x + 5)}$ **4d.** $\dfrac{\cancel{3}\bullet\cancel{(x+5)}\bullet\cancel{2}\bullet\cancel{2}\bullet 2\bullet\cancel{3}}{\cancel{3}\bullet\cancel{2}\bullet\cancel{2}\bullet\cancel{3}\bullet 5\bullet\cancel{(x+5)}}$ **4e.** $\dfrac{2}{5}$ **5.** $\dfrac{1}{2x - 3}$ **6.** $-\dfrac{3}{2x}$

Do the Math 1. $\dfrac{3x}{x+4}$ **2.** $\dfrac{2(n+2)}{3(n-2)}$ **3.** $z + 2$ **4.** $\dfrac{x+2}{x-2}$ **5.** $\dfrac{2}{p}$ **6.** $\dfrac{z+5}{2(z-5)}$ **7.** $\dfrac{9y(y-1)}{2}$ **8.** $\dfrac{3}{2}$

9. $\dfrac{1}{(2x-3)(x+4)}$ **10.** $\dfrac{2(x+5)^2}{45x}$ **11.** $r - 3s$ **12.** $\dfrac{x^2 + 1}{(x+1)^2}$ **13.** $\dfrac{2x^3(x-3)}{(x+3)}$ **14.** $-\dfrac{(p-7)}{(p+2)(p-2)}$ **15.** $\dfrac{b-9}{b-3}$

16. $\dfrac{t(t+3)}{(t+4)(t-3)}$

Five-Minute Warm-Up 1. $\dfrac{3}{5}$ 2a. $\dfrac{13}{3}$ 2b. $\dfrac{5}{2}$ 3a. 1 3b. $\dfrac{5}{8}$ 4. $-\dfrac{1}{2}$ 5. $-2x+3$

Guided Practice 1a. $\dfrac{2x+5x}{x^2-3x}=\dfrac{7x}{x^2-3x}$ 1b. $\dfrac{7x}{x(x-3)}$ 1c. $\dfrac{7\cancel{x}}{\cancel{x}(x-3)}$ 1d. $\dfrac{7}{x-3}$ 2. $\dfrac{5}{x+5}$

3a. $\dfrac{x^2-1}{x^2-5x-6}$ 3b. $\dfrac{(x-1)(x+1)}{(x-6)(x+1)}$ 3c. $\dfrac{(x-1)\cancel{(x+1)}}{(x-6)\cancel{(x+1)}}$ 3d. $\dfrac{x-1}{x-6}$ 4. $x+2$ 5. $\dfrac{(n+5)(n-1)}{(n-5)}$

6. $\dfrac{x+1}{x-3}$

Do the Math 1. $2n$ 2. $\dfrac{5p}{p-1}$ 3. $2(x+2)$ 4. $\dfrac{1}{x-3}$ 5. a 6. $\dfrac{2(x+2)}{x}$ 7. $\dfrac{z+6}{z-1}$ 8. $\dfrac{n+3}{n+1}$ 9. $\dfrac{4(1-2x)}{x-1}$

10. $\dfrac{x^2+x+6}{x-1}$ 11. $\dfrac{x+3}{x+1}$ 12. $\dfrac{m+n}{n-m}$ 13. $\dfrac{3n(n-2)}{2n-1}$ 14. $\dfrac{x+3}{x-3}$ 15. $\dfrac{4s-t}{t-s}$ 16. $\dfrac{n+3}{2n-3}$

Five-Minute Warm-Up 1. $\dfrac{21}{45}$ 2. 180 3. $\dfrac{9}{20}=\dfrac{81}{180}$; $\dfrac{2}{45}=\dfrac{8}{180}$ 4. $3y^2$ 5. $(x-2)^2$ 6. $-3x(x+3)$

Guided Practice 1a. $2\bullet2\bullet2\bullet3$ 1b. $2\bullet2\bullet5$ 1c. $2\bullet2$ 1d. $2\bullet3\bullet5$ 1e. 120 2a. $2\bullet3\bullet x^2$

2b. $3^2\bullet x$ 2c. $3\bullet x$ 2d. $2\bullet3\bullet x$ 2e. $18x^2$ 3. $40a^3b^2$ 4. $14a^2(a-2)$ 5. $(x-3)^2(x+3)$ 6a. $x(3x-1)$

6b. $3x^2(3x-1)$ 6c. $3x$ 6d. $\dfrac{3x}{3x}$ 6e. $\dfrac{x-2}{x(3x-1)}\bullet\left[\dfrac{3x}{3x}\right]=\dfrac{3x^2-6x}{3x^2(3x-1)}$

7. LCD $=36x^2y^2$; $\dfrac{4}{9xy^2}=\dfrac{16x}{36x^2y^2}$; $\dfrac{5}{12x^2}=\dfrac{15y^2}{36x^2y^2}$

Do the Math 1. $49y^2$ 2. $24(x-3)$ 3. $4(x-3)^2(x+3)$ 4. $(x-1)^2(x+1)$ 5. $-3(c-7)(c+7)$

6. $-(z-4)(z+5)$ 7. $\dfrac{7a^2b+ab}{a^2b^2c}$ 8. $\dfrac{3x+9}{(x+2)(x+3)}$ 9. $\dfrac{14a}{6(a+1)(a+2)}$ 10. $\dfrac{7t^2+7}{t^2+1}$ 11. $\dfrac{28}{35n^2}$; $\dfrac{15n}{35n^2}$

12. $\dfrac{8p^3-4p}{24p^2}$; $\dfrac{9p^3+6}{24p^2}$ 13. $\dfrac{(x+2)^2}{x(x+2)}$; $\dfrac{x^2}{x(x+2)}$ 14. $\dfrac{3ab+6b^2}{7a(a+2b)}$; $\dfrac{2a^2}{7a(a+2b)}$ 15. $\dfrac{5}{m-6}$; $\dfrac{-2m}{m-6}$

16. $\dfrac{4a}{(a+1)(a-1)}$; $\dfrac{7a-7}{(a+1)(a-1)}$ 17. $\dfrac{4n^2+8n}{(n+2)^2(n-3)}$; $\dfrac{2n-6}{(n+2)^2(n-3)}$ 18. $\dfrac{3}{(n-3)(2n-1)}$; $\dfrac{4n^2-2n}{(n-3)(2n-1)}$

Five-Minute Warm-Up 1a. LCD $=6$; $\dfrac{3}{2}=\dfrac{9}{6}$; $\dfrac{5}{3}=\dfrac{10}{6}$ 1b. LCD $=84$; $\dfrac{7}{12}=\dfrac{49}{84}$; $\dfrac{5}{28}=\dfrac{15}{84}$

2. $(3z-2)(2z-1)$ 3. $2x-1$ 4. $-\dfrac{x+4}{2x}$ 5. $\dfrac{1}{2x}$

Guided Practice 1a. $3\bullet5$ 1b. 5^2 1c. $3\bullet5^2=75$ 1d. $\dfrac{7}{15}\bullet\left[\dfrac{5}{5}\right]=\dfrac{35}{75}$ 1e. $\dfrac{10}{25}\bullet\left[\dfrac{3}{3}\right]=\dfrac{30}{75}$

1f. $\dfrac{35+30}{75}=\dfrac{65}{75}$ 1g. $\dfrac{13}{15}$ 2a. $2^2\bullet3\bullet x$ 2b. $2\bullet3^2\bullet x^2$ 2c. $2^2\bullet3^2\bullet x^2=36x^2$ 2d. $\dfrac{5}{12x}\bullet\left[\dfrac{3x}{3x}\right]=\dfrac{15x}{36x^2}$

2e. $\dfrac{7x}{18x^2}\bullet\left[\dfrac{2}{2}\right]=\dfrac{14x}{36x^2}$ 2f. $\dfrac{15x+14x}{36x^2}=\dfrac{29x}{36x^2}$ 2g. $\dfrac{29}{36x}$ 3. $\dfrac{6x+8}{(x+2)(x+1)}$ 4a. $x(x-2)$

4b. $\dfrac{2}{x}\bullet\left[\dfrac{x-2}{x-2}\right]=\dfrac{2x-4}{x(x-2)}$ 4c. $\dfrac{4}{x-2}\bullet\left[\dfrac{x}{x}\right]=\dfrac{4x}{x(x-2)}$ 4d. $\dfrac{2x-4-4x}{x(x-2)}=\dfrac{-2x-4}{x(x-2)}$ 4e. $\dfrac{-2(x+2)}{x(x-2)}$

5. 1 6. $\dfrac{2x-10}{x-4}$

Do the Math **1.** $\dfrac{4}{3}$ **2.** $\dfrac{25+12x}{10x}$ **3.** $\dfrac{x^2+3}{(x-1)(x+1)}$ **4.** $-\dfrac{1}{n-4}$ **5.** $\dfrac{x+6}{x+2}$ **6.** $\dfrac{4}{x-4}$ **7.** $\dfrac{22}{105}$ **8.** $\dfrac{-8x}{(x+2)(x-2)}$

9. $\left(\dfrac{x+2}{x+4}\right)^2$ **10.** $\dfrac{2p^2+4p+1}{p(p-2)}$ **11.** $\dfrac{5n-12}{4n^2}$ **12.** $\dfrac{3x+4}{x+3}$ **13.** $\dfrac{4}{3n(n-3)}$ **14.** $\dfrac{a^2-5a+3}{2a^2(a-3)}$ **15.** $\dfrac{x^2-2x-11}{(x-3)(x-2)}$

16. $\dfrac{15}{w(w-3)}$

Section 7.6

Five-Minute Warm-Up **1.** $(2x+3)(x-4)$ **2.** $3(x+5)(x-5)$ **3.** $\dfrac{4}{3(x+2)}$ **4.** x^2-2x+1

5. $3x^2+2x$

Guided Practice **1.** When sums and/or differences of rational expressions occur in the numerator or denominator of a quotient, the quotient is called a complex rational expression. Rational expressions with more than one fraction bar are complex and need to be simplified. **2a.** $5x$ **2b.** $\dfrac{25-x^2}{5x}$ **2c.** $5x^2$

2d. $\dfrac{x^2-25}{5x^2}$ **2e.** $\dfrac{\dfrac{25-x^2}{5x}}{\dfrac{x^2-25}{5x^2}}$ **2f.** $\dfrac{25-x^2}{5x}\cdot\dfrac{5x^2}{x^2-25}$ **2g.** $\dfrac{^{(-1)}\cancel{(25-x^2)}\cdot\cancel{5}\cdot\cancel{x}\cdot x}{\cancel{5}\cdot\cancel{x}\cdot\cancel{(25-x^2)}\cdot 1}=\dfrac{-x}{1}=-x$

3a. Multiplicative Inverse (a number multiplied by its reciprocal is one) or alternately, any quotient with the same numerator and denominator is a representation of one whole. **3b.** Multiplicative Identity

3c. Distributive Property **4a.** x^2 **4b.** $\left(\dfrac{1+\dfrac{1}{x}}{1-\dfrac{1}{x^2}}\right)\cdot\left[\dfrac{x^2}{x^2}\right]$ **4c.** $\dfrac{1\cdot x^2+\dfrac{1}{x}\cdot x^2}{1\cdot x^2-\dfrac{1}{x^2}\cdot x^2}$ **4d.** $\dfrac{x^2+x}{x^2-1}$

4e. $\dfrac{x\cancel{(x+1)}}{(x-1)\cancel{(x+1)}}=\dfrac{x}{x-1}$

Do the Math **1.** $-t(t-2)$ **2.** $\dfrac{1}{x}$ **3.** $\dfrac{3n+2}{(n-2)(n+1)}$ **4.** $\dfrac{2ab}{(a+b)^2}$ **5.** $\dfrac{5c+2d}{2(5c-4d)}$ **6.** $\dfrac{a+8}{4-a}$ **7.** $\dfrac{x-1}{x+1}$

8. $\dfrac{2xy+1}{3x+1}$ **9.** $\dfrac{x-2}{x-3}$ **10.** $\dfrac{6}{y+5}$ **11.** $\dfrac{2x+1}{x-3}$ **12.** $\dfrac{5m+n}{5m}$ **13.** $\dfrac{y}{x}$ **14.** $\dfrac{4(b-1)}{b}$ **15.** $\dfrac{11(2n+3)}{72}$

Section 7.7

Five-Minute Warm-Up **1.** $\left\{\dfrac{8}{3}\right\}$ **2.** $(x-7)(x+4)$ **3.** $\left\{-\dfrac{1}{2},\dfrac{1}{2}\right\}$ **4.** $x=-8$ or $x=2$ **5.** $P=\dfrac{A}{1+rt}$

Guided Practice **1.** the denominator being equal to zero. **2a.** $x=7$, $x=-7$ **2b.** $(x-7)(x+7)$

2c. $(x-7)(x+7)\dfrac{x+5}{x-7}=\dfrac{x-3}{x+7}(x-7)(x+7)$ **2d.** $(x+7)(x+5)=(x-3)(x-7)$

2e. $x^2+12x+35=x^2-10x+21$ **2f.** $x=-\dfrac{7}{11}$ **2g.** $\left\{-\dfrac{7}{11}\right\}$ **3a.** $x=0$ **3b.** $10x$ **3c.** $90+8=7x$

3d. $\{14\}$ **4a.** $x=1$, $x=-1$ **4b.** $(x-1)(x+1)$ **4c.** $x=-1$ **4d.** $\varnothing$ **5a.** $y=0$ **5b.** xyz

5c. $(xyz)\left(\dfrac{6}{z}\right)=\dfrac{2}{x}(xyz)+\dfrac{1}{y}(xyz)$ **5d.** $6xy=2yz+xz$ **5e.** $6xy-2yz=xz$ **5f.** $y(6x-2z)=xz$

5g. $y=\dfrac{xz}{6x-2z}$ **5h.** $y=\dfrac{xz}{6x-2z}$

Do the Math 1. $\left\{\dfrac{12}{13}\right\}$ 2. $\{36\}$ 3. $\left\{-\dfrac{16}{9}\right\}$ 4. { } or $\varnothing$ 5. $\left\{-\dfrac{8}{3}\right\}$ 6. $\{7\}$ 7. $\left\{-\dfrac{3}{2},\dfrac{2}{3}\right\}$ 8. { } or $\varnothing$

9. $\{-3,4\}$ 10. $\{-5\}$ 11. $b=\dfrac{a}{c}-2$ or $b=\dfrac{a-2c}{c}$ 12. $b=\dfrac{4ik}{3k-8i}$ 13. $x=\dfrac{ck-m}{cB}$ 14. $a=\dfrac{bX}{X-b}$

15. after 1 hour and after 3 hours 16. 40 or 125 bicycles

Section 7.8

Five-Minute Warm-Up 1. $\{12\}$ 2. $\left\{\dfrac{2}{3},4\right\}$ 3. $\{3,-1\}$

Guided Practice 1. $\dfrac{3}{x}$ Answers may vary 2. $\dfrac{3}{x}=\dfrac{x+2}{9}$ Answers may vary 3. $\left\{\dfrac{13}{3}\right\}$ 4. about 26.3 million flight hours in 2001. 5. The figures are the same shape, but they are a different size. The corresponding answers are equal and the corresponding sides are proportional. 6a. $\dfrac{6}{3.2}=\dfrac{x}{8}$ 6b. 15 ft

7a. $\dfrac{1}{15}$ 7b. $\dfrac{1}{t}$ 7c. $\dfrac{1}{t+3}$ 8a. $\dfrac{1}{3}$ 8b. $\dfrac{1}{5}$ 8c. $\dfrac{1}{t}$ 8d. $\dfrac{1}{3}+\dfrac{1}{5}=\dfrac{1}{t}$ 8e. It takes 1.875 hours to clean the building when Josh and Ken work together. 9a. $180+w$ 9b. $180-w$ 9c. $\dfrac{1000}{180+w}$ 9d. $\dfrac{600}{180-w}$

9e. $\dfrac{1000}{180+w}=\dfrac{600}{180-w}$ 9f. The speed of the wind is 45 mph.

Do the Math 1. $\left\{\dfrac{20}{9}\right\}$ 2. $\{2\}$ 3. $\{-9\}$ 4. $\{-4,-3\}$ 5. $\{-2,6\}$ 6. $\{-3,6\}$ 7. $\dfrac{n}{2}$ 8. $r+3$ 9. 5 lb

10. 1600 pesos 11. 20 m 12. $\dfrac{28}{11}\approx 2.5$ hr 13. 45 mph 14. 9 mph

Chapter 8 Answers
Section 8.1

Five-Minute Warm-Up 1. See Graphing Answer Section 2. (b) only 3a. -14 3b. 6 3c. 4
4. $y=\dfrac{4}{3}x+4$ 5a. 12 5b. 0 5c. 125

Guided Practice 1. See Graphing Answer Section 2. origin 3. left 4. 2 5. See Graphing Answer Section 5a. $-2;-7;(-2,-7)$ 5b. $-1;-4;(-1,-4)$ 5c. $0;-1;(0,-1)$ 5d. $1;2;(1,2)$ 5e. $2;5;(2,5)$
6. $(a,0)$ and $(0,b)$ 7. $(0,c)$ 8. If one unit is manufactured and sold, there will be a gain (profit) of \$50.
9. 2 sec after the ball leaves the hand of the thrower, it will be 8 ft above the ground.
Do the Math 1A. $(4,-3)$; IV 1B. $(-3,-1)$; III 1C. $(-2,1)$; II 2. See Graphing Answer Section
2D. y-axis 2E. I 2F. x-axis 3. (b) only 4. (a) and (d) 5. (2, 0) and (0, -4)

6 – 9. See Graphing Answer Section 10. $a=\dfrac{7}{3}$ 11. $b=-13$

Section 8.2

Five-Minute Warm-Up 1a. $(-1,0]$ 1b. $(-2,\infty)$ 2a. $0\le x\le 5$ 2b. $x\ge 1$
3 – 5. See Graphing Answer Section
Guided Practice 1. A relation is a mapping that pairs elements of one set with elements of a second set.
2. inputs; x 3. outputs; y 4a. $(-\infty,\infty)$ 4b. $[-3,\infty)$ 5a. $[-3,3]$ 5b. $[-4,4]$
6. (1, -2), (-2, -1), (-3, 0), (-2, 1), (1, 2) See Graphing Answer Section 6a. $[-3,\infty)$ 6b. $(-\infty,\infty)$
Do the Math 1. map: (30, 7.09), (35, 7.09), (40, 8.40), (45, 11.29); domain: $\{30,35,40,45\}$;
range: $\{7.09, 8.40, 11.29\}$ 2. domain: $\{-2,-1,0,1,2\}$; range: $\{-3,0,3,6\}$ 3. domain: $\{-2,-1,0,1,2\}$;
range: $\{-8,-1,0,1,8\}$ 4. domain: $\{-3,0,3\}$; range: $\{-3,0,3\}$ 5. domain: $[-3,3]$; range: $[-2,2]$

6. domain: $\{-2, 0, 1, 2\}$; range: $\{-2, -1, 0, 3\}$ **7.** domain: $(-\infty, \infty)$; range: $[-3, \infty)$

8. domain: $(-\infty, \infty)$; range: $(-\infty, \infty)$ **9.** domain: $(-\infty, \infty)$; range: $(-\infty, \infty)$ **10.** domain: $(-\infty, \infty)$;

range: $[-2, \infty)$ **11.** domain: $(-\infty, \infty)$; range: $(-\infty, 8]$ **12.** domain: $(-\infty, \infty)$; range: $[-2, \infty)$

13. domain: $[2, \infty)$; range: $(-\infty, \infty)$ **14.** domain: $(-\infty, \infty)$; range: $(-\infty, \infty)$

Section 8.3

Five-Minute Warm-Up 1. 17 **2.** -6 **3.** $(-16, \infty)$ **4.** $\{x \mid x \le 100\}$ **5a.** domain: $\{-2, -4, -6, -8\}$

5b. range: $\{1, 3, 5, 7\}$ **6.** $\dfrac{1}{5}$ **7.** -5 **8.** 3 **9.** 108.0 in.^{3}

Guided Practice 1. A function is a relation in which each element of the domain (inputs) corresponds to exactly one element in the range (outputs). **2a.** yes; domain: $\{3, 4, 5\}$; range: $\{-6, -1\}$ **2b.** no

3a. $2x; -2x$ **3b.** no **4a.** yes **4b.** no **5.** A graph represents a function if and only if every possible vertical line intersects the graph in at most one point. **6.** (c) and (d) only **7.** independent; domain

8. dependent; range **9.** 52 **10.** $-6a + 2$ **11.** 4 **12.** $-3k + 1$ **13a.** N, the number of trucks produced

13b. t, time worked in hours **13c.** 300; After 5 hours, the factory produced 300 trucks.

Do the Math **1.** No **2.** No **3.** Yes **4.** Yes **5.** Yes **6.** Yes **7.** No **8.** Yes **9.** No **10.** No

11. Yes **12a.** 10 **12b.** -5 **12c.** $6x + 1$ **12d.** $3x + 7$ **13a.** -9 **13b.** 1 **13c.** $-4x - 3$ **13d.** $-2x - 7$

14. -20 **15.** 3 **16.** $C = 3$ **17.** $B = 5$

Section 8.4

Five-Minute Warm-Up 1. $\left\{\dfrac{1}{2}\right\}$ **2.** $\{6\}$ **3 – 4.** See Graphing Answer Section **5a.** domain: $[-4, 4]$

5b. range: $[-1, 2]$ **6a.** domain: $[-3, 2]$ **6b.** range: $\left[-\dfrac{7}{6}, \dfrac{10}{3}\right]$

Guided Practice 1. zero **2.** $\left\{t \mid t \ne -\dfrac{3}{2}\right\}$ **3.** $(-\infty, \infty)$ $(-2, 8)(-1, 6)(0, 4)(1, 2)(2, 0)(3, 2)(4, 4)$

4. See Graphing Answer Section **5a.** $(-\infty, \infty)$ **5b.** $[-2, \infty)$ **5c.** x-intercepts: $(-2, 0)$, $(2, 0)$; y-intercept: $(0, -2)$ **6a.** yes **6b.** $-7; (6, -7)$ **6c.** $2; (2, 3)$ **7.** x; zero **8.** $(2, 0)$, $(-2, 0)$

Do the Math **1.** $(-\infty, \infty)$ **2.** $\left(-\infty, -\dfrac{1}{2}\right) \cup \left(-\dfrac{1}{2}, \infty\right)$ **3.** $(-\infty, \infty)$ **4.** $\left(-\infty, -\dfrac{5}{6}\right) \cup \left(-\dfrac{5}{6}, \infty\right)$

5. $(-\infty, \infty)$ **6 – 7.** See Graphing Answer Section **8a.** $(-\infty, \infty)$ **8b.** $(-\infty, \infty)$ **8c.** x-intercept: $(3, 0)$;

y-intercept: $(0, -1)$ **8d.** $x = 3$ **9a.** $(-\infty, \infty)$ **9b.** $(-\infty, \infty)$ **9c.** x-intercepts: $(-2, 0)(1, 0)(4, 0)$;

y-intercept: $(0, 2)$ **9d.** $x = -2, x = 1, x = 4$ **10a.** 8 **10b.** 0, 7 **10c.** $(-4, 10)$ **10d.** $(0, 5)$ **10e.** yes; $x = -4$

11a. no **11b.** 17; $(4, 17)$ **11c.** $-3; (-3, -4)$ **11d.** no **12a.** $[0, \infty)$ **12b.** 381.7 cm^3

Section 8.5

Five-Minute Warm-Up 1– 2. See Graphing Answer Section **3.** $y = -3x - 1$ **4.** $\{-0.9\}$ **5.** $\left\{y \mid y \ge -\dfrac{1}{24}\right\}$

Guided Practice 1. linear; line **2.** slope; y-intercept **3a.** $(0, -2)$ **3b.** $\dfrac{3}{2}$ **3c.** See Graphing Answer

Section **4.** $mx + b = 0$ **5a.** $(0, \infty)$ **5b.** 66 ft **5c.** 15 ft **5d.** when the width exceeds 3 ft

6. fixed; a **7a.** 4500 **7b.** negative **7c.** $V(x) = 22{,}500 - 4500x$ **7d.** $[0, 5]$ **7e.** 4500

7f. after 2.75 years **7g.** time, x **7h.** the value, V **8.** 2 **9a.** slope **9b.** $y - y_1 = m(x - x_1)$

Do the Math **1 – 4.** See Graphing Answer Section **5.** $x = 8$ **6.** $x = 4$ **7a.** $\{-4\}$ **7b.** $-\dfrac{1}{3}$

7c. $-\dfrac{1}{3}$ **7d.** $\{x \mid x > -4\}$ **8.** See Graphing Answer Section; $\left(-4, -\dfrac{1}{3}\right)$ **9a.** $g(x) = 3x + 2$ **9b.** -7

10a. age, a **10b.** Birth rate, B **10c.** $[15, 44]$ **10d.** 23.5 per 1000 women **10e.** 37 years old

Five-Minute Warm-Up **1a.** $\{x \mid -4 \le x < -1\}$ **1b.** $[-4, -1)$ **2.** See Graphing Answer Section

3. $(-3, 5]$ **4.** $\{-3\}$ **5.** $\{x \mid x \le -6\}$ **6.** $\{x \mid x > -2\}$

Guided Practice **1.** $A \cap B$; and **2.** $A \cup B$; or **3a – 3b.** See Graphing Answer Section **4a.** $5x < 10$

4b. $x < 2$ **4c.** $x \ge -4$ **4d – 4f.** See Graphing Answer Section **5.** $a < x < b$

6a. $-8 + 3 \le 5x - 3 + 3 \le 7 + 3$ **6b.** $-5 \le 5x \le 10$ **6c.** $-1 \le x \le 2$ **6d.** See Graphing Answer Section

7a. $-\dfrac{3}{2}x > 3$ **7b.** $x < -2$ **7c.** $7x > 14$ **7d.** $x > 2$ **7e – 7g.** See Graphing Answer Section

7h. $(-\infty, -2) \cup (2, \infty)$

Do the Math **1.** $\{2, 3, 4, 5, 6, 7, 8, 9\}$ **2.** $\{4, 6\}$ **3.** $\varnothing$ **4.** $[-2, 2]$ **5.** $(-\infty, \infty)$

6. $(0, 5]$ **7.** $(-\infty, 0) \cup [6, \infty)$ **8.** $x = 1$ **9.** $(-\infty, 2) \cup [5, \infty)$ **10.** $\left(-2, \dfrac{4}{7}\right]$ **11.** $(-\infty, -2] \cup (3, \infty)$

12. $(-\infty, -10) \cup (1, \infty)$ **13.** $(2, 4]$ **14.** $\left(-\dfrac{5}{3}, \dfrac{11}{4}\right]$ **15.** $(-4, 1)$ **16.** $\left[-\dfrac{9}{4}, 3\right)$ **17.** $\left[-\dfrac{7}{3}, 3\right)$

18. $a = -15; b = -1$ **19.** $60 < x < 90$ **20.** approximately 756.7 kwh up to approximately 1953.1 kwh

Five-Minute Warm-Up **1a.** 12 **1b.** 0 **1c.** $\dfrac{3}{4}$ **1d.** 5.2 **2.** $|45|$ **3.** $|-12|$ **4a.** $\{4\}$ **4b.** $\{7\}$

5a. $\{x \mid x > -6\}$ **5b.** $\{x \mid x \le 3\}$

Guided Practice **1.** $u = a; u = -a$ **2.** isolate the absolute value expression **3a.** $|3x - 1| = 2$

3b. $3x - 1 = 2$ or $3x - 1 = -2$ **3c.** $1; -\dfrac{1}{3}$ **3d.** $\left\{1, -\dfrac{1}{3}\right\}$ **4.** $u = v; u = -v$ **5.** $-a < u < a$; $-a \le u \le a$

6a. $-9 \le 4x - 3 \le 9$ **6b.** $-6 \le 4x \le 12$ **6c.** $-\dfrac{3}{2} \le x \le 3$ **6d.** See Graphing Answer Section **6e.** $\left[-\dfrac{3}{2}, 3\right]$

7. $u > a$ or $u < -a$; $u \ge a$ or $u \le -a$ **8a.** $|8x + 3| > 3$ **8b.** $8x + 3 > 3$ or $8x + 3 < -3$

8c. $x > 0$ or $x < -\dfrac{3}{4}$ **8d.** See Graphing Answer Section **8e.** $\left(-\infty, -\dfrac{3}{4}\right) \cup (0, \infty)$

Do the Math **1.** $\left\{-\dfrac{7}{2}, \dfrac{13}{2}\right\}$ **2.** $\{0, 8\}$ **3.** $\{y \mid -10 < y < 2\}$ **4.** $\left\{x \mid -1 \le x \le \dfrac{7}{3}\right\}$

5. $\{x \mid x \le -11 \text{ or } x \ge 3\}$ **6.** $\{z \mid z \text{ is any real number}\}$ **7.** $\varnothing$ **8.** $\left(-\dfrac{4}{5}, 2\right)$ **9.** $\varnothing$ **10.** $(-\infty, \infty)$

11. $\left\{-1, -\dfrac{1}{2}\right\}$ **12.** $\left(-\infty, \dfrac{1}{2}\right) \cup (1, \infty)$ **13.** $\varnothing$ **14.** $\{y \mid y \text{ is any real number}\}$ **15.** $|x - (-4)| < 2$

16. $|2x - 7| > 3$ **17.** below 36.08 lb/in^2 or above 43.92 lb/in^2

Five-Minute Warm-Up **1a.** $\{-5\}$ **1b.** $\left\{-\dfrac{4}{9}\right\}$ **2.** $\{-48\}$ **3 – 4.** See Graphing Answer Section

Guided Practice **1.** $y = kx$ **2.** constant of proportionality **3.** linear; zero **4.** $y = -\dfrac{25}{3}$ **5.** $y = \dfrac{k}{x}$

6. $y = \dfrac{8}{3}$ **7.** $r = 42$

Do the Math **1a.** $k = 5$ **1b.** $y = 5x$ **1c.** $y = 25$ **2a.** $k = \dfrac{1}{5}$ **2b.** $y = \dfrac{1}{5}x$ **2c.** $y = 7$ **3.** $B = 80$

4. $r = 64$ **5.** 10 representative **6.** \$80.50 **7.** 96 feet per second **8a.** $k = 80$ **8b.** $y = \dfrac{80}{x}$ **8c.** $y = \dfrac{16}{7}$

9a. $k = \dfrac{1}{3}$ **9b.** $y = \dfrac{1}{3}xz$ **9c.** $y = 40$ **10a.** $k = \dfrac{21}{10}$ **10b.** $Q = \dfrac{21x}{10y}$ **10c.** $Q = \dfrac{28}{5}$ **11.** 24 amps

12. approximately 0.033 foot-candles

Chapter 9 Answers
Section 9.1

Five-Minute Warm-Up **1.** $\left\{-10, \dfrac{0}{11}, \dfrac{21}{7}, 5\right\}$ **2.** $\left\{-10, -2.3, \dfrac{0}{11}, \dfrac{21}{7}, 5\right\}$ **3.** $\left\{-\dfrac{2}{3}, 1.\overline{6}, 2.718281828...\right\}$

4. $\left\{-10, -2.3, -\dfrac{2}{3}, \dfrac{0}{11}, \dfrac{21}{7}, 1.\overline{6}, 2.718281828..., 5\right\}$ **5.** 25 **6.** 121 **7.** 0.64 **8.** 1.44 **9.** $\dfrac{16}{49}$ **10.** $\dfrac{169}{36}$

Guided Practice **1a.** positive; negative **1b.** radical **1c.** principal **1d.** radicand **2a.** 8 **2b.** 20 **2c.** $\dfrac{2}{5}$

2d. 17 **3a.** -21 **3b.** 9 **3c.** 13 **3d.** 5 **4a.** rational **4b.** irrational **4c.** real **5a.** irrational; 6.93

5b. not a real number **5c.** rational; 16 **5d.** rational; -15 **6a.** 23 **6b.** $\dfrac{1}{4}$ **6c.** $|3y - 2|$ **6d.** $|5x - 3|$

Do the Math **1.** 3 **2.** $\dfrac{2}{9}$ **3.** 0.4 **4.** 3.7 **5.** not a real number **6.** rational; $\dfrac{7}{10}$ **7.** irrational; 4.90

8. irrational; 3.46 **9.** 13 **10.** $|w|$ **11.** $|x - 8|$ **12.** $|3z - 4|$ **13.** 1 **14.** 1 **15.** not a real number

Section 9.2

Five-Minute Warm-Up **1.** 0.5 **2.** $\dfrac{4}{9}$ **3.** $|4x + 3|$ **4.** $|x - y|$ **5.** $\dfrac{1}{49}$ **6.** x^2 **7.** $\dfrac{9x^2}{y^4}$ **8.** $8b^{12}$

Guided Practice **1.** index; radicand; cube root **2.** ≥ 0; any real number **3.** principal root **4a.** -3

4b. not a real number **4c.** $\dfrac{2}{3}$ **5.** ≈ 2.83 **6.** $|2x - 1|$ **7a.** $\sqrt{144} = 12$ **7b.** $\sqrt{-64}$ not a real number

7c. $2\sqrt[3]{x}$ **8.** $\sqrt[n]{a^m}$; $\left(\sqrt[n]{a}\right)^m$ **9a.** 216 **9b.** -1024 **9c.** 16 **10.** ≈ 8.55 **11a.** $(2x)^{\frac{3}{4}}$ **11b.** $\left(2x^2y\right)^{\frac{2}{3}}$

12a. $\dfrac{1}{64^{\frac{1}{2}}} = \dfrac{1}{8}$ **12b.** $2 \cdot 16^{\frac{1}{2}} = 8$ **12c.** $\dfrac{1}{(4x)^{\frac{5}{2}}} = \dfrac{1}{32x^{\frac{5}{2}}}$

Do the Math **1.** 6 **2.** -4 **3.** $\dfrac{2}{5}$ **4.** n **5.** $|2x - 3|$ **6.** 4 **7.** -5 **8.** not a real number **9.** 8 **10.** $\dfrac{1}{11}$

11. 343 **12.** $x^{\frac{3}{4}}$ **13.** $(3pq)^{\frac{7}{4}}$ **14.** 4.40 **15.** 3.16

Section 9.3

Five-Minute Warm-Up **1.** $54z^7$ **2.** $\dfrac{3u^2}{2}$ or $\dfrac{3}{2}u^2$ **3.** $\dfrac{1}{625}$ **4.** $\dfrac{27}{64}$ **5.** $\dfrac{3x^6}{y}$ **6.** $\dfrac{1}{25p^6}$ **7.** $\dfrac{64b^{10}}{a^2}$

8. $\dfrac{1}{27xy^7}$ **9.** $\dfrac{9}{7}$

Guided Practice **1.** All exponents are positive; each base only occurs once; there are no parentheses in the expression; there are no powers written to powers. **2a.** 36 **2b.** $-2a^{\frac{1}{2}}$ **3.** $\dfrac{x^{\frac{11}{8}}}{y^{\frac{15}{8}}}$ **4a.** 9 **4b.** $2x^2|y|\sqrt[4]{8}$

4c. $\sqrt[4]{x}$ **4d.** $\sqrt[6]{p}$ **5.** $2x^{\frac{1}{3}}\left(3x^{\frac{1}{3}}+5x-2\right)$

Do the Math **1.** 9 **2.** 10 **3.** $\dfrac{1}{y^{\frac{7}{10}}}$ **4.** $\dfrac{2}{9}$ **5.** $a^{\frac{1}{2}}b^{\frac{3}{5}}$ **6.** $\dfrac{b^2}{a^{\frac{2}{3}}}$ **7.** $\dfrac{5p^{\frac{1}{5}}}{q^{\frac{1}{2}}}$ **8.** $\dfrac{8m^{\frac{5}{4}}}{n^{\frac{1}{6}}}$ **9.** $x^2+4x^{\frac{1}{3}}$

10. $8p^2-32$ **11.** x^2 **12.** 25 **13.** $5x^2y^3$ **14.** $\sqrt[12]{p^{13}}$ **15.** $3(x-5)^{\frac{1}{2}}(5x-9)$ **16.** $\dfrac{2(6x+1)}{x^{\frac{2}{3}}}$

Section 9.4

Five-Minute Warm-Up **1.** 1, 4, 9, 16, 25, 36, 49, 64, 81, 100, 121, 144 **2.** 1, 8, 27, 64, 125 **3.** 1, 16, 81
4. not a real number **5.** 10 **6.** $|x|$ **7.** $|4x+1|$ **8.** $|2p-1|$ **9.** 13

Guided Practice **1a.** $\sqrt{35}$ **1b.** $\sqrt{x^2-25}$ **1c.** $\sqrt[3]{14x^2}$ **2.** A radical expression is simplified provided that the radicand does not contain factors that are perfect powers of the index. For square roots, there can be no factor with exponent two or higher in the radicand. For cube roots, there can be no factor with exponent three or higher in the radicand. **3a.** 25 **3b.** $\sqrt{25}\cdot\sqrt{3}$ **3c.** $5\sqrt{3}$ **4a.** $16\bullet 3$ **4b.** $\sqrt{16\bullet 3}=\sqrt{16}\bullet\sqrt{3}$

4c. $\dfrac{-6+4\bullet\sqrt{3}}{2}$ **4d.** $\dfrac{2\left(-3+2\sqrt{3}\right)}{2}$ **4e.** $-3+2\sqrt{3}$ **5.** Rewrite the variable expression as the product of two

variable expressions, where one of the factors has an exponent that is a multiple of the index. **6.** $\dfrac{2x\sqrt{3}}{11}$

7. $\dfrac{6}{a^2}$ **8.** Rewrite $\sqrt{6}\bullet\sqrt[4]{48}$ as $6^{\frac{1}{2}}\bullet 48^{\frac{1}{4}}$.

Do the Math **1.** $\sqrt[4]{42a^2b^2}$ **2.** $\sqrt{p^2-25}$; $|p|\geq 5$ **3.** $\sqrt[3]{-3x}$ **4.** $3\sqrt[4]{2}$ **5.** $2|a|\sqrt{5}$ **6.** $-4p$ **7.** $x^2\sqrt[5]{x^2}$
8. -1 **9.** $\dfrac{-3+2\sqrt{3}}{4}$ **10.** 6 **11.** $6x\sqrt{5}$ **12.** $3a\sqrt[3]{2}$ **13.** $6m\sqrt[3]{2mn^2}$ **14.** $\dfrac{\sqrt{5}}{6}$ **15.** $\dfrac{x\sqrt[4]{5}}{2}$ **16.** $-\dfrac{3x^3}{4y^4}$
17. 2 **18.** $\sqrt[6]{392}$ **19.** $\sqrt[8]{45}$

Section 9.5

Five-Minute Warm-Up **1.** $3z^3-5z^2-4z$ **2.** $-3a^2b^2-a^2+6ab-b^2$ **3.** $-8x^4-12x^3y+20x^2y^2$
4. $\dfrac{2}{9}x^5-\dfrac{4}{7}x^4+x^2$ **5.** $18c^2-23c-6$ **6.** a^2b^2-4 **7.** $49n^2-42n+9$

Guided Practice **1.** Like radicals have the same index and the same radicand. **2a.** $9\sqrt{x}$ **2b.** $8\sqrt[3]{3p}$
3a. $-10\sqrt{2}$ **3b.** $-n^4\sqrt{6}+4n^4\sqrt{6n}$ **4.** $18+4\sqrt{6}-27\sqrt{2}-12\sqrt{3}$ **5a.** $(A+B)(A-B)=A^2+B^2$
5b. $49-3=46$

Do the Math **1.** $14\sqrt{3}$ **2.** $7\sqrt[4]{z}$ **3.** $11\sqrt[3]{5}-11\sqrt{5}$ **4.** $8\sqrt{3}$ **5.** $2\sqrt[4]{3}$ **6.** $3\sqrt{3z}$ **7.** $13z\sqrt{7z}$ **8.** $2y\sqrt{3y}$
9. $3(2x-1)\sqrt[3]{5}$ **10.** $5\sqrt{5}+3\sqrt{15}$ **11.** $\sqrt[3]{12}+2\sqrt[3]{9}$ **12.** $15+3\sqrt{5}+5\sqrt{6}+\sqrt{30}$ **13.** $-141-22\sqrt{10}$
14. $7-4\sqrt{3}$ **15.** $-2\sqrt{3}$ **16.** $7-4\sqrt{3}$ **17.** $\sqrt[3]{y^2}-3\sqrt[3]{y}-18$ **18.** $\dfrac{2\sqrt{5}}{25}$

Section 9.6

Five-Minute Warm-Up **1.** 3 **2.** $11a$ **3.** $\dfrac{3\sqrt{2}}{2}$ **4.** 1 **5.** $24-\sqrt{15}$

Guided Practice **1.** The process of rationalizing the denominator of a quotient requires rewriting the quotient, using properties of rational expressions, so that the denominator of the equivalent expression does not contain any radicals. **2.** a perfect square **3a.** $\dfrac{\sqrt{3}}{\sqrt{3}}$ **3b.** $\dfrac{\sqrt{5}}{\sqrt{5}}$ **3c.** $\dfrac{\sqrt{2a}}{\sqrt{2a}}$ **4a.** $\dfrac{\sqrt[3]{25}}{\sqrt[3]{25}}$ **4b.** $\dfrac{\sqrt[3]{18}}{\sqrt[3]{18}}$

4c. $\dfrac{\sqrt[4]{3x^2y^3}}{\sqrt[4]{3x^2y^3}}$ **5.** conjugate **6a.** $3-\sqrt{5}$; 4 **6b.** $2\sqrt{3}+5\sqrt{2}$; -38 **7.** $\sqrt{2}+3$

Do the Math **1.** $\dfrac{2\sqrt{3}}{3}$ **2.** $-\dfrac{\sqrt{3}}{2}$ **3.** $\dfrac{\sqrt{33}}{11}$ **4.** $\dfrac{\sqrt{5z}}{z}$ **5.** $\dfrac{4\sqrt{2a}}{a^3}$ **6.** $-\dfrac{\sqrt[3]{4p^2}}{p}$ **7.** $-\dfrac{\sqrt[3]{15}}{6}$ **8.** $\dfrac{4\sqrt[3]{6z}}{3z}$

9. $2\left(\sqrt{7}+2\right)$ **10.** $10\left(\sqrt{10}-3\right)$ **11.** $\dfrac{\sqrt{5}+\sqrt{2}}{3}$ **12.** $2+\sqrt{3}$ **13.** $\dfrac{4\sqrt{5}}{5}$ **14.** $\dfrac{\sqrt{10}-5\sqrt{5}}{5}$ **15.** $\dfrac{3\sqrt{5}}{5}$

16. $\dfrac{10\sqrt{2}-27}{23}$ **17.** $\dfrac{1}{2\left(2-\sqrt{3}\right)}$ **18.** $\dfrac{a-b}{\sqrt{2a}+\sqrt{2b}}$

Section 9.7

Five-Minute Warm-Up **1.** 12 **2.** n **3.** $\{x\,|\,x\le -3\}$ **4.** -40 **5.** See Graphing Answer Section

Guided Practice **1a.** $4\sqrt{5}$ **1b.** $\sqrt[3]{-9}$ **1c.** $\sqrt{2}$ **2.** ≥ 0 **3.** any real number **4a.** $\left\{x\,\middle|\,x\ge \dfrac{3}{2}\right\}$ or $\left[\dfrac{3}{2},\infty\right)$

4b. $\{x\,|\,x$ is any real number$\}$ or $(-\infty,\infty)$ **4c.** $\{t\,|\,t\le 2\}$ or $(-\infty,2]$ **5a.** $[-3,\infty)$ **5b.** See Graphing Answer Section **5c.** $[0,\infty)$ **6a.** $(-\infty,\infty)$ **6b.** See Graphing Answer Section **6c.** $(-\infty,\infty)$

Do the Math **1a.** 4 **1b.** $2\sqrt{3}$ **1c.** 2 **2a.** 1 **2b.** -3 **2c.** $2\sqrt[3]{2}$ **3a.** $\dfrac{1}{3}$ **3b.** $\dfrac{\sqrt{3}}{3}$ **3c.** $\dfrac{\sqrt{2}}{2}$ **4.** $[-4,\infty)$

5. $\left(-\infty,\dfrac{5}{2}\right]$ **6.** $(-\infty,\infty)$ **7.** $\left[\dfrac{2}{3},\infty\right)$ **8.** $(3,\infty)$ **9a.** $[1,\infty)$ **9b.** $[0,\infty)$ **10a.** $(-\infty,4]$ **10b.** $[0,\infty)$

11a. $[0,\infty)$ **11b.** $[1,\infty)$ **12a.** $(-\infty,\infty)$ **12b.** $(-\infty,\infty)$ **9c. – 12c.** See Graphing Answer Section

Section 9.8

Five-Minute Warm-Up **1.** $\{-3\}$ **2.** $\{1,2\}$ **3.** $2x$ **4.** $2x+10\sqrt{2x}+25$ **5.** $3x+8$ **6.** $4\sqrt{3}$

Guided Practice **1a.** $\sqrt{4x+1}=5$ **1b.** $\left(\sqrt{4x+1}\right)^2=5^2$ **1c.** $4x+1=25$ **1d.** $x=6$ **1e.** yes **1f.** $\{6\}$

2. Extraneous solutions are apparent solutions; they are algebraically correct but do not satisfy the original equation. **3.** Isolate the radical on one side of the equation. If there are two radicals, one radical should be on the left side and the other radical on the right side of the equation. **4a.** $x=1$ **4b.** no **4c.** $\varnothing$ **4d.** The square root function is equal to a negative number. **5a.** $x=4$ or $x=-1$ **5b.** $x=4$, yes ; $x=-1$, no **5c.** $\{4\}$

6a. $(3x+1)^{\frac{3}{2}}=8$ **6b.** $\dfrac{2}{3}$ **6c.** $x=1$ **6d.** $\{1\}$ **7a.** $\sqrt{2x^2-5x-20}=\sqrt{x^2-3x+15}$

7b. $2x^2-5x-20=x^2-3x+15$ **7c.** $x=7$, $x=-5$ **7d.** yes **7e.** $\{7,-5\}$

Do the Math **1.** $\{14\}$ **2.** $\varnothing$ **3.** $\{3\}$ **4.** $\{49\}$ **5.** $\{13\}$ **6.** $\{9\}$ **7.** $\{16\}$ **8.** $\{-2\}$ **9.** $\{6\}$ **10.** $\{-6,3\}$

11. $\{1,5\}$ **12.** $\{12\}$ **13.** $\{-6\}$ **14.** $\{3\}$ **15.** $\{9\}$ **16.** $\{12\}$ **17.** $a=\dfrac{v^2}{r}$ **18.** $S=4\pi r^2$ **19.** $\$1102.50$

Section 9.9

Five-Minute Warm-Up **1a.** $\{8,|-5|\}$ **1b.** $\left\{8,|-5|,\dfrac{0}{-12}\right\}$ **1c.** $\left\{8,|-5|,\dfrac{0}{-12},\dfrac{-6}{3}\right\}$

1d. $\left\{8,|-5|,\dfrac{0}{-12},\dfrac{-6}{3},0.\overline{3},\dfrac{2}{5}\right\}$ **1e.** $\{\pi\}$ **1f.** $\left\{8,|-5|,\dfrac{0}{-12},\dfrac{-6}{3},0.\overline{3},\dfrac{2}{5},\pi\right\}$ **2.** $3x^2-2$

3. $-12p^6+36p^5$ **4.** $-6x^2+13x+28$ **5.** x^4-16

Guided Practice **1.** -1; $\sqrt{-1}$ **2.** $a + bi$; real numbers; standard; 6; -2 **3.** $9i$ **4.** $6 + 2i$ **5.** standard **6.** Add the real parts, then add the imaginary parts together. **7.** $12 + 9i$ **8a.** It cannot be used because $\sqrt{-4}$ and $\sqrt{-9}$ are not real numbers. **8b.** $2i \bullet 3i$ **8c.** -6 **9a.** $4 - 4i$ **9b.** $\dfrac{3 + 6i}{4 + 4i} \cdot \dfrac{4 - 4i}{4 - 4i}$

9c. $\dfrac{12 - 12i + 24i - 24i^2}{16 + 16}$ **9d.** $\dfrac{36 + 12i}{32}$ **9e.** $\dfrac{36}{32} + \dfrac{12i}{32}$ **9f.** $\dfrac{9}{8} + \dfrac{3}{8}i$ **10a.** -1 **10b.** $-i$ **10c.** 1 **10d.** i
10e. -1 **10f.** $-i$ **10g.** 1

Do the Math **1.** $-10i$ **2.** $9\sqrt{2}i$ **3.** $10 + 4\sqrt{2}i$ **4.** $2 - i$ **5.** $-3 + 14i$ **6.** $-4 + i$ **7.** $-3 + i$

8. $-4 - \sqrt{5}i$ **9.** $18 - 6i$ **10.** $5 + 5i$ **11.** $\dfrac{5}{3} + \dfrac{5}{3}i$ **12.** $-21 + 20i$ **13.** $-45 - 28i$ **14.** -12 **15.** $54 + 23i$

16. $-\dfrac{1}{2} - i$ **17.** $\dfrac{8}{17} - \dfrac{2}{17}i$ **18.** i **19.** 1 **20.** $-i$

Chapter 10 Answers
Section 10.1

Five-Minute Warm-Up **1.** $9x^2 - 6x + 1$ **2.** $(x - 2)^2$ **3.** $\left\{\dfrac{1}{3}\right\}$ **4.** $\left\{\dfrac{7}{5}, -\dfrac{7}{5}\right\}$ **5.** $\dfrac{9}{5}$ **6.** $|8x - 3|$

7. $2\sqrt{3}i$ **8.** $2 + \dfrac{1}{2}i$ **9.** $-15 - 7i$

Guided Practice **1.** $x = \sqrt{p}$ or $x = -\sqrt{p}$ $\left(x = \pm\sqrt{p}\right)$ **2.** $\left\{-1 + 2\sqrt{3}, -1 - 2\sqrt{3}\right\}$ **3.** False **4.** False

5a. $n^2 = 144$ **5b.** $\sqrt{n^2} = \pm\sqrt{144}$ **5c.** $n = \pm 12$ **5d.** $\{12, -12\}$ **6a.** integer, rational, irrational

6b. complex; $a + bi, b \neq 0$ **7.** $\left(\dfrac{1}{2}b\right)^2$ **8a.** $49; (p - 7)^2$ **8b.** $\dfrac{81}{4}; \left(n + \dfrac{9}{2}\right)^2$ **8c.** $\dfrac{4}{9}; \left(z + \dfrac{2}{3}\right)^2$

9a. $p^2 - 6p = 18$ **9b.** 9 **9c.** $p^2 - 6p + 9 = 27$ **9d.** $(p - 3)^2 = 27$ **9e.** $\sqrt{(p-3)^2} = \pm\sqrt{27}$

9f. $p - 3 = \pm 3\sqrt{3}$ **9g.** $p = 3 \pm 3\sqrt{3}$ **9h.** $\left\{3 + 3\sqrt{3}, 3 - 3\sqrt{3}\right\}$ **10.** divide both sides of the equation by 3.

11. In a right triangle, the square of the length of the hypotenuse is equal to the sum of the squares of the lengths of the legs; $z^2 = x^2 + y^2$

Do the Math **1.** $\left\{-4\sqrt{3}, 4\sqrt{3}\right\}$ **2.** $\left\{-2\sqrt{5}, 2\sqrt{5}\right\}$ **3.** $\{-1, 5\}$ **4.** $\left\{-\dfrac{7}{2}, \dfrac{1}{2}\right\}$ **5.** $\left\{-\dfrac{3}{2} \pm \dfrac{\sqrt{3}}{2}\right\}$

6. $\{-1, 7\}$ **7.** $4; (p - 2)^2$ **8.** $\dfrac{1}{36}; \left(z - \dfrac{1}{6}\right)^2$ **9.** $\dfrac{25}{16}; \left(m + \dfrac{5}{4}\right)^2$ **10.** $\{-6, 3\}$ **11.** $\left\{-\dfrac{7}{2} \pm \dfrac{\sqrt{21}}{2}\right\}$

12. $\left\{\dfrac{5}{2} \pm \dfrac{\sqrt{37}}{2}\right\}$ **13.** $\left\{5 \pm \sqrt{30}\right\}$ **14.** $\left\{-\dfrac{2}{3}, 2\right\}$ **15.** $\left\{-\dfrac{3}{2} \pm \dfrac{i}{2}\right\}$ **16.** 25 **17.** 3 **18.** $4\sqrt{6} \approx 9.80$

19. $-1 \pm 4\sqrt{2}$ **20.** ≈ 82.284 feet

Section 10.2

Five-Minute Warm-Up **1.** $5\sqrt{5}$ **2.** $\dfrac{5}{2} + \sqrt{2}$ **3.** $2\sqrt{7}i$ **4.** $1 - \dfrac{2}{3}i$ **5.** $3x^2 - 9x + 1$ **6.** $2\sqrt{10}$

Guided Practice **1.** $\dfrac{-b \pm \sqrt{b^2 - 4ac}}{2a}$ **2.** standard form **3a.** $2x^2 - x - 4 = 0$; $a = 2, b = -1, c = -4$

3b. $3x^2 + 6 = 0$; $a = 0, b = 0, c = 6$ **3c.** $3x^2 - 6x = 0$; $a = 3, b = -6, c = 0$ **4a.** 8; -2; -3

4b. $n = \dfrac{-b \pm \sqrt{b^2 - 4ac}}{2a}$ **4c.** $n = \dfrac{-(-2) \pm \sqrt{(-2)^2 - 4(8)(-3)}}{2(8)}$ **4d.** 100 **4e.** $\dfrac{2 \pm 10}{16} = \dfrac{1 \pm 5}{8}$

4f. $\dfrac{1+5}{8}, \dfrac{1-5}{8}$ **4g.** $\left\{\dfrac{3}{4}, \dfrac{-1}{2}\right\}$ **5.** $b^2 - 4ac$ **6a.** 169; two rational **6b.** -20; two complex, not real

6c. 0; one repeated real **7a.** 3 **7b.** $N = \dfrac{2000}{3^2 + 5}$ **7c.** \$142.86 **7d.** \$1714.29

7e. During the third year, Joel spent \$1714.29 on advertising.

Do the Math **1.** $\{-4, 8\}$ **2.** $\left\{-\dfrac{1}{2}, \dfrac{2}{5}\right\}$ **3.** $\left\{1 \pm \dfrac{\sqrt{2}}{2}\right\}$ **4.** $\left\{\dfrac{3}{2} \pm \dfrac{\sqrt{5}}{2}\right\}$ **5.** $\left\{1 \pm \dfrac{\sqrt{10}}{2}i\right\}$ **6.** $\left\{-\dfrac{3}{5} \pm \dfrac{\sqrt{14}}{5}\right\}$

7. 24, 2 irrational **8.** 0, one repeated real **9.** –95, 2 complex, not real **10.** $\left\{\dfrac{7}{2} \pm \dfrac{\sqrt{21}}{2}\right\}$ **11.** $\left\{-2, \dfrac{1}{3}\right\}$

12. $\left\{\dfrac{2}{5} \pm \dfrac{\sqrt{29}}{5}\right\}$ **13.** $\dfrac{5}{2}$ **14.** $1 \pm \sqrt{6}$ **15.** $\dfrac{1}{2} \pm \dfrac{\sqrt{19}}{2}i$ **16a.** $x = -4$ or $x = 2$ **16b.** $x = -2$ or $x = 0$

17. width ≈ 5.307 in. length ≈ 11.307 in. **18.** base≈ 9.426 in.; height≈ 7.426 in. **19.** ≈ 49.0 mph

Section 10.3

Five-Minute Warm-Up **1.** $(a-3)(a+3)(a^2+2)$ **2.** $(2x-5)(3x-5)$ **3.** $\dfrac{25}{x^2}$ **4.** $\dfrac{4}{9}x^6$ **5.** $\left\{\dfrac{3}{2}, -2\right\}$

Guided Practice **1a.** $\sqrt{y}$; $2u^2 - 11u + 15 = 0$ **1b.** $1\,v^2$; $u^2 + 10u + 1 = 0$ **1c.** $(x-1)$; $u^2 - 5u + 6 = 0$

1d. $x^{\frac{1}{3}}$; $u^2 - u - 3 = 0$ **1e.** x^{-1} or $\dfrac{1}{x}$; $4u^2 + u - 3 = 0$ **2a.** x^2 **2b.** $u^2 - 6u - 16 = 0$ **2c.** $(u-8)(u+2) = 0$

2d. $u = 8$ or $u = -2$ **2e.** $x^2 = 8$ or $x^2 = -2$ **2f.** $\sqrt{x^2} = \pm\sqrt{8}$ or $\sqrt{x^2} = \pm\sqrt{-2}$

2g. $x = \pm 2\sqrt{2}$ or $x = \pm\sqrt{2}i$ **2h.** $\left\{2\sqrt{2}, -2\sqrt{2}, \sqrt{2}i, -\sqrt{2}i\right\}$ **3a.** $(x^2 + 3)$ **3b.** $\{1, -1, i, -i\}$ **4a.** $\sqrt{x}$

4b. $\varnothing$ **5a.** $n^{\frac{1}{3}}$ **5b.** $\{-1, 27\}$ **6a.** For $\sqrt{x}$, $x \geq 0$. **6b.** For $\dfrac{1}{x}$, $x \neq 0$.

Do the Math **1.** $\{-3, -1, 1, 3\}$ **2.** $\left\{-1, -\dfrac{1}{2}, \dfrac{1}{2}, 1\right\}$ **3.** $\{3, -4\}$ **4.** $\{36\}$ **5.** $\varnothing$ **6.** $\left\{-\dfrac{1}{5}, \dfrac{1}{3}\right\}$

7. $\left\{-\dfrac{2}{5}, 5\right\}$ **8.** $\{-1, 27\}$ **9.** $\left\{\dfrac{1}{3}, \dfrac{1}{4}\right\}$ **10.** $\{-1, 2\}$ **11.** $\{2, -3\}$ **12.** $\{-2i, -1, 1, 2i\}$ **13.** 81

14. $\left\{\dfrac{7}{8}, 2\right\}$ **15.** $0, \sqrt{5}i, -\sqrt{5}i$ **16.** $-\sqrt{7}i, \sqrt{7}i, -\sqrt{2}, \sqrt{2}$ **17.** $0, -\sqrt{3}, \sqrt{3}$ **18.** $-\sqrt{2}i, \sqrt{2}i, -\sqrt{5}, \sqrt{5}$

19. $-\sqrt{6}, \sqrt{6}, -\sqrt{7}, \sqrt{7}$ **20.** $\dfrac{49}{4}$

Section 10.4

Five-Minute Warm-Up **1 – 2.** See Graphing Answer Section **3.** –29 **4.** 33 **5.** $\{x \mid x \text{ is any real number}\}$

Guided Practice **1.** (b) **2.** (a) **3a.** vertically **3b.** 2 **3c.** down **4a.** horizontally **4b.** 1 **4c.** right **5a.** up

5b. down **6a.** >1 **6b.** $0 < |a| < 1$ **7a.** $f(x) = (3x^2 - 12x) + 7$ **7b.** $f(x) = 3(x^2 - 4x + \underline{\quad}) + 7 + \underline{\quad}$

7c. 4 **7d.** Add the additive inverse of $(3)(4)$ or -12 **7e.** $f(x) = 3(x^2 - 4x + 4) + 7 + (-12)$

7f. $f(x) = 3(x-2)^2 - 5$ **7g.** $(2, -5)$ **7h.** up **7i.** $x = 2$

Do the Math **1 – 6.** See Graphing Answer Section **7.** $h(x) = \left(x - \dfrac{7}{2}\right)^2 - \dfrac{9}{4}$; $V\left(\dfrac{7}{2}, -\dfrac{9}{4}\right)$; $x = \dfrac{7}{2}$

8. $f(x) = 3(x+3)^2 - 2$; $V(-3, -2)$; $x = -3$ **9.** $g(x) = -(x+4)^2 + 2$; $V(-4, 2)$; $x = -4$

10. $h(x) = -4\left(x - \dfrac{1}{2}\right)^2 + 1$; $V\left(\dfrac{1}{2}, 1\right)$; $x = \dfrac{1}{2}$ **11.** $f(x) = \dfrac{1}{2}(x+5)^2$ **12.** $f(x) = x^2 - 5$

Section 10.5

Five-Minute Warm-Up **1.** x-intercept: -4; y-intercept: 3 **2.** $\left\{8, -\dfrac{3}{2}\right\}$ **3.** 6 and -1 **4.** -12

Guided Practice **1.** $-\dfrac{b}{2a}$ **2.** setting $f(x) = 0$ and solving for x. **3a.** 1; 2; -8 **3b.** up **3c.** $x = -1$

3d. $y = -9$ **3e.** $(-1, -9)$ **3f.** $x = -1$ **3g.** -8 **3h.** 36 **3i.** 2 **3j.** $(-4, 0); (2, 0)$

3k. See Graphing Answer Section **4.** y-coordinate **5.** maximum **6.** minimum **7a.** $A = x \cdot y$

7b. $2x + y = 50$ **7c.** $y = 50 - 2x$ **7d.** $A = x(50 - 2x)$ or $A = -2x^2 + 50x$ **7e.** $x = 12.5$ **7f.** $y = 25$

7g. The pen has two sides of 12.5 ft and one side 25 ft. **7h.** 312.5 ft^2

Do the Math **1.** $2; -\dfrac{1}{2}, 4$ **2.** $1; 3$ **3.** $2; \approx -0.28, \approx 1.78$ **4 – 9.** See Graphing Answer Section

10. maximum; 11 **11.** minimum; -6 **12.** 25 and 25 **13.** -5 and 5 **14a.** ≈ 4.84 seconds **14b.** ≈ 383.39 feet **14c.** ≈ 9.74 seconds

Section 10.6

Five-Minute Warm-Up **1.** $[-4, -2)$ **2.** $(-3, 1]$ **3.** $(-2, \infty)$ **4.** $(-\infty, 5]$ **5.** $\{x \mid x \geq 2\}$

6. $\{1 + \sqrt{6}, 1 - \sqrt{6}\}$

Guided Practice **1a.** above **1b.** below **2a.** graphical **2b.** algebraic **3a.** $f(x) = x^2 + 2x - 3$

3b. $(-3, 0); (1, 0)$ **3c.** $(-1, -4)$ **3d.** See Graphing Answer Section **3e.** negative **3f.** $[-3, 1]$

4a. positive **4b.** negative **5a.** $(x+7)(x-5) = 0$ **5b.** $x = -7; x = 5$ **5c.** $(-\infty, -7); (-7, 5); (5, \infty)$

5d. See Graphing Answer Section **5e.** positive **5f.** no **5g.** $(-\infty, -7) \cup (5, \infty)$

Do the Math **1.** $[-1, 8]$ **2.** $(-\infty, 4) \cup (10, \infty)$ **3.** $(-4, -1)$ **4.** $\left(-\dfrac{7}{2}, 1\right)$ **5.** $(-\infty, -2) \cup (3, \infty)$

6. $\left(-\infty, \dfrac{3 - \sqrt{29}}{2}\right] \cup \left[\dfrac{3 + \sqrt{29}}{2}, \infty\right)$ **7.** $\left(-\infty, \dfrac{-3 - \sqrt{69}}{6}\right) \cup \left(\dfrac{-3 + \sqrt{69}}{6}, \infty\right)$ **8.** $(-\infty, \infty)$ **9.** $\varnothing$ **10.** $\{4\}$

11. $(-\infty, -4) \cup (0, \infty)$ **12.** $[-8, 6]$ **13.** $(-\infty, 0] \cup [5, \infty)$ **14.** $(-\infty, -9] \cup [7, \infty)$ **15.** between \$50 and \$70

Section 10.7

Five-Minute Warm-Up **1.** $[-3, 2)$ **2.** $\{x \mid x < -1\}$ See Graphing Answer Section **3.** $\left[-\dfrac{5}{3}, \infty\right)$ **4.** yes

Guided Practice **1a.** 0; 0 **1b.** 0; 0 **2.** positive; negative (alternately: negative; positive) **3.** positive; negative; negative; positive (alternately: negative; positive; positive; negative) **4.** denominator to equal zero **5a.** $x = -2$ **5b.** $x = 4$ **5c.** -3 (answers may vary) **5d.** negative **5e.** negative **5f.** positive **5g.** 0 (answers may vary) **5h.** positive **5i.** negative **5j.** negative **5k.** 5 (answers may vary) **5l.** positive **5m.** positive **5n.** positive **5o.** negative **5p.** $x = 4$ **5q.** See Graphing Answer Section

6. $\dfrac{-2x + 12}{(x-1)(x+1)} > 0$ **7.** $\dfrac{x - 11}{x + 2} < 0$ **8.** See Graphing Answer Section **9.** See Graphing Answer Section

Do the Math **1.** $(-\infty, -8) \cup (-2, \infty)$ **2.** $(-\infty, -12] \cup (2, \infty)$ **3.** $(-5, 10]$ **4.** $(-\infty, -4) \cup \left(\dfrac{2}{5}, 5\right)$

5. $\left(-1, \dfrac{2}{3}\right] \cup [6, \infty)$ **6.** $(4, \infty)$ **7.** $(-2, 11]$ **8.** $(-\infty, -6) \cup (-5, \infty)$ **9.** $(-\infty, -3) \cup \left[-\dfrac{3}{2}, 0\right)$

10. $\left(-\infty, -\dfrac{1}{2}\right] \cup (4, 13]$ **11.** $(-\infty, -3] \cup (8, \infty)$ **12.** $\left(-\dfrac{2}{3}, 4\right)$ **13.** -4 and $\dfrac{5}{3}$ **14.** -3

15. 125 or more bicycles

Chapter 11 Answers
Section 11.1

Five-Minute Warm-Up   **1.** $\{x \mid x \neq 2, x \neq 1\}$ **2a.** -47 **2b.** $-3a^2 + 12a - 11$

2c. $-3x^2 - 6xh - 3h^2 + 1$ **3a.** not a function   **3b.** is a function

Guided Practice   **1.** $(f \circ g)(x)$ **2a.** -3 **2b.** 25   **2c.** 25   **3a.** 39   **3b.** 38   **3c.** 38

4. A function is one-to-one if each unique element in the domain corresponds to a unique element in the range and each unique element in the range corresponds to a unique element in the domain.   **5a.** yes   **5b.** no

6. the horizontal line test

7. one-to-one   **8.** $f^{-1}(x)$; (b, a) **9a.** $\{(15, -3), (-5, -1), (0, 0), (10, 2)\}$ **9b.** $\{-3, -1, 0, 2\}$

9c. $\{15, -5, 0, 10\}$ **9d.** $\{15, -5, 0, 10\}$ **9e.** $\{-3, -1, 0, 2\}$ **10.** $y = x$ **11a.** $y = 4x - 8$

11b. $x = 4y - 8$ **11c.** $x + 8 = 4y$ **11d.** $y = \dfrac{x + 8}{4}$ **11e.** $f^{-1}(x) = \dfrac{x + 8}{4}$

Do the Math   **1.** 253   **2.** 6   **3.** 1   **4.** -94 **5.** $(f \circ g)(x) = 4x - 3$ **6.** $(g \circ f)(x) = \sqrt{x + 2} - 2$

7. $(f \circ f)(x) = \dfrac{2(x - 1)}{3 - x}$; $x \neq 1, 3$ **8.** one-to-one   **9.** not one-to-one   **10.** one-to-one

11. $\{(1, -10), (4, -5), (3, 0), (2, -5)\}$ **12.** $(f \circ g)(x) = (g \circ f)(x) = x$ **13.** $(f \circ g)(x) = (g \circ f)(x) = x$

14. $g^{-1}(x) = x - 6$ **15.** $H^{-1}(x) = \dfrac{x - 8}{3}$ **16.** $f^{-1}(x) = \sqrt[3]{x + 2}$ **17.** $G^{-1}(x) = 3 - \dfrac{2}{x}$

18. $R^{-1}(x) = \dfrac{4x}{2 - x}$ **19.** $g^{-1}(x) = (x + 3)^3 - 2$ **20.** $V(t) = 36\pi t$; $1080\pi \approx 3392.92\,m^3$

Section 11.2

Five-Minute Warm-Up   **1.** 16   **2.** $\dfrac{1}{4}$ **3.** 1   **4.** $\dfrac{1}{10}$ **5a.** 6.0235   **5b.** 6.0234   **6.** $\dfrac{10}{x^2}$ **7.** $\dfrac{2a^6}{5}$

8. $64p^{15}$ **9.** $\left\{-\dfrac{1}{2}, \dfrac{5}{3}\right\}$

Guided Practice   **1.** a positive real number; 1   **2.** ≈ 2.63902 **3.** ≈ 2.66514 **4.** (b)   **5.** (a)   **6.** ≈ 2.718

7a. ≈ 20.09 **7b.** ≈ 0.14 **8.** the exponents are equal   **9a.** $3^{2x + 1} = 3^3$ **9b.** $2x + 1 = 3$ **9c.** $2x = 2$

9d. $x = 1$ **9e.** $\{1\}$ **10.** ≈ 64.7 grams   **11.** $A = P\left(1 + \dfrac{r}{n}\right)^{nt}$; $A = $ final amount; $t = $ years that the interest

accumulates; $r = $ annual interest rate written in decimals; $n = $ number of times per year of compounding

12a. P=$100, r= .07, n=4, t=5   **12b.** $141.48   **12c.** P=$100, r= .07, n=360, , t=5   **12d.** $141.90

Do the Math   **1a.** 9.518   **1b.** 9.673   **1c.** 9.735   **1d.** 9.738   **1e.** 9.739   **2a.** 20.086   **2b.** 4.482

3 – 5. See Graphing Answer Section   **6.** $\{-2\}$ **7.** $\{4\}$ **8.** $\{1\}$ **9.** $\left\{-1, -\dfrac{1}{3}\right\}$ **10.** $\{-2\}$ **11.** $\left\{\dfrac{2}{3}\right\}$

12. $f(2) = 9$; $(2, 9)$ **13.** $x = -4$; $\left(-4, \dfrac{1}{81}\right)$ **14a.** ≈ 6.7 billion people   **14b.** ≈ 7.3 billion people

Section 11.3

Five-Minute Warm-Up   **1.** $\left\{x \mid x > -\dfrac{3}{2}\right\}$ **2.** $\{3\}$ **3.** $\{-4, -3\}$ **4.** $\dfrac{1}{16}$ **5.** 8   **6.** 4   **7.** $\dfrac{1}{4}$

Guided Practice   **1.** $x = a^y$ **2.** $\log_2\left(\dfrac{1}{8}\right) = -3$ **3.** $\log_a 3 = 4$ **4.** $4^p = 30$ **5.** $n^{-5} = 3$ **6a.** $(0, \infty)$

6b. $(-\infty, \infty)$ **6c.** $\{x \mid x < 5\}$ **7.** $y = 5^x$; See Graphing Answer Section   **8.** $x = e^y$

9. $x = 10^y$ **10.** $\{-2\}$ **11.** $e^{-2} \approx 0.1353$ **12a.** decibels (loudness)   **12b.** Richter Scale (earthquakes)
12c. pH (chemistry)

Do the Math   **1.** $\log_8 64 = 2$ **2.** $\log_b 23 = 4$ **3.** $\log z = -3$ **4.** $3^4 = 81$ **5.** $6^{-4} = x$ **6.** $a^2 = 16$ **7.** 2

8. 2   **9.** $(2, \infty)$ **10.** $\left(-\infty, \dfrac{3}{5}\right)$ **11.** -0.108   **12.** -0.693   **13.** $\{6\}$ **14.** $\left\{\dfrac{27}{4}\right\}$ **15.** $\{9\}$ **16.** $\left\{\dfrac{7}{2}\right\}$ **17.** $\{4\}$

18. $\left\{-2\sqrt{2}, 2\sqrt{2}\right\}$ **19.** ≈ 9.2 on the Richter scale

Section 11.4

Five-Minute Warm-Up   **1a.** 1.140   **1b.** 1.139   **2.** $x^{\frac{1}{2}}$ **3.** $a^{\frac{3}{4}}$ **4.** 2^{-4} **5.** $\left(\dfrac{3}{2}\right)^3$ **6.** 1   **7.** 6   **8.** $y = 3^x$

Guided Practice   **1a.** $\sqrt{2}$ **1b.** 0   **1c.** 1   **1d.** 7   **2a.** $\log_a M + \log_a N$ **2b.** $\log_a M - \log_a N$

2c. $r \log_a M$ **3.** $\log 9 + \log x$ **4.** $\ln 2 - \ln x$ **5.** $\log_4\left(\dfrac{1}{x-1}\right)$ **6.** $\dfrac{\log_b M}{\log_b a}$ **7.** ≈ 1.476

Do the Math   **1a.** -3   **1b.** $\sqrt{2}$ **1c.** 10   **2a.** $2a$ **2b.** ab^2 **3.** $\log_4 a - \log_4 b$ **4.** $3\log_3 a + \log_3 b$

5. $3 + \log_2 z$ **6.** $4 - \log_2 p$ **7.** $5 + \dfrac{1}{4}\log_2 z$ **8.** $\dfrac{1}{5}\ln x - 2\ln(x+2)$ **9.** $\dfrac{1}{3}\left[\log_6(x-2) - \log_6(x+1)\right]$

10. $3\log_4 x + \log_4(x-3) - \dfrac{1}{3}\log_4(x+1)$ **11.** 3   **12.** 4   **13.** $\log_2 z^8$ **14.** $\log_2\left(a^4 b^2\right)$

15. $\log_4\left[\sqrt[3]{z}\,(2z+1)^2\right]$ **16.** $\log_7\left(x^2\right)$ **17.** $\ln\sqrt[3]{x^2 - 1}$ **18.** $\log_5(x+1)$ **19.** $\log_4\left(\dfrac{x^4}{16}\right)$ **20a.** 0.827

20b. 1.631

Section 11.5

Five-Minute Warm-Up   **1.** $\{9\}$ **2.** $\{-8, 3\}$ **3.** $\left\{\dfrac{1}{4}, -2\right\}$ **4.** $\{7, 0\}$ **5.** $\{x \mid x < 3\}$

Guided Practice   **1a.** $\left\{\dfrac{5}{2}\right\}$ **1b.** $\left\{\dfrac{1}{3}\right\}$ **1c.** $\{64\}$ **2a.** $x = \dfrac{\log 12}{\log 3} \approx 2.262$ **2b.** $x = \dfrac{\ln 18}{3} \approx 0.963$

3a. $90 = 100\left(\dfrac{1}{2}\right)^{\frac{t}{19.255}}$ **3b.** ≈ 2.927 sec.   **4a.** 3921 people   **4b.** $7500 = 2500e^{0.03t}$ **4c.** 36.6 years or 1986
4d. 23.1 years or 1973

Do the Math   **1.** $\{13\}$ **2.** $\{16\}$ **3.** $\{8\}$ **4.** $\left\{\dfrac{5}{8}\right\}$ **5.** $\{5\}$ **6.** $\dfrac{\log 8}{\log 3} \approx 1.893$ **7.** $\dfrac{\log 20}{\log 4} \approx 2.161$

8. $\ln 3 \approx 1.099$ **9.** $\log 0.2 \approx -0.699$ **10.** $\dfrac{\log 5}{2\log 2} \approx 1.161$ **11.** $\dfrac{\log 5}{\log 4} \approx 1.161$ **12.** 4   **13.** 2   **14.** 2

15. $\ln 4 \approx 1.386$ **16.** 12   **17.** 8   **18.** 6   **19.** 2037   **20.** ≈ 3.766 years

Chapter 12 Answers
Section 12.1

Five-Minute Warm-Up **1.** $2\sqrt{10}$ **2.** $6\sqrt{3}$ **3.** $4p^2\sqrt{2}$ **4.** $|2x-5|$ **5.** -10 **6.** 25 **7.** 6 cm^2 **8.** 12

Guided Practice **1.** $d = \sqrt{(x_2 - x_1)^2 + (y_2 - y_1)^2}$ **2a.** a and c **2b.** b and d **2c.** (a) **2d.** (b)

2e. add (c) and (d) **2f.** take the square root of (e) **2g.** simplify **3.** $4\sqrt{5} \approx 8.94$ **4.** two equal parts

5. $x_1 + x_2$; $y_1 + y_2$ **6.** $(-4, -3)$

Do the Math **1.** 5 **2.** 25 **3.** 2 **4.** $2\sqrt{13} \approx 7.21$ **5.** $2\sqrt{78} \approx 17.66$ **6.** $\sqrt{5.69} \approx 2.39$ **7.** $(3, 5)$ **8.** $(2, 2)$

9. $\left(1, \dfrac{11}{2}\right)$ **10.** $(2, -2)$ **11.** $\left(2\sqrt{6}, 4\sqrt{2}\right)$ **12.** $(-0.7, 1.95)$ **13a.** See Graphing Answer Section

13b. $d(A, B) = 5$; $d(B, C) = 3\sqrt{5}$; $d(A, C) = \sqrt{58} \approx 7.07$ **14.** $(-16, -3)$ and $(8, -3)$

Section 12.2

Five-Minute Warm-Up **1.** $49; (x - 7)^2$ **2.** $\dfrac{25}{4}; \left(y - \dfrac{5}{2}\right)^2$ **3.** $(y + 8)^2$ **4.** $2(x - 3)^2$

5a. $\dfrac{225\pi}{4} \approx 176.71$ in.^{2} **5b.** $15\pi \approx 47.12$ in.

Guided Practice **1a.** center **1b.** radius **1c.** $d = 2r$ **2.** $(x - h)^2 + (y - k)^2 = r^2$

3. $(x + 1)^2 + (y - 3)^2 = 25$ **4a.** $(2, -3)$ **4b.** 2 **4c.** See Graphing Answer Section

5. $x^2 + y^2 + ax + by + c = 0$ **6a.** 9; 1; 9; 1 **6b.** 3; 1; 9 **6c.** $(-3, 1)$; 3 **6d.** See Graphing Answer Section

Do the Math **1 – 8.** See Graphing Answer Section **1.** $x^2 + y^2 = 25$ **2.** $(x - 1)^2 + y^2 = 4$

3. $(x + 4)^2 + (y - 4)^2 = 16$ **4.** $(x - 5)^2 + (y - 2)^2 = 7$ **5.** $C(0, 0), r = 5$ **6.** $C(5, -2), r = 7$

7. $C(6, 0), r = 6$ **8.** $C(2, -2), r = 0.5$ **9.** $C(-1, 4), r = 3$ **10.** $C(-2, 6), r = 2$ **11.** $C(7, -5), r = 8$

12. $x^2 + (y - 3)^2 = 25$ **13.** $(x - 2)^2 + (y + 3)^2 = 9$ **14.** $(x - 1)^2 + \left(y + \dfrac{1}{2}\right)^2 = \dfrac{169}{4}$

15. $A = 64\pi$ square units; $C = 16\pi$ units

Section 12.3

Five-Minute Warm-Up **1.** $(2, 1)$ **2.** up **3.** $x = 2$ **4.** $25; (x + 5)^2$ **5.** $-12; -3(x - 2)^2$ **6.** $\{8, 0\}$

Guided Practice **1a.** left or right **1b.** right **1c.** left **1d.** up or down **1e.** up **1f.** down **2a.** down

2b. right **3a.** left **3b.** $y^2 = -4ax$ **3c.** $y^2 - \dfrac{1}{2}x$ **4a.** $x^2 - 8x = -4y - 20$

4b. $x^2 - 8x + 16 = -4y - 20 + 16$ **4c.** $x^2 - 8x + 16 = -4y - 4$ **4d.** $(x - 4)^2 = -4(y + 1)$ **4e.** down

4f. $(4, -1)$ **4g.** See Graphing Answer Section

Do the Math **1.** $x^2 = 20y$ **2.** $y^2 = -32x$ **3.** $y^2 = 2x$ **4.** $y^2 = 16x$ **5.** $x^2 = -8y$

6 – 13. See Graphing Answer Section **6a.** $V(0, 0)$ **6b.** $F(0, 7)$ **6c.** $y = -7$ **7a.** $V(0, 0)$, **7b.** $F\left(0, \dfrac{5}{2}\right)$

7c. $x = -\dfrac{5}{2}$ **8a.** $V(0, 0)$ **8b.** $F(0, -4)$ **8c.** $y = 4$ **9a.** $V(-4, 1)$ **9b.** $F(-4, 0)$ **9c.** $y = 2$ **10a.** $V(-5, 2)$

10b. $F(-2, 2)$ **10c.** $x = -8$ **11a.** $V(-1, 3)$ **11b.** $F(-1, 5)$ **11c.** $y = 1$ **12a.** $V(2, 4)$ **12b.** $F(-2, 4)$

12c. $x = 6$ **13a.** $V(2, 0)$ **13b.** $F\left(2, \dfrac{-5}{2}\right)$ **13c.** $y = \dfrac{5}{2}$ **14.** 20 feet

Sullivan/Struve/Mazzarella, *Elementary & Intermediate Algebra, 2e*

Five-Minute Warm-Up 1. $\dfrac{81}{4}; \left(y-\dfrac{9}{2}\right)^2$ 2. $36; (x+6)^2$ 3. $\dfrac{1}{4}; 4\left(x-\dfrac{1}{4}\right)^2$ 4. $y=9(x+3)^2-6$

5. $(-3,-6)$ 6. up 7. $x=-3$

Guided Practice 1a. foci 1b. major axis 1c. minor axis 1d. center 1e. vertices 2a. a^2 2b. a
2c. $2a$ 2d. $2b$ 2e. major 2f. a^2-b^2 2g. the origin 3a – 3b. See Graphing Answer Section

4. $\dfrac{x^2}{144}+\dfrac{y^2}{169}=1$ 5a. $\dfrac{(x+5)^2}{9}+\dfrac{(y-2)^2}{25}=1$ 5b. $C(-5,2)$ 5c. $V_1(-5,7); V_2(-5,-3)$

5d. $F_1(-5,6); F_2(-5,-2)$ 6a. $\dfrac{(x-1)^2}{9}+\dfrac{(y-3)^2}{4}=1$ 6b. $C(1,3)$ 6c. $V_1(4,3); V_2(-2,3)$

6d. $F\left(1\pm\sqrt{5},3\right)$ 7a. $\dfrac{(x-4)^2}{36}+\dfrac{(y+3)^2}{64}=1$ 7b. $C(4,-3)$ 7c. $V_1(4,-11); V_2(4,5)$

7d. $F\left(4,-3\pm 2\sqrt{7}\right)$

Do the Math 1 – 4. See Graphing Answer Section 1a. $V(\pm5,0)$ 1b. $F\left(\pm\sqrt{21},0\right)$ 2a. $V(0,\pm6)$

2b. $F\left(0,\pm 2\sqrt{5}\right)$ 3a. $V(\pm8,0)$ 3b. $F\left(\pm3\sqrt{7},0\right)$ 4a. $V(0,\pm9)$ 4b. $F\left(0,\pm6\sqrt{2}\right)$ 5. $\dfrac{x^2}{25}+\dfrac{y^2}{21}=1$

6. $\dfrac{x^2}{24}+\dfrac{y^2}{25}=1$ 7. $\dfrac{x^2}{45}+\dfrac{y^2}{49}=1$ 8. $\dfrac{x^2}{100}+\dfrac{y^2}{64}=1$ 9 – 10. See Graphing Answer Section

11a. $\dfrac{(x+3)^2}{9}+\dfrac{(y-4)^2}{25}=1$ 11b. $C(-3,4)$ 11c. $V(-3,-1)$ and $(-3,9)$ 11d. $F(-3,0)$ and $(-3,8)$

12a. $\dfrac{x^2}{900}+\dfrac{y^2}{256}=1$ 12b. yes

Five-Minute Warm-Up 1. $\{-4,4\}$ 2. $\{-1,-5\}$ 3. $16; (x+4)^2$ 4. $\dfrac{4}{9}; \left(y-\dfrac{2}{3}\right)^2$ 5. See Graphing

Answer Section
Guided Practice 1a. foci 1b. transverse axis 1c. center 1d. conjugate axis 1e. vertices 2a. a^2 2b. a
2c. $2a$ 2d. $2b$ 2e. left and right 2f. up and down 2g. a^2+b^2 2h the origin 3a. center: $(0,0)$
3b. $a=4, b=3$ 3c. $c=5$ 3d. vertices: $(\pm4,0)$; foci: $(\pm5,0)$. 3e. $(\pm5,9),(\pm5,-9)$
3f. See Graphing Answer Section 4. A boundary line that the graph approaches but does not cross when
moving towards $+\infty$ or $-\infty$. 5a. $\dfrac{b}{a}x$ 5b. $\dfrac{a}{b}x$

Do the Math 1 – 4. See Graphing Answer Section 1. $V(\pm3,0)$ 1b. $F(\pm5,0)$ 2a. $V(0,\pm9)$

2b. $F\left(0,\pm 3\sqrt{10}\right)$ 3a. $V(\pm6,0)$ 3b. $F\left(\pm2\sqrt{10},0\right)$ 4a. $V(0,\pm3)$ 4b. $F\left(0,\pm\sqrt{13}\right)$ 5. $x^2-\dfrac{y^2}{15}=1$

6. $\dfrac{y^2}{36}-\dfrac{x^2}{28}=1$ 7. $\dfrac{y^2}{16}-\dfrac{x^2}{4}=1$ 8. $\dfrac{x^2}{8.1}-\dfrac{y^2}{72.9}=1$ 9. parabola 10. hyperbola 11. hyperbola 12. circle

13. parabola 14. ellipse 15a. $(0,5)$ and $(0,-5)$ 15b. $\left(0\pm\sqrt{29}\right)$ 16. $y=\pm x$

Section 13.1

Five-Minute Warm-Up **1a.** -5 **1b.** -9 **2a.** 1 **2b.** 1 **2c.** -3 **2d.** 5 **3a.** $\dfrac{1}{9}$ **3b.** $-\dfrac{1}{27}$ **3c.** $\dfrac{1}{81}$ **4.** $\dfrac{25}{24}$

Guided Practice **1a.** terms **1b.** ellipsis **1c.** finite **2.** a_n **3.** $1, \dfrac{3}{2}, \dfrac{7}{3}, \dfrac{15}{4}, \dfrac{31}{5}$ **4a.** $a_n = 3n$

4b. $a_n = (-1)^{n+1}\left(\dfrac{1}{6}\right)^n$ **5.** $1; 2; 3; 4; 4; 7; 12; 19; 42$ **6.** $-5 + (-3) + (-1) + 1 + 3 + 5 = 0$ **7.** $\displaystyle\sum_{i=0}^{6}(2i)$

Do the Math **1.** $-3, -2, -1, 0, 1$ **2.** $5, 3, \dfrac{7}{3}, 2, \dfrac{9}{5}$ **3.** $2, 8, 26, 80, 242$ **4.** $\dfrac{1}{2}, 2, \dfrac{9}{2}, 8, \dfrac{25}{2}$ **5.** $a_n = 5n$

6. $a_n = \dfrac{n}{2}$ **7.** $a_n = n^3 - 1$ **8.** $a_n = \left(-\dfrac{1}{2}\right)^{n-1}$ **9.** 55 **10.** 50 **11.** 120 **12.** 4 **13.** 16 **14.** 69

15. $\displaystyle\sum_{k=1}^{9}(2k-1)$ **16.** $\displaystyle\sum_{k=1}^{16}\dfrac{1}{2^{k-1}}$ **17.** $\displaystyle\sum_{i=1}^{15}(-1)^{i+1}\left(\dfrac{2}{3}\right)^i$ **18.** $\displaystyle\sum_{k=1}^{12}\left[3\cdot\left(\dfrac{1}{2}\right)^{k-1}\right]$ **19a.** \$5033.33

19b. \$5415.00 **19c.** \$11,098.20

Section 13.2

Five-Minute Warm-Up **1.** 4 **2.** $-\dfrac{9}{5}$ **3a.** $(14, 4)$ **3b.** $(1, -4)$ **4.** -36

Guided Practice **1a.** d **1b.** a **2.** yes; $a = 5$; $d = 3$ **3.** $3, 6, 11, 18, 27, 38; 3, 5, 7, 9, 11$

4a. $a_n = 5n - 8$ **4b.** $a_n = 32$ **5a.** $a = 12; d = 3$ **5b.** $a_n = 3d + 12$ **6a.** $a_n = 4n + 8$ **6b.** $a_{10} = 48$

6c. $S_{10} = 300$ **7a.** $a_1 = 3$, $a_{10} = -87$ **7b.** $S_{10} = -420$

Do the Math **1.** $d = 10; 11, 21, 31, 41$ **2.** $d = \dfrac{1}{4}; 1, \dfrac{5}{4}, \dfrac{3}{2}, \dfrac{7}{4}$ **3.** $a_n = 3n + 5; a_5 = 20$

4. $a_n = -3n + 15; a_5 = 0$ **5.** $a_n = \dfrac{1}{2}n - \dfrac{7}{2}; a_5 = -1$ **6.** $a_n = 4n - 9; a_{20} = 71$ **7.** $a_n = -6n + 26; a_{20} = -94$

8. $a_n = -\dfrac{1}{2}n + \dfrac{21}{2}; a_{20} = \dfrac{1}{2}$ **9.** $a_n = 3n - 8$ **10.** $a_n = 4n - 17$ **11.** $a_n = -5n + 22$ **12.** $a_n = \dfrac{1}{4}n + \dfrac{15}{4}$

13. 5500 **14.** $10,425$ **15.** -9200 **16.** 5440 **17.** -2905 **18.** -413 **19.** $x = 1$ **20.** 1600 seats

Section 13.3

Five-Minute Warm-Up **1a.** $\dfrac{2}{3}$ **1b.** $\dfrac{4}{9}$ **1c.** $\dfrac{8}{27}$ **2a.** 3 **2b.** 12 **2c.** 27 **3a.** $\dfrac{8x^3}{5}$ **3b.** $9r^8$ **4.** 2

Guided Practice **1a.** r **1b.** a **2.** yes; $a = 36$; $r = \dfrac{1}{2}$ **3.** $1, \dfrac{2}{5}, \dfrac{4}{25}, \dfrac{8}{125}; r = \dfrac{2}{5}$

4a. $\{a_n\} = \left\{2 \cdot \left(-\dfrac{1}{3}\right)^{n-1}\right\}$ **4b.** $-\dfrac{2}{2187}$ **5a.** $a = 6, r = 4$ **5b.** $2,097,150$ **6a.** $a = 6; r = -\dfrac{1}{3}$ **6b.** $\dfrac{9}{2}$

7. \$99,658.27

Do the Math **1.** $r = -2; -2, 4, -8, 16$ **2.** $r = 2; \dfrac{2}{3}, \dfrac{4}{3}, \dfrac{8}{3}, \dfrac{16}{3}$ **3.** $r = \dfrac{1}{6}, \dfrac{1}{3}, \dfrac{1}{18}, \dfrac{1}{108}, \dfrac{1}{648}$ **4.** arithmetic

5. neither **6.** geometric **7.** neither **8.** $a_n = 30 \cdot \left(\dfrac{1}{3}\right)^{n-1}; a_8 = \dfrac{10}{729}$ **9.** $a_n = (-4)^{n-1}; a_8 = -16,384$

10. $177,147$ **11.** -1280 **12.** 0.0000000004 **13.** $88,572$ **14.** $40,950$ **15.** $\dfrac{3}{2}$ **16.** $\dfrac{48}{5}$ **17.** 5 **18.** $\dfrac{1}{3}$

19. $\dfrac{5}{11}$ **20.** \$10,497.60

Five-Minute Warm-Up   **1.** $x^2 + 4x + 4$ **2.** $y^2 - 6y + 9$ **3.** $16x^2 - 40xy + 25y^2$

4. $9n^2 + 4n + \dfrac{4}{9}$ **5.** 35

Guided Practice   **1a.** 151,200   **1b.** 15   **2a.** 10   **2b.** 1716   **3.** $p^4 + 8p^3 + 24p^2 + 32p + 16$

Do the Math   **1.** 120   **2.** 360   **3.** 45   **4.** 1   **5.** 10   **6.** 21   **7.** 50   **8.** 1   **9.** $x^4 - 4x^3 + 6x^2 - 4x + 1$

10. $x^5 + 25x^4 + 250x^3 + 1250x^2 + 3125x + 3125$ **11.** $16q^4 + 96q^3 + 216q^2 + 216q + 81$

12. $3w^4 - 432w^3 + 864w^2 - 768w + 256$ **13.** $y^8 - 12y^6 + 54y^4 - 108y^2 + 81$

14. $243b^{10} + 810b^8 + 1080b^6 + 720b^4 + 240b^2 + 32$ **15.** $p^6 - 18p^5 + 135p^4 - 540p^3 + 1215p^2 - 1458p + 729$

16. $81x^8 + 108x^6y^3 + 54x^4y^6 + 12x^2y^9 + y^{12}$ **17.** 1.00501

Graphing Answer Section

Section 1.3 Guided Practice

4.

Section 1.3 Do the Math

7.

Section 2.7 Guided Practice

7b.

	Rate, mph	Time, hours =	Distance, miles
Slower boat	r	2.5	$2.5r$
Faster boat	$r + 4$	2.5	$2.5(r + 4)$
Total			50 miles

Section 2.7 Do the Math

5.

	Rate, mph	Time, hours =	Distance, miles
Beginning of trip	r	2	$2r$
Rest of the trip	$r - 10$	3	$3(r - 10)$
Total		5	580

Section 2.8 Warm-Up

7.

Section 2.8 Do the Math

2.   **7f.**

Section 2.8 Guided Practice

1. $(5, \infty)$

2. $(-\infty, 6]$

3. $[-2, \infty)$

4. $(-\infty, -3)$

9. $\{x \mid x < 3\}; (-\infty, 3)$

10. $\{x \mid x > 3\}; (3, \infty)$

11. $\{x \mid x \le -4\}; (-\infty, -4]$

12. $\{x \mid x > -2\}; (-2, \infty)$

13. $\{x \mid x \ge 5\}; [5, \infty)$

14. $\{x \mid x \ge -1\}; [-1, \infty)$

15. $\left\{x \mid x > \dfrac{11}{2}\right\}; \left(\dfrac{11}{2}, \infty\right)$

16. $\varnothing$ or $\{\ \}$

17. $\{p \mid p \text{ is any real number}\}; (-\infty, \infty)$

Section 3.1 Warm-Up

1.

Section 3.1 Guided Practice

1.

Section 3.1 Do the Math

1.

2.

8.

x	y	(x, y)
-3	-17	$(-3, -17)$
1	-1	$(1, -1)$
2	3	$(2, 3)$

9.

x	y	(x, y)
-2	2	$(-2, 2)$
2	-1	$(2, -1)$
4	$-\dfrac{5}{2}$	$\left(4, -\dfrac{5}{2}\right)$

Section 3.2 Warm-Up

6.

Section 3.2 Guided Practice

1.

5c.

6.

7.

Section 3.2 Do the Math

3.

4.

11.

12.

13.

14.

Section 3.3 Guided Practice

9.

Section 3.3 Do the Math

3a., 3b.

4a., 4b.

7.

8.

Section 3.4 Guided Practice

4c.

5d.

Section 3.4 Do the Math

5.

(0, −1)

6.

(0, −3)

7.

(0, 2)

8.

(0, −2)

15e.

Section 3.5 Do the Math

1.

(4, 1)

2.

(6, −3)

3.

(−8, 2)

4.

(−7, −1)

11b.

(30, 3600)
(20, 3150)

Section 3.6 Do the Math

1–3.

Slope of the Given Line	Slope of a Line Parallel to the Given Line	Slope of a Line Perpendicular to the Given Line
$m = 4$	4	$-\dfrac{1}{4}$
$m = -\dfrac{1}{8}$	$-\dfrac{1}{8}$	8
$m = \dfrac{5}{2}$	$\dfrac{5}{2}$	$-\dfrac{2}{5}$

Section 3.7 Warm-Up

4.

Section 3.7 Guided Practice

6h.   **7c.**

Section 3.7 Do the Math

5.   **6.**   **7.**   **8.**

9.   **10.**   **11.**   **12.**

Section 4.1 Warm-Up

1a.   **1b.**

Section 4.1 Guided Practice

2g.   **3.**

Section 4.1 Do the Math

3.
(3.5, −7)

4.

5.
(1, 0)

6.

11.

Speedy
(500, 130)
Cheap

Section 4.4 Guided Practice

4c., 4d.

	Distance (miles)	Rate (mph)	Time (hours)
With the wind	2400	$a + w$	6
Against the wind	2400	$a - w$	8

Section 4.5 Guided Practice

1a–c.

	Number	Cost per Person in Dollars	Amount
Adults	a	7.50	$7.5a$
Students	s	4.00	$4s$
Total	40		202

2a–c.

	Number of coins	Value per Coin in Dollars	Total Value
Quarters	q	0.25	$0.25q$
Dimes	d	0.10	$0.1d$
Total	42		6.75

3a–c.

	Price \$/Pound	Number of Pounds	Revenue
Almonds	6.50	a	$6.5a$
Peanuts	4.00	p	$4p$
Mix	6.00	50	300

4a–c.

	Number of ml	Concentration	Amount of Pure HCl
25% HCl solution	x	0.25	$0.25x$
40% HCl solution	y	0.40	$0.4y$
30% HCl solution	90	0.30	27

Section 4.5 Do the Math

1.

	Number	•	Cost per Item	=	Total Value
Bracelets	b		10		$10b$
Necklaces	n		15		$15n$
Total	69				895

2.

	Principal	•	Rate	=	Interest
Savings Account	s		0.0275		$0.0275s$
Certificate of Deposit	c		0.02		$0.02c$
Total	1700				37.75

3.

	Number of Pounds	Price per Pound	=	Total Value
Peanuts	p	5		$5p$
Trail Mix	t	2		$2t$
Total	40	3		$3(40)$

Section 4.6 Warm-Up

3a.   **3b.**

Section 4.6 Guided Practice

7.   **8d.**

Section 4.6 Do the Math

3.   **4.**   **5.**   **6.**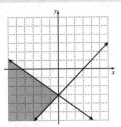

7a.

(graph: Number lbs. hamburger (h) vs Number lbs. bratwurst (b))

Section 6.2 Guided Practice

3a.

Factors whose product is –56	1, –56	2, –28	4, –14	7, –8	8, –7	14, –4	28, –2	56, –1
Sum of factors	–55	–26	–10	–1	1	10	26	55

4a.

Factors whose product is –24	1, –24	2, –12	3, –8	4, –6	6, –4	8, –3	12, –2	24, –1
Sum of factors	–23	–10	–5	–2	2	5	10	23

Section 8.1 Warm-Up

1.

Section 8.1 Guided Practice

1.

5.

Section 8.1 Do the Math

2.

6.

7.

8.

9.

Section 8.2 Warm-Up

3.

4.

5.

Section 8.2 Guided Practice

6.

Section 8.4 Warm-Up

3.

4.

4.

Section 8.4 Do the Math

6.

7.

Section 8.5 Warm-Up

1.

2.

Section 8.5 Guided Practice

3c.

Section 8.5 Do the Math

1.

Section 8.5 Do the Math (continued)

2.

3.

4.

8.

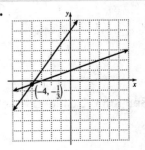

$\left(-4, -\frac{1}{3}\right)$

Section 8.6 Warm-Up

Section 8.6 Guided Practice

2.

3a.

3b.

4d-f.

Section 8.6 Guided Practice (continued)

6d.

7e-g.

Section 8.7 Guided Practice

6d.

8d.

Section 8.8 Warm-Up

3.

4.

Section 9.7 Warm-Up

5.

Section 9.7 Guided Practice

5b.

6b.

Section 9.7 Do the Math

9c.

10c.

11c.

12c.

Section 10.4 Warm-Up

1.

2.

Section 10.4 Do the Math

1.

2.

3.

4.

5.

6.

Section 10.5 Guided Practice

3k.

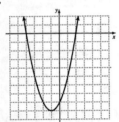

Section 10.5 Do the Math

4.

5.

6.

7.

8.

9.

Section 10.6 Guided Practice

3d.

5d.

Interval	$(-\infty, -7)$	$x = -7$	$(-7, 5)$	$x = 5$	$(5, \infty)$
Test Point	-8	-7	0	5	6
Sign of $x + 7$	$-$	0	$+$	$+$	$+$
Sign of $x - 5$	$-$	$-$	$-$	0	$+$
Sign of product	$+$	0	$-$	0	$+$
Conclusion	Included	Not Included	Not Included	Not Included	Included

Section 10.7 Warm-Up

2.

Section 10.7 Guided Practice

5q.

8.

Interval	$(-\infty, -4)$	-4	$(-4, 2)$	2	$(2, 3)$	3	$(3, \infty)$
Test Point	-5	-4	0	2	2.5	3	4
Sign of $x + 4$	$-$	0	$+$	$+$	$+$	$+$	$+$
Sign of $x - 3$	$-$	$-$	$-$	$-$	$-$	0	$+$
Sign of $x - 2$	$-$	$-$	$-$	0	$+$	$+$	$+$
Sign of quotient	$-$	0	$+$	Undef.	$-$	0	$+$
Conclusion	Not Included	Included	Included	Not Included	Not Included	Included	Included

9.

Section 11.2 Do the Math

3.

4.

5.

Section 11.3 Guided Practice

7.

Section 12.1 Do the Math

13a.

Section 12.2 Guided Practice

4c.

6d.

Section 12.2 Do the Math

1.

2.

3.

4.

5.

6.

7.

8.

Section 12.3 Guided Practice

4g.

Section 12.3 Do the Math

6.

7.

8.

9.

10.

11.

12.

13.

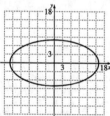

Section 12.4 Guided Practice

3a.

3b.

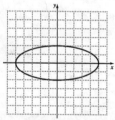

Section 12.4 Do the Math

1.

2.

3.

4.

9.

10.

Section 12.5 Warm-Up

5.

Section 12.5 Guided Practice

3f.

Section 12.5 Do the Math

1.

2.

3.

4.